Cultural Heritage as a Legal Hybrid

Alicja Jagielska–Burduk

Cultural Heritage as a Legal Hybrid

Between Public and Private Law

Springer

Alicja Jagielska–Burduk
Opole, Poland

ISBN 978-3-031-04945-3 ISBN 978-3-031-04946-0 (eBook)
https://doi.org/10.1007/978-3-031-04946-0

This Springer imprint is published by the registered company Springer Nature Switzerland AG
The registered company address is: Gewerbestrasse 11, 6330 Cham, Switzerland

Acknowledgements

I would like to acknowledge the funding and support provided by the University of Opole for this project through the UNESCO Chair on Cultural Property Law, City of Bydgoszcz, and UNIDROIT, where I conducted my research within the visiting scholar programme. I am grateful to Piotr Stec, University of Opole, and Wojciech Szafrański, Adam Mickiewicz University, Poznań, for their valuable comments and for inspiring me in my scientific endeavours. I am thankful for the consultations with my colleagues at the UNESCO UNITWIN Chairs Network and especially the UNESCO chairholders, who were there for me when I needed it most, as well as the International Art Market Studies Association. I also wish to thank the editors at Springer for their commitment and advice during the preparation of this book.

Contents

Chapter 1
Introduction

Cultural heritage as a subject of regulation is a perfect example of where private law and public law meet. The observation of tensions between public and private elements allows us to trace changes in the construction of cultural heritage protection over the years. In this regard, the formation of cultural heritage protection is undoubtedly similar to the history of property law.[1] On the example of cultural heritage and cultural property, we can think of the new global property order, where culture and cultural resources have a complex role.[2] The book examines the role of private law in cultural heritage protection, which from the outset was of a public nature. It considers the problem of defining cultural heritage as a legal concept and providing protective mechanisms based on private law, with an emphasis on moments when the merger of public and private elements is necessary to safeguard and transmit cultural resources to future generations. The aim was to look beyond existing public and private law on cultural heritage and examine its complex status as a legal hybrid.

The book's core research problem centers on the role of civil law in shaping the system of cultural heritage protection. To this end, an attempt will be made to answer the questions of whether the law facilitates or hinders the future protection of cultural heritage, and whether the available institutions, either in their present form or after some adaptation, will be fit for use in the service of cultural heritage protection. It seems that civil law can be seen not only as a historical anchor for cultural heritage in the well-known division of goods into tangible and intangible categories and the right of ownership of things (if we consider only tangible heritage), but also as a starting point to change the status of cultural heritage or its selected components within the system of goods itself.[3] Searching for the directions in which changes occur is justified by the differentiation of heritage components, both in the case of

[1] Rozwadowski (1984).

[2] Turner (2017), pp. 39–44.

[3] Macmillan (2020), pp. 86–88.

A. Jagielska-Burduk, *Cultural Heritage as a Legal Hybrid*,
https://doi.org/10.1007/978-3-031-04946-0_1

tangible and intangible goods, and repeated for years in the literature going beyond the boundaries inherent in things as objects of property.[4]

Moving past the debates publicized in the media—concerning the owner of a Picasso painting putting his knee through the canvas,[5] a painting being partially destroyed during an auction through a shredder built in the frame,[6] or setting a valuable work of art as a target in a game of darts[7]—we should examine private and public cultural heritage law from a different perspective. In this way, it is possible to enrich the discussion on the participation of private entities in the guardianship of heritage and the perception of the State Treasury or other public holders of historic resources as "natural" guardians of heritage. The perspective proposed in this book conceives of cultural heritage as a hybrid between public and private law and discusses the "emancipation" process of cultural property.

During the initial work on the 1995 UNIDROIT Convention[8] in 1989, attention was drawn to the interrelationship between private law, private international law, and public international law in the protection of cultural heritage.[9] Defining cultural heritage by reference to private law is crucial when it comes to its protection. This is not only true for tangible heritage, but also for selected elements of intangible heritage, as well as cultural property that exists only in digital form. Civil law, and more specifically the introduction of additional protective measures in national civil codes, has been identified as a complementary source of obligations for the process of strengthening heritage protection systems and implementing the 1970 UNESCO Convention.[10] The Analytical Summary of National Reports Received on the Implementation of the 1970 Convention,[11] published in 2019, states that the provisions on property in particular, including archaeological monuments, are of great importance in the adaptation of national civil codes for cultural heritage protection. As important achievements in private law, changes relating to the extension of limitation periods

[4] Crewdson (1984), p. 126; Carpenter et al. (2009).

[5] Glaister (2006).

[6] Martin (2018).

[7] Sax (1999).

[8] Unidroit Convention on Stolen or Illegally Exported Cultural Objects, Rome 24 June 1995.

[9] L. V. Prott reported that she disagreed with the opinion of one of the participants in the Working Group, who felt that the group should deal only with private law and not with issues of private international law or public law. She argued that private law and private international law issues should be in one UNIDROIT legal instrument, Travaux préparatoires, 1989, Doc. 13, p. 1.

[10] UNESCO Convention on the Means of Prohibiting and Preventing the Illicit Import, Export and Transfer of Ownership of Cultural Property, No. 11806, 823 UNTS. 231, Nov. 14, 1970.

[11] Seventh Session of the Subsidiary Committee of the Meeting of States Parties to the Convention concerning the Means of Prohibiting and Preventing the Illicit Import, Export and Transfer of Ownership of Cultural Property (UNESCO, Paris, 1970), C70/19/7.SC/6 Paris, April 2019, p. 5.

or the inclusion of provisions on due diligence in the codification[12] were also mentioned.

Initially, reflections on cultural heritage law were national in nature and concerned only tangible goods.[13] Then, because of the need to secure the components of heritage in emergency situations, particularly threats caused by military actions, solutions were introduced at the international level.[14] The emergence of international law on the protection of cultural property in peacetime has had a noticeable impact on international trends, used in turn in national laws. For instance, initiatives for model provisions on state ownership of undiscovered cultural objects[15] or ongoing works on model provisions implementing the 1970 UNESCO Convention.[16] Yet another relationship takes place regarding intangible cultural heritage regulated at the international level, which in the case of Poland, was previously nearly absent from national law. In this case, the protection and identification of this heritage has, as it were, its origin at the international level, while national efforts are often the result of accession to the 2003 UNESCO Convention.[17]

Both tangible and intangible cultural heritage pose a challenge for national legislation regarding the legal history of respective countries, obligations deriving from international law, and the independence of each nation's own search for a bespoke protection model. Although the notion of cultural heritage transcends civil law regulation and property rights, it must be taken into account when building a coherent cultural heritage protection system. It seems that in national legislation, we can observe an increased interest in leveraging civil law or private law to strengthen the existing cultural heritage protection framework.

The main focus of work in this area will remain on the subject of regulation, which is not uniform and has long provided numerous challenges. At the same time, new legal initiatives are still more focused on tangible goods, and only address intangible goods in a limited way (depending on the relevant national legislation). As a result, cultural heritage protection law is currently subject to continuous erosion and fragmentation. Persistent problems in defining cultural heritage and valuing its individual components affect, among other things, the effective application of the law. A traditional emphasis on the material dimension of heritage and placing

---

[12] Seventh Session of the Subsidiary Committee of the Meeting of States Parties to the Convention concerning the Means of Prohibiting and Preventing the Illicit Import, Export and Transfer of Ownership of Cultural Property (UNESCO, Paris, 1970), C70/19/7.SC/6 Paris, April 2019, pp. 5–6.

[13] Frigo (2004); Merryman (1986).

[14] Convention for the Protection of Cultural Property in the Event of Armed Conflict. The Hague, 14 May 1954.

[15] Expert Committee on State Ownership of Cultural Heritage, Model Provisions on State Ownership of Undiscovered Cultural Objects. Explanatory Report with model provisions and explanatory guidelines, UNESCO, UNIDROIT, 2011. https://en.unesco.org/sites/default/files/unesco-unidroit_model_provisions_en_0.pdf. Accessed 1 June 2022.

[16] Initiative on Draft model provisions on the prevention and fight against the illicit trafficking of cultural property.

[17] Vaivade and Wagener (2017).

heritage in the category of things is now giving way to a new perception of heritage in both its tangible and intangible dimensions, both in terms of its importance for the community as well as a holistic approach. This broad perception of cultural heritage and the qualification of its individual components is the aim of the considerations presented in this book.

Additionally, EU law creates a certain concept of collective cultural heritage of the European Union, while highlighting national cultural property that cannot be moved outside the borders of a Member State.[18] In the context of phenomena related to population migration, the issues of cultural migration and the need to protect the cultural space of migrants are also considered. As a result of the changes caused by COVID-19 and in view of the partial transfer of access to heritage to the online space, as well as access to heritage in the physical dimension, the construction of access to cultural space on the Internet has also emerged.

The core of the book deals with cultural heritage that is or is meant to be under legal protection. It is essential to address the process of defining cultural heritage and initiatives at the international level that have affected national legislation. The criminal and human rights law perspectives are also presented to show recent cases and argumentation in the field of cultural heritage (for example, the ICC's landmark ruling in the Al Mahdi case[19]).

Therefore, this book does not present a complete discussion of the problems cultural heritage faces in civil law, but is rather intended to determine the current stage of the relevant legal framework and use of civil law institutions, using Poland's legal system to illustrate these themes. The search for a national concept of cultural heritage protection in Poland does not take place in a vacuum. On the contrary, external circumstances, including international trends, have had a significant impact on the creation of new legislative solutions, such as activities related to the implementation of EU law or the implementation of international obligations. Thus, in my research I will refer to specific acts of international and EU law to demonstrate the proper context and the ongoing process of change in the law.

The book aims to show how current problems referred to in international debates are mirrored in national legislation. Poland is used as a practical example, referring to other countries' solutions as well as EU and international law instruments. This approach enables the reader to examine the creation of national legislation at the operational level and provides a template for all national lawyers concerning issues to be tackled in national laws regarding current challenges and emerging trends. In my opinion, it is necessary to take a bird's-eye view while studying the legal concept of cultural heritage, to better understand the short-, medium-, and long-term consequences of regulation. In this way, the problems discussed in the book could be of interest to lawyers and policymakers responsible for culture-related issues in their respective countries.

---

[18] Weller (2018).

[19] The Prosecutor v. Ahmad Al Faqi Al Mahdi, ICC-01/12-01/15.

The idea is to demonstrate how the hybridization of cultural heritage occurred and what the current challenges are, as some must be addressed together at the international level (e.g., AI, space cultural heritage). However, others can and should be solved at the national level. I argue that certain solutions can be used regardless of the history of each legislation within a country's legal system, focusing rather on the subject of the regulation (cultural heritage). Taking this approach, together with an examination of the ongoing publicization of private law, makes it possible to pinpoint how hybridization has taken place.

The second chapter concentrates on civil law and the division of tangible and intangible goods. It examines the concept of "res" and the construct of collections and their integrity as a civil law object. The notion of cultural heritage is presented from both the international law and Polish law perspectives. The chapter presents the ongoing processes of decodification of civil codes and publicization of private law with the aim to show how they affect cultural property protection. The current effect of publicization on private law is depicted using examples of civil law principles.

Chapter 3 includes sections devoted to less traditional cultural heritage forms with a focus on legal challenges posed by such components, including space cultural heritage, AI-generated and digital art, which will at some point constitute a part of cultural heritage in general. Additionally, the complex status of the human body as a heritage component is depicted. The fragmentation of national cultural heritage legislation and the reasons behind it are demonstrated using the example of the Polish Fryderyk Chopin Law.

The idea of the common good is presented in Chap. 4, where I describe resources that do not constitute a civil law thing (animals, minerals, waters); here, I also refer to public trusts and special regimes of natural heritage used in India, Australia, and New Zealand. This chapter shows how tangible assets such as waters, minerals, and similar elements that are treated as resources are regulated and how the distribution of rights is applied. This is followed by a debate on the legal status of animals. The idea behind the different ownership model shows how resources are prioritized and how the public interest is secured. The last two sections focus on a holistic approach to cultural heritage and the cultural dimension of nature in international and Polish law.

Chapter 5 addresses the protection of cultural heritage with the use of private law instruments in Poland. The landmark notion of *res extra commercium*, museums and archive collections are all examined. Additionally, the legal provisions of ownership acquisition regarding found historical objects and the institution of national treasures are presented in the context of how they complement the existing legal protection. The evolution of the law is shown through new provisions for purchasing a movable property with the added special protection of objects entered in the National Register of Lost Cultural Property and national treasures belonging to public collections, constituting a new legal development as a result of implementing the EU 2014/60 directive.[20]

The book covers cultural heritage law (in both its public and private modalities), emphasizing a search for new solutions in national legislations (e.g., cultural heritage as the fourth estate). The sixth and final chapter first examines shared responsibility for cultural heritage and the role of private actors in cultural heritage protection. The chapter ends with a proposal and assessment on the possible extent of the dereification of cultural property for the reader's consideration. This attempts to answer if dereification is actually real or whether it will remain a myth used in arguments to strengthen the protection of a particular category of cultural property.

The scope of the publication forced me to choose Polish legislation while discussing some specific legal solutions. The famous dichotomy of source countries and import countries could be supplemented by the division between heritage-rich and heritage-deprived countries. In this context, Poland could offer a new perspective as a post-dependency country. However, this analysis did not result in only one legislative example; the cases referred to in the book derive from different jurisdictions to provide the reader with a broad picture of the situation and how certain developments can be effectively introduced into national legislation. The example focuses on many problems that are not only limited to the European Union, and was meant to serve as a basis for a pilot action to search for a new legal standing of cultural heritage. Therefore, the presentation of universal problems is shown through the example of this country, which previously faced enormous cultural heritage losses during the twentieth century and now faces similar challenges regarding technological developments and the COVID-19 pandemic, regarding the central role of culture and cultural heritage in the economic and social recovery process.

References

Carpenter KA, Katyal SK, Riley A (2009) In defense of property. Yale Law J 118(6):1022–1125

Crewdson R (1984) Cultural property – a fourth estate? Law Soc Gazette 18:126–129

Frigo M (2004) Cultural property v. cultural heritage: a "battle of concepts" in international law? Int Rev Red Cross 86(854):367–378. https://doi.org/10.1017/S1560775500180861

Glaister D (2006, 19 Oct) Tycoon rips £75m Picasso. The Guardian. https://www.theguardian.com/world/2006/oct/19/arts.artsnews. Accessed 1 June 2022

Macmillan F (2020) Intellectual and cultural property: between market and community. Routledge, London

Martin G (2018, 31 Dec) Clues and Legal Liabilities: What Happened After Banksy Shredded His Own $1.4 Million Artwork. Forbes Life. https://www.forbes.com/sites/guymartin/2018/12/31/clues-and-legal-liabilities-what-happened-after-banksy-shredded-his-own-1-4-million-artwork/?sh=6095b361c7d2. Accessed 1 June 2022

[20] Directive 2014/60/EU of the European Parliament and of the Council of 15 May 2014 on the return of cultural objects unlawfully removed from the territory of a Member State and amending Regulation (EU) No. 1024/2012 (Recast), OJ L 159, 28.5.2014, pp. 1–10.

Merryman JH (1986) Two ways of thinking about cultural property. Am J Int Law 80(4):831–853. https://doi.org/10.2307/2202065

Rozwadowski W (1984) Definicje prawa własności w rozwoju, dziejowym. CPH 36(20):1–26

Sax JL (1999) Playing darts with a Rembrandt: public and private rights in cultural treasures. University of Michigan Press, Ann Arbor. doi:https://doi.org/10.3998/mpub.16038

Turner B (2017) The anthropology of property. In: Graziadei M, Smith L (eds) Comparative property law. Global perspectives. Edward Elgar Publishing, Cheltenham, pp 26–47

Vaivade A, Wagener N (2017) National laws related to intangible cultural heritage: determining the object of a comparative study. SAACLR 2(3):91–108. https://doi.org/10.4467/2450050XSNR.17.024.8425

Weller M (2018) Rethinking EU Cultural Property Law: Towards Private Enforcement. Nomos, Dike, Facultas, Zurich–Vienna–Baden-Baden. https://doi.org/10.5771/9783845290140

Chapter 2
Cultural Heritage: Legal Concepts and Protection

2.1 Introduction

Cultural heritage constitutes a particular type of property that is protected by law. Its status in private law is the result of an evolution in domestic law, but has also been influenced by international law in the form of international commitments and changing standards of protection contained in documents of "soft law." This first part examines the components of cultural heritage divided into material and intangible property, and defines things and sets of things within the scope crucial for research on the status of the cultural heritage. These reflections are preceded by a discussion of the concept of cultural heritage. The chapter ends with sections on the publicization of private law and selected principles of civil law related to the protection of cultural heritage.

The aim of this chapter is to present the concept of cultural heritage in civil law relations, within the context of evolving perceptions and emerging new forms of cultural heritage. Therefore, it is important to determine whether the division into movable and immovable things serves to protect cultural heritage, where the materiality or immateriality of property takes on special significance due to new forms of the concept arising. Further, cultural heritage, whether material or intangible, always has a certain inherent intangible value that makes it worthy of being preserved. In addition, particular attention must be paid to the issue of collections and how these can be protected or managed under private law, where a collection may consist of a set of material or intangible property (e.g., CryptoArt).

Given the various positions put forward by experts in legal doctrine concerning how to determine what is an object of a civil law relationship, it is necessary to specify how property that is part of cultural heritage resources is to be considered. Cultural property, as it is broadly understood, can be treated as the subject of a civil law relationship.

The chapter was translated from Polish into English by Anthony Sloan and the author.

A. Jagielska-Burduk, *Cultural Heritage as a Legal Hybrid*,
https://doi.org/10.1007/978-3-031-04946-0_2

Cultural heritage is presented considering how it may comprise an element of the subject of a civil law obligation, or the subject of property rights. At this point, it should be indicated that some of the components analyzed will be the subject of an absolute subjective right other than ownership, and that their status as an element of trade is atypical. Some of the cultural property discussed, e.g., archaeological artefacts extracted from the ground that constitute property of the State Treasury, may be handed over as museum property according to the decision of a provincial conservator of historical objects. The transfer of ownership takes place pursuant to an administrative decision having civil law effects, not as the result of a (contract). Consequently, the types of legal relationships that can actually exist concerning a given component of heritage are limited. Also, that part of cultural heritage does not occur in nature or take place in trade entirely, as a thing. Hence, the need to define the status of such property and its place in the civil law system; this is discussed in detail in Chap. 3.

In every case involving cultural heritage protection, the definition of the property to be protected must be considered. Additionally, this entails classifying the property within a mosaic of heritage components and determining what detailed provisions apply to that particular part of the set. The property must be qualified as a material object, and an assessment of whether it meets the criteria for being considered things must be made. Next, it must be determined whether a given object can be included among those circulating in trade or whether it warrants exclusion, for certain reasons. When examining the status of heritage, it is important to realize that its status may change as the result of legislative intervention. For example, it may be acknowledged that a given item is not a material object (thing), but another type of material property. The most radical solution is to classify property of this type as being outside the traditional scope of things.

2.2 Cultural Heritage as a Legal Concept

This chapter presents selected elements of the discussion on how heritage is defined, with reference to the definitions in force in Polish law on the protection of cultural heritage. I begin by looking at cultural heritage solutions discussed internationally. There have been many changes in how cultural heritage is defined, and new categories of heritage are created systematically.[1] One can even get the impression that how heritage is defined serves new goals other than protection. These include using cultural heritage in economic development and the creative sector. Moreover, in the case of intangible heritage, we can observe that the driving force behind creating a framework for its protection is international law, which has led to the introduction of new solutions in domestic law, including in Poland. One cannot speak, however, of a process that is uniform. In countries that introduced legislation

[1] Prott and O'Keefe (1989), pp. 26–30.

designed to protect indigenous peoples and their cultures, this notion appeared earlier. Can international law on cultural heritage, then, replace domestic regulations on heritage protection? It seems this is not possible in the "basic" dimension, although in the past, voices have called for the creation of a protective regime at the international level solely for the most valuable cultural objects.[2] Yet projects aimed at helping secure cultural heritage or supporting the process of rebuilding it where it has been destroyed (e.g., intentional terrorist attacks in Mosul and Timbuktu) show the importance of international cooperation. Nor can one ignore the fact that the system of state parties to a convention submitting reports makes it possible for them to share new achievements and best practices with other states, who can then consider implementing certain regulations in their own domestic law.

The debate over the essence of cultural heritage is enriched by various arguments. These may result from the scope of cultural heritage, its nature, and how it transforms. For example, expanding the concept of heritage to include its intangible dimension, and granting protection thereto, is a key moment in how heritage is defined. An example of a milestone within this scope is the acceptance of the definition of intangible heritage in the UNESCO Convention for the Safeguarding of the Intangible Cultural Heritage.[3] Cultural heritage need not be individual in character or important solely for a single group; it can serve to connect representatives of various cultures living in a given region. Cultural heritage is also a sensitive area, since it involves the rights of indigenous peoples, family heirlooms and objects important in religious rites and rituals. The idea of the commonality of cultural heritage in international law, raised later in this book, confirms how broad the concept of cultural heritage actually is, and how difficult it is to accurately reflect its importance.

Lyndel Vivien Prott and Patrick O'Keefe have written on the phenomenon of "cultural property" with reference to property rights and objects of ownership, and on "cultural heritage," which involves a gradual dereification of heritage.[4] A more recent summary of the subject, often quoted in scholarly literature, has been prepared by Janet Blake.[5] This shift in direction for the concept of cultural heritage and its partial transformation can be considered in several contexts. The first concerns the scope of cultural heritage and its components resulting from the perception of heritage as an element of the human environment and attributing to it certain specific functions in the development of society. The second context addresses the right to own components of cultural heritage; this is the result of putting together the notions of "culture" and "property," and entails a potential conflict arising from their separate meanings. The third context refers to the specific nature of common law and statutory law systems. In many countries having a statutory legal system, cultural property is understood not only as movable things, but also as real estate

[2] Williams (1978), p. 202.

[3] Lixinski (2013), pp. 7–8.

[4] Prott and O'Keefe (1992).

[5] Blake (2000).

or intangible cultural heritage.[6] New terminology is invented partly to conceal the fact that not all resources can be protected as legal instruments and definitions currently stand. Decision-makers accept the creation of new forms of protection and special regimes as a way of solving the problem without revealing its scale to the wider public.[7]

Regarding the first variant, it should be noted that many studies accept that the broadest of the available concepts is "cultural heritage." Meanwhile, in the discussion over how to define cultural heritage, issues arose concerning indigenous rights, cultural rights, and the participation of individuals in managing cultural heritage. The idea of intangible heritage, whose definition is also fraught with difficulty, was further added to the concept of material heritage.[8] The view was expressed that defining intangible heritage represents not only an undeniable development in international law on the protection of cultural heritage, but also an important step towards a more multidimensional view of heritage.[9] Furthermore, the approach to heritage has fundamentally changed; specifically, it has come to include development and management elements, and its permanent task is to prepare long-range plans for managing cultural heritage at the national and regional levels, as well as plans for cultural policy at the level of the European Union (EU) and the 2030 Agenda for Sustainable Development.[10]

Whether we are dealing with cultural property or cultural heritage, there is no doubt that these concepts are largely unstable, even fluid. The term "fluid modernity" was coined by Zygmunt Bauman, and his theory is vital for understanding the concept of cultural heritage and its place in international and domestic legal frameworks. Bauman wrote about the continuous reconstruction of culture and changes in how products of culture are perceived because of new approaches and interpretations.[11] Under this notion, the meaning of culture is constantly changing. How might this affect the concept of cultural heritage? After all, there are some elements whose importance will not change significantly, but can only grow over time, as in the case of *Lady with an Ermine* by Leonardo da Vinci. However, others—such as works of modern art initially derided as offensive or pornographic—have been recognized as heritage components in the years or decades since their creation. One such example is the painting *Frenzy* by Władysław Podkowiński, or the contemporary works of Iwona Demko which, despite being accompanied by a theoretical basis prepared by their author, are not comprehensible for every viewer. On the one hand, there are

[6] Frigo (2004), p. 369.

[7] Szafrański (2017), p. 317.

[8] More on defininition cultural heritage and intangible cultural heritage Francioni (2020), pp. 56–57.

[9] Francioni (2020), pp. 56–57.

[10] Resolution 70/1. Transforming Our World: The 2030 Agenda for Sustainable Development, Adopted by the General Assembly on 25 September 2015, A/RES/70/1. https://www.un.org/en/development/desa/population/migration/generalassembly/docs/globalcompact/A_RES_70_1_E.pdf. Accessed 1 June 2022.

[11] Bauman (2011), pp. 27–31.

resources passed on to future generations who have no choice about what kind of cultural heritage they receive. On the other hand, there is a need to make a determined selection, which means that "one can speak of a kind of thought loop—we protect certain kinds of remnants of the past because they are cultural property, and cultural property is protected due to its very nature."[12] We are faced, then, with the impossibility of doing away with the entirety of cultural heritage and the need to select which components are to be given special attention. It is the law that provides a formula for making such a selection and ensuring that resources are passed down appropriately to future generations.

The purpose of the revisions being made in how heritage is defined is to keep up with inevitable change. Cultural heritage continues to grow as new human and natural property is created, and this means that only some elements can be fully protected. There is an advantage in not having a fixed single legal definition of heritage, which is visible in international legal instruments. For example, the definition of cultural heritage found in UNESCO documents, including conventions and recommendations, is adapted in each case to serve the goals of a given document.[13] In turn, the range of a legal definition in domestic law usually covers both the act itself and secondary legislation to ensure continuity,[14] unless another definition is proposed in the latter. In applicable literature and case law, numerous attempts have been made to connect "property" with "heritage" (cultural heritage property[15]), while other proposals act as a kind of bridge between legal or ownership rights and those based on a relationship with the state, such as cultural patrimony or cultural objects.[16] A constant element of considerations on heritage, regardless of its ownership status, is its relationship with the environment, location and humankind.[17]

Insofar as components of culture represent value, they remain connected to the notion of property; that is, rights of an individual over a given object.[18] The aversion to the term "cultural property" that exists in the case of exceptional objects of religious significance or those connected with deceased persons results from the additional spiritual value stemming from external tradition or beliefs and attributed to certain components of the cultural heritage. The terminological inconsistencies found in academic works and state documents result from an overlapping of the scope of meaning of some concepts and from an intuitive understanding of the meaning of a given term within a specific statement.

The way heritage is defined affects its commodification, which is fraught with risk, as indicated in the introduction. The phenomenon of the commodification of

[12] Szafrański (2017), p. 316.

[13] Cf. O'Keefe (1999), p. 44.

[14] Zieliński (2002), pp. 201–202. This is in case of the Polish definition.

[15] Sax (2007).

[16] Fincham (2011), p. 676.

[17] Lixinski (2013), pp. 5–7.

[18] Gerstenblith (1995), p. 567.

cultural heritage comes up in the debate over the future of the art market, and in the new perception of heritage as an element of the development of the European Union.[19] For instance, the growth in tourism linked to cultural heritage sites is economically beneficial for regions. Unfortunately, it does not always occur with the needs of the local community in mind. It is well-known that cities rich in historical objects, such as Venice, are now considered as being exclusively geared towards tourists, while the inhabitants and their needs take a back seat. On the other hand, examples can be found of immovable components of cultural heritage being adapted and used for new purposes while stimulating job creation and economic activity. This trend appears to be increasingly important. Combining new functions of immovable historical objects with a dialogue involving the local community and heritage stakeholders was the core of the Forget Heritage project conducted using funds from Interreg Central Europe in the years 2015–2019.[20] Certainly, the course charted in that project for adapting heritage to meet the needs of people today is gaining in importance at the global scale, and is affecting how heritage is commonly perceived, not only in terms of ownership, but also in terms of the meaning of heritage for the community.[21]

Reaping benefits from cultural heritage has another dimension in the case of indigenous peoples.[22] Participants in the debate over who is entitled to commercialize certain products and launch them on the market include representatives of businesses, indigenous communities and, of course, lawyers, all of whom assess the commercial value of and the right to exploit cultural heritage components. The example of the Quileute tribe, which gained popularity in connection with the books of Stephanie Meyer (in which members of the tribe are werewolves) shows the power of the business built on *The Twilight Saga* and products targeted at its fans.[23] This case, embedded in the reality of the film business, reveals how many problems are connected with the commercial exploitation of elements of the culture of the indigenous peoples of America, and forces the questions of who should profit from and who should set the rules for such activity.

Cultural heritage can also be defined by looking for its function in a developing society and its role in strengthening the local economy. This can also involve identifying a section of heritage, valuating it, and granting it more effective, and therefore more costly, protection than that granted to other elements. The multi-dimensionality of heritage allows for this, which makes cultural heritage an attractive resource in terms of building mutual understanding, supporting economic

[19]Communication from the Commission to the European Parliament, the Council, the European Economic and Social Committee and the Committee of the Regions Towards an integrated approach to cultural heritage for Europe. Brussels 22.7.2014. COM/2014/0477 final.

[20]Forget Heritage, https://www.interreg-central.eu/Content.Node/Forget-heritage.html. Accessed 1 June 2022.

[21]Jagielska-Burduk (2019), pp. 259–263.

[22]Carpenter et al. (2010), p. 582.

[23]Carpenter et al. (2010), pp. 581–582.

progress in the cultural sector, and developing tourism. Cultural competences are acknowledged as vital to building the future; these include appropriate mechanisms for managing cultural heritage. The elasticity of cultural heritage manifests in its continuous transformation, and in the discovery of new dimensions, including the use of new technologies and the appearance of new entities on the map of cultural heritage stakeholders.[24]

The existence of conflicts of interest over heritage—not only the basic conflict between private and public interests—is manifest in the large number of entities having different needs, which do not always overlap and are not solely focused on preserving heritage.[25] This is why attempts to reconcile conflicting or competitive interests (e.g., those of local communities versus the international community) and to hand resources down to future generations in the best possible condition run into difficulties connected with the new dimensions of heritage and its new functions. For example, in a report on public space and the exercise of cultural rights, it was stated that cyberspace is also a public space. The argument was that, to discharge their responsibilities regarding human rights, public authorities must take steps to guarantee all citizens access to and participation in cyberspace, and further, that the scope and importance of the problem require a separate study.[26] Given the current tendency of art—and therefore cultural heritage—to move into the digital sphere, which was forced upon creators in 2020 due to the COVID-19 pandemic, questions also arise in private law over access to property available online.

In the Polish legal debate, the basic definitions discussed are those of cultural heritage and monuments. It is necessary to address this here, as the evolution of legal definitions regarding cultural heritage differs from country to country.

The most popular definition is the one proposed by Jan Piotr Pruszyński:

> resources constituting immovable and movable things together with the spiritual values associated therewith, historical and moral phenomena acknowledged as worthy of legal protection for the good of society and its development and of being transmitted to subsequent generations due to their understandable and accepted historical, patriotic, religious, scientific or artistic value, which are significant for identity and the continuity of political, social and cultural development, for demonstrating truths and commemorating historical events, cultivating the sense of beauty and community as a civilisation.[27]

The definition of cultural heritage was acknowledged in 2007 for the purpose of deliberations by the Constitutional Tribunal.[28] In my view, that definition's limitation of cultural heritage to resources constituting immovable and movable things is its greatest weakness. This can be eliminated by assuming that the author had a broad understanding of "things" in mind. A reference should be made to a ruling by the

---

[24] Gaweł (2016), pp. 34–44.

[25] Vadi (2014).

[26] Report of the Special Rapporteur in the field of cultural rights, A/74/255, p. 24.

[27] Pruszyński (2001), p. 50.

[28] Polish Constitutional Court, Judgement of 8 October 2007, K 20/07, OTK-A 2007/9/102. Polish Official Journal (Dz. U.) 2007, No. 192, item 1394.

Provincial Administrative Court in Warsaw, which drew attention to the large number of definitions of cultural heritage and stated that

> although this is only one of many definitions of a broad semantic concept, there is no doubt that it refers to items inherited from the past and functioning today that are inextricably linked with the culture and history of a given country.[29]

The reference in the definition to movable and immovable things as real estate, however, suggests that the author used the word "things" in the strict sense, and made a division between movable things and real estate. Thus, the definition proposed in 2001 seems inadequate to today's challenges, 20 years and myriad cases later. Heritage is increasing not only in the sense that new components similar to previous ones are being created; new types of property that were previously unknown or never before considered as part of heritage are also emerging. For this reason, it is more fitting to employ a definition that refers to material and intangible property so that neither elements that have long been considered heritage resources nor those that have enriched it only relatively recently due to technological progress fall outside of the scope of the definition.

This conforms to the need to set the terminology used in cultural heritage protection in order at the national level. The proposal to introduce a definition of cultural heritage as an object of protection in the legal system could serve to tighten up legislation concerning cultural property. Wojciech Szafrański argues that this scattering of definitions is one of the main causes of the lack of systemic cohesion in this area.[30] A similar purpose may be achieved by adopting new legislative acts relating to museums, libraries, archives, monuments, and the art market and introducing them separately into a single heritage code. So far, there are separate legal acts covering these issues. It seems that working in parallel would make it possible to build a coherent system. The central part of that system should be a general section containing key principles and the subject of the regulations. Including a definition of cultural heritage in this part might be appropriate. In my view, it would be best to focus primarily on defining protection and guardianship, the purpose of the act, legal principles, and definitions of what property is subject to protection in libraries, museums, and archives in the general section. By establishing a definition of cultural heritage at the doctrinal level to be used in assessing the constitutionality of legal provisions or the effectiveness of the system as a whole, there would be no need to create a separate legal definition.

The legal regulations covering cultural heritage in administrative law and administrative activities have effects in the sphere of civil law, specifically concerning civil law relationships.[31] The forms and mechanisms of protection and guardianship were analyzed in the context of the concepts of historical objects, intangible cultural

---

[29] Voivodship Administrative Court in Warsaw, Judgement of 3rd December 2020, VII SA/Wa 1156/20, LEX no. 3161886.

[30] Szafrański (2019), p. 64.

[31] Zalasińska (2010), p. 164.

property, family souvenirs and what are known as "cult objects." Piotr Dobosz pointed to a "private" element, that

> with regard to cultural heritage as broadly understood, and within the scope of its protection, guardianship and formation, the reality around us does not lead solely to forms and methods of a public law nature. The reflections quoted indicate that such mechanisms may also have a private law dimension.[32]

A second key definition concerning cultural heritage protection in Poland is the legal definition of a monument (historical object), contained in Article 3 pt. 1 of the Act on the Protection and Guardianship of Monuments (APGM):

> real estate or movable things, or parts or sets thereof, which were made by people or in connection with human activity and which constitute evidence of a bygone era or events and whose preservation lies in the interest of society due to their historical, artistic or scientific value.[33]

Without a doubt, the legal definition of a monument only encompasses that part of cultural heritage which is granted protection in the APGM. Given the fact that cultural heritage comprises more than monuments, the second chapter deals with property that also constitutes components of cultural heritage, but which cannot always be considered monuments or historical objects. The mosaic of components of cultural heritage will be completed in the Chap. 5, with a reflection on archaeological artefacts, national cultural property, and public collections.

A third definition which should be addressed is that of cultural property. A definition of this term is contained in the no-longer binding Act on Protection of Cultural Property (APCP 1962).[34] Under Article 2 APCP,

> cultural property in the meaning of the act is every movable or immovable object, from the past or contemporary, that is significant for the heritage and cultural development due to its historical, scientific or artistic value.

Cultural property also appears in the conceptual framework of constitutional law,[35] specifically in Article 73 of the Polish Constitution, which concerns the freedom to enjoy the products of culture.[36] The newest legal definition of cultural property is contained in the Act on the Restitution of National Cultural Property[37] (ARNCP), discussed in Chap. 5. Here, though, it is worth pointing out that the definition proposed therein in a way constitutes a combination of the 1962 definition and the current definition of a monument, encompassing not only monuments but also movable things that are not monuments

---

[32] Dobosz (2018), p. 64.

[33] More on defining historical monument in APGM: Jagielska-Burduk (2011), pp. 68–84.

[34] Act on Protection of Cultural Property of 15 February 1962, consolidated text. Polish Official Journal (Dz. U.) 1999, No. 98, item 1150.

[35] Izdebski (2019), pp. 112–115.

[36] Cf. Frankiewicz-Bodynek (2019).

[37] Act of 15 May 2017 on the Restitution of National Cultural Property, consolidated text. Polish Official Journal (Dz. U.) 2019, item 1519.

as well as their components parts or sets thereof, whose preservation lies in the interest of society due to their artistic, historical or scientific value, or due to their importance for heritage and cultural development (Article 2 pt. 1 ARNCP).

All of the above definitions are centered on tangible things.

In this work I use the concept of cultural property within the meaning of the definitions cited and with reference to the relevant legal acts, but also a broader concept of cultural property understood as components of cultural heritage that include both material and intangible property. I use the term cultural heritage in the meaning ascribed in a given act of international law with an indication of what that act is, or in the meaning accepted by Jan Piotr Pruszyński when discussing Polish law. In the latter case, components of cultural heritage will also include property that does not constitute things.

2.3 Tangible and Intangible Assets

Civil law distinguishes material property from intangible property. This makes it possible to define what material property is and how it differs from intangible property. Both may be the object of a civil law relationship, but only material objects can be classified as things. Apart from things, other types of material property exist, such as water in its free state, mineral deposits, and air: these only become things when isolated. Intangible property includes works, computer programs, industrial designs, and personal rights. Specific regulations exist in relation to some of them. The division of *res* into *corporales* and *incorporales* and the Romanist tradition have been used to analyze changes in private law and in the search for a "new order."[38] The usefulness of separating intangible property as objects of human dominion is just one important example of that use. Wojciech Dajczak states that "the evolutionary tendency reconstructed makes it possible to question the sense of using the criterion of materiality as an objective restriction of property."[39] He also notes that the integration of "material and intangible objects of legal control does not rule out differences in specific regulations."[40] This division is also very important when evaluating the changes taking place in the legal protection of cultural heritage in private law.

The division into material and intangible property is not identical to the division into "material" cultural heritage and intangible cultural heritage. There is no overall binding and accepted definition of cultural heritage, and concerning the needs of a given act of law or international convention what cultural heritage is, how we define the scope of its components in the form of cultural property and how we define

[38] Dajczak (2008), pp. 92–95.

[39] Dajczak (2007), p. 219.

[40] Dajczak (2007), p. 223.

intangible cultural heritage are assumed.[41] Without doubt, the border between cultural heritage and intangible cultural heritage is a hazy one. The development of copyright and granting protection to works have meant that the importance of intangible property in civil law trading has grown, while such property has become an object of civil law relations. The issue of preserving intangible property on material media has been discussed in the context of copyright.[42]

Moreover, a decision to acquire property in the form of a sculpture is not based on the object itself, but in the artistic statement expressed by the object.[43] It sometimes happens that a decision to acquire a work is caused by intangible connections with the object as a carrier of memories or a witness to history. Here I have in mind, for example, the auction sale of an Omega art deco watch from 1934 that once belonged to the artist at *Władysław Szpilman. The Virtuoso's Study* in September 2020 at DESA Unicum.[44] The value of the item, which sold for 210,000 zlotys, was certainly affected by the fact that the watch had been in Szpilman's possession since the war.[45] In this case there is no work-medium relationship, but the undeniable intangible value of the material object and its history determined its material value and its value as part of the cultural heritage.

Some intangible property, such as stories and folk songs, may be handed down from generation to generation without ever being recorded.[46] Only inventorying activities aimed at preserving them for future generations led to their being saved in some tangible form. This is an important element of cultural heritage protection. Certainly, it protects important assets for a given group. Mechanisms for protecting industrial property are now evidently becoming one of the instruments that can be used to protect intangible heritage, although they are not a complete "tailor-made" solution. Intangible heritage and its cultivation may lead to material results. The basis for the creation of some cultural heritage known to us is creative thought; the objects are the *corpus mechanicum* of the work. Where it is impossible to identify the author, this does not affect the justification for granting protection to a work as a cultural heritage component; that protection extends beyond the interest of the creator and is for the purpose of protecting the interests of the future generations to whom the heritage components are to be transmitted.

The question arises: can cultural heritage exist purely in the form of intangible property? It seems that it can, if we consider works accessible solely in digital form stored in the Internet cloud.[47] Further, nowadays the classic division into work and carrier does not always apply. This applies regarding works created in the web and

[41] Definitions in the UNESCO cultural conventions.

[42] Zoll (1947), p. 26.

[43] Katner (2014), Art. 45 [Commentary].

[44] https://desa.pl/pl/wyniki/memorabilia-wladyslawa-szpilmana/c2o5/. Accessed 1 June 2022.

[45] https://desa.pl/pl/historie/zegarek-i-wieczne-pioro-wladyslawa-szpilmana/. Accessed 1 June 2022.

[46] Katner (2012), p. 1359.

[47] Art works stored in the e-cloud: Stec (2015b), p. 89, footnote 29.

stored not only on an ordinary medium but only in the cloud, on an external server. The creation of works designated solely for an Internet audience, without being preserved in any material form, or the co-creation of works of art by the artist as initiator and the public as participants, go beyond the work-carrier scheme. In the case of cultural heritage, not only material property can act as a medium. This is easily demonstrated by the protection of cultural heritage in the form of traditions, customs, and craftsmanship. All of these are centered on a human being who possesses the requisite knowledge and skills.

In this connection, situating cultural heritage in the civil law system must first take account of its multitude of forms and its continually expanding character, not only in those dimensions already known, but also in forms that are impossible to foresee today or related to technological progress. The cultural heritage may be seen as the set of both material and intangible property. The unlimited forms it can take on mean that, in private law, it will appear in either purely intangible forms of property or as intangible property fixed as an object. It will also appear in nature as material property constituting things and as material property not having that character. One example discussed further on in this book is the status of archaeological artefacts before their excavation in private law.[48]

The private law system and protection of material and intangible property affect the scope of protection granted to cultural heritage provided by private law. Other claims will serve to prevent infringements of intangible property, such as cultural property constituting works, as well as other material property. By this I mean existing protection apart from the mechanisms contained in the legal acts protecting historical objects and the provisions of EU and international law concerning cultural heritage. The division into material and intangible property reflects the division into material cultural heritage and intangible cultural heritage only to a certain extent. The value that carries over this division is the value of heritage for future generations, but also its importance for current generations. That importance need not be universal or national; it is enough for a community to have a bond with a certain kind of heritage at the local level. When we see a relationship between the intangible value incorporated in cultural heritage and its value as material property, it will not be possible to make a clear distinction between material and intangible property in the case of cultural heritage.

It is precisely this intangible value that can be of primary importance when locating a given item in trade within the system of protection. At present, as regards a clear majority of cultural heritage components, control that is effective *erga omnes* is based on ownership. Perhaps the right path for cultural heritage is to recognize that the division into material and intangible property is the common factor of the very essence of the cultural heritage. Reversing the order and concentrating on the essence of heritage will make it possible to deal with issues on a different plane. It may be that such an approach will have important practical consequences. It will

---

[48] The notion of tangible property that does not constitute a thing will be developed further in the chapter on state-ownership of archaeological property.

make it possible to create a kind of base of values that can transform the status of property into that which is deserving of being preserved by and for future generations. It will make it possible to quickly verify the location of a given element in the system of protection.

The meaning of the word "value" has undergone a far-reaching semantic decomposition. In the past, the words "value" and "valuable" did not have such a strong economic connotation. Yet today, the word "valuable" has become "linguistically lost," with its meaning approaching that of "costly"—from which the economization of the term requires but one more step to arrive at "price"—the price of cultural property.[49] Nowadays the concepts of value and valuation are often confused. Valuations of cultural property are usually made for the needs of the art market, that is, to determine not the value, but the price of art works in trade; such valuations usually take publicly available historical market data as a starting point.[50] At present, there is no standard for the valuation of cultural property, although these are essential (even when no trade is involved), for example, in the insurance process. The developing art market began to capitalize cultural property (even that which was excluded from trade) and to build a new level of economic value of cultural property as a determinant of non-economic value—its "importance" or "weight" (the more expensive the item, the more valuable and important). At the same time, two additional elements were imposed that had already been observed by the turn of the 19th and 20th centuries in connection with the emergence of the Austrian School in the theory of property (and later, American property theory)[51]—and in this way attempts were made to answer the question of whether things (here cultural property) have a defined value in and of themselves (the theory of objective value) or whether we attribute value to them depending on our preferences or needs (the theory of subjective value).[52] Resolving this problem of whether cultural property has its own value or derivative value (borrowed from other cultural property) is the key to the possibility and legitimacy of classifying cultural property.

In the 1960s in Poland, a campaign to classify historical objects began. It was conducted by the Monuments Documentation Centre (headed by Kazimierz Malinowski) and involved a special base of instructions on how to classify particular objects into one of five classes (the most valuable being those in class zero). There was no economic criterion, however. The particular class in which an object was grouped was determined by various evaluation criteria—its value at the global, regional, or national scale; the concept of representativeness; stylistic purity; substantial physical condition; and technical criteria. That system is no longer binding in Poland. However, in the "culture of valuation," the importance of economic valuations has grown immensely, and this often leads to moral hazard as a derivative of

[49] Tatarkiewicz (1968), pp. 11–15.

[50] Szafrański and Wilk (2017), pp. 139–141.

[51] Works of Ch. Ehrenfelsa, M. Urabna and O. Krausa from 1893–1937 were important for development of the theory of value.

[52] Tatarkiewicz (1968), pp. 15–20.

the non-transparency of the art market and the gigantic asymmetry of information on that market.

While it is the norm today for the real estate market in Anglo-Saxon countries, Fair Market Value (FMV) should perhaps be utilized in the field of cultural property. FMV is not only for commercial purposes (the purchase or sale of real estate), but also provides information on the value of real estate in general. There is no doubt that when there is an "economization" of all areas of life, economic valuation will also take place in the area of heritage. Even today, insurance, compensation for damage, theft, etc. of cultural property necessitate a shift from attributing value to making a specific valuation, and therefore to develop standards for doing so. In relation to cultural property, or components of the material and intangible heritage in general, the concept of FMV (along with the procedure and system it entails) may become a remedy for the deformation of the classic market formula for the valuation of cultural property (perpetrated by intermediaries, sellers, and buyers on the art market). This is vital in that there are heritage components, including especially those constituting public property, that are considered "priceless" or "invaluable." Their removal from trade due to their ownership structure calls into question the idea of applying valuation as known on the art market without any additional safety valve. FMV could provide such additional security, from both the objective side (ways of determining value) and the subjective side (persons are authorized to perform a valuation provided certain criteria and the public trust are fulfilled).

In seeking to attribute heritage in general to the categories of material and immaterial property, what comes to the fore is the importance and role of heritage in the intangible and impalpable context. This is confirmed each time by the definitions of cultural property and historical objects in Polish acts of law, recognizing value criteria and thereby acknowledging property as a part of cultural heritage.[53] Only afterwards will a component be ordered according to the criteria of materiality and intangibility. The right to the component, though, will be invariable, and will be formally similar to ownership. Yet it will not always be possible to qualify property protected by law within the dichotomous division between movable and immovable things. The next step, then, will be to classify material property constituting, or not constituting, things. In the case of intangible property, the problem will be one of assigning components to intangible heritage or virtual/digital cultural heritage.

[53] Cf. Zajęcki (2012); Zeidler (2008).

2.4 The Legal Concepts of Res (Material Objects) and Collection

2.4.1 Things

The definitions of "thing" and "set of things" are vital for cultural heritage in private law. Determining the relationship between the legal construction of things and cultural heritage and its components, including monuments within the meaning of the APGM, will make it possible to determine what subjective rights may apply to a given component. This in turn will make it possible to answer the question of whether one can consider a subjective right *in rem* in each case or whether, due to the properties of a given component, these will be rights similar to rights *in rem*, or other absolute property rights.

Under Article 45 of the Polish Civil Code (CC),[54] only material objects can be things. The definition of "thing" adopted in the Code states that the key features of things are their material character and their separateness.[55] Things constitute autonomous legal property.[56] Although one can say that the definition of "thing" accepted in the legal sciences is well established, Polish authors keep returning to it in the literature. Bronisław Ziemianin states that

> a doubt may arise, however, as to whether that definition fits the content of Article 45 CC, since that provision does not indicate the second characteristic of things, that is, their separation from nature.[57]

In Ziemianin's opinion, that doubt disappears upon an analysis of the definition of an object as a separate element of reality we perceive through our senses.[58] That division constitutes a framework for creating laws on material and intangible property. Some components of material property are things. Other components that cannot be separated from nature, such as mineral deposits and water resources, are not things. The detailed provisions governing the status of such property establish how they are to be managed and the scope of the civil law relationships that can concern them.[59]

The influence of the concept of things on the development of the civil law system has been examined in the context of Polish law. The adoption in Polish law of a narrow understanding of things[60] led to "the development of subjective rights to

[54] Act of 23 April 1964 Civil Code, consolidated text. Polish Official Journal (Dz. U) 2020, item 1740 with later amendments.

[55] Bednarek (1997), p. 47.

[56] Grzybowski (1985), p. 411.

[57] Ziemianin (2007), p. 429.

[58] Ziemianin (2007), p. 430.

[59] See Sect. 4.2.

[60] Ignatowicz (2000), p. 17.

control various types of property."[61] A too-narrow understanding of things is reflected in the institution of property rights.[62] The definition of a thing accepted in a given legal system results in either property rights or other rights being applied to property.[63] Such other rights concern material property not constituting things (e.g., water) or intangible property in the form of works, such as works of art. Edward Gniewek argues that "due to the deficiencies in the legal terminology, here we use the term 'other property' ('intellectual property')."[64] Thus, apart from the right of ownership, in the case of works we have another absolute property right.[65]

How a thing is defined is crucial to determine ownership, and when it comes to components of cultural heritage, the discussion on the object of an ownership right comes back like a boomerang. It has been argued that public law alone is not enough to form a legal framework of protection. It is then worth considering a return to a sharp division between movable and immovable things, as well as the criteria for making that division. One must also attend to the issue of material property not constituting things and the right thereto. This need is justified by the advancement seen in the current debate on the law of cultural heritage and the necessity of finding solutions in civil law that will allow new protective regimes to be established.

Today, the division of things into movable and immovable differs from past divisions. The division has not always been based on the very nature of a given thing. In the law of Mazovia, a herd of more than ten mares was treated as real estate, as was the amount obtained from a sale of real estate.[66] Certain types of property considered valuable, such as weapons and jewellery, were counted as real estate.[67] This division was intended to emphasize the importance and value of certain types of property. Real estate was treated as being the most valuable, but some types of movable property that were either more precious or held in large quantities were equated with it. The search for new protective regimes for components of cultural heritage may also involve changes in the object of ownership or based on new legal structures deriving from new divisions.

The problem of classification continues to arise, including in relation to multi-component property. Since only things can be objects of ownership, how should one define an absolute right to other property of a multi-component nature that is often distinguished through the prism of its function and purpose? Here I have in mind something similar to enterprises, agricultural holdings or inheritances' that are complex in terms of components but carved out in the provisions of civil law. The problem of the abolition of co-ownership of a farm or enterprise has been addressed

[61] Żabiński (1974), p. 256.

[62] Stelmachowski (1969), p. 207.

[63] Żabiński (1974), p. 254.

[64] Gniewek (2013), p. 349.

[65] About intellectual property right: Czajkowska-Dąbrowska (2007).

[66] Borkowska-Bagieńska et al. (1994), p. 139.

[67] Maciejewski (2007), p. 299.

by Bronisław Ziemianin,[68] while the problem of enterprises has also been discussed by Andrzej Stelmachowski. He emphasized the material and intangible dimensions of an enterprise and its components.[69]

In the interbellum, Fryderyk Zoll wrote that

> a thing is part of nature in the natural or a processed state—it takes up space, and because it can be perceived by the senses, in Polish terminology it is sometimes called a sensorial thing (*res corporalis*).

Even then, Zoll pointed out that this was "an imprecise name, since things that exist only as ideas, such as works of art, also act on the senses."[70] This is why an attempt was made to depart from the traditional object of ownership in a draft property law, which, however, was not successful.[71] Intangible property is divided into objects of intellectual or industrial property rights. Continuing the line of thought on sensorial things that owe their existence to creative activity, they can be seen to function in two dimensions (as works and as things). In the meaning of civil law, however, a thing must have material form and be potentially subject to control. Apart from the attempt Fryderyk Zoll writes about, in the years that followed no efforts were made to introduce new legal solutions. Legislative activity and the legal sciences focused on specifying and adapting rights to material property not constituting things and intangible property to systemic changes; absolute rights arose in relation to such property.

Regarding the appropriation of material objects, Jan Wasilkowski also spoke out:

> a broader scope of ownership in civil law would lead to a blurring of the fundamental difference between the right, which is the basis of all property rights institutions, and the rights that derive from it.[72]

Wasilkowski assumed that the existence of other rights would be derivative in relation to ownership. Yet it should be considered whether this blurring of the differences between rights mentioned above is not already slowly taking place, where at least those rights to other material and intangible property are similar to ownership. Andrzej Stelmachowski asked "does the engagement of the public interest favour such a legislative separation of those rights as would exclude the application of civil law?"[73] His answer was negative, although he categorically pointed to another existing practice, including the laws on seed, forests, weapons and ammunition, and pharmaceutical products.[74] In this context, he pointed to problems arising from the appearance of new types of property or an additional element of the public interest, whereas Hubert Izdebski has observed a clear reversal

[68] Ziemianin (2007), p. 432.

[69] Stelmachowski (1994), pp. 107–108.

[70] Zoll (1920), p. 20.

[71] Zoll (1947), p. 22–26

[72] Wasilkowski (1965), p. 815.

[73] Stelmachowski (1994), p. 110.

[74] Stelmachowski (1994), p. 108.

from a culture of ownership to a culture of paid use. He bases his findings on the emergence of new institutions such as leasing and time-sharing, and argues that these are leading to a "blurring" of ownership and, potentially, to the "self-liquidation of property."[75] It should be mentioned that this blurring of ownership, and specifically the element of temporary use, often comes up in discussion on ownership or other rights to cultural heritage, where it is frequently considered in the context of current and future generations.[76]

The definition of a thing has not been completely accepted in legislation on the protection of historical objects. It seems, though, that this was not due to a search for additional non-sensorial values in historical objects subject to protection, but to the issue of how to describe and keep records of them. Piotr Dobosz addressed the relationship between the category of things (movables and immovables) and the conceptual category of a historical object in the period when the APCP was in force. In his opinion, "the object of consideration should be described in the language of the branch of law to which it belongs, in this case the language of administrative law."[77] He pointed to the incompatibility of the definition of a historical object with the dichotomous division into movable and immovable things. The issue of treating a movable part or component part (e.g., polychrome decorations) as a separate historical object has been raised many times, and is involved in striving to maintain the integrity of historical objects.[78]

This position must be verified once more due to the discussions taking place over the emergence of a branch of the cultural heritage law and to the current structure of protective regulations, in which private law is beginning to play a key role. Furthermore, Wojciech Kowalski has indicated that the APCP

> does not provide a decisive, consistent chapter of regulations concerning movable and immovable property, even though their different natures necessitate an entirely different method of protecting them, making them available, supervising and conserving them, etc.[79]

What is noticeable is not only that the division of historical objects into movables and immovables is divorced from the science of civil law, but also that, as regards the provisions intended to create protective mechanism, that division is blurred.

When the legislator's artificial division of historical objects into movables and immovables is confronted with the civil law division into movable things and real estate, a lack of connection between the two divisions appears. Article 6 par. 1 APGM lists sample monuments that are immovable, movable and archaeological, where archaeological artefacts can take the form of movable or immovable historical objects.[80] Moreover, one can get the impression that this procedure was not fully

[75] Izdebski (2004), p. 175.

[76] Jagielska-Burduk (2016b), pp. 60–65.

[77] Dobosz (1997), pp. 72–73.

[78] Jagielska-Burduk (2011), pp. 197–210.

[79] Kowalski (1986), p. 173.

[80] 6.1 APGM The protection and care are subject, regardless of the state of preservation:

thought out, and that the method is flawed for being highly arbitrary.[81] This indicates that

> the norm refers to historical objects in the material sense, and so the guarantees resulting from the regulation in question apply to objects, goods and property that are historical objects in the meaning of the act and that have not been disclosed in the register of monuments and regional records of monuments.[82]

Without going further into the problem of protecting historical objects not covered by the forms of protection granted to historical objects or not disclosed in the register,[83] we should still pause over the first part of the above citation. Indirectly, it follows from that passage that historical objects will not only be things within the meaning of the Civil Code (objects mentioned above), but also property of a

---

(1) immovable monuments being, in particular:

  (a) cultural landscapes,
  (b) urban and rural arrangement and building complexes,
  (c) works of architecture and construction,
  (d) works of defence engineering
  (e) technical installations, in particular mines, steelworks, power stations and other industrial plants
  (f) cemeteries,
  (g) parks, gardens and other forms of designed greenery,
  (h) places commemorating historical events or the activity of prominent personalities or institutions;

(2) movable monuments being, in particular:

  (a) works of plastic arts, artistic crafts and applied arts,
  (b) collections constituting collections of objects collected and arranged according to the ideas of people who created these collections,
  (c) numismatic and historical memorabilia, in particular militaria, flags, seals, badges, medals and orders
  (d) technical products, in particular machines, means of transport, machines and tools bearing witness to material culture, characteristic of old and new forms of the economy, documenting the level of science and the development of civilisation
  (e) library materials referred to in Article 5 of the Act of 27 June 1997 on libraries (Polish Official Journal [Dz. U.] 2019, item 1479),
  (f) musical instruments,
  (g) folk art and handicraft products and other ethnographic objects,
  (h) objects commemorating historical events or the activity of prominent personalities or institutions;

(3) archaeological monuments which are, in particular:

  (a) field remains of prehistoric and historical settlement,
  (b) cemeteries,
  (c) barrows,
  (d) relics of economic, religious and artistic activity.

[81] On the similarities between APMG and APCP: Golat (2004), p. 27.

[82] Michalak and Ginter (2016), pp. 87–88.

[83] About model of the dilligent holder: Jagielska-Burduk (2014), pp. 311–318.

different nature. One can distinguish three basic issues, regarding: ensuring protection in cases of illegal trading, detaching the object of protection from things in the civil law meaning, and granting property not strictly constituting things protection under the APGM.

First, it is necessary to discuss the unsuitability of the division into movable and immovable historical objects, which results from the need to protect some historical objects in the form of statues, mouldings, and murals. Under the binding law, components of cultural heritage (understood as historical objects) are treated in principle as things, including movable things and real estate. The legislator referred appropriately to the basic concepts of civil law in the legal definitions of movable and immovable historical objects found in the APGM. The practice of classifying historical objects as movable or immovable, however, extends beyond the civil law division.[84] This stems mainly from the purpose of identifying a historical object and how it is recorded in, for example, the register of historical objects; that is, how it is secured. Entering "movable" elements in the form of sculptures and statues fixed to the buildings makes it possible to quickly begin the search for a lost object and to identify it.

Second, based on the enumeration found in the APGM, it is difficult to define what a historical object (monument) is. For example, the immovable historical objects listed include parks and gardens, which means that protection is granted to the park, not to the real estate on which it located. In this way, the historical object is divorced from the real estate.[85] One can look at the protection of a cultural landscape in yet another way, as an area identified by people that contains both natural elements and products of civilization, historically formed by natural factors and human activity (Article 3 pt. 14 APGM). Defining a cultural landscape as an immovable historical object, as in the example above, does not fit in at all with the definition of real estate. Furthermore, space is also formed by intangible elements, which will also be protected under that provision. An example of this is where a given space is associated with specific practices or ceremonies. Just to note that in applications for inclusion on the World Heritage List, the element of intangible heritage is also very significant to the evaluation.

Third, a no less important element is that of material property not constituting things. The structure of the definitions of a historical object, movable historical object, and immovable historical object, in which direct reference is made to things, presents the greatest practical challenge. An analysis of the act permits the conclusion that protection is afforded to property in material form but not necessarily constituting a thing in the strict sense.[86] An example of this is archaeological artefacts before being discovered and excavated,[87] as well as before and after

[84]Cf. Jagielska-Burduk (2011), pp. 197–211.

[85]More about distinction between immovable monuments and estate: Drela (2002), p. 61.

[86]When it comes to the intangible values the APGM mentions geographical, historical, and traditional names of construction objects, squares, streets, and settlement units that may be protected under this act.

[87]See Sect. 5.5.

receiving protection through entry in the register of historical objects. Similar problems with classification as things in the strict sense of the term crop up in the case of the space heritage[88] or the human body[89] as property that is protected and constitutes a component of the cultural heritage.

The impossibility of exercising control over certain components of cultural heritage means that these cannot be treated as things (e.g., some components of the space heritage[90]). In previous studies, no attention was paid to the multitude of other heritage components that do not fit within the definition of a thing, yet are material property deserving of protection, as is discussed further on. For example, as presented later in this book studies on the protection of the human body after death and works of modern art that involve new technologies and means of expression are shifting the borders of the materiality of cultural heritage. Thus, the components of cultural heritage do not only constitute things. Further, some of them fall within the set of non-things without losing their material character.

Under Article 6 par. 2 APGM, "Geographical, historical and traditional names of construction objects, squares, streets and settlement units may also be protected." Thus, the legislator has seen the need to protect certain intangible property under the principles foreseen for historical objects. Katarzyna Zalasińska rightly observes that, in allowing the entry of geographical, historical or traditional names of objects in the register of historical objects (Article 9 par. 2 APGM), the legal effects this would entail were not foreseen, and in particular did not provide adequate means of preventive and follow-up supervision corresponding to the specific character of such objects.[91] It is worth adding that here the protection is similar to that granted to historical objects, although the specifics of the protected property will require an appropriate application of the law; for example, the provisions concerning the obligation to obtain a permit (Article 36 APGM). This legal procedure is important in that it shows how the legislator acts and, in a way, its awareness of the heterogeneity of cultural property. The very application of a basic form of protection to a non-historical object permits the supposition that, similarly, based on the appropriate legal provision, non-things, for instance a satellite or other device located in outer space, could also be entered in the register of historical objects.

Certain changes connected with how the most valuable heritage components are viewed in the legal system can be seen in the ARNCP. In it, the minister responsible for culture and the protection of national heritage is indicated as the entity who decides on and coordinates the management of cultural property. Such management involves exercising rights of the State Treasury regarding cultural property covered through restitution (Article 12 par. 1 ARNCP), including transferring ownership thereof (Article 13 ARNCP) and the possibility of entrusting the performance of

---

[88] See Sect. 3.3.

[89] See Sect. 3.2.

[90] Bednarek (1997), p. 47.

[91] Zalasińska (2020), p. 26.

certain activities to third parties (Article 12 par. 5 ARNCP). The guidelines have been issued on proper management that include the principles of the integrity of sets and collections and the place of origin or discovery of archaeological artefacts. In the Polish language, management [*gospodarowanie*] means administering resources or deciding how to use what you have.[92] Management in the broad sense appears in the Water Law and in reference to mineral deposits (Sect. 4.2.1). At this point it should be added that, overwhelmingly, this refers to the management of resources that are vital to the public interest, and at times concerns only property owned by the State Treasury.

The term management appears in several provisions of the ARNCP. Without going into the details of the regulations on national cultural property, it is noteworthy that the term management is used as a model of how the minister should act. The possible return of cultural property to the resources of the State Treasury in the event of the liquidation of a cultural institution (Article 13 par. 4 ARNCP) confirms that such property leaves those resources only provided that the entities to which it is entrusted provide proper care and continue to exist. Thus, the State Treasury figures as the guarantor of this section of the cultural heritage, which is managed in accordance with specific supplementary principles alongside the fundamental principles concerning historical objects, library materials and archival materials.

It can be argued that management is an activity aimed at maintaining resources of cultural property, and can be used with regard to both material heritage and intangible cultural heritage. It does not matter whether an object constitutes material or intangible property; what is crucial is the existence of certain management principles resulting from the value and importance of a given item and from the public interest as expressed in the use of that item. It seems, however, that in the field of cultural heritage, most of the material and immaterial property subject to management comprises heritage resources belonging to the State Treasury.

2.4.2 Sets of Things

An important problem connected with where cultural heritage is situated in private law is the structure of sets of things and the consequences in terms of managing collections. A set of objects does not constitute a thing, whereas the objects in the set are things.[93] In terms of the durability of cultural heritage, what raises most interest is the issue of the integrity of a collection. Jerzy Ignatowicz considered *universitas rerum* to mean "a certain whole composed of things usually of the same type, such as a herd of sheep or a library."[94] One may wonder at the freedom with which a herd of

---

[92] *Gospodarowanie* – cf. *Gospodarować*. Definition in: Słownik języka polskiego PWN, https://sjp.pwn.pl/sjp/gospodarowac;2462513.html. Accessed 1 June 2022.

[93] Bednarek (1997), pp. 47–48.

[94] Ignatowicz (2000), p. 19.

animals or a library collection can be set next to each other as examples of sets of things. Perhaps these examples are the most picturesque, or academic. There should be no doubt, though, that a library collection, or certain breeds of animal, may have considerable economic value.

Wojciech Katner defined a set of things as

> autonomous things which, when gathered together, form a certain whole, e.g., a collection of paintings by one painter, or from a certain period, of a given style, etc., or a library of a specific person, institution or field of knowledge.[95]

Here Katner clearly indicates the intangible values that are present "around" a set when he refers to "a certain whole." Those values may include, for example, the profile of the collection as regards the artist or period, or the thought that determined what elements were included in the case of a library. Similarly, in analyzes of organized sets of things, reference is often made to sets of furniture or libraries having historical or museological value.[96] The element of organization, which does not result from the fact that the structure of a given set is determined at the moment it is created (e.g. a coffee service), is of paramount importance. The fact that some parts of a collection are gathered according to a certain key, although not always according to a concept that can be clearly identified,[97] constitutes additional value of the set and may even greatly increase its value.

The view, once widely accepted, that real estate is the most valuable type of property is no longer grounded in reality, given the measurable and verifiable value attained by some heritage components, for instance in auctions. In foreign markets, the prices paid for objects have frequently exceeded real estate prices. In 2017, a private collector paid $450,300,000 for a painting depicting Jesus Christ entitled *Salvator Mundi*, attributed to Leonardo da Vinci.[98] The scale of the advertising campaign for the auction at Christie's is illustrated by the fact that the promotional film included an appearance by Leonardo di Caprio.[99] In 2019, a painting from Claude Monet's *Haystacks* series sold for $111 million. On the Polish art market, the most expensive items sold include not just old works, but also modern ones (Roman Opałka's *Detal 3546421-3562392* from the series *1965/1-∞* sold for 3,658,000 zlotys; Wojciech Fangor's *M22*, 1969 for 731,600 zlotys[100]). One may wonder whether, if collections of such objects were available in the world for sale, the prices paid for them would not be multiples of the sum of their individual prices. Most such works, though, are sold individually.[101] On the other hand, in 2019 a set of

---

95 Katner (2012), p. 1316.

96 Katner (2012), p. 1316.

97 Legal definition of collection in APMG.

98 The attribution was questioned, the object has not been made available to the public in the Abu Dhabi Louvere Museum. Cf. Kirkpatrick (2019); Smee (2019).

99 Crow (2017).

100 Kamecki (2021).

101 There are sales of single objects from private collections.

sculptures by Magdalena Abakanowicz was sold at auction for more than 8 million zlotys. Her installation *Caminando* consists of twenty figures made of bronze.[102] The sculptures were part of an artistic installation, and were once part of the collection of Marsha and Robin Williams. The installation has never been divided. Recognition of *Caminando* as a single work preserves its integrity. We will probably never learn whether the sale of each sculpture separately would be more profitable. Given that individual pieces by Abakanowicz achieve prices well above 500,000 zlotys, this is highly probable. Similar situation occurred in 2021 regarding the sale of another installation *Tłum III (Crowd III)* authored by Abakanowicz consisting of 50 sculptures. The sale price 13.2 million zlotys.[103]

A further issue arises when acquired objects are included in a specific set and a collection is created: how this affects the value of the whole and how the collection should be managed. Much space has been devoted in the literature to the problem of sets of things, especially in the context of private collections.[104] One concept suggests that legal actions concern each component of a set, and therefore each element of a collection separately.[105] Wojciech Katner supports a way of managing collections (however defined) that is more favorable for collectors, within a single legal action, as is the case with the sale of an enterprise.[106] These postulates for changes in the law have not been met with interest by legislative officials. The last such occasion was the implementation of Directive 2014/60, when it was possible to introduce provisions on collections and the trade in them. These supplemented the provisions on public collections.[107] It is very disappointing that there was no discussion whatsoever on this subject during the legislative process.

As to the history of the regulation of collections in Polish law, it must be said that one chapter of the APCP concerned collections.[108] Article 55 APCP also contained a legal definition of a collection (or set) as an agglomeration of movable cultural property stored in one place and not constituting a museum. Currently, apart from this statement in the binding act that a collection comprises a movable historical object, there are no other provisions that exclusively concern collections. Under Article 6 par. 1 pt. 2 letter b APGM, movable historical objects as collections constitute "sets of objects collected and arranged in accordance with the concept of the persons who established these collections." A set of things in the form of a collection—a movable historical object entered in the register of historical objects—is therefore given additional protection. Interestingly, considering the law on the protection of historical objects, in such a case we are faced with a single item of property, but under civil law with a number of separate things. To date, the APGM

[102] Kaźmierska (2019).

[103] https://desa.pl/pl/aukcje-dziel-sztuki/rzezba-i-formy-przestrzenne-21pazdziernika2021/magdalena-abakanowicz/crowd-iii-50-figur/.

[104] For example: Stec and Maniurka (2015).

[105] Grzybowski (1985), p. 458; Jagielska-Burduk (2011), p. 209.

[106] Katner (2012), p. 1317.

[107] See: Sect. 5.4.

[108] About collections in the Polish legal system: Kowalski (2015), pp. 208–211.

regulation on collections has had no equivalent in the provisions on collections that do not consist solely of movable historical objects;[109] nor has any detailed provision yet been introduced governing the sale or rental of collections.

Regarding transactions in collections and their status as sets of things, various authors invoke the structure of the sale of an enterprise, pointing to the heterogeneity of the components involved.[110] Such a sale includes both the material and intangible elements of the enterprise,[111] which further strengthens the argument that material property and intangible property are integrated. Under Article 55^2 of the Civil Code,

> a legal act whose object is an enterprise covers everything that is part of the enterprise, unless it follows otherwise from the substance of the legal act or from specific regulations.

Parties, then, may freely shape the object of an agreement, although the starting point is an assumption as to the completeness of that object, i.e., all the elements of which the enterprise is composed.

A collection can also be seen in the context of copyright and treated as a work.[112] This approach does not guarantee, however, the durability of the collection, but only shifts the weight of protection to the author of the collection rather than its parts. Nor is integrity secured by the existing provisions concerning databases.[113] In addition to providing some protection of integrity, however, these are an excellent tool to govern the use of collections. One can imagine a collection of sculptures by Wacław Bębnowski put together by one person and later donated to a foundation along with documentation. The documentation contains information on the guiding thought behind the collection and a specific date on which the collector completed the process of creating the collection, which they considered to be a closed whole in that form. For our purposes here, this allows us to suppose that the collection can be treated as a work—and this has been confirmed in case law.[114] The recipient

---

[109] Cf. Kowalski (2015), p. 214.

[110] Stelmachowski (1994), pp. 107–108.

[111] Article 55^1 [Enterprise – definition].

An enterprise is an organized set of intangible and tangible components intended for conducting business activity. It includes in particular:

(1) a designation individualizing the enterprise or its separated parts (enterprise name);
(2) ownership of real property or movables, including equipment, materials, goods and products, as well as other rights in rem to real property or movables;
(3) rights arising from lease and tenancy agreements of real estate or movable property and rights to use real estate or movable property arising from other legal relationships;
(4) receivables, rights from securities and cash;
(5) concessions, licenses and permits;
(6) patents and other industrial property rights;
(7) Property copyrights and property related rights;
(8) company secrets;
(9) books and documents related to the conduct of business activities.

[112] Stec (2015b), pp. 80–81.

[113] Stec (2015b), p. 89, footnote 29.

[114] Polish Supreme Court, Judgement of 8 November 1932, II K 1092/32; Polish Supreme Court, Judgement of 5 July 2001, II CKN 907/99, Lex 551 102; Jankowska-Sabat (2015), p. 42.

foundation will therefore be restricted in the scope of how it is able to manage the collection.

Unfortunately, the application of copyright law to managing collections does not facilitate their growth, and often acts as a barrier or results in conflicts between the author or their legal successors and a new owner. If we accept the idea of a collector-author and treat a collection as a work, we cannot deny the collector's right to complete the collection at the moment they acquire a particularly sought after work or deem that the purpose of the collection has been achieved for other reasons.[115] The example mentioned above confirms that copyright may limit the future development of or changes occurring in a collection. Most often, though, a collection ceases to grow upon the death of the collector, or when they cannot afford to expand it further. In the case of museum collections, when purchases are being made it is common practice to take account of economic copyrights. The importance of transferring the economic copyrights to a work is evident from the provisions found in regulations by the Minister of Culture and National Heritage programs, including those of the National Collection of Contemporary Art (2021 and 2022) programme[116] and the National Collections of Contemporary Art (2019).[117] Among those programs' qualified costs, we find the category "Purchase of works of art, objects, licences, instruction." In the detailed description of costs, the following information on purchases is given: civil law agreement, agreement for specific work with transfer of economic copyrights, license, invoice, bill. True, in the criteria for assessing applications there is no information on additional points awarded for the transfer of ownership to the carrier of a work along with the economic copyrights; nevertheless, this fact can be considered when evaluating a purchase from the perspective of planned educational or popularization activities that go beyond fair use by the museum.[118]

One can also say regarding collections that their integrity is subject to protection in two dimensions. The first is based on the material components of the set. The second consists of the intangible values connected with the creation of the set, and potentially, copyrights to particular parts of it. If we add to this certain features of a work evident in the concept according to which the collection was amassed, then there automatically arises a need to consider the issue of the author's personal rights, including the integrity of the work. The right of the author's collection to have the

[115] About risks and copyright law in the exhibition's protection from the management perspective Jagielska-Burduk, Jakubowski (2020).

[116] Program Ministra Kultury i Dziedzictwa Narodowego 2021, Narodowa kolekcja sztuki współczesnej, Regulamin i specyfikacja (Guidelines and specification), attachment 4.18. https://www.gov.pl/web/kultura/narodowa-kolekcja-sztuki-wspolczesnej. Accessed 1 June 2022; Program Ministra Kultury i Dziedzictwa Narodowego na rok 2022, Narodowa kolekcja sztuki współczesnej, Regulamin i specyfikacja (Guidelines and specification), attachment 4.18. https://www.gov.pl/web/kultura/narodowa-kolekcja-sztuki-wspolczesnej2. Accessed 1 June 2022.

[117] Program Ministra Kultury i Dziedzictwa Narodowego 2019, Narodowe kolekcje sztuki współczesnej 14 Załącznik nr 3, http://www.mkidn.gov.pl/media/po2019/Regulaminy%20i%20wytyczne/20181029_REG_Programy_2019_Narodowe_kolekcje_sztuki_wspolczesnej__publikacja_PDF.pdf. Accessed 1 June 2022.

[118] Gredka-Ligarska et al. (2019), pp. 198–206.

integrity of their work preserved coincides to a certain extent with their intention in this regard. That right would be infringed every time one of the collection's components was sold or a new "mismatched" element was added by the new owner of the collection. This makes it difficult to see how the creation of a concept or the application of a copyright mechanism can protect collections, when usually they are not permanent but rather undergo many changes. Furthermore, copyright as a mechanism would not prevent a collection from being traded as a set.

I believe copyright protection should be rejected in favor of protecting collections based on the property existing in both the material and intangible dimensions. The latter element, in my opinion, can refer to the link between individual objects and the additional intangible value they acquire as a set. In principle, a collection as a set of things may be subject to numerous changes, not all of which involve accumulation. Domestic and foreign auction houses often conduct sales of collections of individuals, for example that of Anda Rottenberg in 2017,[119] or even "clearance auctions";[120] auctions can also be used to refresh a collection or obtain funds for purchasing new objects. One cannot ignore that there are many instances in which only part of a collection is put up for auction, where the most valuable pieces having been previously sold off, usually to private entities. On the other hand, it is also possible to sell a "tweaked" collection; that is, one from which objects of lesser value or doubtful provenance have been removed so they do not tarnish the collection as a whole.

The maintenance and protection of public collections and, for some time now, private collections, are being discussed more and more frequently in the academic community.[121] Although the problems in applying Polish law have been pointed out, there have been no changes in its provisions so far. Work on a new act on cultural heritage should provide an excellent opportunity for regulating the management of collections. It seems it will also be worth creating a new definition that emphasizes the dual nature of collections and treats them as organized sets of both material and intangible components after the model of an enterprise. It was in this regard that Jerzy Stelmachowski wrote of the need to develop an operational regulation that includes management, encumbrance, and protection. He pointed out that "active assets have a completely different function than their passive counterparts. An inactive enterprise constitutes an ordinary *universitas rerum* (like a library)."[122] Stelmachowski believed that an inactive enterprise should be governed by the

---

[119] Anda Rottenberg collection. Auction of contemporary art, 4 April 2017, https://desa.pl/pl/aukcje/kolekcja-andy-rottenberg-aukcja-sztuki-wspolczesnej/. Accessed 1 June 2022.

[120] For instance Sale Auction. From the Collection, 23 Sept 2020, https://rempex.com.pl/wydarzenia/512-25-aukcja-wyprzedazowa-ze-zbiorow-kolekcjonera/przedmioty. Accessed 1 June 2022.

[121] Conference Private Collections. Historical and Legal Perspective within International conferences on cultural heritage protection, 6–7 June 2019 and the UNIDROIT Convention Academic Project.

[122] Stelmachowski (1994), p. 111.

ordinary rules of civil law, while others should apply to an active enterprise due to its different economic value.

Following this lead in relation to collections, one can propose that an operational regulation such as that mentioned above be applied. In essence, a collection may seem to be like a living organism that undergoes change, when in fact, nothing is further from the truth. In Poland, there are collections not subject to expansion whose original set has been "frozen." I am thinking, for example, of the private art collections of the Poznan Society of the Friends of Science[123] or the Płock Scientific Society,[124] which are not increased, and where the role of associations is to guard that heritage as is. Regarding an operational regulation, then, one should assume that the equivalent of the increased economic value of an enterprise due to its active status will be the aforementioned intangible value of a collection. That value somehow attests to the "activity" of the collection, its active dimension, and does not rule out viewing the collection as a certain economic whole. The example of a collector making objects from their collection available to the public commercially emphasizes the commercial dimension of collections.[125] On the other hand, if we accept the fiction of a collection being active, the concept of operational regulation can be applied more broadly, and it is noteworthy that Jerzy Stelmachowski considered a library to be an ordinary *universitas rerum*.

Over the years, changes have taken place in how collections are perceived. First, it should be mentioned the perception from a protective perspective was contained in the APCP. This can be viewed as embedding collections in the structure of the protection of the cultural heritage system and public law. A second way of perceiving collections is through the prism of copyright. Here a collection can be deemed to be a work, and the collector as its author; a second thread is the copyrights held by the authors of the individual works contained in the collection. The third, and probably the most promising way of perceiving collections for the future is to base the collection on the dimension of ownership and concentrate on the management of that property. This will be possible in part by treating collections as property having both a material and an intangible dimension, as well as by the operational regulation discussed above. However, this does not mean abandoning the idea of building a new regime for collections based on a right of ownership, or that the role of the collector as the author of the collection will cease to be crucial. The legislative activity should be directed towards strengthening collecting and the collector's position as an owner, not only towards regulations of a passive character.[126]

An important problem indirectly related to collections that is certainly less heard of in the national and international discussion is the institution of historical art studios.[127] A model worth examining for managing historical studios is an initiative

[123] http://ptpn.poznan.pl/en/. Accessed 1 June 2022.

[124] http://www.tnp.org.pl/. Accessed 1 June 2022.

[125] Drela (2006), p. 84.

[126] Kowalski (2015), p. 216.

[127] Cf. Kasprzak (2019), pp. 36–40.

taken by the City of Warsaw in 2014 in appointing a Team for Warsaw Historical Art Studios.[128] While the word "studio" mainly denotes a particular place, in reality, after an artist stops using their studio (for example, upon their death), what remains within the studio are numerous articles associated with the artist's life. The problem to be solved, then, is what to do with the premises, since any existing agreements are no longer in force. To care for the legacy of artists, new rules have been introduced regarding such premises. The resolution defines a Warsaw historical art studio as:

> premises rented in the past as an art studio which, due to the activity carried on within them or the collections or artistic output of the person who used the studio, require that the character of the studio be maintained and that it be made available as a place of particular historical or artistic value.

Whether a studio is of a historical nature is determined based on an evaluation made by the Team for Warsaw Historical Art Studios, following which a relevant resolution is adopted by the city council.[129]

One can risk the statement that, in its operational dimension, such a studio is more like an enterprise than a collection. What is striking is the phrase "collections or artistic output," which can include souvenirs, furnishings, and equipment, works by the artist, and even works by other artists. These may comprise a set of things organized or simply amassed by the artist. Certainly, they may also comprise an art collection gathered by the artist that contains their own works and those of others. Or they may comprise a stool, a bucket for mixing paints, or notes on a wall, as referred to in an interview by one of the Team members.[130] Combining premises in the capital city of Warsaw, which are undoubtedly "saturated" with creativity of additional intangible value, with the property found within them is a curious endeavor. On the one hand we have units of local government, and on the other hand property (undefined at the level of the resolution) that may be private (owned by heirs or third parties who allowed the artist to use their property temporarily) or state-owned (to be taken account of in this case, the acquisition of the inheritance by the district in which the artist last resided). Undoubtedly, one goal is to ensure the continuation and functioning of such studios and the preservation of their unique meaning and aura.[131] This solution, then, is one of the institutionalized methods to protect heritage at the local government level, which means that the relevant unit can create special programs to finance it. Here, the intangible element is distributed differently than in the case of a collection. It appears spatially, in the premises, yet arises out of the

[128] About the initiative: Żakowska (2014), p. 70.

[129] Art Studios in Warsaw: https://um.warszawa.pl/waw/zabytki/pracownie-artystyczne. Accessed 1 June 2022.

[130] Stelmach (2018).

[131] Activities related to historic artistic studios funding are undertaken, e.g., under the task: Popularization of Warsaw art studios in 2020. Call for proposals in 2020 for Art Studios dissemination projects: https://um.warszawa.pl/waw/zabytki/-/konkurs-popularyzacja-warszawskich-pracowni-artystycznych-przydatne-informacje. Accessed 1 June 2022.

interaction between the space, any elements added by the artist (stained glass, reliefs), and the movable property left in the studio.

Importantly, the city council resolution assumes the continuation of the "activity" of the studio as an entity worthy of protection and its availability to the public. The priority to conclude a lease of such a studio goes to the artist's spouse, descendants, ascendants, siblings, stepchildren, children-in-law, and students, if these are artists themselves and will use the premises only as a studio. An agreement is concluded under the condition of "maintaining the character of the art studio and making it available to the public as a place of particular historical or artistic value" (Clause 16 par. 1 of the resolution). If no one exercises their priority right or there are no eligible persons, the studio can be rented to a legal or natural person who must, however, continue the program of activity in the studio. Only after approval by the Team does the relevant district council handle the signing of an agreement, while the manner of using the studio is subject to control, as well as to a reporting obligation (Clauses 20, 21 of the resolution).

The object of the agreement, therefore, is a certain organized whole, which seems to make it similar to actions whose object is an enterprise. Thus, alongside collections there appears a new, important legal structure concerning art studios, to which no separate attention was paid. Taking action at the local government level may be an excellent starting point for creating a best practice model. When premises in a district take on new value due to the artistic activity performed within them, the person of the artist, and the things left behind, are worthy of being preserved. Other important elements of such studios are the possibility of conducting further creative activity in them, and the assumption of preserving the legacy they contain. In this way, a studio does not lose its "living" character; it does not become a cabinet of curiosities, a memorial room, or a museum, but has a clear operational dimension. Where such a studio is entered in the register of historical objects, any changes to it require a permit from the provincial monument's conservator, and since control and reporting obligations are also in place, the whole institution resembles a project of cultural heritage management.

2.5 Publicization of Private Law and the Protection of Cultural Heritage in the Civil Code

John Henry Merryman, a civil law expert and distinguished researcher of the law as it concerns the art market and the protection of cultural heritage, explored the relationship between private and public law.[132] He wrote on the distinction between these two areas as being inscribed in the genetic code of European lawyers and their

[132] Merryman (1968), pp. 3–19.

attempts to perpetuate this dichotomy, in stark contrast to the approach taken by American lawyers.[133] He stated that it was possible

> to see fundamental private law concepts as having been modified by the addition of social or public elements, and such terms as the 'socialisation' or 'publicisation' of private law are frequently encountered. Although a more traditional doctrinal writer may insist that the legal content, as distinguished from the social and economic content of private rights, remains unchanged under the new government, such a distinction is unconvincing. In fact, the content of private rights has been substantially altered.[134]

These observations could have influenced Merryman's innovative works on cultural property and analyzes of the trade in cultural property from a national or international perspective that were published later. In his 1986 article "Two Ways of Thinking about Cultural Property," Merryman presented two ways of looking at heritage that were independent (although convergent concerning preservation).[135] In the first view, heritage appears as an element of trade and exchange, and continues nowadays in proposals for protection through market participation.[136] In the second view, heritage constitutes an integral element of national heritage, and is therefore connected with a given nation or country. Certainly, one can look at cultural property or, more broadly, cultural heritage from a private law perspective and the private interest associated with it,[137] or from a public law perspective and the public interest—these are all defined in various ways.[138] Every item of cultural property can be seen in terms of protecting the interest of whoever is in possession of it at the moment, or the interest of future generations. This justifies referring to the discussion on the publicization of private law, which involves a gradual departure from traditional civil law.

The presence of a public element in private law is the result of that departure. The source of the publicization of private law should be seen in the appearance of new areas of regulation at the point of contact between private law and public law, and in the necessity of adjusting regulations to the standards of EU law and, within a certain scope, to technological progress. This phenomenon can be viewed in two ways. First, as one more step in the development of private law. Second, as an intervention in the existing system of private law norms and the entities subject thereto, which is leading to a segmentation of private law.[139] We can look at the publicization of civil law as one aspect of the internal decomposition of the Civil Code through the inclusion of elements from external private law within its provisions, such as issues related to heritage protection.[140]

---

[133] Merryman (1968), pp. 3–4.

[134] Merryman (1968), p. 16.

[135] Merryman (1986).

[136] Szafrański (2015), pp. 125–140.

[137] Cf. Merryman (2005), pp. 11–39.

[138] Cf. Merryman (1994), pp. 61–76.

[139] Safjan (2012), p. 51.

[140] Stec (2015a), p. 33. The author points out different status of the art market actors.

In considering the hybridization of legal institutions, Bartosz Liżewski takes yet another stance on the publicization of private law:

> ... it is a mistake to try to define what the content of public law in private law is, or the reverse. Obviously, one can speak here of a lasting process of the publicization of private law and the privatization of public law, but in my conviction, connecting feature of public law with those of private law within specific legal institutions illustrates the emergence of a 'third way' in the law.[141]

Liżewski points to a certain mixing of shades of what is considered private and public in legal institutions. It seems that, in the case of cultural heritage, one can hypothesize that many legal institutions, although contained in the Civil Code, can be treated as hybrid in nature. In pursuing this idea of the hybridization of legal institutions, the problem of the protection of components of cultural heritage, which has always been at the point of contact between public and private law, provides a perfect example for tracing the process of the changes taking place in private law.

At the outset, it must be emphasized that new private law regulations on the protection of cultural heritage began to appear only relatively recently, along with Poland's accession to the European Union.[142] They introduced new provisions, whether related to cultural property illegally removed from the territory of Member States or the right to reuse images of [143] museum exhibits[144]) pursuant to the Act on the Reuse of Public Sector Information.[145] These constitute proceedings that combine public and private elements.[146] Proceedings on the return of cultural property initiated by Member States are conducted in accordance with a defined procedure, and the requesting state pays compensation upon the return of the object, regardless of the legal situation of the owner. What is more, the time period within which a claim for return can be made is not counted from when the owner of the stolen property (who may be a private entity) learned of the theft, but rather from the moment when "the competent central authority of the requesting Member State became aware of the location of the cultural object and of the identity of its possessor or holder" (Article 8 of the Directive on the return of cultural objects unlawfully

[141] Liżewski (2018), p. 59.

[142] Cf. Council Directive 93/7/EEC of 15 March 1993 on the return of cultural objects unlawfully removed from the territory of a Member State , OJ L 74, 27.3.1993, pp. 74–79 followed by Directive 2014/60/EU of the European Parliament and of the Council of 15 May 2014 on the return of cultural objects unlawfully removed from the territory of a Member State and amending Regulation (EU) No. 1024/2012 (Recast), OJ L 159, 28.5.2014, pp. 1–10.

[143] Directive 2013/37/EU of the European Parliament and of the Council of 26 June 2013 amending Directive 2003/98/EC on the re-use of public sector information Text with EEA relevance OJ L 175, 27.6.2013, pp. 1–8 repealed by Directive (EU) 2019/1024 of the European Parliament and of the Council of 20 June 2019 on open data and the re-use of public sector information PE/28/2019/REV/1, OJ L 172, 26.6.2019, pp. 56–83. The latter should lead to changes in the law in 2021.

[144] Cf. Mileszyk (2019).

[145] Act of 25 February 2016 on the Re-use of Public Sector Information, consolidated text. Polish Official Journal (Dz. U) 2019, item 1446.

[146] Liżewski (2018), p. 61.

removed from the territory of a Member State and amending Regulation (EU) No. 1024/2012 (Recast). However, under Article 13 of the Directive, ownership of the cultural object after return shall be governed by the law of the requesting Member State.

Certainly, a further impetus for legislative action connecting private and public law is provided by the need to combat the illegal trade in cultural property and the new threats emerging in connection with cultural property being smuggled out of areas of armed conflict. At the same time, the maturity of the Polish art market and activities promoting the protection and importance of heritage mean that the issue of due diligence is part of the discussion at the national and international levels, and provides a desirable model to be incorporated in domestic law.[147] This phenomenon can be read as a gradual shift of cultural heritage protection instruments to the level of private law, which is intended to complement the norms contained in public law. The ongoing publicization of private law in this scope seems to be inevitable, and will likely lead at least to an amendment of the APGM, if not to the inclusion of a new provision in the Civil Code, in the near future.

It cannot be ignored that over the years there has been a change in the profile of private law entities, with separate regulations addressed to entrepreneurs and special protection granted to consumers. Joanna Helios argues that

> the publicisation of private law is visible in the context of the expansion of instruments of consumer protection, which are situated both in the public and private law spheres.[148]

Such a differentiation has also been made concerning the object of trade. In accordance with the principle of certainty in trading and the core institution of acquiring ownership of movable property from an unlawful vendor, new detailed provisions concerning property entered in the National Register of Lost Cultural Property (presented in Chap. 5) are currently appearing.[149] Cultural property entered in the register cannot be acquired in good faith from an unauthorized person, nor do the provisions on prescription apply. Cultural property as an object of trade therefore requires the application of provisions that will not protect the certainty of trade, but whose foundation is to protect the public interest and to ensure that the trade in cultural objects is secure. Thus, the autonomy of parties is subject to numerous restrictions, in this case justified by the need to protect the public interest. Yet here we have a situation where the interest of the individual coincides with the public interest;[150] it is in the interest of the rightful owner of the property and in the public

---

[147] Due Diligence (C70/19/7.SC/8a) Subsidiary Committee of the Meeting of States Parties to the UNESCO Convention on the Means of Prohibiting and Preventing the Illicit Import, Export and Transfer of Ownership of Cultural Property (UNESCO, Paris, 1970). https://unesdoc.unesco.org/ark:/48223/pf0000368565. Accessed 1 June 2022.

[148] Helios (2013), p. 25.

[149] Act of 4 November 2016 on amending the Act on the Protection and Guardianship of Monuments and the Act on museums. Polish Official Journal (Dz. U.) 2016, item 1887.

[150] Helios (2013), p. 22.

interest to prevent the property from becoming an object of trade or changing owners.

The protection of cultural heritage found in the provisions of the Polish Civil Code concerning the acquisition of ownership and found objects, as well as in draft amendments to the code[151] (which will be presented later) reflects this phenomenon. It also attests to the legislative progress made, the introduction of provisions on the protection of monuments, and the observation that private law norms concerning the acquisition of ownership are important instruments for protecting cultural heritage. Exceptions are made to universal solutions to secure selected property for future generations. For the underlying assumption is to protect property—that is, components of cultural heritage—and only afterwards to protect entities that participate in trade. In both material and procedural civil law, new provisions on cultural heritage are being formulated that undoubtedly contain a tinge of public law.

On the existing complexity of private law relationships, a strengthening of the regulatory protection of the cultural heritage is being imposed. First, this stems from the increasing awareness of the need to protect cultural heritage and from international commitments, including obligations related to the implementation of EU law and international conventions to which Poland is a party. In a certain sense, those conventions often force a discussion on new solutions or the need to draw on those that have already proven effective in other legal systems and lend themselves to introduction within the Polish legal order.

The attention paid to cultural heritage, even if unsystematic or at times merely superficial, is greater today than in the past. The question arises over the extent to which private law, and which of its institutions, can be supplemented by solutions from public law. The imperative method has penetrated into private law and will be used many times for the needs of systemically regulating cultural heritage, thereby arriving at hybrid legal institutions. It seems that, when reinforcing the presence of elements related to cultural heritage in civil law, a more well-thought-out strategy is needed. Amending the Civil Code, which is based on the public interest and under which property is in a certain sense treated as public, requires precision and a guarantee that the required activities are coordinated by public entities.

The publicization of civil law as it pertains to cultural heritage attests to the "strength" of the Civil Code and to a conviction that the protective measures introduced in this way will be effective. At present, the search for new solutions is being made by analyzing the degree to which the protection granted in public law is effective. Protection in the meaning of public law will also take place at a certain time. For example, property begin to be subject to the regime of the APGM at the moment when a decision on its entry into the register of monuments becomes final. To protect objects before the end of the procedure in 2017, an amendment to the

[151] For instance, Act on amending the Civil Code Act, the Civil Procedure Code Act and the Private International Law Act, Senate IX term, Print 760. https://www.senat.gov.pl/prace/proces-legislacyjny-w-senacie/inicjatywy-ustawodawcze/inicjatywa,62.html. Accessed 1 June 2022.

APGM[152] introduced a new institution guaranteeing temporary protection before entry in the register of historical objects. Under Article 10a APGM,

> from the day a proceeding is initiated on the entry of a historical object in the register to the day on which a decision in the matter becomes final, it is forbidden to carry out conservation, restoration, construction works or other activities at the monument the proceeding concerns which could cause a harm to the substance or changes in the appearance of the historical object.[153]

This shows that initiating a proceeding had not previously stopped entities from deciding to demolish an object; in fact, the initiation of a proceeding could stand in conflict with a decision previously issued allowing the demolition to move forward.

Describing the history of the development of administrative law, it was noted that "the development of administrative law on the continent was always burdened with the prism of civil law," and over time "people began… to see in administrative law and civil law two equal planes of the law."[154] The protection of cultural heritage is addressed in acts from the area of administrative law. This does not mean, though, that private law issues have been neglected. On the contrary, for some time now there has been an observable shift in the direction of private law, property rights and a search for the new status of property. For example, over the years mature art markets (France, United Kingdom) have created internal legal rules for the functioning of entities in the cultural sector, including experts, case law concerning liability and forgeries. It has not proved possible, though, to create a model legal regulation for the art market. Today, the large number of new legal regulations is the result of membership in the European Union and of the binding instruments for combating money laundering and the illegal trade in cultural property. The enforcement of the statutory obligations imposed, for example, on the holder of a historical object may be perceived as guaranteeing effective protection at the operational level. Nor can it be excluded that the special regime laid down in private law, or a completely new legal category, may be equally or more effective.

2.6 Civil Law Principles and Cultural Heritage Protection

In 2018, a proposal was made in the legal sciences for a catalogue of principles for the legal protection of cultural heritage in Poland.[155] In earlier literature, the cultural heritage protection principle was rightly considered a meta-principle.[156] Completing the catalogue was a large undertaking, since the list is an open one and, being

[152] Act of 22 June 2017 on amending the Act on the Protection and Guardianship of Monuments. Polish Official Journal (Dz. U.) 2017, item 1595.

[153] Zalasińska (2020), pp. 40–42.

[154] Szczaniecki (1985), p. 602.

[155] Zeidler (2018); Węgrzak and Zeidler (2020), pp. 292–302.

[156] Zeidler (2014), p. 29.

relatively new, has not yet been discussed or analyzed by other researchers. One can assume that the catalogue will be added to and changed, similar to the catalogue of principles of private law. Moreover, in differentiating these principles from cultural heritage law at the international level, it will be necessary to look for a new branch of law in Polish law and to reconstruct the catalogue of principles in place internationally.

When making cultural heritage in private law a priority, it is necessary to verify to what extent certain civil law principles affect the status of cultural heritage. Below, I present core principles of civil law: the principle of autonomy of will, the principle of trade certainty and security, and the principle of equity. These principles are discussed within the scope where they affect the status of cultural heritage and the security thereof in private law. Additionally, mention is made of the principle of the unity of civil law, whose history is of particular importance considering the fragmentation of cultural heritage law.

The catalogue of principles of civil law was compiled over many years, and there are certain discrepancies between the principles proposed by doctrinal experts.[157] As mentioned above, a number of catalogues of principles of civil law were proposed in the literature much earlier than in the case of the protection of cultural heritage.[158] When creating a catalogue, some authors invoke traditional principles of civil law,[159] others the fundamental principles of Polish civil law[160] or, in the context of private law, directive fundamental principles of private law.[161] Without doubt, the form of a catalogue is affected by technological progress, systemic transformations and the standards of international and EU law. And certainly, the existence of principles of private law constitutes an important foundation at the stage of establishing, interpreting, and applying the law. Without undertaking a theoretical and legal analysis of the principles of the law that have already been examined in the literature on the subject,[162] it is worth juxtaposing selected civil law principles with the needs of cultural heritage protection.

The principle of autonomy of will is considered one of the basic principles of civil law. Marek Safjan has shown that this principle has three dimensions: axiological, formal, and pragmatic.[163] The axiological dimension refers to the freedom of the individual, while the formal dimension encompasses an entity's freedom to shape its legal situation. The pragmatic dimension primarily concerns freedom of contract.[164] This principle, similarly conceived, is described by Stefan Grzybowski, who highlights the freedom to decide to perform a legal action and shape its content, including

[157] Safjan (2012), p. 319.
[158] Cf. Stefaniuk (2016).
[159] Stelmachowski (1969), p. 81.
[160] Grzybowski (1985), p. 50.
[161] Safjan (2012), p. 329.
[162] Kordela (2012); Tkacz (2014); Wronkowska et al. (1974).
[163] Safjan (2012), p. 319.
[164] Safjan (2012), pp. 329–340.

by choosing the other party to an agreement. As to limitations of this principle, he argues that these do not constitute separate principles.[165]

The principle of freedom of contract is acknowledged as a decisive link in the autonomy of will of the parties.[166] Using that freedom, they may shape the content of legal actions as they see fit. This does not mean, however, that their range of competence is completely unlimited.[167] Outside professional trade, where consumers participate, special provisions apply to cultural property. These are related to the creation of a special position of art market participants (museums), to the contract's provisions, and to restrictions on transferring ownership of certain types of property.

For example, to support museums' function of gathering collections, museums were given privileges as art market participants. This was accomplished through two means: priority of purchase from entities offering historical objects for sale, and a pre-emption right to purchase items put up for auction at sale price (Article 20 MA).[168] Pertaining to the purchase of objects by registered museums, the act introduces the invalidity of legal acts performed in violation of their priority of purchase or pre-emption right.

Additionally, when museums wish to dispose of its exhibits by way of exchange, sale, or donation (a process known as deaccession), they must abide by a formal procedure requiring them to obtain a permit from the minister responsible for culture and the national heritage. An application for a permit is submitted by the museum director based on an opinion by the museum board. The minister issues a decision after obtaining an opinion from the Council for Museums (Article 23 MA). Apart from the provisions typical of the public finances sector, the legislator also restricted the freedom to dispose of museum property or to conclude agreements that transfer ownership.

And in relation to agreements concerning cultural property, additional contractual limitations are provided for. These additional contractual provisions, which also appear in agreements establishing a right of perpetual usufruct, are often seen as an unnamed form of protection of historical objects, and are certainly mechanisms that strengthen protection.[169] Under Article 26 par. 1 APGM, however,

> in an agreement for the sale, exchange, donation or lease of an immovable historical object entered in the register that constitutes property of the State Treasury or a local government unit, when defining the manner of use of that historical object it must be stipulated that, if the condition of the historical object so requires, the acquirer or lessee is obligated to carry out all necessary conservation work on the historical object in a timely manner.

This exemplifies the requirement to include additional provisions in the form of an obligation to perform defined work on a historical object. The protection

---

[165] Grzybowski (1985), p. 50.

[166] Stelmachowski (1969), p. 81.

[167] Machnikowski (2005), p. 165 et seq.

[168] Jagielska-Burduk and Markowski (2013); Stanulewicz (2007).

[169] Jagielska-Burduk (2016a), p. 184; Sienkiewicz (2013), pp. 245–259.

requirements imposed on a purchaser, donee or lessee mean that, within this scope, the freedom of contract of the parties involved is limited. This undoubtedly results from the fact that such cases involve property of the State Treasury or a local government unit that has historical value. Under Article 13 par. 4 of the Act on the Management of Real Estate[170] (AMRE), a permit from the provincial conservator of historical objects is required for the sale, exchange, donation, handover for perpetual usufruct or in-kind contribution of real estate entered in the register of monuments to a company. Similarly, the consent of the provincial conservator is required for agreements on the sale, exchange, donation or lease of real estate constituting the property of the above entities, if the real estate is a cemetery entered in the provincial record of historical objects (Article 13 par. 5 AMRE).[171] In a certain sense, this last solution shows the complexity of cultural heritage's structure is, since protection is granted to both cemeteries and the human remains located within them.

The legal principle of trade certainty and security, which coexists with that of autonomy of will, occupies a special place in the normative framework. It was noted that

> the variety and flexibility of civil law institutions require at the same time particularly high respect for values relating to legal security... It is therefore encumbent upon the legislator, as directly results from the provisions of the Constitution, to implement private law mechanisms that ensure the certainty of legal relationships formed.[172]

In other words, to a large extent civil law institutions permit parties to freely create the content of legal actions. On the other hand, structures that protect certainty and security in trading should be created. These provide market participants with a certain ability to predict the effects of their legal relationships.

Some provisions of private law, then, are designed to strengthen the security of trade. Although others, to protect the greater good or the good of a weaker entity, make exceptions to that security or, in a sense, complement it. Irrespective of the freedom private law grants to contractual parties, certain values are protected, including consumer interests and the security of cultural heritage. The principle of consumer protection results in a differentiation in the positions of contract parties.[173] And similar provisions have been introduced concerning the protection of cultural property and, indirectly, owners of such property. An amendment to the Civil Code, specifically the institution of the acquisition of ownership of movable things from an unauthorized entity, in a way constitutes a weakening of certainty and security in trading in favor of the special place held by cultural property in private law. A participant's trust in the rules of trading, which involves certain actions entailing

[170] Act of 21 August 1997 on the Management of Real Estate, consolidated text. Polish Official Journal (Dz. U.) 2021, item 1899.

[171] See more on the implementation of this regulation and the linkt to the Potomski Potomska v. Poland case: Zalasińska (2020), p. 97.

[172] Safjan (2012), p. 345.

[173] On consumers' regulations cf. Mojak (2016), p. 158.

specific legal effects, here yields to the need to protect the integrity and inviolability of cultural heritage.

These provisions are aimed at protecting the legal situation of a rightful owner who, for example, lost possession of an object as the result of theft. The protection afforded to good faith and certainty in trading is weakened with regard to the protection of cultural property. Acquisitions made in good faith from an unauthorized entity and acquisitions by prescription do not apply to cultural property entered in the National Register of Lost Cultural Property. That register was designed as an open register and was meant to be kept in an ICT system; its accessibility means that all potential buyers can use it to verify objects before purchasing. Article 169 par. 3 and 174 par. 2 of the Civil Code provide for the protection of particular values incorporated in property subject to trade.[174] There is no need, though, for national cultural property in public collections to be disclosed in the register. Under Article 46 ARNCP, it is not possible to acquire such property from an unauthorized entity or through prescription, meaning that registration does not serve its intended purpose. In the past, the provisions of Articles 171 and 177 CC[175] excluded the application of certain provisions to such property to protect public property.[176]

In a certain sense, the measures taken by the law on the protection of cultural heritage to protect cultural property are a response to the overall private law principle of trade certainty and security. On the other hand, this branch of law encompasses not only public law, but also private law. According to Kamil Zeidler, this principle

> in various states is manifested in a different degree of intervention by the legislator in market freedom when the object of trade is works of art or historical objects.[177]

It seems that this principle, whose supranational nature is emphasized, is complementary to the principle of certainty and security. Regarding trust in the other party to an agreement in the case of cultural property (the "know your client" model), the introduction of a responsible art market model[178] and regulations on combating money laundering[179] all take on increasing importance. As technology develops in

---

[174] Comment to the Art. 171 Polish Civil Code: Grzybowski (1985), p. 53.

[175] Article 171 of the Civil Code The provisions on the protection of a good faith purchaser do not apply in the case of the sale of a movable item belonging to the objects of permanent equipment of a state organizational unit.

Article 177 of the Civil Code The provisions on acquisition of property by acquisitive prescription shall not apply if the property is subject to state ownership.

[176] Kowalski (2004), p. 97.

[177] Zeidler (2018), p. 153.

[178] Responsible Art. Market (RAM), http://responsibleartmarket.org/. Accessed 1 June 2022.

[179] Cf. Directive (EU) 2018/843 of the European Parliament and of the Council of 30 May 2018 amending Directive (EU) 2015/849 on the prevention of the use of the financial system for the purposes of money laundering or terrorist financing, and amending Directives 2009/138/EC and 2013/36/EU (Text with EEA relevance), PE/72/2017/REV/1, OJ L 156, 19.6.2018, pp. 43–74 and Directive (EU) 2015/849 of the European Parliament and of the Council of 20 May 2015 on the prevention of the use of the financial system for the purposes of money laundering or terrorist

the future, the issue of security of contracts may be reinforced further still using block chain in registering transactions that concern cultural property or make it possible to invest in such items by acquiring ownership interests in them.[180]

For some types of cultural property, legal actions are required to be in written form and with a certain date; otherwise they are invalid. Under Article 45 ARNCP,

> a legal act involving a transfer of ownership or encumbrance of national cultural property of the Republic of Poland belong to public collections is made in written form with a certain date.

One can assume that a written form will soon be required not only for particular components of public collections, but also for other types of cultural property. Regarding agreements concerning immovable historical objects, the issue of the public register also arises; that is, land and mortgage registers. Under Article 9 par. 4 APGM

> the entry of an immovable historical object in the register is disclosed in the land and mortgage register for that real estate at the request of the provincial conservator of historical objects.

The entry in the land and mortgage register is made pursuant to a decision on the entry of that historical object in the register. This obligation to note in the land and mortgage register that a real property has been entered in the register of historical objects allows contractual parties to verify the status of the property before concluding a sale. This information is vital for buyers, who are aware of their obligations resulting from the provisions of law concerning immovable historical objects.

The special nature of private law is manifest in its respect for the principles of equity. This character is no doubt connected to the ability of parties to form their situation in accordance with the principles of autonomy of will and certain and security in trading. Civil law is geared towards the interests of parties to a legal relationship, where their positions are generally equal. Civil law regulations are therefore based on autonomy of will, freedom of contract, and the achievement of the purposes and interests of contracting parties. As Marek Safjan has observed,

> this difference in perspectives between private and public law does not mean that in the realm of private law no solutions or mechanisms can appear that involve values important for society as a whole. On the contrary. Private law, and its mechanisms and institutions, are necessary for society as a whole to function, while a strictly individualistic approach is supplemented by structural elements that carry general values.[181]

Some of the mechanisms connected with those general values concern cultural heritage. There are various methods of implementing equity elements in private law.

---

financing, amending Regulation (EU) No. 648/2012 of the European Parliament and of the Council, and repealing Directive 2005/60/EC of the European Parliament and of the Council and Commission Directive 2006/70/EC (Text with EEA relevance), OJ L 141, 5.6.2015, pp. 73–117.

[180] Cagnoli (2020).

[181] Safjan (2012), p. 319.

First, a distinction is made between invoking general clauses, principles of equity, undefined expressions, and normative solutions to protect certain values.

In private law, the notion of an abuse of right may be used to recover components of cultural heritage that have been lost. An abuse of the law may be considered when an entity (museum) invokes the limitation on the deadline for seeking release of an object based on a claim for possession. Such situations may occur where an owner or their heirs know about and attempted to recover objects belonging to the family but did not file a lawsuit at the right time or what they believed to be the proper time. The fate of the Sanguszko family's collection confirms the complicated factual status of most cases related to the implementation and effects of agricultural reform in Poland. Here, it is worth citing the Supreme Court's rationale for its verdict:

> there is no doubt that, in certain, exception circumstances, raising the charge of time barring may constitute an abuse of right. The application of Article 5 CC may be supported by the reasons for which the obliged party did not raise a claim (see rulings of the Supreme Court of 13 November 1997, I CKN 323/97, OSNC 1998 No. 5 item 79, and of 27 June 2001, II CKN 604/00).[182]

While in the case referred to above the court found there had been no abuse of right, this is a very important indicator for similar cases in the future in which heirs begin looking for objects in state or local government museums, or in all other cases concerning cultural heritage.

A further example is provided by Article 355 par. 1 CC, which refers to the due diligence required in a given type of relationship. The importance of this provision in relation to trading in cultural property was emphasized in a report Poland submitted to UNESCO. Under Article 355 par. 1 CC, "a debtor is obliged to exercise the diligence generally required in relations of a given type (due diligence)." Article 355 par. 2 CC contains a clarification of the procedural model in commercial transactions, in accordance with which

> the due diligence of a debtor within the scope of the economic activity it conducts is defined by taking account of the professional nature of that activity.

In the report referred to above, titled Analytical Summary of National Reports Received on the Implementation of the 1970 Convention,[183] it was indicated that, in some states, the due diligence model is introduced by requiring sellers to keep a register of transactions. This element, though, is not relevant to the search for a due diligence model for buyers of cultural property, for it only involves the seller, while the buyer merely agrees to it. As to a concrete general clause concerning cultural heritage, it seems there is a need to refer to a specific procedural model, as is the case in the ARNCP. Article 33 par. 2 ARNCP implements Article 10 of the Directive of the European Parliament and of the Council 2014/60/EU of 15 May 2014 on the

---

[182] Jagielska-Burduk and Mularski (2015), pp. 201–216.

[183] Seventh Session of the Subsidiary Committee of the Meeting of States Parties to the Convention concerning the Means of Prohibiting and Preventing the Illicit Import, Export and Transfer of Ownership of Cultural Property (UNESCO, Paris, 1970), C70/19/7.SC/6 Paris, April 2019, p. 2.

return of cultural objects unlawfully removed from the territory of a Member State in Polish law,[184] and stipulates that

> when evaluating due caution and diligence, a court considers all the circumstances of the acquisition, particularly documentation concerning the foreign origin of national cultural property as referred to in Article 18 par. 1, the existence of a permit for the export of that property as required by the provisions of the EU Member States making a claim, the type of parties participating in the transaction, the price paid, whether the holder checked the available register of stolen cultural property, and all other pertinent information and documents the holder could have obtained exercising due diligence, as well as all other activities that would be justified in the circumstances of a given case.[185]

This model can also be used when considering what constitutes due diligence in legal relations arising in the field of culture or on the art market.

Finally, it is worth mentioning the principle of the unity of civil law, which assumes the existence of a single civil law. This is a reflection of the functioning of the Civil Code, which in a way constitutes the core, or even the heart, of civil law, and which nevertheless is not complex in nature.[186] The Civil Code is supplemented with specialized legal acts, while the regulation of certain spheres in separate acts does not necessarily mean that they do not form part of civil law. It is generally accepted that all the provisions that regulate civil law relationships are provisions of civil law.[187] In accordance with the initial assumptions of the Act, the Civil Code also governed relationships between units of the socialist economy.[188] The principle of the unity of civil law was adopted as an opposition to the concept of economic law.[189] Andrzej Stelmachowski, observing the development of private law over time, came to the conclusion that "the principle of the unity of civil law... did not stand the test of life – at least in the legislative plane"[190] and that "it was the product of a certain myth."[191]

Even if we accept the principle of the unity of civil law, this does not prevent or affect the growing number of legal acts outside the Civil Code. These are caused by the emergence of new regulatory areas, and by maintaining the assumption that the Civil Code should not be changed frequently. The organizational and ordering function of the material of civil law is discussed by Piotr Stec, who asserts that

---

[184] Directive 2014/60/EU of the European Parliament and of the Council of 15 May 2014 on the return of cultural objects unlawfully removed from the territory of a Member State and amending Regulation (EU) No. 1024/2012 (Recast), OJ L 159, 28.5.2014, pp. 1–10.

[185] Article 18 (1) The provisions of this Chapter shall apply to the return of foreign national cultural treasure unlawfully removed from the territory of a Member State as of January 1, 1993 and located in the territory of the Republic of Poland.

[186] Stec (2015a), p. 32.

[187] Grzybowski (1985), p. 51.

[188] Cf. Szczepaniak (2016), p. 108; Wolter (1986), pp. 20–21.

[189] Wasilkowski (1964), p. 739.

[190] Stelmachowski (1980), p. 39.

[191] Stelmachowski (1980), p. 43.

> the principle of the unity of civil law made it possible to preserve those areas of trade that the legislator wanted to treat, somewhat by force, as autonomous within the orbit of private law, to which they belong given the method of regulation adopted.[192]

The principle of the unity of civil law, while important at the stage of creating a binding civil code, has not withstood the test of time. Causes include systemic and political changes, the growth of certain areas of regulation, and the emergence of new values subject to protection. A decodification of private law is noticeable in the provisions concerning heritage components. These are scattered among various acts of law. Further, the changes made to grant special protection to public collections give the impression of not being coordinated with existing solutions, including those present in the Civil Code (see Sect. 5.4).

Among the premises for making changes in private law and progressive decodification, Wojciech Dajczak mentioned "important technological and economic changes, the growing importance of constitutional jurisprudence, and progress in the European process."[193] Decodification consists of "a set of phenomena and processes detrimental to the elements constituting the Code in a given understanding of it."[194] The broad range of regulations outside the Civil Code suggests an ongoing decomposition of civil law. Examples of this include acts of law related to consumer sales, separate title to premises, and pledge rights.[195] A separate act is devoted to copyright, whose object of regulation is close to cultural heritage. It is pointed out that, when analyzing specific cases, one can determine the extent to which we are dealing with a deliberate decodification or one that is made for practical reasons.[196] In considering the Civil Code and the regulations connected with cultural heritage, it seems we are faced with a decodification that is taking place out of practical considerations and perhaps as a kind of prognosis to a Code of Cultural Heritage.

An example of the fragmentation of civil law related to cultural heritage, including in this case civil proceedings, is the fact that the principles on the return of cultural property illegally removed from the territory of EU Member States is located outside of the Code of Civil Procedure.[197] Initially, Council Directive 93/7/EEC of 15 March 1993 on the return of cultural objects unlawfully removed from the territory of a Member State was implemented by adding a new chapter to the APGM.[198] In turn, Directive 2014/60/EU of the European Parliament and of the Council of 15 May 2014 on the return of cultural objects unlawfully removed from

---

[192] Stec (2015a), p. 32.

[193] Dajczak (2008), p. 95.

[194] Longchamps de Bérier (2019), p. 13.

[195] Radwański (2009), p. 138.

[196] Rudnicki (2019), p. 171.

[197] Stec (2015a), p. 33.

[198] Council Directive 93/7/EEC of 15 March 1993 on the return of cultural objects unlawfully removed from the territory of a Member State, OJ L 74, 27.3.1993, p. 74.

the territory of a Member State[199] was implemented in the legal system through the adoption of the Act on the Restitution of National Cultural Property. Tomasz Giaro argues that "the piecemeal intervention of Community law has strongly deepened the decodification of civil law in Member States,"[200] where, in the case of the directives that have been implemented, each system uses its own regime of legal production.[201] While the implementation of Directive 2014/60/EU occurred through the inclusion of a new act in the legal system, attention should be paid not only to the effects of decodification, but certainly also to the disintegration of the law on heritage protection.

It should be added that a draft Act on an amendment to the Civil Code, the Code of Civil Procedure and the International Private Law Act of 2018—unprocessed since 2018—foresaw important changes in the scope of exclusion from trade in good faith and prescription for works of art plundered from the territory of the Republic of Poland during the Second World War, and exclusive domestic jurisdiction in cases of property rights or the possession of movable things constituting works of art plundered from the territory of the Republic of Poland during the Second World War; these changes were to be introduced to the Civil Code and the Code of Civil Procedure, as appropriate (as will be presented more in detail in the Sect. 5.3). This confirms that the legislative solutions considered are being introduced chaotically. Certainly, the unity of civil law is not being taken into consideration, with fragmentation proceeding as a secondary phenomenon that is not always analyzed in relation to how the changes that are made affect cultural heritage.

It can be said that cultural heritage is throwing down the gauntlet to the principles discussed above. It cannot be held, though, that the changes made in the Polish Civil Code and other legal acts concerning the status of cultural heritage in civil law are the effect of a game of catch-up with reality solely within the scope of technological progress. What can be said with certainty is that those changes are part of an attempt to catch up with, or to take part in, the race to find a new model of protection for cultural property at the international level. This does not merely imply looking for solutions identical to those in force in other countries, but may also entail introducing unique legal institutions designed to strengthen the protective regime.

The principles of autonomy of will and trade certainty and security have been altered significantly as regards their application to the cultural heritage in the area of private law. Those changes result from international commitments, the implementation of EU law, and an independent evolution of the law on the protection of the cultural heritage. Some provisions concerning cultural heritage emerged in private law only in recent years. There is no doubt that the issues of artistic and historical value and the protection of property incorporating these were foreseen already in the

---

[199] Directive 2014/60/EU of the European Parliament and of the Council of 15 May 2014 on the return of cultural objects unlawfully removed from the territory of a Member State and amending Regulation (EU) No. 1024/2012 (Recast), OJ L 159, 28.5.2014, pp. 1–10.

[200] Giaro (2017), p. 23.

[201] Giaro (2017), p. 24.

provisions on finds and treasure. It must be emphasized, therefore, that there was an awareness of the important value of cultural heritage at the time the Polish Civil Code was enacted.

Moreover, it can be stated that components of cultural heritage have always occupied a special place in the Civil Code, and that subsequent amendments have confirmed that heritage protection is part of the axiology of private law. In all of the above-discussed principles, cultural property appears as property protected by law, regardless of whether it constitutes an object of private or public property. The need to combat the illegal trade in cultural property has led to a supplementation of the principle of certainty and security in trading by the introduction of provisions that prohibit such acquisitions even when made in good faith and acquisitions by prescription. Regarding the procedural model applicable to cultural heritage, the provisions concerning both the object and the place of regulation are mostly found outside the Civil Code.

2.7 Conclusions

When defining cultural heritage, reference should be made to both material and intangible property. Both types are worthy of preservation not because of their material or intangible form, but because of the intangible values they incorporate. The view that such a definition should be limited to things as material objects separated from nature is no longer defensible because of the growing number of heritage resources and our inability to foresee what forms they take on in the future.

Decision-makers cannot decide to protect only material heritage or only that part of it that constitutes things. It is possible, though, for only a portion of heritage to be granted protection if the legislator considers the value of a given type of property to future generations and provides it with an enhanced protective regime. Although the definition of a historical object in the APGM focuses on protecting movable and immovable historical objects, Article 6 par. 2 of the same act stipulates that "Geographical, historical and traditional names of construction objects, squares, streets and settlement units may also be protected."

The private law element—or perhaps the "proprietary" element—has been gradually eliminated in favor of the idea of cultural heritage. Today, one can observe a reverse tendency that justifies an examination of just how much of the old "property" remains in the concept of cultural heritage. Without doubt, an important element of every regime related to heritage protection is to determine who the owner is. At this point it is worth noting, though, that some heritage elements cannot be objects of ownership, such as the above-mentioned geographical names and other property not constituting things. Cultural heritage is protected irrespective of issues of property rights, as has been emphasized, for example, in the definition of cultural heritage adopted in the Faro Convention (Article 2)[202] or in the Convention Concerning the Protection of the World Cultural and Natural Heritage (Article 6 (1).[203]

The definition of cultural heritage proposed by Polish doctrinal experts and adopted by the judiciary did not address the need for a flexible definition that takes account of the many possible forms of cultural heritage. Certainly, though, while the legal definitions of a historical object, including that in the APCP, were created on the assumption that a given act would be in force for a long time, there can be no such expectation with regard to an all-encompassing definition of cultural heritage. This results from the fact that the legal regulations at both the domestic and international levels are usually prepared to resolve a specific problem (e.g., illegal trade) or to protect a particular part of the resources of the cultural heritage.

An important consideration concerning the materiality and intangibility of heritage in private law is how a "thing" and "set of things" are defined. The existing definitions do not fit the definition of a historical object. Moreover, the multidimensional nature of cultural heritage means that some of its elements are not things. Here, it should be pointed out that private law will not regulate the legal relations of the entirety of cultural heritage. For example, given the restrictions of private law regulations, components of space heritage located outside of the Earth's orbit remain outside the interest of the legislator, whereas meteorites do not. Yet it may turn out that, as human beings become increasingly active in space, this too may change.

Material cultural heritage is imbued with undeniable intangible value. It needs to be stated categorically that a fragment, or perhaps a layer, of cultural heritage that is non-sensorial exists. It can be treated as a kind of common denominator, the core of material and intangible heritage. Often, intangible heritage results in the creation of material property, and so we see the material dimension of the intangible heritage in the form of, say, decorations, painted Easter eggs and Christmas nativity scenes. It seems that, in the case of cultural heritage constituting things, one can separate the *corpus mechanicum* from the additional value that exists in the intangible dimension. Treating this as an "intangible" component of the thing indicates a relationship between that value and the carrier. Just as a component part cannot be removed without affecting the whole, value so incorporated is also impossible to "uproot."

The idea of a set of things is of key importance with regard to collections, including museum collections. A collection's existence, expansion, completion, or introduction to trade are important to determine how it can be managed and what

---

[202] Art. 2. A cultural heritage is a group of resources inherited from the past which people identify, independently of ownership, as a reflection and expression of their constantly evolving values, beliefs, knowledge and traditions. It includes all aspects of the environment resulting from the interaction between people and places through time.

[203] Art. 6.1. Whilst fully respecting the sovereignty of the States on whose territory the cultural and natural heritage mentioned in Articles 1 and 2 is situated, and without prejudice to property right provided by national legislation, the States Parties to this Convention recognize that such heritage constitutes a world heritage for whose protection it is the duty of the international community as a whole to co-operate.

changes to it are permissible. Above all, before a set of objects is added to public collections, it is necessary to support the owner's use of collection management mechanisms and to recognize the collection as a separate object of trade. The civil law construction of the collection as a whole that acknowledges its intangible layer makes it possible to treat the collection like an enterprise and as a separate object of a legal agreement.

An interesting legal structure adopted for the needs of managing certain resources of the city of Warsaw is that relating to historical art studios. Again, like an enterprise, a studio comprises real property or a part thereof (premises) together with movable things consisting of equipment, memorabilia and objects the artist wished to be surrounded by when working. In terms of heritage protection, a historical art studio lies somewhere between a typical creative place and a historical object, in which changes are permissible only to the extent they do not disrupt the historical substance. In this way, a studio becomes a place that connects the past with the present—provided it is made publicly available.

From the example of the provisions of law on cultural property, we can see there has been a publicization of private law: the public element related to the cultural heritage protection, while present in the Civil Code from the beginning, has recently intensified. The intensification I have in mind concerns not only new legal provisions, but also legislative initiatives. It seems that, as may not be the case with other objects of regulation, what is most natural with regard to the use of cultural property, or even expected, are hybrid regulations. For the public element inherent in the values and importance of a given object for present and future generations cannot be ignored, and in principle is of a permanent nature.

The principles of civil law of autonomy of will, trade certainty and security, and equity all apply to cultural heritage. Yet, it sometimes happens that the provisions concerning cultural property place certain values above those that express the fundamental principles of civil law, such as, for example, the principle under which participants in trade are guaranteed certainty over acquisitions made in good faith. Depending, then, on how we define those provisions—whether as disrupting that principle or as a formative element of it—in every case what will remain at the center of protection is cultural property, not the parties to a legal transaction or their freedom to form its content. And so, autonomy of will is affected by: granting pre-emption rights, priority, the obligation to preserve a defined form of a legal transaction, or even the conclusion of particular contractual provisions designed to ensure the protection of a monument.

The decodification of civil law will result in the Civil Code having a new function as a central act, and there is no way to halt that process. In the case of cultural heritage protection, at least at the level of postulates, one can anticipate that in the future a code of cultural heritage will arise. The current dispersion of provisions across many acts of law relating to heritage, and the fragmentary regulation in other acts whose core is, for example, the investment process or the management of real estate, pose a challenge and at the same time should mobilize forces to create a comprehensive code. The example of the normative acts regulating the problem of cultural heritage confirms this fragmentation of the law, but also highlights the power of private law solutions for protecting cultural heritage. The role of the Civil Code as the heart of private law makes it necessary to locate cultural heritage elements, or at least those constituting things, in civil law.

References

Bauman Z (2011) Kultura w płynnej nowoczesności. Wyd. Narodowego Instytutu Audiowizualnego. Agora SA, Warszawa

Bednarek M (1997) Mienie. Komentarz do art. 44–55 Kodeksu cywilnego. Zakamycze, Kraków

Blake J (2000) On defining the cultural heritage. International and Comparative Law Quaterly 49(1):61–85

Borkowska-Bagieńska E, Krasowski K, Lesiński B, Walachowicz J (1994) Historia państwa i prawa Polski. Zarys wykładu. Ars Boni et Aequi, Poznań

Cagnoli MV (2020, 16 June). Blockchain for the Art Market: applications and implications. http://www.medialaws.eu/blockchain-for-the-art-market-applications-and-implications/. Accessed 1 June 2022

Carpenter KA, Katyal SK, Riley AR (2010) Clarifying cultural property. IJCP 17:581–598. https://doi.org/10.1017/S0940739110000317

Crow K (2017, 16 Nov), Leonardo da Vinci Painting 'Salvator Mundi' Smashes Records With $450.3 Million Sale. The Wall Street Journal. https://www.wsj.com/articles/leonardo-da-vinci-painting-salvator-mundi-sells-for-450-3-million-1510794281. Accessed 1 June 2022

Czajkowska-Dąbrowska M (2007) Własność czy własności (intelektualnej)? In: Kidyba A, Skubisz R (eds) Współczesne problemy prawa handlowego. Księga jubileuszowa dedykowana prof. dr hab. Marii Poźniak-Niedzielskiej. Wolters Kluwer, Warszawa, pp 46–53

Dajczak W (2007) Rzymska res incorporalis a kształtowanie się pojęć „rzeczy" i „przedmiotu praw rzeczowych" w europejskiej nauce prawa prywatnego. Wydawnictwo Naukowe Uniwersytetu im. Adama Mickiewicza, Poznań

Dajczak W (2008) Poszukiwanie „nowego ładu" prawa prywatnego w okresie jego „dekodyfikacji" i „instrumentalizacji". Uwagi z perspektywy tradycji romanistycznej. In: Radwanowicz-Wanczewska J, Niczyporuk P, Kuźmicz K (eds) Jednostka a państwo na przestrzeni wieków. Temida 2, Białystok 2008, pp. 83–95

Dobosz P (1997) Administracyjnoprawne instrumenty kształtowania ochrony zabytków. Dajwór, Kraków

Dobosz P (2018) Formy, mechanizmy ochrony i opieki a pojęcia: zabytek, niematerialne dobro kultury, pamiątka rodzinna i tzw. przedmiot kultowy. In: Dobosz P, Górny W, Mazur A, Mazurek B, Kozień A (eds) Samorząd terytorialny, architektura, dzieła sztuki, prawo. Kraków, Studio Cubus, pp 55–65

Drela M (2002) Dobro kultury jako przedmiot ochrony prawnorzeczowej. PiP 11:56–65

Drela M (2006) Własność zabytków. C.H. Beck, Warszawa

Fincham D (2011) The distinctiveness of property and heritage. Penn State Law Rev 115(3): 641–684

Francioni F (2020) Art. 2(1) [commentary]. In: Blake J, Lixinski L (eds) The 2003 UNESCO intangible heritage convention: a commentary. Oxford University Press, Oxford, pp 56–57

Frankiewicz-Bodynek A (2019) Konstytucyjna regulacja dziedzictwa narodowego oraz dóbr kultury. Wydawnictwo Adam Marszałek, Toruń

Frigo M (2004) Cultural property v. cultural heritage: a "battle of concepts" in international law? Int Rev Red Cross 86(854):367–378. https://doi.org/10.1017/S1560775500180861

Gaweł Ł (2016) Zarządzanie dziedzictwem i jego interesariusze. In: Jagielska-Burduk A (ed) Mechanizmy prawne zarządzania dziedzictwem kultury. Wolters Kluwer Polska, Wydawnictwo Uniwersytetu Gdańskiego, Gdańsk–Warszawa, pp 26–44

Gerstenblith P (1995) Identity and cultural property: the protection of cultural property in the United States. BUL Rev 75:559–668

Giaro T (2017) Dekodyfikacja. Uwagi historyczno-teoretyczne. In: Longchamps de Bérier F (ed) Dekodyfikacja prawa prywatnego. Szkice do portretu. Wydawnictwo Sejmowe, Fundacja "Utriusque Iuris", Warszawa, pp 13–37

Gniewek E (2013) Przedmiot prawa własności. In: Gniewek E (ed) Prawo rzeczowe. System Prawa Prywatnego, vol 3. C.H. Beck, Warszawa, pp 347–362

Golat R (2004) Ustawa o ochronie zabytków i opiece nad zabytkami. Komentarz. Zakamycze, Kraków

Gredka-Ligarska I, Gwoździewicz-Matan P, Kowalski WW (2019) Umowy w działalności muzeów. Prawo cywilne. Prawo autorskie. Wydawnictwo Uniwersytetu Gdańskiego, Gdańsk

Grzybowski S (ed) (1985) System prawa cywilnego, vol 1: Część ogólna. Zakład Narodowy im. Ossolińskich, Wydawnictwo Polskiej Akademii Nauk, Wrocław–Warszawa

Helios J (2013) Publicyzacja prawa prywatnego – prywatyzacja prawa publicznego w kontekście rozważań nad prawem europejskim. Acta Wratislaviensis, Przegląd Prawa i Administracji 92: 11–36

Ignatowicz J (2000) Prawo rzeczowe. Wydawnictwa Prawnicze PWN, Warszawa

Izdebski H (2004) Własność. Pomiędzy doktryną a dogmatyką prawa. CPH 56(1):161–175

Izdebski H (2019) Komentarz do Konstytucji RP. Art. 6, 70, 73. Difin, Uniwersytet SWPS, Warszawa

Jagielska-Burduk A (2011) Zabytek ruchomy. Wolters Kluwer Polska, Warszawa

Jagielska-Burduk A (2014) Koncepcja świadomego dysponenta zabytków w polskim prawie ochrony zabytków. In: Zeidler K (ed) Prawo ochrony zabytków. Wolters Kluwer, Wydawnictwo Uniwersytetu Gdańskiego, Warszawa–Gdańsk, pp. 311–318

Jagielska-Burduk A (2016a) Formy ochrony zabytków jako mechanizm zarządzania dziedzictwem kultury. In: Jagielska-Burduk A (ed) Mechanizmy prawne zarządzania dziedzictwem kultury. Wolters Kluwer Polska, Wydawnictwo Uniwersytetu Gdańskiego, Gdańsk–Warszawa, pp. 171–212

Jagielska-Burduk A (2016b) Nowy wizerunek dziedzictwa – między ochroną a zarządzaniem. In: Jagielska-Burduk A (ed) Mechanizmy prawne zarządzania dziedzictwem kultury. Wolters Kluwer Polska, Wydawnictwo Uniwersytetu Gdańskiego, Gdańsk–Warszawa, pp. 44–65

Jagielska-Burduk A (2019) Cultural heritage, education, and research in the European Union. In: Jakubowski A, Hausler K, Fiorentini F (ed) Cultural Heritage in the European Union. A Critical Inquiry into Law and Policy. Brill Nijnhoff, pp 241–265. https://doi.org/10.1163/9789004365346_012

Jagielska-Burduk A, Jakubowski A (2020) "Narrative museums" and curators' rights: the protection of a museum exhibition and its scenario under polish law. SAACLR 2(6):151–176. https://doi.org/10.4467/2450050XSNR.20.014.13017

Jagielska-Burduk A, Markowski D (2013) Wybrane zagadnienia dotyczące sposobów nabywania własności dzieł sztuki i zabytków przez muzea. Acta Universitatis Nicolai Copernici. Zabytkoznawstwo i Konserwatorstwo 44:531–545. https://doi.org/10.12775/AUNC_ZiK.2013.022

Jagielska-Burduk A, Mularski K (2015) Problematyka reprywatyzacji zabytków ruchomych. Uwagi na marginesie wyroku Sądu Najwyższego z 16 lutego 2012 r. (III CSK 208/11). Wydział Teologiczny Uniwersytetu Opolskiego, Opole 2015, pp. 201–216

Jankowska-Sabat M (2015) Pojęcie kolekcji w orzecznictwie sądowym. In: Stec P, Maniurka P (eds) Kolekcje i zbiory muzealne. Problematyka prawna. Redakcja Wydawnictw Wydziału Teologicznego Uniwersytetu Opolskiego, Opole, pp. 41–62

Kamecki R (2021, 4 Jan) Artinfo.pl ogłasza wyniki rynku sztuki za 2020 rok. https://artinfo.pl/artinformacje/artinfo-pl-oglasza-wyniki-rynku-sztuki-za-2020-rok Accessed 1 June 2022

Kasprzak A (2019) Warszawskie historyczne pracownie artystyczne. Spotkania z Zabytkami 11–12:36–40

Katner W (2012) Dobra niematerialne. In: Safjan M (ed) (2012) Prawo cywilne – część ogólna. System Prawa Prywatnego, vol 1. C.H. Beck Warszawa, pp 1358–1376

Katner W (2014) Art. 45 [Commentary]. In: Księżak P, Pyziak-Szafnicka M (eds) Kodeks cywilny. Komentarz. Część ogólna, 2nd ed. Lex

Kaźmierska M (2019, 30 Oct) Rzeźby Magdaleny Abakanowicz sprzedane za ponad 8 mln zł. Należały do Robina Williamsa. Gazeta Wyborcza. https://poznan.wyborcza.pl/poznan/7,36000,25362347,rzezby-magdaleny-abakanowicz-sprzedane-za-ponad-8-mln-zlotych.html?disableRedirects=true. Accessed 1 June 2022

Kirkpatrick DD (2019, 30 March) A Leonardo Made a $450 Million Splash. Now There's No Sign of It. The New York Times. https://www.nytimes.com/2019/03/30/arts/design/salvator-mundi-louvre-abu-dhabi.html. Accessed 1 June 2022

Kordela M (2012) Zasady prawa. Studium teoretycznoprawne. Wydawnictwo Naukowe UAM, Poznań

Kowalski W (1986) Miejsce ochrony dóbr kultury w systemie prawa. OZ 3:171–178

Kowalski W (2004) Nabycie własności dzieła sztuki od nieuprawnionego. Zakamycze, Kraków

Kowalski W (2015) Dawne i współczesne uwarunkowania prawne kolekcjonerstwa w Polsce. In: Rosset TF de, Kluczewska-Wójcik A, Tołysz A (eds) Kolekcjonerstwo polskie XX i XXI wieku. Narodowy Instytut Muzealnictwa i Ochrony Zbiorów, Warszawa, pp. 204–219

Lixinski L (2013) Intangible cultural heritage in international law. Oxford University Press, Oxford

Liżewski B (2018) Prawo publiczne a prawo prywatne – wybrane uwagi teoretyczne na temat hybrydyzacji instytucji prawnych. Zeszyty Naukowe Katolickiego Uniwersytetu Lubelskiego Jana Pawła II 61(4):47–63. https://doi.org/10.31743/zn.2018.61.4.47-63

Longchamps de Bérier F (2019) Wstęp. In: Longchamps de Bérier F (ed) Dekodyfikacja prawa prywatnego w europejskiej tradycji prawnej. Wydawnictwo Uniwersytetu Jagiellońskiego, Kraków

Machnikowski P (2005) Swoboda umów według art. 353[1] KC. Konstrukcja prawna. C.H. Beck, Warszawa

Maciejewski T (2007) Historia powszechna ustroju i prawa. C.H. Beck, Warszawa

Merryman JH (1968) The public law-private law distinction in European and American law. J Public Law 17(3):3–19

Merryman JH (1986) Two ways of thinking about cultural property. Am J Int Law 80(4):831–853. https://doi.org/10.2307/2202065

Merryman JH (1994) Nation and the object. IJCP 3(1):61–76

Merryman JH (2005) Cultural property internationalism. IJCP 12(1):11–39

Michalak A, Ginter A (2016) Ustawa o ochronie zabytków i opiece nad zabytkami. Komentarz. Wolters Kluwer, Warszawa

Mileszyk N (2019) Ponowne wykorzystanie informacji sektora publicznego w działalności muzeów w związku z ustawą o reuse. NIMOZ, Warszawa https://nimoz.pl/files/publications/56/Ponowne_wykorzystywanie_ISP_w_dzialalnosci_muzeow_2019.pdf

Mojak J (2016) Ewolucja zasad współczesnego polskiego prawa cywilnego – zasada bezpieczeństwa obrotu. Studia Iuridica Lublinensia 25(1):147–159. https://doi.org/10.17951/sil.2016.25.1.147

O'Keefe R (1999) The meaning of 'cultural property' under the 1954 Hague convention. Netherlands Int Law Rev 46(1):26–56. https://doi.org/10.1017/S0165070X00002084

Prott LV, O'Keefe PJ (1992) 'Cultural heritage' or 'cultural property'? Int J Cult Prop 1(2): 307–320. doi:https://doi.org/10.1017/S094073919200033X

Prott LV, O'Keefe PJ (1989) Law and Cultural Heritage, vol 3: Movement. Butterworth & Co, London

Pruszyński J (2001) Dziedzictwo kultury Polski. Jego straty i ochrona prawna, vol 1. Kantor Wydawniczy Zakamycze, Kraków

Radwański B (2009) Kodyfikacja prawa cywilnego. RPEiS 2:131–142

Rudnicki J (2019) Polska i historyczne fazy dekodyfikacji prawa cywilnego. In: Longchamps de Bérier F (ed) Dekodyfikacja prawa prywatnego w europejskiej tradycji prawnej. Wydawnictwo Uniwersytetu Jagiellońskiego, Kraków, pp. 165–207

Safjan M (ed) (2012) Prawo cywilne – część ogólna. System Prawa Prywatnego, vol 1. C.H. Beck, Warszawa 2012

Sax JL (2007) Legal concepts of cultural heritage property. J Rare Books Manuscripts Cult Herit 8(1):67–74. https://doi.org/10.5860/rbm.8.1.279

Sienkiewicz T (2013) Umowa o oddanie gruntu w użytkowanie wieczyste jako nienazwana forma ochrony zabytków. In: Jagielska-Burduk A, Szafrański W (eds) Kultura w praktyce. Zagadnienia prawne, vol 2: Wokół problematyki prawnej zabytków i rynku sztuki. Wydawnictwo Poznańskiego Towarzystwa Przyjaciół Nauk, Poznań, pp 245–259

Smee S (2019, 15 Oct) The Louvre wants this $450 million 'Leonardo' in its big show. But its mystery owner appears to be balking. The Washington Post. https://www.washingtonpost.com/entertainment/museums/the-louvre-wants-this-450-million-leonardo-in-its-big-show-but-its-mystery-owner-appears-to-be-balking/2019/10/15/85bc5094-eec2-11e9-b648-76bcf86eb67e_story.html. Accessed 1 June 2022

Stanulewicz M (2007) Szczególne uprawnienia muzeów do nabywania zabytków w świetle art. 20 ustawy o muzeach. In: Szafrański W (ed) Wokół problematyki prawnej zabytków i dzieł sztuki, vol 2. Poznań, Wydawnictwo Poznańskie, pp 109–123

Stec P (2015a) Kodeks cywilny – między dekodyfikacją a rekodyfikacją. In: Stec P, Załuski M (eds) 50 lat Kodeksu Cywilnego. Perspektywy rekodyfikacji. Wolters Kluwer, Warszawa, pp 25–44

Stec P (2015b) Kolekcja jako przedmiot obrotu cywilnoprawnego. In: Stec P, Maniurka P (eds) Kolekcje i zbiory muzealne. Problematyka prawna. Redakcja Wydawnictw Wydziału Teologicznego Uniwersytetu Opolskiego, Opole, pp 79–95

Stec P, Maniurka P (eds) (2015) Kolekcje i zbiory muzealne. Problematyka prawna. Redakcja Wydawnictw Wydziału Teologicznego Uniwersytetu Opolskiego, Opole

Stefaniuk K (2016) Zasady prawa w systemach i podręcznikach prawa cywilnego. Studia Iuridica Lublinensia 25(1):137–141. https://doi.org/10.17951/sil.2016.25.1.137

Stelmach M (2018, July) Miejsce po Artyście. Rozmowa z Michałem Krasuckim. Dwutygodnik. Strona kultury, ed. 242. https://www.dwutygodnik.com/artykul/7918-miejsce-po-artyscie.html. Accessed 1 June 2022

Stelmachowski A (1969) Wstęp do teorii prawa cywilnego. PWN, Warszawa

Stelmachowski A (1980) Zasada jedności prawa cywilnego. Przegląd Ustawodawstwa Gospodarczego 2:37–43

Stelmachowski A (1994) Przedmiot własności w prawie cywilnym. Studia Iuridica 21:105–111

Szafrański W (2015) Ochrona dziedzictwa kulturalnego a rynek sztuki Zagrożenia, korzyści, perspektywy. In: Pływaczewski W, Gadecki B (eds) Ochrona dziedzictwa kulturalnego i naturalnego. Perspektywa prawna i kryminologiczna. Wydawnictwo C.H. Beck, Warszawa, pp 125–140

Szafrański W (2017) Koncepcje nacjonalistyczne i internacjonalistyczne w prawie ochrony dziedzictwa wielokulturowych dzieł sztuki/dóbr kultury. In: Szwarc AJ (ed) Panorama prawnych aspektów wielokulturowości społeczeństwa. Wydawnictwo Wyższej Szkoły Bankowej w Poznaniu, Poznań, pp 315–327

Szafrański W (2019) Aktualne problemy i zagrożenia związane z obrotem dobrami kultury na rynku sztuki w Polsce z perspektywy prawnej ochrony zabytków. SAACLR 1(5):41–68. https://doi.org/10.4467/2450050XSNR.19.003.10804

Szafrański W, Wilk D (2017) Sposoby czy metody? Aspekty podmiotowe i przedmiotowe wycen dzieł sztuki w Polsce. SAACLR 1(3):115–156. https://doi.org/10.4467/2450050XSNR.17.009.7381

Szczaniecki M (1985) Powszechna historia państwa i prawa. PWN, Warszawa

Szczepaniak R (2016) Węzłowe problemy stosowania prawa prywatnego w sektorze publicznym. RPEIS 78(4):107–121. https://doi.org/10.14746/rpeis.2016.78.4.9

Tatarkiewicz W (1968) O pojęciu wartości. Co historyk filozofii ma do zakomunikowania historykowi sztuki. In: Ryszkiewicz A (ed) O wartości dzieła sztuki. Materiały II Seminarium Metodologicznego Stowarzyszenia Historyków Sztuki, Radziejowice 19-21 maja 1966. "Desa", "Arkady", Warszawa

Tkacz S (2014) O zintegrowanej koncepcji zasad prawa w polskim prawoznawstwie: od dogmatyki do teorii. Wydawnictwo Adam Marszałek, Toruń

Vadi V (2014) Cultural heritage in investment law and arbitration. Cambridge University Press, Cambridge

Wasilkowski J (1964) Metoda opracowania i założenia kodeksu cywilnego. PiP 5–6:737–745

Wasilkowski J (1965) Pojęcie własności w świetle kodeksu cywilnego. PiP 12:815–828

Węgrzak M, Zeidler K (2020) The principles of cultural heritage law based on the polish law as an example. Revista de Direito Internacional 17(3):292–302. https://doi.org/10.5102/rdi.v17i3.7028

Williams SA (1978) The International and National Protection of Movable Cultural Property. A Comparative Study. Oceana Publications, Dobbs Ferry–New York

Wolter A (1986) Prawo cywilne. Zarys części ogólnej. PWN, Warszawa

Wronkowska S, Zieliński M, Ziembiński Z (1974) Zasady prawa. Zagadnienia podstawowe. Wydawnictwo Prawnicze, Warszawa

Żabiński Z (1974) Wpływ pojęcia rzeczy na kształtowanie się systemu prawa cywilnego. ZNUJ PWiOWI 1:251–261

Zajęcki M (2012) Definiowanie pojęć podstawowych prawa kultury w kontekście zasad wykładni prawa polskiego. In: Jagielska-Burduk A, Szafrański W (eds) Kultura w praktyce. Zagadnienia prawne, vol 1. Wydawnictwo Poznańskiego Towarzystwa Przyjaciół Nauk, Poznań, pp. 23–41

Żakowska M (2014) Miejskie pracownie warszawskich artystów. Warszawa w Budowie 6:64–75. https://issuu.com/muzeum_sztuki_nowoczesnej/docs/mw_uc4_booklet_web_2. Accessed 1 June 2022

Zalasińska K (2010) Prawna ochrona zabytków nieruchomych w Polsce. Wolters Kluwer Polska, Warszawa

Zalasińska K (2020) Ustawa o ochronie zabytków i opiece nad zabytkami. Komentarz. C.H. Beck, Warszawa

Zeidler K (2008) Wartość zabytku jako kategoria normatywna. In: Szafrański W (ed) Wokół problematyki prawnej zabytków i dzieł sztuki, vol 2. Wydawnictwo Poznańskie, Poznań, pp 37–48

Zeidler K (2014) Prawo ochrony dziedzictwa kultury jako nowa gałąź prawa. In: Zeidler K (ed) Prawo ochrony zabytków. Wolters Kluwer, Wydawnictwo Uniwersytetu Gdańskiego, Warszawa–Gdańsk, pp 23–33

Zeidler K (2018). Zasady prawa ochrony dziedzictwa kultury – propozycja katalogu. RPEIS 4:147–154. https://doi.org/10.14746/rpeis.2018.80.4.11

Zieliński M (2002) Wykładnia prawa. Zasady. Reguły. Wskazówki. Wydawnictwo Prawnicze LexisNexis, Warszawa 2002

Ziemianin B (2007) Prawo własności. In: Kidyba A, Skubisz R (eds) Współczesne problemy prawa handlowego: księga jubileuszowa dedykowana prof. dr hab. Marii Poźniak-Niedzielskiej. Wolters Kluwer, Warszawa, pp 429–435

Zoll F (1920) Prawa rzeczowe na ziemiach polskich, part 1. Księgarnia J. Czarneckiego, Warszawa–Kraków

Zoll F (1947) Prawo cywilne w zarysie, vol 2: Prawo rzeczowe, issue 1. Księgarnia Powszechna, Kraków

Chapter 3
Cultural Heritage Forms: Legal Challenges

3.1 Introduction

This section concerns private law challenges relating to the expansion of heritage resources and the emergence of new categories of cultural heritage components. Those challenges are divided according to the nature of a component as determined using an objective criterion. This makes it possible to examine components of cultural heritage as separate property to which detailed provisions of the law apply. Additionally, it makes it possible to determine what segment of cultural heritage currently requires the legislator's urgent attention. It is true that some of the types of property described herein, such as NFTs and CryptoArt, are relatively new. However, they deserve to be addressed even at this early stage because the process of heritagization is proceeding rapidly. No "age limit" has been set, therefore, on property whose status as components of cultural heritage is considered in this section, since this could be detrimental to the findings and might make it impossible to capture the essence of the current issues concerning cultural heritage.

Among those elements that are especially challenging for private law, we distinguish the following as material property: the human body, human remains, and space heritage. We then examine intangible heritage, where how a given component is expressed determines whether it exists in material or intangible form. Next, we look at art created by artificial intelligence and heritage in cyberspace, which must be treated separately with regard to additional legal regulations and means of protection.

The multitude of forms within the scope of intangible heritage makes it very difficult to think of heritage as a resource that is relatively uniform. This is evident in the definition accepted for the needs of the UNESCO Convention for the Safeguarding of the Intangible Cultural Heritage 2003, in accordance with which "intangible heritage" means

---

The chapter was translated from Polish into English by Anthony Sloan and the author.

A. Jagielska-Burduk, *Cultural Heritage as a Legal Hybrid*,
https://doi.org/10.1007/978-3-031-04946-0_3

> the practices, representations, expressions, knowledge, skills – as well as the instruments, objects, artefacts and cultural spaces associated therewith – that communities, groups and, in some case, individuals recognize as part of their cultural heritage.

In addition, the emergence of new property from practices and customs means that some of these have commercial value. And at the same time, questions arise concerning the commercial exploitation of that heritage—whose cultural heritage is it and how the risks of abuse can be limited. The common denominator in private law may prove to be the intangible value of cultural heritage, and that part of it which we are able to record digitally in the form of files. Since a digital version of a component of cultural heritage is known as a digital twin, it is worth considering whether a similar mechanism and connection might not be made between material and intangible heritage.

Some of these challenges have been with us for some time now, but a change in how certain phenomena are perceived has intensified the debate, or even changed its result. It should be added that the discussion does not always concern the history of the national heritage of a particular country (e.g., human remains in museums). For example, the silence in the Polish law may be justified by the fact that the most dynamic discussion on this subject concerns places where the original inhabitants of a given territory or indigenous peoples live, or where goods obtained during the colonial period are now located in universal museums.[1] Nevertheless, the technological progress we are currently witnessing and its use in the fine and applied arts (e.g., diamonds made of human remains) mean that this problem cannot go unaddressed.

Finally, I discuss problems related to a specific regulation for the safeguarding of the cultural heritage connected to Fryderyk Chopin. My aim is to show that, when commemorating particular persons important to the history of the Polish nation, even over 20 years ago the legislator was looking for new, unique solutions in the area of both material and intangible values. This enables us to answer the question of the usefulness of this legislative solution, which can be considered in a broader scope and used as a foundation for new acts of law.

As is always the case before a change in legal regulations, the introduction of changes as to how legal relations in civil law are classified may be sped up or slowed down by the legal and social debate. The debate on changing the status of property as an element of a legal relationship may lead to such a good or right being situated anew. Technological progress and social change can certainly be deemed a cause of the new property being identified and created. For example, at one time the growth in airline services, particularly in the private commercial sector, led to an intensification of interest in those subjects of legal relations connected with aviation.[2] Within this scope, a continual expansion of new services and the increased availability of existing services to a wider customer base are foreseen.[3]

[1] Fiskesjö (2014).

[2] Katner (2012), p. 1331.

[3] Katner (2012, p. 1334) gives example of commercial space tourism.

Taking this further, we can expect that cultural heritage will also expand due to technological progress; this will include components of space cultural heritage,[4] the exploration of that heritage, and the development of artificial intelligence.[5] In addition, irrespective of technological progress, a parallel process is underway whereby the total amount of heritage artefacts is increasing. One element connecting such new items is their intangible and cultural value. It can be assumed, then, that the expansion of resources will take place ever more rapidly, hence the urgent need for an internal classification of cultural property. This will make it possible to determine the moment at which it is justifiable for the legislator to intervene, possibly by granting certain types of property a new place in the system of material property. In each case, such actions may be based on an accepted system of values that affects how a particular item of cultural property is perceived and where its place is on the "ladder" of cultural heritage.

3.2 The Human Body and Cultural Heritage

The status of human remains has come up many times in discussions on the safeguarding of cultural heritage in connection with the functioning of museums. In the sphere of cultural heritage, the discussions that captured the most interest worldwide concerned Maori preserved heads. Earlier, *toi moko* had come up for auction and found their way into private collections. In 2010, in France, an act was passed pursuant to which, as of the day of its entry into force, all the Maori preserved heads stored in French National Museums (Musées de France) no longer formed part of their collections. In this way, Maori heads were excluded from the French public collections' regime (*res extra commercium*), and, with the participation of a special commission, a declassification system was introduced. The purpose of the changes introduced by the act was to effect the return of Maori heads to New Zealand.[6] Ten years later, the act is not rated very favorably; Sophie Vigneron has pointed out that in other countries, including Great Britain and Germany, the process of repatriation is being carried out within a broader scope.[7] It is important to bear in mind that issues concerning the repatriation of human remains are perceived differently because of the nature of the goods involved, and decision-makers (although not always, as discussed further in this chapter) are more inclined to return human remains than other cultural artefacts located in European museums. Yet an analysis of the French model shows that there, even a special act of law did not resolve the problem or make the introduction of a special procedure possible.[8]

---

[4] See Sect. 3.3.

[5] See Sect. 3.5.

[6] Paterson (2010), pp. 643–647.

[7] Vigneron (2020), pp. 314–315.

[8] Vigneron (2020), pp. 331–332.

Another matter of significance when considering the human body in the context of the cultural heritage is the medieval cult of relics, i.e., fragments of the bodies of saints[9]; the cult still exists, for example, regarding relics of the blood of Pope John Paul II.[10] Heated emotions were raised by an examination of the heart of Fryderyk Chopin, which is certainly treated in Polish culture as an exceptional artefact.[11] There is even an act in force to protect the composer's heritage;[12] nevertheless, Chopin's heart remains beyond its scope of application. Can Chopin's heart be treated as a component of cultural heritage? And if so, under Polish law, does it constitute a historical object? It is justifiable to maintain that a heart, which constitutes human remains, can be a component of cultural heritage? As to the second question, the answer may be twofold, depending on how human organs are classified. In the definition of a historical object contained in the APGM, reference is made to a civil-law construction of things (*res*). In this light, those who do not consider parts of the human body (constituting internal organs) to be things would not acknowledge that a heart can be a historical object. For the body of a deceased person cannot be adequately categorized using the traditional dichotomy between "person" and "thing."[13]

The status of corpses and human remains is not treated in a uniform manner in different legal systems. In many acts of law, human remains can be considered as components of cultural heritage, and a cautious approach is taken towards their "reification." Of key importance here are domestic acts of law, including those that concern cemeteries and the burial of the dead, as well as those regulating the protection of cultural heritage. To take an example of a foreign regulation, in the Native American Graves Protection and Repatriation Act (NAGPRA),[14] the US legislator deliberately avoids the reification of human remains located in museums. The UNESCO Convention on the Protection of the Underwater Cultural Heritage also treats human remains as a separate category.[15] Under Article 2 par. 2 of the Convention, Parties shall cooperate in the protection of underwater cultural heritage. Each country seeks its own ways of doing so, taking account of its own legal system and legal culture. A management model is considered that includes rights similar to property rights with respect to a deceased person's right to be buried by relatives.[16]

---

[9] Nieroba (2012), p. 152.

[10] Red. (2015).

[11] Dębowska (2014); Kowalski (2017).

[12] Act of 3 February 2001 on the Protection of the Heritage of Fryderyk Chopin. Polish Official Journal (Dz. U.) 2001, No. 16, item 168, as amendmed.

[13] Cf. Pietrzykowski (2015), p. 250.

[14] 25 U.S.C. § 3005(a) (2000).

[15] Convention on the Protection of the Underwater Cultural Heritage adopted on 2 November 2001, Records of the General Conference, 31st session, Paris, 15 October to 3 November 2001, v. 1: Resolutions, 31 C/Resolutions + CORR.

[16] See on "no-property rule" and "quasi property rights": Gallagher (2010).

The cultural dimension of graves and human remains is uncontested. Doubts do arise, however, over human remains being categorized as material goods that can be subject to ownership. For this reason, in the NAGPRA act referred to above, when discussing human remains located in museums, reference is made to a museum's existing control over those exhibits ("control of a museum"). The act constitutes an example of a conscious use of a broad network of concepts concerning the cultural heritage and its components to deal with the issue of human remains located in American museums.[17] While the NAGPRA act is not considered flawless, its adoption constituted a milestone in the perception of human remains as property constituting part of the cultural heritage of certain groups, and undermined the idea of treating them as things.[18]

It is universally accepted that the body of a living human being does not constitute a thing. The problem of classification arises after a person's death in relation to a corpse, human remains, and organs removed during life or after death. Various views exist concerning organs that can be used to save the health or life of another person. Moreover, assuming that a transplanted organ is a thing after it has been removed from a donor's body, it loses that status after being transplanted into a recipient.

In the case of a human body after death and the forms in which it can exist, science considers the following: human remains, mummies, and preparations preserved in containers. In Polish science, the following position has been presented. According to Stefan Grzybowski, "skeletons, mummies and anatomical preparations may be objects of trade, rights *in rem*, and legal circulation."[19] Corpses constitute things, but are excluded from trade and, as such, cannot be subject to rights *in rem.*[20] This leads to the assertion that corpses constitute ownerless things.[21] According to Stefan Rudnicki and Stefan Dmowski, "human organs separated from a donor's body, skeletons, mummies and anatomical preparations, as material objects, are things in the meaning of Article 45 of the Civil Code."[22] Jerzy Ignatowicz, in turns, believes that corpses are not things, but research preparations are.[23] Wiesław Daszkiewicz has stated that exceptions permitting human remains to be treated as things "may be, for example, mummies as museum exhibits, or bones or other body parts located in medical offices."[24] Zbigniew Radwański proposed that corpses, human cells separated from the body, tissues, organs and blood are not things, but are subject to separate regulation.[25]

---

[17] Fincham (2011), pp. 675–678.

[18] Brown and Bruchac (2006), p. 194.

[19] Grzybowski (1985), p. 411.

[20] Grzybowski (1985), p. 411.

[21] Bednarek (1997), p. 82.

[22] Rudnicki and Dmowski (2001), p. 138. The object is no longer a thing after transplantation and being integrated into the human body.

[23] Ignatowicz (2000), p. 18.

[24] Daszkiewicz (1989), pp. 63–64.

[25] Radwański (2002), p. 114.

From a cultural heritage perspective, this last view most fully reflects the specific nature of such goods. One cannot help but notice that it is possible to distinguish at least two perspectives, one scientific (research preparations, DNA samples and scientific progress) and the other relating to human dignity, respecting the rights of families or communities, and guaranteeing proper burial. Accepting one or the other as prevalent results in a different view of the human body after death. In the case of exhibits that have been in museums for years, the problem is even more complicated, for a political element appears. It is connected with the shaping of attitudes on the art market; additionally, the legal regulations concerning collections in force in a given country must be considered.

It should be pointed out that attitudes towards mummies and exhibits have momentous consequences in museum practice. For example, in Great Britain, in the Human Tissue Act[26] the return of human remains is limited by the provision of Section 47, pursuant to which deaccession from the collections of relevant institutions applies only to the remains of persons who died less than 1000 years ago;[27] in other words, ancient mummies remain beyond the scope of that regulation. This is not tantamount to a reification of mummies, but only a reflection of the deaccession policy decided upon for relevant institutions. For research preparations to be museum exhibits, they must be acknowledged as things. Whether such a status is conferred or not involves considerations of a moral nature. Along with scientific progress and the possibility of using human body parts to save lives, comes the problem of determining how to classify such property and whether it can be subject to trade. Wojciech Katner suggests that the principle of organs being excluded from trade may be departed from in the case of organ donations, which are an expression of a person's will to provide assistance and save the life of another human being. That principle, then, is that the human body and its components are excluded from trade. Non-remuneration also arises in connection with the use of human cadavers and organs for research purposes or to save human life.[28]

When considering cultural heritage, yet another element appears, that of the public interest as an inherent component of the discussion over heritage. For example, it is difficult to agree with a categorical commodification of mummies if we consider that, in fact, they constitute the bodies of deceased persons, prepared in a ritual manner, and placed in special containers after the mummification process. Taking another stance requires us to assert that a mummy may be an object of trade. At the time when the latter view was expressed, the issues of trade restrictions and treating mummies both as components of cultural heritage and as human remains were not as prevalent as they are today. The return of the mummy of Ramses I from the Michael Carlos Museum in Atlanta to Egypt was particularly hailed as a

[26]Human Tissue Act 2004 (c. 30), Explanatory Notes. https://www.legislation.gov.uk/ukpga/2004/30/pdfs/ukpgaen_20040030_en.pdf. Accessed 1 June 2022.

[27]Gallagher (2010), p. 68.

[28]Katner (2012), p. 1318.

breakthrough, and the mummy was placed in the museum in Luxor.[29] Also, where a mummy is recognized and attributed to a particular historical ruler, national and religious elements enter into the discussion. Even if an object was acquired in accordance with the law and taken out of the country before this was prohibited under Egyptian law, claims for repatriation often find support in the nature of the artefact concerned.

A different case is that of the Broken Hill skull (or Kabwe Man) in the Museum of Natural History in London.[30] This particular exhibit cannot be attributed to a specific person, only to a particular territory. Nevertheless, Zambia argues that the case connects different considerations pertaining to human remains; that is, affiliation with a group inhabiting a particular area, and with the civilization that existed there at the time. That argument goes beyond the current status of property rights under British law, and is based on the idea of an intangible bond and of an artefact's importance due to its connection with the history of the heritage of humankind.[31] At Zambia's initiative, the matter was submitted in 2016 to a meeting of the International Commission for Promoting the Return of Cultural Property to Its Countries of Origin or Its Restitution in Case of Illicit Appropriation (ICPRCP).[32] In 2018, the Commission addressed the causes of the claim for repatriation in its recommendations. It held that the existence or non-existence at the time an artefact is taken out of a country of a law prohibiting such activities is not the only fact to be considered when determining whether objects should be returned to their country of origin; further, the ICPRCP recommended that the two states concerned should enter into bilateral talks.[33] During the session in 2021 the ICPRCP noted "that the two bilateral meetings have not yet resolved the case but both the United Kingdom and Zambia are committed to further and fruitful dialogue" and inscribed the item on the next session's agenda.[34]

On the 23rd session in May 2022 the Secretariat informed that a letter was sent "on 4 March 2022 to Zambia and the United Kingdom of Great Britain and Northern Ireland expressing its availability for a constructive exchange of information to facilitate dialogue".[35] A special approach must be taken towards property

---

[29] Ikram (2011), p. 145.

[30] See more: Musonda (2013), pp. 199–203.

[31] The International Commission for Promoting the Return of Cultural Property to Its Countries of Origin or Its Restitution in Case of Illicit Appropriation, 20th session, http://www.unesco.org/new/fileadmin/MULTIMEDIA/HQ/CLT/pdf/Zambie.pdf. Accessed 1 June 2022.

[32] Final Report(ICPRCP/16/20.COM/Report, par. 16. https://unesdoc.unesco.org/ark:/48223/pf0000369036. Accessed 1 June 2022.

[33] ICPRCP/18/21.COM/Decisions, Recommendation 21.Com 8, par. 10.
https://unesdoc.unesco.org/ark:/48223/pf0000369026. Accessed 1 June 2022; about negotiations: M. Balley,. After 48 years, Zambia still wants Rhodesian Man back, The Art Newspaper, vol. XXIX, no 321, 1 June 2022.

[34] ICPRCP/21/22.COM/Decisions, Recommendation 22.Com 7, Accessed 1 June 2022: https://unesdoc.unesco.org/ark:/48223/pf0000379856.

[35] ICPRCP/22/23.COM/5.REV, Report of the Secretariat, https://unesdoc.unesco.org/ark:/48223/pf0000381584, Accessed 1 June 2022.

made from processed fragments of the human body, one example being books whose covers are made out of human skin.[36] In the days when human skin was used for book covers, the practice was considered unusual.[37] The degree of processing involved can be misleading as to the provenance of the material used, which constitutes only one material element of the object. In this regard, it seems fitting to agree in part with the view that parts of the human body may be things, and to acknowledge that in such cases we are dealing with a thing (a book), and that in this context a processed corpse or human remains should be categorized as things. This should not, however, deprive them of the special place they occupy in relation to other types of property. The historical and emotional value of such things, and the obligation to cultivate the memory of the dead, permit the assertion that, for moral reasons, such things should be excluded from trade.

Yet another approach is required when the body of a living person is used in the creation of a work of art. For example, a contract with a minor for the creation of a tattoo depicting the Eiffel Tower and a rose was deemed invalid under French law for violating the public order. The tattoo itself was removed.[38] In another context, it is worth looking at a work of contemporary art that also includes an element of the body of a living person. The artist Wim Delvoye entitled his work *Tim* (from the name of the man, Tim Steiner, on whose back the work exists). The artist rented the man's back to tattoo it. The tattoo depicts a haloed Madonna beneath a Mexican skull. Currently, the "work" is part of the collection of the German collector Rik Reinking, who, when asked about his decision to make the purchase, replied that *Tim* simply fit the profile of his collection.[39] The work was sold to Reinking in 2008 for EUR 150,000, out of which Tim Steiner received EUR 50,000. In an interview, Steiner said that "now my skin belongs to Rik Reinking"; he compared his back to a canvas, and himself to the frame. Under his contract, Tim Steiner is obliged to take part in exhibitions three times per year. He has shown the work in the Louvre, among other places.[40] Other works of art include animals (pigs) whose torsos have been tattooed. Only after the natural death of the animals (the pigs live on a farm) do the buyers receive their treated hides.[41] It should be added that the film *The Man Who Sold His Skin*, which tells the story of Tim Steiner, was nominated for an Oscar, and in respect of the film Wim Delvoye said: "The fact Tim got sold is more important than the tattoo itself," adding that the film's main subject is the "commodification of art, humans, etc. But in this film it also deals with love, migration and so much else."[42]

---

[36] Kersten (1910), p. 363; Verheyen (2016), p. 74.

[37] Z (1930), pp. 8–19.

[38] Vigneron (2020), pp. 319; Court of Cassation (France), First Civil Chamber, Case No. 70–12.490, Judgment of 23 February 1972, Bulletin civ. 1 n. 61, p. 54.

[39] TIAMSA meeting "Drivers of Collecting Contemporary Art – A Perspective from Germany" with Bettina Steinbrügge, Katharina zu Sayn-Wittgenstein and Rik Reinking; Moderator: Dieter Dahlhoff, 11 February 2021.

[40] Interview Tattoo Tim, lifesize artwork (2017, 8 February). https://www.slow-words.com/tattoo-tim-lifesize-artwork/. Accessed 1 June 2022.

[41] Low (2017).

[42] Cascone (2021).

At present, many more legal problems concerning human remains are being analyzed. In the Polish legal system, the definitions of "corpse" and "human remains" can be derived from the content of the Regulation of 7 December 2001 on the handling of bodies and human remains issued on the basis of the Act of 31 January 1959 on Cemeteries and Burials[43] ("ACB"). Under the act, the bodies of deceased persons, and of stillborn children—regardless of the length of the pregnancy—are deemed to be corpses (Clause 2 of the Regulation). Clause 8, in turn, concerns human remains and how they are to be handled. It also addresses the question of whether human remains other than those set out in pt. 1–3 exist.[44] It seems that a catalogue constructed in this way should contain a full enumeration. Moreover, the category "remains of corpses extracted by digging up a grave or in other circumstances" is rather broad in scope and could encompass other doubtful forms of human remains.

Defining the terms "human remains" or "corpse" in a regulation is not the correct legislative procedure. Those concepts do appear in the ACB but are not defined. Article 20 ACB provides a statutory delegation for the issuance of a relevant regulation by the minister responsible for health. The delegation encompasses defining the concept of a corpse in the meaning of the ACB, the handling of corpses and human remains, and the conditions for the exhumation and movement of corpses and human remains. The content of the statutory delegation concerning the definition of the concept of a corpse raises serious doubts. Further, the delegation of defining a key concept of the ACB in a regulation issued on the basis of the delegation is improper. Both "corpse" and "human remains" should be regulated in the act itself.

In my view, the enumeration of human remains provided in the act is incomplete; it should include, for example, processed human remains in the form of a diamond.[45] In light of the technological progress being made in the field of funeral services, the issue of how to handle human remains processed into decorative stones deserves serious consideration. This is not a marginal matter; today such services are available in practically every crematorium. After post-cremation, the ashes are processed, where they not only irretrievably lose their original character, but also become a new material object. After such a transformation into what is known as a "memory diamond," are we faced with an object that has intrinsic value, and should therefore be classified as a thing? For the family or loved ones of the deceased person, such an object is important as a carrier of sentimental value. On the other hand, if a ring

[43] Act of 31 January 1959 on Cemeteries and Burials, consolidated text. Polish Official Journal (Dz. U.) 2020, item 1947.

[44] Remains shall mean the ashes resulting from the incineration of a corpse, the remains of a corpse, excavated when digging a grave or in other circumstances, parts of the human body, detached from the whole.

[45] In almost every region there is a company where you can turn cremated ashes into diamonds. The order requires only 200 grams of remains. See the article: W Polsce robią diamenty z prochów zmarłych (2015, 10 June). Fakt. https://www.fakt.pl/wydarzenia/polska/w-polsce-mozna-zrobic-diament-z-prochow-zmarlych/9eb436b. Accessed 1 June 2022.

bearing such a diamond is stolen, for a potential fence it will be nothing more than an ordinary ring containing a gemstone.

Another form of processing human remains for a different purpose, namely that of burial, is composting. In this regard, it is also necessary to refer to the regulations permitting this type of burial. After a body is composted, the family of the deceased receives soil that they can use,[46] for example, to grow a "memory tree."[47] Compared with cremation, composting consumes much less energy, making it a more ecological method. However, while this type of burial is permitted in the United States, it is not allowed in Poland. Nevertheless, the issue of the processing of human bodies arises. Under the ACB, in Poland only burial is permitted. Under Article 14 par. 1 ACB, "corpses can be buried by being placed in earthen graves, in masonry graves or catacombs, or by being submerged at sea." It is permissible for remains deriving from the cremation of a body to be deposited in a columbarium. Burial in a grave or catacomb may take place solely in a cemetery. In the future, the acceptance of new forms of burial may lead to a change in approach towards a processed body as a component of heritage and towards places of commemoration. Technological processes with regard to how the dead are buried, new methods of using human remains, and above all the interest society takes in these, will force an amendment of the ACB.

A full treatment of this issue is beyond the scope of this study; however, it is worth noting that the "additional" or "outstanding" value of a ring may be seen as a *pretium affectionis*. Nor can it be ruled out that a ring could be deemed a monument in the meaning of the APGM. A similar view should be taken of other unusual transformative uses of human ashes, such as their being pressed into recordings of favorite music, an interview, or memoirs.[48] One can easily imagine that, like an element of jewellery, a record made from the ashes of a well-known person could have both high material and affective value.

Another problem lies in determining whether human remains can be deemed archaeological artefacts. The most detailed examination of this problem to date was performed in Poland by Maciej Trzciński, who studied excerpts from decisions by authorities in charge of the protection of artefacts pertaining to archaeological research and exhumations resulting from the search for the burial places of victims of war crimes.[49] Trzciński also pointed to the problem of mementos located in burial places, and the difficulties encountered in classifying these as family mementos or archaeological artefacts.[50] No normative changes have been adopted since these gaps in the law were pointed out.

[46] Herzog (2015).

[47] Kraskowska (2019).

[48] Grygiel (2019).

[49] Trzciński (2017), p. 8.

[50] Trzciński (2017), p. 10.

In accordance with the definition of a monument contained in the APGM,[51] it seems impossible to give an affirmative answer the question of whether human remains can meet the criteria for becoming a historical object. Furthermore, one legal basis applies to exhumations, whereas other provisions apply to archaeological research. Maciej Trzciński states that, even when not conducting archaeological work, archaeological research methods may apply, or the presence of an archaeologist may be required.[52] Two solutions may therefore be considered. The first involves including human remains—that is, objects that do not constitute things—within the scope of the terms "historical object" and "archaeological artefact." The second, which comes into play during searches conducted at the scenes of past crimes and battlefields, should consider the relationship between archaeological research and exhumation, and should separately consider archaeological exhumation works, which in each case require a permit from the provincial conservator of historical objects.[53]

A similar stance was presented in the past for the needs of research conducted within the National Programme for the Protection and Guardianship of Monuments during the years 2014–2017 for the National Institute for Museums and Public Collections. The arguments raised therein refer to the definition of human remains provided in the Regulation of 7 December 2001 on the handling of bodies and human remains (discussed above), but also to the absence of a time limit for archaeological artefacts, to bioethical constraints, and to issues of grave rights.[54] A similar perception of human remains is found in the document *Wytyczne do prowadzenia badań archeologicznych. Badania inwazyjne* [*Guidelines for Conducting Archaeological Research. Invasive Research*].[55] The document emphasizes the role of human remains as archaeological sources of scientific and historical significance, the need for proper collection of human remains, and an evaluation of whether they should be reburied or may be used for research purposes.[56]

It has been shown in the literature, it is true, that the phrase contained in the definition of a historical object, "connected with their activity" may be of key importance when classifying human remains as historical objects. The remains of an individual "that were not buried and resulted from the death of the individual from natural causes" would remain outside the scope of what can be categorized as a historical object.[57] In my opinion, such an interpretation of the provisions of law and the scope of the definitions involved leads to an untenable result. First, assuming that

[51] Article 3.3 APGM Monument: immovable or movable object or part of group of thereof, made by man, or connected with their activity, and constituting a testimony of the past epoch or event, the preservation of which is in the social interest because of historical, artistic, or scientific value.

[52] Trzciński (2017), p. 8.

[53] Trzciński (2017), p. 9.

[54] Trzciński (2016), p. 91.

[55] Misiuk et al. (2019).

[56] Misiuk et al. (2019), pp. 37–38.

[57] Jastrzębska (2015), p. 185.

a human body and human remains are not things, no further consideration need be given to a possible overlapping of the semantic scope of the names involved. Second, even if we assume that human remains may be treated as things, classifying them as historical objects (or not) depending on how the person lost their life (in connection or not with human activity) leads to absurd conclusions. The current definition does not correspond in any way with the status of human remains in private law or the need to protect them as potential components of cultural heritage. The protection of those components may, however, be ensured using additional legal instruments contained in the acts of law cited below.

Human remains benefit indirectly from the protection provided in the APGM if they are situated on the site of an immovable historical monument. Under Article 6 par. 1 APGM, cemeteries are protected as immovable historical monuments. Cemeteries gain such protection by being entered in the register of historical monuments, most often because of their inherent historical value; additionally, many cemeteries are of indisputable artistic value (the issue of individual tombstones being registered). The body of a person after their death is then protected along with their grave and/or tombstone. Thus, answers must also be found for the question of how human bodies or remains should be classified when they form part of a historical cemetery or tomb. Is their status independent of their location, and if so, how is it regulated? A certain dependence exists between a historical monument, the form and value given to it, and the dead people buried within it. If not for the families of the deceased, or the activities of the deceased while still alive, such a grave or tombstone would not have been commissioned.

A similar dependence arises concerning memorabilia. The value of an object is affected by intangibles—such as the person who used it, its history, and the context in which it was used. Such factors partly determine the market value of memorabilia. Identical objects, each used by a different person, can have different values. A letter opener that once belonged to Winston Churchill would be valuated differently than one belonging to Marilyn Monroe. Moreover, the groups of those eager to possess one or the other object will be different, although certainly they could overlap. Both objects could have historical value from the perspective of protecting cultural heritage. One can also speak of a "special quality" as something intangible attached to an object due to its significance for future generations. Monika Drela proposes the terms "component part" and "affiliation" for an element of intangible heritage and its connection with a particular place.[58] In the case of souvenirs, one can further identify a *corpus mechanicum*, that is, a thing that is affiliated not with a place, but with a person or an event.

One example of art whose creation is strictly connected with a place or event is trench art.[59] The accepted definition of trench art is objects associated with military operations, created not only by soldiers, but also by civilians or prisoners of war. Trench art need not be created at the moment a particular event occurs, but can

[58] Drela (2017), pp. 41–42.

[59] Saunders (2000), pp. 44–46; (2011), pp. 14–15.

involve the use of materials such as shells, helmets and canteens.[60] It thus involves a combination of two elements—the utilitarian and the symbolic.[61] The Polish archaeologist Dawid Kobiałka has said that "trench art is therefore a material medium that combines the living and the dead, the past and the present, and a spiritual dimension commemorated/fixed in material."[62] This indisputably important additional value in the intangible dimension may be treated as an "immaterial" component part of a thing that cannot be separated from the object without causing an essential change to the whole.

In addition, who a deceased person was and the role they played in the history of their nation or humanity affects whether their tomb is considered to have historical value. This is particularly so in the case of historic graves and cemeteries. This relationship, however, has no legal effect on how human remains should be classified, although it may be significant as an auxiliary argument. As a rule, a monument is of a unique character, and is usually located in a separate quarter. When an urn containing ashes, a heart or a body is placed in a grave, they become connected in a technical way with the tombstone, whereas a tombstone erected on a real property constituting a cemetery may be treated as a component part of that real estate.

In looking for protective regimes, a person's right to worship the memory of a deceased relative or loved one, which is considered a personal right, must be considered. It is acknowledged that "this is an inherent right of people close to the deceased," while "the right of a loved one resulting therefrom encompasses the entitlement to bury, move or exhume the remains,[63] to erect a tombstone and determine what is inscribed on it, to visit and take care of the grave, and to engage in religious ceremonies."[64] In a certain sense, then, the right to a grave would seem to be an additional personal right.[65] It is accepted that such a right is of a mixed character, containing both property and non-property elements. The Supreme Court stated in a ruling that "the personal right to revere the memory of a deceased person is dominant in relation to the property entitlements resulting from a contract concluded with the cemetery administration; such a contract cannot be performed in

[60] Polish works on trench art: Kobiałka (2018), pp. 114–129; (2019), pp. 272–276.

[61] Kobiałka (2018), p. 121.

[62] Kobiałka (2018), p. 129.

[63] A famous foreign example of exhumation is the case of the grave of General Francisco Franco and the transfer of his remains from the Valley of the Fallen. However, the administrative procedure that was initiated was not stopped by the family of the deceased. The Spanish Supreme Court did not grant the family's request to halt the exhumation. The context of the case although politically embedded shows the relationship between the public interest (perceived in one way or another) and the family's right to burial. As a result, two reasons clash, one public law related to the administrative procedure and the other rooted in the family's right to ensure burial and respect for the deceased family member.

[64] Pazdan (2012), p. 1260.

[65] Cf. Rudnicki (1987), p. 109. The author points out that "right to a grave consists of a number of specific rights arising from the agreement concluded (Article 56 of the Civil Code)."

a manner that infringes personal rights. At the moment the latter arise, the exercise of existing property rights becomes subject to certain limitations."[66]

Without going into a detailed discussion on burial rights, reference should be made to how they affect the protection granted to human bodies and remains, as well as the preservation of graves. One of those entitlements is the right to prepare and construct a suitable burial place. This right is exercised by concluding an agreement with the administrator of a cemetery on the legal status of the tombstone itself. The Supreme Court has addressed this issue, and stated that a masonry tombstone is permanently associated with the ground on which it stands, and as such cannot constitute an object of property separate from that ground.[67] Pertaining to the use of a grave, the provisions on co-ownership apply per analogiam.[68] What is important for the object of protection is whether the holders of the right to the grave must jointly decide such matters as, for example, the maintenance of the tombstone. It seems that, by taking actions that go beyond the ordinary scope of the law, this would be justified.

To continue, the justification for submitting an application for the subsidy of conservation work by the holder of a right to a grave is worth mentioning. In practice, such applications are drawn up and submitted by the cemetery administration.[69] Where the right holder believes that a monument should be entered in the register of historical objects, but the requirements for making such an entry ex officio are not met, it is necessary for the cemetery administrator to take part as the applicant in each case, as set out in Article 2 ACB.[70] The decision in the matter is delivered to the cemetery administration. Nevertheless, the participation of the persons holding the right to the grave is also necessary. This, therefore, is a special case of who disposes of a historical object.

Yet, it would be difficult to agree with leaving the persons who hold the right to a grave out of a procedure, since their entitlements include maintenance of the grave, where repairs or modifications involve significant financial outlays. In my view, persons who hold a right to a grave can be treated as keepers of a historical object whose title stems from a right other than ownership. It should be added that any material intervention in the appearance of a historical object constitutes an infringement of the provisions of the APGM and requires a permit from the competent provincial conservator of historical objects (Article 36 APGM). If an object requires repair, the problem of who pays the bill arises. Under the APGM, the entity that should apply for a permit or submit an application is the cemetery administrator. Yet,

[66] Polish Supreme Court, Judgement of 24 June 2019, III CSK 267/17, LEX no. 2684205.

[67] Polish Supreme Court, Resolution of 29 September 1978, III CZP 56/78, LEX no. 2309.

[68] Polish Supreme Administrative Court, Judgement of 15 December 2016, I OSK 435/15, LEX no. 2205409; Polish Supreme Court, Judgement of 8 May 2015, III CSK 305/14, LEX no. 1723776.

[69] In the context of the entity authorized (municipality as the manager of a municipal cemetery) to apply for permission to cut down a tree in a cemetery listed in the register of historic monuments. Regional Court in Olsztyn, Judgement of 10th January 2019, IX Ca 761/18, LEX no. 2620842.

[70] Voivodship Administrative Court, Decision of 5th November 2009, III SAB/Kr 29/09, LEX no. 626237.

in a situation where a natural person wishes to renovate a tombstone, the two parties must work together.[71] Cemetery regulations commonly contain a provision that, where the cemetery is entered in the register of historical objects, the holder of the right to a grave must apply through the agency of the cemetery administrator. In the case where an entire cemetery is entered in the register of historical objects, a permit will also be needed to locate and erect a tombstone, for the historical arrangement of the cemetery is also subject to protection, and any disruption of that arrangement could undermine the site's historical value.

The ACB provides for the entry of an individual tombstone or monument in the register of historical objects.[72] It is therefore worth considering whether a single tombstone constitutes movable or immovable real property. Under Article 7 par. 5 ACB, a grave that has significant historical or artistic value cannot be reused. The legislator included a definition in parentheses and explained that, when classifying a grave as a historical object, account must be taken of its "antiquity, the persons buried within it, or events with which it is connected" (Article 7 par. 5 ACB). The Act of 28 March 1933 on military graves and cemeteries (AMGC)[73] contains a detailed regulation on the costs incurred in maintaining a military cemetery or graves of outstanding historical value. Such outstanding value may be confirmed by granting the grave or cemetery one of the forms of protection specified in the APGM, although this is not a necessary condition. Under Article 6 par. 4f AMGC, if outstanding historical value can be attributed to a cemetery or graves, then the works specified in Article 6 par. 4d AMGC[74] may be subsidized in an amount up to 100% (if the situation is severe and could lead to destruction of the grave, in regular situations up to 50%) of the outlays necessary to perform those works.

In several places, the ACB refers to the issue of the historical value and sites where cemeteries are protected within the system of protection of cultural heritage. Under Article 6 ACB, even the closure of a cemetery or the use of its grounds for another purpose may cause damage to historical objects located there. It is permissible to move historical objects to another place, provided that the consent of the provincial conservator of historical objects is obtained. The procedure for this should take place under Article 36 par. 1 pt. 1 APGM. The ACB also contains a provision that regulates the scope of the act's application in relation to archaeological works.

---

[71] About cooperation between the family of deceased and monuments authorities Baniukiewicz (1994), p. 25.

[72] On the protection of cultural property in case of conflict Dobosz (1998), p. 212.

[73] Act of 28 March 1933 on military graves and cemeteries, consolidated text. Polish Official Journal (Dz. U.) 2018, item 2337.

[74] A grant for the subsidizing of tasks related to the care of war graves and cemeteries may include expenditures necessary to:

(1) performing activities related to the search for, construction, repair, relocation, and maintenance of graves and war cemeteries;
(2) necessary additional activities leading to the realization of the objectives mentioned in item 1;
(3) conducting scientific research, exhumations, and archaeological studies related to war graves and cemeteries.

Within the scope concerning exhumation and the movement of bodies, the act does not apply "to archaeological excavations concerning graves and cemeteries located beyond cemetery grounds" protected under the ACB. The new draft on the Act on Cemeteries and Burials does not bring much to the debate[75] and is now under consultations procedure. The main aim is to reinforce protection of cemeteries with historical value and old cemeteries that have not yet been listed in the register of monuments. The information on the entry of the grave in the register of monument or in the commune records of monuments is to be revealed in the cemetery records. Additionally, the decision to close the cemetery shall be send to the regional authority (wojewoda). The proposed changes provides protection mechanisms, however do not cover all challenges.

In the Act on Museums, there are no detailed provisions concerning the display of human remains or biological preparations. However, in the ICOM Code of Ethics, there is a passage that deals with "sensitive cultural material." Decisions on this subject are found in the sections on collection, research, and exhibition. Human remains and objects associated with religious worship are considered culturally sensitive material. They may be collected, provided that this will result in their safeguarding. Moreover, they should be treated with respect. An additional restriction is that the collection of such objects must be carried out in accordance with professional standards and the interests and beliefs of the groups the objects concern. Within this scope, the Code refers to communities, ethnic groups, and religious groups. In this way, a partial assumption is made that the museum acquiring the objects need not be connected with a given culture. Those standards, however, while important for the future, do not resolve the problems posed by collections already located in museums (2.5 of the Code). Detailed rules concern research on materials having religious significance; such research should be conducted in accordance with professional standards (3.7 of the Code).

A reference to the principles of professional conduct is also made regarding exhibitions. Exhibitions and the display of human remains should be prepared "with great tact and respect for the feelings of human dignity held by all peoples" (4.3 of the Code).

> Human remains and materials of sacred significance must be displayed in a manner consistent with professional standards and, where known, taking into account the interests and beliefs of members of the community, ethnic or religious groups from whom the objects originated. They must be presented with great tact and respect for the feelings of human dignity held by all peoples.

In relation to both exhibitions and research, reference is made to the interests and beliefs of the groups concerning these objects. The issue of displaying human remains arises when parts of collections are being prepared. For example, the Museum of Forensic Medicine at Wrocław Medical University plans to divide its

[75] Governmental draft of the act on cemeteries and burials, Warsaw, 23 September 2021 https://legislacja.rcl.gov.pl/projekt/12351755/katalog/12819378#12819378. Accessed 1 June 2022.

exhibition into two parts, including one with limited public access.[76] For purposes of the exhibition, the scientific and historical context prevails.

In an artistic context, in turn, we have the example of human remains being used in the Body World Vital[77] exhibition created by Gunther von Hagens.[78] The exhibition involves the use of prepared fragments of human bodies,[79] and combines scientific and artistic elements.[80] The work of Grzegorz Klaman provides another example of this in his *Katabasis* (1993), located in the collection of the Arsenal Gallery in Białystok. The work consists of three boxes of steel and aluminium that contain human organs in formaldehyde (an eye, an ear, and a tongue), as well as a speaker and a gas cylinder with a burner. The problem of bioart thus arises in the sphere of law, and also with respect to records of works (inventories) and conservation work. For this reason, it is critical to examine domestic law in this scope when creating legal frameworks for the protection of the cultural heritage.

When seeking an international standard for handling human remains as a component of cultural heritage, it is necessary to consult international documents. With the aim of unifying and supporting domestic legal systems, the document entitled *UNESCO – UNIDROIT Model legislative provisions on State ownership of undiscovered cultural objects (2011)*, prepared by experts, refers to classifying human remains as *undiscovered cultural objects*. In accordance with the relevant definition, such objects are those which, under the law of their country of origin, are significant for archaeology, prehistory, history, literature, art, or science, and which are situated in the soil or under water. (Provision 2 – Definition. Undiscovered cultural objects include objects which, consistently with national law, are of importance for archaeology, prehistory, history, literature, art, or science and are located in the soil or underwater). In the *Explanatory Guidelines*, it is stated that this catalogue is not exhaustive, and states may add to it other objects they treat as undiscovered cultural property, including human remains. The concept of being located in the soil should be understood as broadly as possible, to also include, for example, under the ice or under a building.[81]

In my view, human organs, bodies, and remains do not constitute things in the meaning of civil law, but do constitute material objects regulated according to the

[76] Wysocki (2019).

[77] https://bodyworlds.com/exhibitions/. Accessed 1 June 2022.

[78] The exhibition was not organized in France. Vigneron (2020), p. 319.

[79] Exhibits have been prepared in plastination technique https://bodyworlds.com/plastination/plastination-technique/. Accessed 1 June 2022.

[80] The public showing of a sculpture by R.N. Gibson entitled Human earrings created using two fetuses resulted in a lawsuit alleging that the creator and curator's public showing of the sculpture violated norms (R. v. Gibson (1991) 2 QB 619. http://irep.ntu.ac.uk/id/eprint/20114/1/219253_PubSub1820_Lewis.pdf. Accessed 1 June 2022). More: Lewis (2002), p. 50 et seq.

[81] Expert Committee on State Ownership of Cultural Heritage, Model Provisions on State Ownership of Undiscovered Cultural Objects. Explanatory Report with model provisions and explanatory guidelines, UNESCO, UNIDROIT, 2011, p. 5. https://en.unesco.org/sites/default/files/unesco-unidroit_model_provisions_en_0.pdf. Accessed 1 June 2022.

principles set out in binding provisions of law, including those concerning cemeteries and burial. I base this view on certain elements of a non-legal nature, including the religious and cultural context of those objects. Yet I see no obstacle to products of the epidermis, such as hair, being treated as things when separated from the body.[82] This is the proper stance concerning, for example, the lock of George Sand's hair in the collection of the Chopin Institute.

It seems reasonable to stop considering the ownership of such objects in favor of a particular type of control. As the keeper of an object, a museum must observe the particular provisions regulating the protection of collections. Of course, not all provisions concerning museum exhibits will apply directly to human remains. In their case, it is not possible to apply provisions on deaccession, but it will still be permissible to transfer such objects between museums. An auxiliary application of the manner sovereignty is exercised can be found in the provisions of Articles 5 and 28 APGM. From these provisions, one can decipher a model of a conscious keeper/holder of historical objects concerning the protection of historical objects entered in the register.[83] This particular type of sovereignty will be similar to ownership. It seems fitting here to cite certain statements made on the crime of trafficking in human organs and the desecration of corpses, to the extent that this is helpful in formulating how these are to be managed under civil law.

Protection of the special sovereignty over an object resounds in the provisions of criminal law concerning trafficking in human organs. Commenting on Article 44 of the Act of 1 July 2005 on the collection, storage and transplantation of cells, tissues and organs[84] (ACSTCTO), which penalizes the collection or disposal of cells, tissues and organs, acting as an agent in their acquisition or disposal or taking part in their being obtained in contravention of the law, Magdalena Budyn-Kulik refers to organs as being excluded from regular trade. She points out that

> acquisition should be understood as gaining factual control over a cell, tissue or organ separated from the body of a donor. This concept cannot be interpreted in a purely civil way because cells, tissues, and organs are excluded from normal commercial trade. Trading them, apart from those cases set out in the act and in the manner foreseen therein, is not legal, and therefore one cannot speak of obtaining ownership or any other property right foreseen by the law, e.g., by way of a contract.[85]

Julia Kapelańska-Pręgowska and Piotr Chrzczonowicz, when analyzing the classification in criminal law of human organs as objects subject to protection under Article 44 as referred to above, mention not only human dignity, respect for corpses and the integrity of transplant medicine, but also the bodily integrity of a living human being.[86]

---

[82] For example, hair used in the wig or hairdressing industry.

[83] Jagielska-Burduk (2014), pp. 311–318.

[84] Act of 1 July 2005 on the collection, storage and transplantation of cells, tissues and organs, consolidated text. Polish Official Journal (Dz. U.) 2020, item 2134.

[85] Budyn-Kulik (2017).

[86] Kapelańska-Pręgowska and Chrzczonowicz (2015), p. 97.

Under Article 262 par. 1 of the Polish Criminal Code,[87] the desecration of a human corpse, ashes or a burial place is a punishable offence. Anyone who digs up a corpse, a grave or other burial place is also guilty of a crime. It is accepted that, in criminal law, the term "corpse" should be understood broadly to include human remains.[88] This broad understanding stems from the definition contained in the Regulation of 7 December 2001 on the handling of bodies and human remains. Human dignity, reverence and respect are listed as protected values. In the case of the desecration of a corpse, an element of ownership does arise in relation to the decorative form of the grave and valuables buried along with the deceased person. It is not possible, though, to commit the crime of stealing a corpse or human remains. Based on the previous criminal code, Wiesław Daszkiewicz has shown that

> a perpetrator who removes a corpse cannot in principle be held responsible – as regards the body itself – for theft under Article 203 of the Criminal Code, or for seizing communal property, e.g., under Article 199 of the Criminal Code, since a corpse cannot constitute movable property.[89]

In both the ACSTCTO and the current Criminal Code, there is a direct reference to the human body and its parts as being subject to protection.

The media attention paid to the "theft" of the body and remains of Charlie Chaplin show that "grave robbing" continues to exist in the modern world. Moreover, in the case of people who played an important role in history, it is even more likely. In the case of the body of Charles Chaplin, the perpetrators were hoping for a ransom; the whole story of the stolen coffin and body was depicted in the film *The Price of Fame*. Without a doubt, the perpetrators were driven by the fame of the deceased and by his family's desire to protect his memory. In my conviction, such events—the phenomenon of the sale of relicts—force us to think about cultural heritage in new ways. They should lead to legislative changes aimed at affording these components of the cultural heritage a legal position that is clearly articulated.

Human remains can be treated as components of cultural heritage. They do not constitute things within the meaning of the Civil Code, and therefore do not constitute historical objects within the meaning of the APGM; thus, they do not form part of the collection of archaeological historical objects. Nor do human remains constitute museum exhibits within the meaning of the MA, and they should not be included in museum inventory. Human remains located in museum collections should be recorded on special, separate lists. Current museum practice is the expression of an approach to recording the objects found in a museum, in which for years the most important role has been played by the inventory of museum exhibits.[90] Yet it is worth pointing out that even an entry in a museum inventory does not change the status of an object or of its ownership. The idea of considering such

[87] Act of 6 June 1997 Criminal Code, consolidated text. Polish Official Journal (Dz. U.) 2021, item 2345.

[88] "It should be assumed, however, that under Article 262 the term "corpse" refers to both the whole body and its parts (remains) resulting from decomposition, dismemberment, etc." (Mozgawa 2020).

[89] Daszkiewicz (1989), pp. 63–64.

[90] Jagielska-Burduk and Mularski (2015), pp. 201–216.

objects as things is founded merely on the supposition that they constitute the property of the museum.

The absence of uniformity among attitudes towards human remains weakens the protection they receive as components of the cultural heritage. When properly exercised, the existing right to burial can strengthen the protection granted to historical objects connected with a burial place, but this is not enough. Treating persons who have the right to a grave as the keepers of a tombstone constituting a historical object allows the protection to be shifted to the regime of the legal protection of historical objects. Certainly, however, this does not exhaust the internal divisions that exist in this category of objects. Enacting suitable legislative changes that separate this part of cultural heritage will make it possible to protect such objects more effectively.

Proposals have been made to introduce provisions concerning status and protection into acts regulating cemeteries or the protection of cultural heritage. Faced with the variety of situations appearing in the area of law that deals with cultural heritage, at present we are not able to regulate everything legally. Here, it is important to note sets of good practice, or soft law sources (e.g., the ICOM Code). Yet there are certain spheres where the legislator should not remain inactive. I am convinced that one such area is the legal regulation of human remains and their place in the system governing cultural property.

A distinction should be made between human remains that should be buried and those which are or should be found in cultural institutions to bear witness to the history of humankind. Yet it is not possible to make such an exact distinction. Claims brought against foreign museums concern objects to which one can attribute a cultural affiliation with a particular group of people or a society, as well as those whose affiliation, according to its foreign keeper, is based solely on a territorial link (such as the human skull mentioned above).

Perhaps a distinction should be made in the MA regarding objects that do not constitute museum exhibits understood as things. To this end, separate records could be kept, resulting in a different form of protection. Another, less invasive solution would be to apply the provisions concerning museum exhibits accordingly, but to amend how exhibits are defined. In practice, cultural property is already included in inventories of museum exhibits. In this respect, it should be borne in mind that foreign museums are already dealing with problems from the past and how objects were originally obtained. For example, over time, the practice of trading Maori heads on the art market came to be condemned, which led to changing attitudes among participants in that market. Creating procedures to return objects and policy documents that also meet the needs of cultural institutions has shown how complicated and time-consuming these processes are.

This is why, if the legislator cannot stay ahead of current trends, it should at least keep abreast of the progress being made in this area. The future seems to be of key importance in the debate over human remains. New forms of processing and using human remains, the human body and body parts are appearing, and these carry new ways of perceiving the problem. In the case of body parts used in artistic exhibitions or installations, attention must also be paid to the issue of the conservation and management of such property. Even when incorporated into an installation consisting of various components, they do not lose their outstanding character. If body parts can be used in various contexts, this may not always be in accordance with the will of the deceased person. An exception would be a situation where a body is allocated for artistic purposes in accordance with the will of the deceased or, as in the case of Tim Steiner, the person who signed a contract to that effect while still alive. Archaeological heritage, including that encompassing human remains, cannot be treated as historical objects within the meaning of the APGM. Pertaining to this part of the archaeological heritage, consideration can be given to an appropriate application of the provisions of the APGM to the greatest extent possible when read together with the ACB.

3.3 Cultural Heritage in and from Outer Space

As technology, scientific progress, and human beings travel to new places, the resources of cultural heritage grow. Apart from the issue of threats to cultural heritage on this planet, for some time researchers, and particularly archaeologists, have turned their attention to what lies beyond the Earth. Beyond existing space law[91] and the debate over civilization's future use of outer space, questions are being raised over how far human heritage extends and to what extent we can speak of space heritage as such.[92] A consequence of the development in thought on space heritage and its treatment as a separate area is the need to classify objects attesting to humanity's presence in space within civil law.

It is worth noting that outer space has only become a subject of interest in international law relatively recently.[93] As to cultural heritage, this seems to have been the last thread to appear in the discussion over space law. Provisions of international law concerning outer space, the commencement of commercial aviation projects, the question of liability for damage caused by satellites, and the debate over natural resources and their exploitation all preceded the discussion on the importance of space and space exploration for the cultural heritage of humankind.

We can identify a number of aspects of space cultural heritage, each of which requires a distinct statutory approach, and in many cases a different level of regulation: meteorites that have fallen to the Earth, space heritage in the form of devices located on the Earth in museums or in outer space, places of historical importance for civilization that contain relics of humanity's presence there (moon landing sites), and resources that are brought down to the Earth through cooperation between states. Unfortunately, there is no single private law solution that can be proposed for all these goods, since the problem relates not just to a given object's location, but also to its origin and properties (meteorites).

It is accepted that material objects originating beyond the Earth are things. It is further assumed that they acquire this attribute at the moment they reach the Earth, or

[91] O'Leary (2009a), p. 34.
[92] Seddon (2015), p. 158.
[93] Grochalski (2019), p. 214.

when possession of them is taken using appropriate technical means.[94] A meteorite is deemed ownerless property within the meaning of Article 181 of the Civil Code, that is, it is deemed to be an item that "never belonged to anyone" (is "originally" no one's).[95] In principle, shards of meteorites constitute separate movables.[96] From the literature, we know that meteorite fragments cannot be classified as adhering to or being appurtenances of real property, nor can they be treated as profits.[97] In the case of meteorite shards discovered after many years in deeper layers of the soil, similar to the way in which archaeological artefacts are uncovered, the idea that they constitute movables may be doubted. Meteorite shards embedded in deeper layers of the Earth are certainly connected with the other layers of the soil. Yet, as in the case of archaeological finds, due to their inherent properties, they must be separated and legally classified in a different manner than layers of earth or minerals.[98]

A meteorite that falls to the Earth does not become a component part of the soil when lying on the surface. Paweł Księżak argues, however, that

> one can hold that such a consequence occurs with the passage of time, especially when the meteorite is located beneath the surface of the ground. As long as it remains on the surface, though, it should be treated as a separate object that belongs to no one. This issue, however, is highly controversial.[99]

According to Bartosz Guzowski, in the case where a meteorite becomes part of a mineral deposit, it becomes the property of the owner of the deposit (the State Treasury or the owner of the property).[100] In terms of their importance to science, meteorite shards are of the same, high value, whether they are located on or beneath the soil surface. To grant a different private law status to each, then, will not serve the cause of granting them protection.

In the literature, a number of analyses have been made on the acquisition of meteorites and their ownership. A possible connection with real property or its location between different layers of the soil have led to ownership of the meteorite being attributed to the owner of the real property. In most studies, it is accepted that a meteorite may constitute ownerless property, in which case ownership of it is acquired on the basis of Article 181 of the Civil Code,[101] pursuant to which "The ownership of an ownerless movable is acquired by the movable being taken in an owner-like possession." It has been rightly pointed out that Article 189 of the Civil Code, which states that ownership is acquired when a search for an object's owner would clearly be futile, cannot apply to meteorites. Yet it should be noted that the proposed construction, whereby ownership is acquired in equal parts by the finder and the owner of the real property, could prove more effective in practice. Especially

[94] Piasecki (1989), p. 58, argument 4.
[95] Rudnicki (2011), Art. 181 [Commentary].
[96] Kotowiecki (2006).
[97] Kotowiecki and Skórka (2002), p. 105.
[98] Kotowiecki and Skórka (2002), p. 106.
[99] Księżak (2005).
[100] Guzowski (2011), p. 82, footnote 13.
[101] Guzowski (2011), p. 84.

since, in the case of hunting for meteorites that may be located beneath the soil surface, the search may lead to damage being caused to the ground.

Interesting contributions to the discussion over the acquisition of ownership of meteorites have been made by Jan Rudnicki. He points to the importance of the Civil Code and the fundamental principles of acquiring ownership. Using the example of meteorites, Rudnicki emphasizes the importance of the institution of acquiring ownerless property. He argues that applying other legal provisions to meteorites, i.e., those modelled on the State Treasury's acquisition of ownership over archaeological artefacts,

> would in fact mean depriving this whole category of originally ownerless property of virtually any economic significance whatsoever, since then perhaps the last economically significant things that originally belonged to no one would be... pieces of amber.[102]

Rudnicki states that, when looking for the ownership status of meteorites, many authors begin with the detailed acts of public law, and then refer to the Civil Code,[103] which is the result of a decodification of civil law. Every researcher intuitively perceives the specific nature of an object, its importance for science and history, and its undoubted material value. This indirectly attests to their correctly and intuitively including meteorites among material objects that are atypical. It also supports the correctness of the legislative activities of other states whose provisions of civil law contain a separate manner of acquiring ownership over meteorites.[104]

The construction of the Polish definition of a historical object (monument) makes it impossible to count a fragment of a meteorite that has fallen to Earth in that category, and therefore it cannot be deemed an archaeological artefact.[105] While the properties of archaeological artefacts are specified in the definitions of historical object and archaeological artefact, in the case of meteorites, a key property is certainly their extraterrestrial origin. At present, there are no regulations in the APGM that can be directly applied to meteorites. Nor can the construction of the State Treasury's acquisition of ownership of archaeological artefacts or the protection mechanisms provided in other acts of law be applied. Experts point to the need to create legislative protection due to the hunt for meteorites and the trade that exists among collectors.[106] A meteorite shard may be a component of a collection, that is, a set of objects gathered together and arranged in accordance with the conception of the creators of the collection. On that basis, such a fragment may be subject to protection as a movable historical object, or a movable historical object entered in the register of historical objects. At the domestic level, the protection granted to fragments that constitute museum exhibits[107] or parts of a collection entered in the

[102] Rudnicki (2014), p. 22.

[103] Rudnicki (2014), p. 25.

[104] Schmitt (2002), p. B8; Kotowiecki and Skórka (2002), pp. 93–103.

[105] Grajewski (2017), p. 55.

[106] Grajewski (2017), pp. 60–61.

[107] On the assumption that musealium is not only monument entered in the inventory.

register of historical objects also applies to the National Register of Lost Cultural Objects,[108] discussed further below. This is just a partial solution that can be applied only under certain conditions; it cannot be said to form a proper system for protecting meteorites.

The legislator has been unambiguous, though, in restricting the free movement of such objects outside of Poland. Under Article 121 par. 1 of the Nature Protection Act[109] (NPA), taking meteorites or fossil plant or animal remains out of the country requires a permit from the minister responsible for environmental matters. It has been pointed out that this provision is an instrument that aims to protect inorganic natural objects. Krzysztof Gruszecki holds that this provision should specify "what type of fossil plant or animals remains and meteorites are covered by the obligation to obtain a permit for export."[110] Of particular interest is the scope of application of the above provision, and the fact that it regulates both fossil plants and animals and meteorites as examples of inorganic natural objects.

Under Article 36 TFEU, a restriction on exports may be made if there are justifiable considerations of public morality, public order, public security, protection of the health or life of humans, animals or plants, the protection of national cultural treasures having artistic, historical, or archaeological value, or the protection of industrial or commercial property. In this way, the importance of such objects is emphasized; they are situated apart from goods whose export is prohibited, but among those whose export is controlled. Unfortunately, the regulations concerning a ban on exports or the obligation to obtain an export permit are not the only instruments for protecting and controlling historical objects, including meteorites. For example, the APGM provides a right to conduct research on a historical object, but when such an object is entered in the register of historical objects, numerous obligations are imposed pertaining to any disturbance of the object's substance or the possibility of conducting scientific research on it. It seems that similar regulations should also apply to meteorites, at least with respect to their access for scientific research purposes.

In accordance with information obtained under the procedure of access to public information, only two applications were made on the basis of Article 121 par. 1 of the NPA during 2015–2020. In both cases, a decision permitting the requested export was issued.[111] Undoubtedly, the number of meteorites that have been taken out of the country is higher than that. This attests to a low level of awareness among

[108] Grajewski (2017), p. 60.

[109] The Nature Protection Act of 16 April 2004, consolidated text. Polish Official Journal (Dz. U.) 2018, item 142 as amended.

[110] Gruszecki (2020), Art. 121 [Commentary].

[111] The questions sent to the ministry:

In the last five years, broken down by individual years (2020, 2019, 2018, 2017, 2016), how many applications referred to in the provision of Article 121, paragraph 1 of the Law on Nature Protection export abroad regarding the export of meteorites?

In the last five years, by year (2020, 2019, 2018, 2017, 2016), how many decisions allowing export of meteorites abroad were issued?

those who acquire such objects and the need for an awareness-raising campaign. Perhaps it would be worth combining such a campaign with one on the security of the art market. In this way, while popularizing responsible collecting, the protection of cultural heritage could be extended to include space heritage as well as fossilized plants and animals. The starting point could be the idea of a "cabinet of curiosities" containing various objects which, despite their diversity, were equally important for collectors.

Apart from the issue of whether a meteorite constitutes a thing, consideration must be given to their value, which necessitates the creation of a new model for dealing with meteorite fragments that are found accidentally. Is there any justification for the absence of special provisions concerning meteorites? First, falling meteorites are a relatively rare phenomenon. Second, the provisions of civil law on acquiring ownership over ownerless things apply. Under civil law, however, studies of meteorites to date show that the existing legal instruments for determining ownership are inadequate.[112] This is particularly so concerning the issues of hunting and trading in meteorites, and including them in collections. There is merit in the proposals being made to grant separate normative protection to meteorites, or to at least situate them differently within the legal system.

From a private law perspective, the findings made at the beginning of the discussion on the legal regulation of meteorites are very interesting. A working group established in 1964 resulted in the publication of recommendations for this phenomenon regarding legal status, interesting proposals were made for resolving these issues at the level of an international convention, not at the level of domestic law. Moreover, the group accepted that the ownership of a meteorite should rest with the state, not with the owner of the property on which the meteorite landed.[113] Express reference was made for the need to create a single legal model. This idea was never enacted, and at the domestic level the ownership of a meteorite is determined based on general rules, or specific rules aimed at protecting property.

In agreements concerning outer space, there is a general lack of provisions regulating the legal status of meteorites. In the Agreement Governing the Activities of States on the Moon and Other Celestial Bodies of 1979, there is a brief reference to meteorites.[114] Although under Article 1 par. 3 of that Agreement, the document does not apply to meteorites that reach in Earth in a natural way. But this limitation does not apply to fragments of meteorites found and obtained on the moon; this example is given by Matthieu Gounelle and Max Gounelle.[115] In this way, we may encounter meteorites possessing a different status depending on where they come

In the last five years, by year (2020, 2019, 2018, 2017, 2016), how many decisions have been issued refusing to grant permission to export meteorites abroad?

[112] Grajewski (2017), p. 52.

[113] Gounelle and Gounelle (2019, p. 2889) and the documents referred in the text.

[114] Agreement Governing the Activities of States on the Moon and Other Celestial Bodies, UN Doc. A/Res/34/68.

[115] Gounelle and Gounelle (2019), p. 2891.

from and how human beings took possession of them. Taking possession will also include a space probe controlled by humans that finds, gathers, and takes samples of meteorites.

Finally, reference should be made to Antarctica and meteorites located there. In 2006, referring to Antarctica as a "meteorite Eldorado,"[116] Andrzej Kotowiecki wrote that

> people are collecting meteorites only from the surface of icebergs and the snow. A separate problem is whether meteorites collected in Antarctica can be legally sold on... And then there's the question of how Antarctic meteorites came to be in the possession of dealers and are offered for sale at mineral markets and fairs.[117]

He is of the opinion that this should not be possible, even in the absence of a specific provision on this issue in the TFEU. As to introducing meteorite shards within regular trade, this should involve exchanges among scientific institutions involved in research.[118]

The Antarctic Treaty signed in Washington on 1 December 1959, which regulates cooperation among states,[119] contains no provisions on meteorites. As material objects, meteorites attract the attention of researchers for the information they may provide about the cosmos. The preamble to the Treaty states that it constitutes "the establishment of a firm foundation for the continuation and development of such cooperation on the basis of freedom of scientific investigation in the Antarctica," based on the exchange of data and the results of scientific observations in the Antarctic and free access thereto (Article III par. 1 letter c). Outside the Antarctic Treaty itself, the issue of conducting research, including for the purpose of finding meteorites, also arises in the Protocol on Environmental Protection to the Antarctic Treaty.[120] Under its Article 7, with regard to the mineral resources of Antarctica, all activities other than scientific research are prohibited. It is worth pointing out that different views exist on whether meteorites belong to the mineral resources of Antarctica.[121] In relation to the problem of private expeditions hunting for meteorite shards and introducing them to trade, including in online auctions,[122] in 2001 the parties to the Treaty adopted Resolution 3 (2001) on dealing with meteorites located

[116] Kotowiecki (2006), p. 83.

[117] Kotowiecki (2006), pp. 79–80.

[118] Kotowiecki (2006), pp. 79–80.

[119] Antarctic Treaty signed 1 December 1959 in Washington 402 UNTS 71, 12 UST 794, 19 ILM 860 (1980), Cmnd 1535, ATS 12 (1961).

[120] The Protocol on Environmental Protection to the Antarctic Treaty was signed in Madrid on October 4, 1991 *(XI ATSCM/2/3/2), reprinted in (1991) 30 ILM 1460.*

[121] Gounelle and Gounelle (2019, p. 2894) present the approach to treat meteorites as mineral resources of different opinion is Kotowiecki (2006, p. 79).

[122] Report of the Committee for Environmental Protection, Report from the Committee's fourth meeting (CEP IV) July 9–13, 2001, p. 4.

in the territory of Antarctica.[123] In that resolution, fears are expressed over the loss to science that could be caused by the unrestricted collection of Antarctica's meteorites. At the same time, states are called on to take the legal or administrative measures[124] necessary to ensure that meteorites are collected and exploited in accordance with scientific standards and made available for scientific purposes.

As regards the international protection of meteorites, it has been acknowledged that meteorites are included in the catalogue of objects recognized in the 1970 UNESCO Convention. In the meaning of Article 1 of the Convention, cultural property consists of objects that meet two criteria. First, they are recognized by a state as being significant for archaeology, prehistory, history, literature, art, or science for sacred or secular reasons. Second, they have an affiliation with one of the categories set out in Article 1. It should be mentioned that some researchers see the proper category as Article 1.a (rare collections and specimens of fauna, flora, minerals and anatomy, and objects of palaeontological interest), accenting the value of minerals.[125] Others see a further basis in Article 1.b, that is, property relating to a nation's history (including the history of science and technology and military and social history, history related to the life of national leaders, thinkers, scientists and artists and to events of national importance) and the historical importance of meteorites.[126]

The status of meteorites brought back from the moon will be determined by international public law, similar to the case of meteorites found in the Antarctica, whereas in the case of a meteorite that falls to the Earth, the general provisions on the acquisition of ownership apply, or possibly also the binding provisions of a given country concerning the acquisition of ownership of meteorites, considering their value and scientific importance. This dualism is not a proper solution. Given humankind's increasing activity in space, a need will arise to regulate the issue of meteorites in a comprehensive way, especially since some states are more capable of exploring outer space than others. The growing opportunities for space exploration mean that it will become possible to obtain meteorites commercially; it will then be necessary to determine on what basis (if at all) they can be introduced to trade, including for collection purposes.

Another important element of space heritage will be all those devices created by humans that are now situated in outer space (e.g., satellites), or those whose journey is over and are now found in museums. It is generally accepted that space vehicles

[123] Resolution 3(2001) Collection of meteorites in Antarctica, https://www.ats.aq/devAS/Meetings/Measure/283.

[124] Gounelle and Gounelle (2019), p. 2893.

[125] Similar findings can be made with regard to Annex 1 of the UNIDROIT Convention: Schmitt (2002), pp. B8–B9.

[126] Gounelle and Gounelle (2019), p. 2890.

are things as long as they remain under human control.[127] Wojciech Katner speaks along these lines when he says that

> all cosmic devices are similar to aircraft, and so by their nature are movable things subject to the legal regime governing such things. If being subject to human control is a condition of being a thing, then including space vehicles in the category of movable things must be limited to situations where that condition is fulfilled. Therefore, a device in space that self-destructs or over which human control has been lost (whether from the Earth or from space) cannot be an object of a civil law relationship, with certain exceptions such as a meteorological probe, a telecommunications satellite, etc.[128]

In accordance with this assumption, at the moment people lose control over a spaceship—understood as the absence of communication by technical means—the spaceship ceases to be a thing. In the literature, a more general view has also been expressed that contains no restrictions concerning human control over a spaceship.[129] It may be that for the authors of the above commentary the element of control was obvious, but whether one view or the other is accepted is of key importance when classifying "space cultural heritage" in the system of civil law. This is even more crucial in that international regulations regulating responsibility for objects in space and their ownership make no reference to the element of control.

The issue of space heritage raised by researchers also concerns the "mobility" of that heritage, i.e., whether its components are movables. This problem is discussed in relation to moon landing sites and the positions of satellites in relation to the Earth.[130] The inability to establish a clear dichotomy between movable and immovable heritage results in a need to adapt the means of protection granted to cultural heritage in general to the specifics of space heritage. The "instability" of space heritage in outer space thus constitutes an additional criterion that forces a new approach to protection.

Space cultural heritage is gradually making a name for itself in the academic debate over cultural heritage. Astronomical heritage is analyzed separately, although the first attempts to diagnose this heritage and its place in the system of conventions on protecting world heritage also included space heritage. In 2003, the World Heritage Thematic Programme "Archeo-Astronomical Sites and Observatories" was initiated.[131] It now continues as part of the program "Astronomy and the World Heritage. A Thematic Initiative." Its purpose is to identify heritage sites associated with astronomy.[132] The work has been joined by the International Astronomical Union based on an understanding signed with UNESCO in 2008.[133] The

[127] Grzybowski (ed) (1985), p. 416.

[128] Katner (2014), Art. 45 [Commentary].

[129] Rudnicki and Trzaskowski (2014), Art. 45 [Commentary].

[130] Marov (2010), p. 237; Cotte and Ruggles (2010), p. 264.

[131] https://whc.unesco.org/en/astronomy/. Accessed 1 June 2022.

[132] Gounelle and Gounelle (2019), p. 2890.

[133] https://whc.unesco.org/en/news/498/. Accessed 1 June 2022. The MOU was renewed in 2013 r. while celebrating its 10th anniversary (https://whc.unesco.org/en/news/1005. Accessed 1 June

first report prepared under the initiative drew attention to the already existing World Heritage List and to the astronomical dimension and value of some sites on that List. That value was not determined, though, by an assessment of outstanding universal value of the sites.

The report also addressed the issue of World Heritage Sites that have an astronomical dimension. Examples include Stonehenge, the Royal Observatory in Greenwich, the Ulugh Beg Observatory in Samarkand, and the pyramids at Giza. In similar cases, there should be a gradual recognition of their additional value, resulting in increased protection.[134] Incidentally, it is worth adding that some authors argue that conventions should apply to places where a meteorite lands. In their research, they point to the possibility of regarding meteorites and their surroundings as potential natural world heritage sites. This is a particularly interesting option, since the area in which a large meteorite is located would be subject to protection.[135] This aspect, however, has not been developed during the work undertaken within the Thematic Initiative.

Independently of UNESCO's work, the concepts of "Starlight Reserves" and "Dark Sky Parks" have been developed. However, UNESCO's current position is that neither of these ideas can be accepted by the World Heritage Committee. The effect of a dark sky can be perceived as an element of culture or of the natural environment. But it is not a sufficient basis for attributing to such places an outstanding universal value or authenticity required for their entry on the World Heritage List. Heritage sites connected with the science of astronomy and having centuries of tradition undoubtedly combine material heritage with elements that are intangible, in a way that is particularly striking in contrast to other sites.[136] Further work in this area resulted in a second report, which does not refer to space heritage, but focuses solely on astronomical heritage in the context of the requirements for World Heritage Sites.

In a certain sense, the discussion over astronomical elements of world heritage was brought on by the problem of space heritage. Space heritage was discussed in the first report, but, as mentioned above, this analysis was not continued in the second report.[137] Given the specific nature of space heritage, its scientific value, and its connection to technology, a second working group was established and charged with preparing a report devoted solely to space heritage. At the 36th session of the World Heritage Committee in 2012, conducting research on space heritage was

2022). In 2015 UNESCO and the IAU signed MOU regarding the cooperation (consultative status, cf. p. 1). Ruggles and Cotte (2017), p. 1.

[134] The authors suggest that states should be encouraged to introduce changes in the site's description to stress and recognize the astronomical element (Cotte and Ruggles (2010), p. 262).

[135] Gounelle and Gounelle (2019), p. 2890. Cf. Vredefort Dome in South Africa inscribed on the UNESCO list in 2005.

[136] Cotte and Ruggles (2010), p. 263.

[137] Ruggles (2017), pp. 292–293.

recommended, including the technological heritage related to space exploration.[138] While those activities are focused on determining what may be subject to protection as a fragment of the world heritage of humanity, the results may prove very useful to studies of that part of heritage in private law.

Apart from determining whether components of space heritage are things, further questions arise concerning ownership and other rights. At the level of the Convention on the Protection of the World Heritage, the problem of heritage components located beyond state borders has already come up on several occasions. Regarding components of the underwater heritage located in areas outside territorial waters on or beneath the sea or ocean floor, it has been proposed that the UNESCO principles of protection should apply. Certainly, in the case of space heritage, it is known that some objects will be situated beyond the borders of any state. Similar challenges arise in Antarctica, whose status is regulated by the Antarctic Treaty.[139] In all these situations, it is recommended that sites be given protection. It has been recommended that the World Heritage Committee take appropriate measures aimed at protecting sites of outstanding universal value located outside the borders of states.[140]

The components of space heritage include: equipment connected with a human presence in space, spacecraft and devices, samples of scientific importance gathered from extraterrestrial sites, and the historical context and ground-breaking nature of certain events connected with space explorations and the locations where they took place.[141] Technological progress and the presence of humans and their equipment in outer space attest to a part of human history that is of fundamental importance.[142] An analysis has already been made regarding the cultural value regarding the Moon landing sites, known as "Apollo culture."[143] Different approaches towards these sites (as a whole and individually) have been considered, as well as towards equipment left behind, changes that have taken place since the landings, and their political context (the Cold War era).[144] The principles of protecting those sites, however, have not been worked out in detail. What is more, the legal status of particular elements of space heritage will differ.

Under Article II of the Treaty on the Principles Governing the Activities of States in the Exploration and Use of Outer Space, including the Moon and Other Celestial

[138] WHC-12/36.COM/19, Decision: 36 COM 5D, point 7. https://whc.unesco.org/en/decisions/4611/. Accessed 1 June 2022.

[139] Antarctic Treaty signed 1 December 1959 in Washington 402 UNTS 71, 12 UST 794, 19 ILM 860 (1980), Cmnd 1535, ATS 12 (1961).

[140] Ruggles (2017), p. 292.

[141] Marov (2010), pp. 234–237.

[142] Marov (2010), p. 233.

[143] Cf. O'Leary (2009b), pp. 757–780.

[144] Gorman (2016).

Bodies,[145] "outer space, including the moon and other celestial bodies, is not subject to national appropriation by claim of sovereignty, by means of use or occupation, or by any other means." Thus, no consideration can be given to exerting ownership over space itself, or even a part of it. Some researchers take a cautious approach to interpreting Article II of the Outer Space Treaty, pointing out that an absolute prohibition on the appropriation of space could hinder technological development and the acquisition of resources.

The treaty does not deal with the concept of shared human heritage, which is well established in research on cultural heritage. In the preamble, however, this clause does appear: "the common interest of all mankind in the progress of the exploration and use of outer space for peaceful purposes." The use of outer space for peaceful purposes, or in the interests of future generations, can easily be connected with cultural heritage. Like space, the whole of human heritage is to be passed on to future generations, and so the present generation should use it with the interest of future generations in mind.

In the Outer Space Treaty, the issue of the ownership of objects released in space is not addressed. Under Article VIII of the treaty,

> Ownership of objects launched into outer space, including objects landed or constructed on a celestial body, and of their component parts, is not affected by their presence in outer space or on a celestial body or by their return to the Earth. Such objects or component parts found beyond the limits of the State Party to the Treaty on whose registry they are carried shall be returned to that State Party, which shall, upon request, furnish identifying data prior to their return.

From a civil law perspective, such objects are things, since they are subject to human control. At the same time, they are material property that can be dangerous, and whose removal or destruction may be considered to ensure the safety of human endeavors in space.[146]

Interestingly, from the perspective of environmental protection, in her analysis of this provision Dagmara Kuźniar points out that "the treaty does not regulate the conditions of liability for damage caused in the space environment, hence the reference to the construction contained in Articles VI and VII."[147] Article VII concerns liability for an object released against another state, or its natural or legal persons.[148] It is difficult to see how this provision can be interpreted as a reference to liability for the space environment or celestial bodies. It will be even more difficult to determine whether it can apply to liability for the destruction of components of

---

[145] Treaty on Principles Governing the Activities of States in the Exploration and Use of Outer Space, including the Moon and Other Celestial Bodies, Moscow, London and Washington on 27 January 1967, entered into force 10 October 1967; 610 UNTS 205, 6 ILM 386 (1967).

[146] Cf. Gorman (2009), pp. 391–392.

[147] Kuźniar (2019), p. 84.

[148] Kuźniar (2019, pp. 84–85) indicates the liability for governmental and non-governmental organizations operating in space under the authority and supervision of the state and others operating without state's authority (strict liability).

cultural heritage, although a starting point might be the definition provided for the entirety of human achievement. Under Article I of the Treaty,

> The exploration and use of outer space, including the moon and other celestial bodies, shall be carried out for the benefit and in the interests of all countries, irrespective of their degree of economic or scientific development, and shall be the province of all mankind.

Without a doubt, in the future the provisions of existing treaties will prove inadequate, and new solutions for protecting the space heritage will be required.

The assumption concerning the common interest was repeated in the Agreement Governing the Activities of States on the Moon and Other Celestial Bodies, concluded in 1979.[149] Those determinations go farther still. Under Article 11 of the Agreement, the moon and its natural resources constitute part of the common heritage of humankind. In this context, it is acknowledged that, while the moon cannot be appropriated, humanity is responsible for managing it, including by protecting the human landing sites on it.[150] Consequently, in the meaning of Article 11 par. 5 of the Agreement, states are obliged to create an international regime for the purpose of managing natural resources acquired in space. Both now and in the future, it has already been determined that such resources are to be used based on the principles of equality and cooperation. For this reason, the Agreement cannot be seen as less important than the Treaty in terms of which solutions are created in the future for managing space exploration.[151] Irrespective of the above, it should be emphasized that the Agreement refers directly to humankind heritage, of which the moon and its natural resources constitute a part. However, many states have not ratified the Agreement,[152] mainly due to the resource management model it proposes and because it prevents states from expanding their activities within the scope of acquiring resources.

The reluctance of states concerning the concept of the common heritage as set out in the Agreement is justified by the fact that it prevents private and state entities from appropriating outer space. For Dennison Butler, in this case the idea of *res communis* is incompatible with the essential nature of outer space and its importance for humanity's development. As examples of common property, he points to resources that are necessary for survival or whose nature does not admit their being classified as private property (e.g., flowing water).[153] The moon and other celestial bodies are also described as *res extra commercium.*[154] Some researchers argue, though, that this perception of the moon and other celestial bodies may turn out to be temporary. Analyses refer to the model of *terra nullius* and the existing manner in which states cooperate over Antarctica. The possibilities for appropriation these put forward are

---

[149] Agreement Governing the Activities of States on the Moon and Other Celestial Bodies, UN Doc. A/Res/34/68.

[150] Reynolds (2015), p. 119.

[151] Turrini (2019), p. 176.

[152] Polkowska (2020), p. 123.

[153] Butler (2017), p. 509.

[154] Lyall and Larsen (2018), p. 193.

close to civil law structures, and employ the concept of *res nullius* in relation to natural resources.[155]

Paolo Turrini shows that as long as the international community remains in accord over the solutions accepted and decides to use a given resource or not, it makes no difference whether *res extra commercium, terra nullius* or the common heritage is applied.[156] Yet this does not mean that these constructions cannot coexist; for example, *res extra commercium* and common heritage in outer space. It is worth pointing out that, in the case of *res extra commercium*, an object may constitute the property of a particular entity (for example, a state). In turn, in regulations concerning outer space the ban on appropriation is meant to indicate the regime for permissible exploitation.

The present lack of a uniform position and the risks that arise in relation to human activity in space mean that the legal regulation of components of heritage will occupy a secondary importance. It cannot be ruled out that similar constructions will be considered first in relation to commercial activities, and then cultural heritage. After determining what is possible regarding the use or possession of resources that have been found or acquired, another element will appear: how to protect the existing landscape and movable objects brought to Earth. This element, though, will be secondary; prime consideration will be given to commercial use. On the other hand, one can see opportunities for the development of joint research on the protection of space heritage as an element that brings states together. One can even image that, once the scope of space heritage has been defined, states will come to an agreement over its components faster than they will over commercial activity.

States should determine now what the rules of cooperation will apply in the future. Certainly, such real cooperation may stand in the way of states' unequal technological and economic progress. The idea that all states will have a share in resources, even states that do not contribute to research, would be very difficult to put into practice. One can see a certain analogy between Article 2 of the Convention on the High Seas and outer space. Under Article 2 of the Convention: *"The high seas being open to all nations, no State may validly purport any part of them to its sovereignty."* In turn, the freedom to use the high seas is exercised under the conditions set forth in the convention and other norms of international law. Such a foundation is also possible for future regulations protecting space heritage, with the important reservation that further exploration of space will be regulated separately.

"Remains" left behind after human sojourns into space, where these are in constant motion, can pose a serious threat. Alice Gorman has put forward a conception of space archaeology and of the importance of human devices left in space to archaeological science. She shows that the realm of space in which such remains exist constitutes a changing "landscape" that is the result of humans interacting with their surrounding environment.[157] She adds that certain objects have already been

---

[155] Butler (2017), p. 513.

[156] Turrini (2019), p. 187.

[157] Gorman (2005a), pp. 338–339.

displayed in thematic museums and possess cultural value. Further, some of them are traded, and even come up for sale in auctions.[158] They constitute material evidence of the presence of human beings in space. Yet the question of whether they should stay in space arises; for example, should a satellite no longer in use be brought back to Earth to please the public?

Gorman considers that the demand that such objects be left in their current location and protected in situ represents an application of the protection granted to the cultural landscape to space heritage. She also reflects on how such a "landscape" should be managed, arguing that attempts to remove or destroy such objects could be seen in the future as an irretrievable loss for humanity.[159] Gorman proposes that work should begin on developing a model for managing space heritage and the space "landscape," using existing methods for managing cultural heritage.[160] The creation of such a model (inventorying, preserving and using the space heritage)[161] will result in the need to classify certain objects as subject to protection.

Here we are faced with the changing status of a heritage component and, in a certain sense, with the "death of a thing" at the moment control over it is lost. The object's status as a component of cultural heritage, though, does not change. It also remains independent of control potentially being regained over the satellite, since it attests to the development of civilization. Certainly, states' different levels of participation in space exploration, and their desire to reap benefits from space, are not conducive to the development of a model for managing the space heritage.

Under Article 3 of the Treaty on the Principles Governing the Activities of States in the Exploration and Use of Outer Space, including the Moon and Other Celestial Bodies,

> States Parties to the Treaty shall carry on activities in the exploration and use of outer space, including the moon and other celestial bodies, in accordance with international law, including the Charter of the United Nations, in the interest of maintaining international peace and security and promoting international co-operation and understanding.

This provision could be a starting point for cooperation on identifying and protecting space cultural heritage.

At this point, reference should again be made to the law of the high seas and the UNESCO Convention on the Protection of the Underwater Archaeological Heritage. Components of underwater archaeological heritage are beyond the jurisdiction of states, as are elements of space heritage.[162] For this reason, a useful example of the development of the law regarding the protection of heritage outside state jurisdiction is the law of the sea or, to be precise, the UN Convention on the Law of the Sea.[163] It

[158] Cf. O'Leary (2009a), p. 33.

[159] Gorman (2005a).

[160] Gorman (2005b).

[161] Cf. Gorman (2009), pp. 394–395.

[162] Doyle (2009), pp. 749–750.

[163] UN General Assembly, *Convention on the Law of the Sea*, 10 December 1982; Doyle (2009), p. 747.

contains only two articles concerning the underwater heritage, and these are rather general (Articles 149 and 303).[164] Further international work resulted in the adoption of the UNESCO Convention on the Protection of the Underwater Archaeological Heritage, aimed at creating a comprehensive system of protection whose "essence involves cooperation among states."[165] A basic assumption of the convention is that the underwater heritage "shall not be commercially exploited" (Article 2 par. 7).[166] In the context of the current commercial use of outer space, it is worth pointing out that in the preamble to the convention, concern is expressed over the commercial exploitation of underwater cultural heritage, including transactions involving components of that heritage.[167] Similar doubts may arise over the use of resources and the resulting disturbance of the "spacescape," or over the removal of devices orbiting the Earth where these do not pose a threat to the safety of ongoing activities.

At present, Polish activities in space are mainly focused on research and commerce. The element of cultural heritage continues to hold little interest. It therefore seems fitting to demand that the tasks of the Manfred Lachs Polish Centre for Space Law should include research on a model of heritage protection, so that the voices of Polish experts are heard in the international arena and are connected with the Polish Space Agency. It is worth noting that the Ministry of Culture and National Heritage was not mentioned among "important Polish players in space activity."[168] This all the stranger in that, as early as 2012, UNESCO appealed for all states to cooperate concerning research on the technical heritage related to space exploration.

After a stage of awareness-raising[169] and bottom-up initiatives for research on heritage, the next stage will be legislative activities. The issue of determining the status of components of space heritage will be a direct result of these activities. The purpose of such legislative activities will be to regulate the right to acquire resources, the right to components of cultural heritage other than devices sent into space by a

[164] Cf. Convention on the Protection of the Underwater Cultural Heritage 2001. In: O'Keefe and Prott (2011), p. 131.

[165] Kowalski (2014), p. 320.

[166] Kowalski (2014), p. 337.

[167] Cf. Miligan (2015), pp. 125–126.

[168] "In particular, the relevant parties of the Polish space activity are: Chancellery of the Prime Minister, Ministry of Development, Ministry of National Defence, Ministry of Science and Higher Education, Ministry of Foreign Affairs, Ministry of Internal Affairs and Administration, Ministry of Digitalization,Ministry of Agriculture, Ministry of Environment, Ministry of Infrastructure and Construction, Ministry of Energy, Ministry of Science and Higher Education, Ministry of Foreign Affairs, Ministry of Interior and Administration, Ministry of Digitalisation, Ministry of Agriculture, Ministry of the Environment, Ministry of Infrastructure and Construction, Ministry of Energy, Ministry of Marine and Inland Navigation, Polish Agency for Enterprise Development (PARP), Space Research and Satellite Committee of Polish Academy of Sciences, Space Sector Employers' Union, National Centre for Research and Development, National Science Centre, General Geodesy and Cartography Office, Polish Air Navigation Services Agency, Space Research Centre of Polish Academy of Sciences." (https://polsa.gov.pl/o-agencji/misja-wizja-i-zadania. Accessed 1 June 2022).

[169] Fewer (2007), p. 5.

state, and the rights and obligations parties may have to cultural sites located in outer space. At the same time, analyses should be made of the principles of governing, and possibly conserving, space heritage. Two roads are open; the first involves diagnosis and identification without interfering in preservation, while the second relates to conservation and activities aimed at preserving the integrity of the space heritage.[170]

With regard to objects located on Earth, it will be necessary to verify whether they can be exploited commercially—the regime of *res extra commercium* may apply. It may be that, due to the value meteorites may have for science and our knowledge about the cosmos, the concept of *res nullius* should apply first, with acquisition of ownership being possible only under certain conditions. Meeting such conditions would involve going through a procedure similar to that used when notifying the relevant authorities about archaeological finds and receiving confirmation of the finder's acquisition of ownership if the authority does not exercise its right to acquire the object concerned. I do not agree with the view that special provisions on acquiring certain types of property that are scientifically or culturally valuable weaken the institution of the acquisition of ownership. The deficiencies in the system for controlling the export of meteorites shows there is a need for regulation in this area. Perhaps provisions governing the acquisition of archaeological artefacts and meteorites could be introduced if the former were moved to the Civil Code. In that case, the other provisions concerning them would remain in the detailed legislation of public law.

As to the future of cultural heritage left in outer space and "locations" associated with the human presence in space, it will be necessary to develop methods of managing these that do not involve how they are classified under civil law.[171] True, objects left in space, such as those from the Apollo missions, are still the property of the United States of America,[172] but the same cannot be said of the parts of the moon on which Americans landed. This is why it will be necessary in the law of the future to combine currents in international law, the issue of the appropriation or non-appropriation of outer space, and elements of private law expressed in the right of ownership over space probes and space stations. I am convinced that it will not be enough just to amend the Convention on the Protection of the World Heritage[173] because, in the case of space heritage that includes elements of the space landscape, protected sites in space will be intertwined with movable components (which may be in circulation) or those no longer in orbit. The creation of a single, comprehensive act of law regulating these areas will provide a solid guarantee[174]; furthermore, it will not rule out the application of the protection granted to World Heritage Sites.

---

[170] Cotte and Ruggles (2010), p. 265; Lyall and Larsen (2018), p. 202.

[171] Elements of private law appear in space tourism.

[172] O'Leary (2015), p. 9; Reynolds (2015), pp. 121–122.

[173] Reynolds (2015), pp. 121–126.

[174] Lixinski et al. (2021), pp. 1–45.

Creating new legislation requires time, and most likely an opportune moment that involves both social and political factors. Certainly, there are some good signs in this respect: UNESCO's establishment of working groups, the preparation of the first studies on heritage, and recent academic publications. The issues of underwater heritage and Antarctica's heritage were regulated only relatively recently, and it appears that the process of regulating space heritage has already begun. These efforts will certainly accelerate the progress being made in science and technology, which are now advanced enough that we can imagine an expansion of public and private entities into outer space. Since states and international organizations now perceive the importance of acting in space and of space technologies for protecting the Earth's cultural heritage,[175] the next stage will be an intensification of activities to protect space heritage.

To conclude, attention must be given to certain rapidly changing aspects related to the presence of states in outer space. First, some states are creating their own legal regulations connected with space exploration—this is part of US policy, for example. A key aspect here is space mining and the acquisition of resources. Second, there has also been a noticeable intensification of activities at the level of the European Union,[176] while at the same time, the Committee on the Peaceful Uses of Outer Space (COPUOS) has adopted Guidelines for the Long-term Sustainability of Outer Space Activities,[177] which states may choose to apply. Third, private sector entities are now being included in space exploration activities.[178] It may be that cooperation on cultural heritage may act as a much-needed bridge between private and public activities in outer space. In a certain sense, this was the message of a resolution by the UN General Assembly on the use of science and technology in cultural development and in achieving the goals of Agenda 2030.[179]

In her latest publication, *Dr Space Junk* vs *the Universe*, Alice Gorman discusses the process of colonization, analyzing the future management of outer space. She shows that the potential process of space colonization and "marking territory" may lead to problems. As an example, she offers the use of the American flag on the moon. Gorman also points out that lessons should be learned from the colonization of Africa and Australia pertaining to the appropriation of certain territories and when searching for a best practice model of cooperation.[180] There is a real need to find a way to include a cultural element in the technological race, international politics, and private entities' plans to take part in exploiting extraterrestrial resources. That

---

[175] Declaration on the fiftieth anniversary of the Treaty on Principles Governing the Activities of States in the Exploration and Use of Outer Space, including the Moon and Other Celestial Bodies. A/RES/72/78, par. 7.

[176] See more Polkowska and Toumi (2020), pp. 439–441.

[177] Guidelines for the Long-term Sustainability of Outer Space Activities of the Committee on the Peaceful Uses of Outer Space, cf. Polkowska (2020), p. 127.

[178] See more Polkowska and Toumi (2020), pp. 443–447.

[179] Resolution adopted by the General Assembly on 7 December 2018 International cooperation in the peaceful uses of outer space, A/RES/73/91.

[180] Gorman (2019), pp. 218–219.

element of culture, or more broadly, cultural heritage and the management thereof, should be considered along with what is determined concerning the economic exploration of space; in fact, elements of culture can act as signposts for decision-makers.

3.4 Intangible Cultural Heritage

There is no doubt that a clear majority of legal regulations at both the domestic and international levels concern tangible heritage. Historically, material heritage was the first to be granted legal protection. Gradually, international efforts were made concerning the need to protect intangible heritage, which constituted a complex process that culminated in the adoption of the UNESCO convention on intangible heritage in 2003. During the work on the convention,

> it was realised that some components of that heritage are of a very delicate nature, sometimes even somewhat ephemeral; they are particularly sensitive to numerous threats and at times are difficult to fix in a way that guarantees their survival.[181]

I agree with Anna Przyborowska Klimczak that protecting intangible heritage is "a serious challenge for the international community,"[182] and would add that that challenge is faced at the level of private law, as well. In this chapter, I examine intangible heritage in its private law dimension, and separately from tangible heritage within the scope crucial to investigating cultural heritage's place in private law.

Cultural heritage constitutes an internally non-uniform set of components, both domestically and globally, and the variety of phenomena contained under the umbrella of intangible heritage confirms the hypothesis that cultural heritage is heterogeneous even within a single category. Thus, there can be no dichotomy in the sense of a complete division between material and intangible heritage, for they overlap. Elements of intangible cultural heritage constitute an important fragment of material heritage.[183] There is no legal definition of intangible heritage in Polish law, though one is included in the UNESCO Convention on the Safeguarding of the Intangible Cultural Heritage (UNESCO 2003 Convention). Under Article 2 par. 1 thereof, intangible cultural heritage, transmitted from generation to generation, is constantly recreated by communities and groups in response to their environment, their interaction with nature and their history. Three basic components for describing intangible cultural heritage are proposed in the convention: how that heritage manifests itself, communities and groups, and cultural space.[184]

[181] Przyborowska-Klimczak (2011), p. 166.

[182] Przyborowska-Klimczak (2011), p. 166.

[183] Schreiber (2014), p. 403.

[184] Cf. Scovazzi (2012), p. 180.

Intangible heritage manifests itself in oral traditions and expressions, in language as a vehicle of that heritage, in the performing arts, customs, rituals and ceremonies, in knowledge and practices concerning nature and the universe, and in traditional craftsmanship. Intangible heritage is also associated with practices, images, the transfer of knowledge and skills, as well as objects, artefacts, and cultural spaces. In many cases, components of intangible heritage can also be classified in several of the areas set out in Article 2 par. 2 of the convention.

The cultural context in which certain products of cultural heritage arise is provided by intangible heritage. With regard to the "properties" and ways of dealing with cultural heritage, a division can be made between intangible heritage as a living element and tangible heritage as a "dead" one. Yet in both cases, the intangible value of those components, their bond with a given place, community or nation, and their history all mean it is in the interest of society to preserve them. The intangible value of both material and intangible cultural heritage is undeniable, and this impalpable but key element is present in both cases. Material heritage incorporates cultural values which, by virtue of their preservation, can be passed on to future generations. Intangible heritage cannot always take on a lasting material form but remains at the level of intangible values in the form of oral traditions, expression, and practices.

The goal of protecting intangible heritage is to maintain the continuity of those traditions; this can only be achieved through the efforts of individuals or groups to cultivate them. Continuity also includes changes that take place in elements of intangible heritage, which, like any "living organism," evolve. This is why one cannot speak of the permanence of intangible heritage, for change is an inherent part of it. Taking stock of intangible heritage occurs through the creation of national registers, which should be updated regularly. Indirect knowledge about intangible heritage and information enabling its preservation are also provided by archives and libraries. The activities of such institutions constitute an important support in intangible heritage protection. Documentation work is also important in disseminating knowledge of intangible heritage and making it understandable to people from outside the circle where it is cultivated.[185]

The role of the local community in protecting intangible heritage is underlined in the convention,[186] and differs from the accepted role of communities in protecting material cultural heritage in the form of, e.g., a historic palace. In the preamble to the convention, mention is made of the role of communities in creating, protecting, preserving, and continuing intangible cultural heritage. This is a reversal of the situation we are faced with in the case of material heritage. The role people play in managing material heritage is confined to activities aimed at preserving it. In this way, it is difficult to speak of any "ownership" of the components of intangible heritage. Nevertheless, the group that is most strongly connected with a given

[185] On cultural diversity and acceptance Frankiewicz-Bodynek (2014, footnote 23) about Śmigus Dyngus (tradition of spilling water on the Easter Monday, initially boys were chasing girls with buckets of water).

[186] Brzezińska (2013), p. 115.

component of intangible heritage has a stronger bond with it than do people from another region or part of the world. What is more, certain groups will be more privileged as depositaries to reap benefits from the commercial exploitation of material products that incorporate their intangible heritage.

Under Article 11 pt. b of the convention, a state is obliged to define and describe elements of intangible heritage within its territory and, in doing so, may draw on help from communities, groups, and non-governmental organizations. The participation of communities, groups and individuals also encompasses their taking an active role in managing that heritage. In this scope, people who have the requisite knowledge and skills to transfer the heritage to future depositaries must be included in heritage management and conservation. Often, these are skills that require many years of preparation and patience, and are very time-consuming. In the case of intangible heritage, this element of transferring traditional knowledge and skills is a very important one. The importance of groups in protecting the intangible heritage is also reflected in the procedure for preparing applications for the domestic and global intangible heritage lists. Every application is submitted by depositaries of that heritage.[187] The convention contains an element on the participation of communities and societies;[188] this will be vital for heritage protection, whether in the form of documented practices, obtaining consent for use, or taking part in managing heritage.

Another issue worth mentioning is the hierarchization of intangible heritage. What has been part of the organized protection of cultural heritage from the very beginning in the form of categories, additional forms of protection, or special forms of protection has not been present with regard to protecting intangible heritage. Every element of cultural heritage is important, and its value is not subject to dispute. The convention emphasizes the importance of communities, groups and individuals taking part in protecting cultural heritage, yet there are no mechanisms for locating elements of intangible heritage in a hierarchy or ranking them in terms of their relative importance.[189] In this scope there is a difference from the World Heritage List and the entry procedures involved there.

[187] Wytyczne dotyczące składania wniosków o wpis oraz procedury wpisywania elementów dziedzictwa niematerialnego na Krajową listę. In: Krajowa lista niematerialnego dziedzictwa kulturowego. Narodowy Instytut Dziedzictwa, p. 3. https://nid.pl/en/dziedzictwo-niematerialne/. Accessed 1 June 2022.

[188] Blake (2017), p. 56.

[189] Cf. Operational Directives for the Implementation of the Convention for the Safeguarding of the Intangible Cultural Heritage Adopted by the General Assembly of the States Parties to the Convention at its second session (UNESCO Headquarters, Paris, 16 to 19 June 2008), amended at its third session (UNESCO Headquarters, Paris, 22 to 24 June 2010), its fourth session (UNESCO Headquarters, Paris, 4 to 8 June 2012), its fifth session (UNESCO Headquarters, Paris, 2 to 4 June 2014), its sixth session (UNESCO Headquarters, Paris, 30 May to 1 June 2016)and its seventh session (UNESCO Headquarters, Paris, 4 to 6 June 2018), par 1.2. https://ich.unesco.org/doc/src/ICH-Operational_Directives-7.GA-PDF-EN.pdf. Accessed 1 June 2022.

The procedure for entry on the list brings new mechanisms of protection. The UNESCO 2003 Convention did not create a separate regime for protecting components of intangible heritage, but rather created conditions conducive to its identification, documentation, promotion, and education.[190] The variety of forms is present in intangible heritage results in a wide range of material and intangible property and can be considered part of intangible heritage as a whole. Some of those elements may take on material form, whereas others will always remain separate from material parts of the world (things). One example is traditional knowledge or skills as intangible values transmitted over generations. Instruments, in turn, may be protected as historical objects, and at the same time as part of intangible cultural heritage (e.g., traditional musical practices or oral storytelling).[191]

A debate on creating a framework for protecting this part of heritage arose while the convention was being drafted. Ultimately, no separate right to traditional knowledge was created; the central aims of the convention remain confined to collecting, preserving, promoting, and educating people about the components of intangible heritage.[192] Article 3 of the convention defines the relationship between the protection of world heritage and intellectual property rights, as well as the use of biological and ecological resources. First, the protection of world heritage under the 1972 Convention concerning the Protection of the World Cultural and Natural Heritage is not restricted or amended, and the convention has no effect on the rights or obligations of the parties, where those rights or obligations stem from international instruments concerning intellectual property rights or biological or ecological resources.

A comprehensive analysis of the tools used to protect intangible heritage is not the main goal of this study, so I will limit myself to mention only those elements that demonstrate the multi-dimensional nature of cultural heritage, and which necessitate the use of different legal instruments that come up in the international debate, paying particular attention to intellectual property rights. This is a starting point in the search for new legal methods of protecting intangible heritage.

Even before the work on the UNESCO 2003 Convention began, voices were already being raised concerning the protection of intangible heritage and its products by means of intellectual property rights. In a recommendation of 15 November 1989 on the protection of traditional culture and folklore,[193] reference was made to the issue of intellectual property and its importance in protecting intangible values. It was shown that folklore constitutes a manifestation of both individual and collective creativity. The recommendation draws attention to the work going on at that time at UNESCO and the WIPO, and constitutes only one method of protection. Certainly,

[190] Forrest (2010), pp. 386–397.

[191] About music instrument Lixinski (2020).

[192] Jodełka (2005), p. 173.

[193] Recommendation on the Safeguarding of Traditional Culture and Folklore, 15 November 1989.

the recommendation refers to joint work that resulted, for example, in the publication of a *Draft Treaty for the Protection of Expressions of Folklore Against Illicit Exploitation and Other Prejudicial Actions* in 1982,[194] as well as in the submission of a draft convention,[195] on which the work was discontinued. In 1998, the WIPO began independent work on searching for protective regimes based on intellectual property law.

It was the task of the Intergovernmental Committee on Intellectual Property and Genetic Resources, Traditional Knowledge and Folklore, established in the year 2000,[196] to continue that work. The committee prepared two sets of model provisions on protecting traditional knowledge and traditional expressions of culture; these were adopted in 2014.[197] Both documents have been discussed in detail in the literature.[198] By a decision of the Assemblies of the Member States of WIPO, it was agreed that in the years 2020–2021 the Committee would continue working on legal instruments for protecting genetic resources, folklore and traditional knowledge.[199] The drafts propose a new *sui generis* right based on intellectual property law, considering the specific nature of the subject of protection. The problems caused by the need to find a legal solution include: the impossibility of identifying an author; authorship being attributed to a numerically undefined group; the collective ownership of a given group over a product; the element of conscious consent by the rightsholders; and the difficulty in demonstrating novelty in the case of traditional knowledge (e.g., recipes) known for years. In 2021 the Committee was supposed to submit the results of its work; after evaluating the results, the General Assembly was expected to decide whether to continue the work or convene a diplomatic conference.[200] The General Assembly agreed to renew the IGC's mandate for the 2022/

---

[194] Model Provisions for National Laws on the Protection of Expressions of Folklore Against Illicit Exploitation and Other Prejudicial Actions. UNESCO/WIPO, Paris–Geneva 1982, WIPO 1985. https://www.wipo.int/export/sites/www/tk/en/folklore/1982-folklore-model-provisions.pdf. Accessed 1 June 2022.

[195] Draft Treaty for the Protection of Expressions of Folklore Against Illicit Exploitation and Other Prejudicial Actions. UNESCO/WIPO, Paris–Geneva 1984.

[196] Decision, Assemblies of the Member States of WIPO Fifty-Ninth Series of Meetings September 30 to October 9, 2019 Agenda Item 20 Report on the Intergovernmental Committee on Intellectual Property and Genetic Resources, Traditional Knowledge and Folklore (IGC). https://www.wipo.int/about-wipo/en/assemblies/2019/a_59/doc_details.jsp?doc_id=443934. Accessed 1 June 2022.

[197] Blake (2017), p. 50.

[198] Blake (2015), pp. 259–270.

[199] TCESREV.2 The Protection of Traditional Cultural Expressions: Draft Articles Rev. 2 (March 22, 2019) https://www.wipo.int/edocs/mdocs/tk/en/wipo_grtkf_ic_40/facilitators_text_on_tces.pdf. Accessed 1 June 2022; TKREV. 2 The Protection of Traditional Knowledge: Draft Articles Rev. 2 (March 22, 2019). https://www.wipo.int/edocs/mdocs/tk/en/wipo_grtkf_ic_39/wipo_grtkf_ic_39_facilitators_text_tk_rev_2.pdf. Accessed 1 June 2022.

[200] Report on the Intergovernmental Committee on Intellectual Property and Genetic Resources, Traditional Knowledge and Folklore (IGC). Decision, Assemblies of the Member States of WIPO. Fifty-Ninth Series of Meetings, September 30 to October 9, 2019. Agenda Item 20. https://www.wipo.int/export/sites/www/tk/en/igc/pdf/igc_mandate_2020-2021.pdf. Accessed 1 June 2022.

2023 biennium and encouraged to continue work the available documents, inter alia, WIPO/GRTKF/IC/40/6, WIPO/GRTKF/IC/40/18, WIPO/GRTKF/IC/40/19, and the Chair's Text on a Draft International Legal Instrument Relating to Intellectual Property, Genetic Resources and Traditional Knowledge Associated with Genetic Resources. The decision taken sets out the work program including thematic, cross-cutting, and stocktaking sessions. The General Assembly in 2023 will decide on the further steps as follows.[201]

In these acts, issues concerning the protection of intangible cultural heritage are regulated alongside others, and do not constitute the main objective of the regulations. The use of traditional knowledge appears, for example, in the Convention on Biological Diversity.[202] Under Article 8 letter j of that convention, each state must

> subject to its national legislation, respect, preserve and maintain knowledge, innovations and practices of indigenous and local communities embodying traditional lifestyles relevant for the conservation and sustainable use of biological diversity and promote their wider application with the approval and involvement of the holders of such knowledge, innovations and practices and encourage the equitable sharing of the benefits arising from the utilization of such knowledge, innovations and practices.

The Nagoya Protocol[203] sets out ways of dividing benefits deriving from the use of traditional knowledge. Under Article 5 par. 5 of the Protocol,

> each Party shall take legislative, administrative or policy measures, as appropriate, in order that the benefits arising from the utilization of traditional knowledge associated with genetic resources are shared in a fair and equitable way with indigenous and local communities holding such knowledge. Such sharing shall be upon mutually agreed terms.

In turn, access to such knowledge and its availability should take place "with the prior and informed consent or approval and involvement of these indigenous and local communities" (Article 7 of the Nagoya Protocol). Pertaining to artistic performances that can constitute manifestations of folk culture, it is worth referring to the Agreement on Trade-Related Aspects of Intellectual Property Rights (TRIPS),[204] which sets out minimum standards but without protecting moral copyrights, and is therefore of limited use in protecting intangible heritage.[205] The WIPO Copyright

---

[201] Report on the Intergovernmental Committee on Intellectual Property and Genetic Resources, Traditional Knowledge and Folklore (IGC). Decision, Assemblies of the Member States of WIPO Sixty-Second Series of Meetings October 4 to 8, 2021 Agenda Item 18. https://www.wipo.int/export/sites/www/tk/en/documents/pdf/igc mandate-2022-2023.pdf. Accessed 1 June 2022.

[202] UN Convention on Biological Diversity on 5 June 1992 1760 UNTS 79, 31 ILM 818 (1992).

[203] Nagoya Protocol on Access to Genetic Resources and the Fair and Equitable Sharing of Benefits Arising from their Utilization to the Convention on Biological Diversity, OJ L 150, 20.5.2014, pp. 234–249 and Regulation (EU) No 511/2014 of the European Parliament and of the Council of 16 April 2014 on compliance measures for users from the Nagoya Protocol on Access to Genetic Resources and the Fair and Equitable Sharing of Benefits Arising from their Utilization in the Union Text with EEA relevance, OJ L 150, 20.5.2014, pp. 59–71.

[204] Uruguay Round of Multilateral Trade Negotiations (1986–1994) – Annex 1 – Annex 1C – Agreement on Trade-Related Aspects of Intellectual Property Rights (WTO), OJ L 336, 23.12.1994, pp. 214–223.

[205] Blake (2015), p. 243.

Treaty, in turn, deals with artistic performances and phonograms in its Article 5, where it foresees protection that is independent of property rights[206] for artistic audio performances, whether live or recorded.

In the applicable literature, mention is often made of the need to come up with unique forms of protection and create a legal framework appropriate to the subject of protection.[207] The protection given to intangible heritage under the current intellectual property rights framework is inadequate. The main thrust of the law at present is to protect the fruits of human creativity, thereby supporting progress and creativity; it is not to protect intangible values, and so this occurs only incidentally, as it were.[208] Traditional knowledge may be protected using available mechanisms only insofar as it meets the criteria of novelty and innovation. Yet such knowledge usually originated decades or centuries ago, and therefore does not qualify for protection under intellectual property law. Patents, trademarks, industrial marks and protected geographical designations have all been suggested as potential institutions for protecting intangible heritage, while much also depends on the legal system and legal culture of a given country. The legal orders of countries in which the participation of indigenous peoples and communities in culture is significant contain solutions in the form of case law[209] or legislation. Manifestations of traditional culture may also be protected by means of copyrights and related rights, particularly with regard to performances of traditional songs or music, as well as contemporary works containing folk elements. As in the case of traditional knowledge, patent and geographical designation protection may apply, while other protective mechanisms are also being considered related to business secrecy and unfair competition.[210]

Some states have decided to adopt their own legal regulations. It should be added that, before the adoption of the UNESCO Convention, only some states had domestic regulations related to intangible heritage,[211] while others began giving the issue consideration during the work on the convention. Globally, however, it was the adoption of the convention in 2003 that marked a breakthrough in the complex process of creating national regulations in this scope. Anita Vaivade and Noé Wagener rightly point out that "the novelty of the 2003 Convention should be assessed in dialogue with national conceptual and institutional histories, and with the evolution of national policy measures."[212] They argue that there has been a visible shift from an object-centered approach to one anchored in the recognition of the outstanding value of intangible cultural heritage.[213] In this respect, the search for

---

[206] *WIPO* Performances and Phonograms *Treaty* adopted in Geneva on *December 20, CRNR/DC/ 95.*

[207] Blake (2015), p. 245 et seq.

[208] Cf. Lixinski and Blake (2020).

[209] About Australia Lixinski (2013), pp. 120–121.

[210] Lixinski (2013), pp. 194–196.

[211] Vaivade and Wagener (2017), pp. 99–101.

[212] Vaivade and Wagener (2017), p. 101.

[213] Cornu and Vaivade (2020), p. 1.

protective regimes should consider the context and history of a given country, and its current legal framework for protecting cultural heritage. The presence of intangible elements in existing domestic law[214] may strengthen activities in this direction, or alternatively, serve as a starting point. On the other hand, systems are noticeably being revised in terms of their compliance with the requirements of international law; new domestic models are currently being sought. Bolivian law has been cited as a regime that effectively protects the intangible heritage *erga omnes*; it enshrines the right of the state to intangible heritage, excluding products of craftsmanship but including products within a specific *public domain* regime. This, however, does not give communities the right to reap benefits from the use of their intangible heritage. For products of craftsmanship, the regulations foresee protection through registration under the rules applicable to trademarks.[215]

Applying the above observations to Polish law, the first thing to do is to look for grounds for the protection of intangible heritage in binding acts of law. It is generally accepted that Articles 5 and 6 of the Polish Constitution lay down "a directive that all elements of heritage be perceived collectively" and that they constitutionally strengthen the area of culture.[216] This integrated perception, however, is not reflected in a comprehensive protection of culture, although certain possibilities are provided by some forms of protection granted to immovable historical objects. In the context of cultural space, reference can be made to the protection of the cultural landscape and protection in the form of a cultural park.

There is no special act in the Polish legal system devoted to the problem of intangible heritage. There are, however, certain measurable ways of protecting the "material" part of intangible heritage, that is, externalizations thereof, as already contained in the APGM.[217] Examples given of movable historical objects are provided in Article 6 par. 1 pt. 2 letter g APGM, and include products of folk art, handicrafts, and other ethnographic objects. The catalogue contained in Article 6 APGM is open, although it is worth noting that components of cultural heritage connected with the intangible heritage are identified separately. In this way, elements of intangible heritage can be protected. Objects that constitute evidence of intangible heritage may be subject to protection as historical objects if they fit the definition of a "historical object." In line with this definition, a historical object must constitute evidence of a bygone era. At present, the discussion continues over how old an object must be to qualify as "historical"; protection is being increasingly granted to younger movable and immovable objects, while as time passes, that threshold is constantly shifting. Objects made in modern times while cultivating

---

[214] Article 6 par. 2 APGM "Geographical, historical and traditional names of construction objects, squares, streets and settlement units may also be protected." The category was not mentioned in the APCP 1962 and was added in the to provide protection for the intangible property entered to the monuments register (Golat 2004, p. 27).

[215] Lixinski (2013), p. 122.

[216] Zalasińska (2017), p. 319.

[217] Zalasińska (2017), p. 320.

traditional practices—such as embroidery, pottery, and weaving—cannot be treated as historical objects.

To the extent that an object is a work and constitutes an expression of the creative work of an individual person, it may be protected by copyright. The same goes for a work that is inspired, e.g., one that bears creative and individual traits. A work created by a folk artist is protected as a work.[218] The use of all or part of a work on products traded commercially without the consent of the author of the work is an infringement of copyright.[219] Under Article 3 of the Copyright and Related Rights Act (CRRA),

> collections, anthologies, selections and databases having the features of a work are subject to copyright, even if they contain unprotected materials, provided that the selection, arrangement or compilation is of a creative nature, without prejudice to the rights to use the works they contain.

Thus, a collection of works of folk art that in themselves do not constitute works can be subject to protection, provided that the way in which they are selected and composed is of a creative nature. Nevertheless, the qualification of works of folk art is fraught with difficulty.[220] In a ruling, the Supreme Court made a distinction between the level of protection afforded to works of folklore not subject to copyright protection and other works of folk art. The scale of infringements that occur is a result of the low level of awareness that such works may be subject to protection. This is why educational campaigns aimed at drawing attention to this problem align with the foundations of the UNESCO 2003 Convention.[221]

Artistic performances are also subject to protection. Under Article 85 par. 1 of the CRRA, "every artistic performance of a work or work of folk art remains under protection, regardless of its value, purpose or means of expression." Protection is granted to artistic performances, in particular "the activities of actors, reciters, conductors, instrumentalists, vocalists, dancers and mimes, as well as other persons who creatively contribute to a performance" (Article 85 par. 2 CRRA). A performer has the right to the protection of their personal rights and the use of their artistic performance, and to dispose of those rights in the fields of exploitation set out in the Act.[222] That right expires after 50 years. Protection of folk-art performances was added by the Act of 9 June 2000 Amending the Copyright and Related Rights

[218] Polish Supreme Court, Verdict of 17 November 2011, III CSK 30/11 LEX no. 1129116.

[219] Examples known from the media include the use of cut-outs from the Łowicz region on chocolate's box (judgment of the Supreme Court of November 17 2011 III CSK 30/11, LEX no. 1129116) and on an occasional medal of the Mint of Poland SA. (Mennica Polska SA). The latter was solved by a settlement (Klepczarek (2012).

[220] Bieczyński (2011), p. 244.

[221] About the National Action for the Protection of Copyright of Folk Artists "Catch the Thief!" Rutkowska (2018), p. 354.

[222] The listing is enumerative Czajkowska-Dąbrowska (2007), p. 332.

Act.[223] In the amendment, the term "work of folk art" is used, with the proviso that not every manifestation of folk creativity can obtain the status of a work. For example, in relation to some works created by folk artists, there is no way to determine who their author was, and since they have existed in the culture of a given region for years, a full identification of their provenance is impossible. Performers may seek additional protection in the protection of personal rights provided by the Civil Code.

Folk artists may also seek protection of their individual rights through a collective management organization. For example, the Folk Artists' Association runs a Copyright Agency which can be entrusted with the management of rights or authorized to collect, distribute, and pay remuneration to performers for the use of the effects of their work. Similarly, folk art performers hold copyright in their performances (Article 85 CRRA). That right "arises in relation to a performance or work of folk art that possesses artistic features."[224] Protection additionally applies to performances whose authorship cannot be specifically attributed and which do not in themselves constitute a work.

With regard to manifestations of intangible heritage in the form of traditional knowledge, the issues of recipes and methods of treatment come up. The basic form of protection for this heritage may be that of trademark protection or, in the case of the use of technology to prepare a drug, patent law. The names of products can also comprise elements of intangible heritage. For instance, the Polish cheeses "oscypek" and "bryndza podhalańska" are registered and protected designations of origin.[225] The essence of such protection, though, does not secure a product's connection with Polish culture or a particular region, but primarily serves to secure the interests of local entrepreneurs.

In relation to patterns used for many years without change, the problem of whether they can be used commercially and whether they remain in the public domain arises. In the Polish legal system, there is no such model as *domaine public payant*. That model foresees payment for the use of elements in the public domain, where the funds gathered as a result are used to support activities connected with preserving traditional culture. Some authors see a certain potential of this institution to protect intangible heritage, where such protection is effective in the hands of the state,[226] and where introducing the model internationally would increase its effectiveness.[227]

---

[223] Act of 9 June 2000 Amending the Copyright and Related Rights Act. Polish Official Journal (Dz. U.) 2000, No. 53, item 637.

[224] Barta and Markiewicz (2019), p. 243.

[225] Act of 17 December 2004 on Registration and Protection of Names and Designations of Agricultural Products and Foodstuffs and on Traditional Products, consolidated text. Polish Official Journal (Dz. U.) 2019, item 915.

[226] Lixinski (2013), p. 199.

[227] Konach (2014), pp. 36–37.

Can such an outline of the protection of intangible heritage be confronted with the question of whose heritage it is? In the case of material heritage and the absence of private law ties therewith (if, for example, it does not occur in tangible form, and we are not dealing with an artistic performance of a work of folk art) does the issue of how to dispose of such heritage become relevant? One can imagine that not all members of a group or community will be interested in cultivating traditions or taking part in such activities, or in managing and protecting that heritage. For example, such a position has been expressed in a Latvian act of law,[228] in accordance with which members of a community have the right to refuse[229] to take part in protecting their intangible heritage. Under Section 7 pt. 3 of that act, a community has the right to refuse to take part in measures aimed at securing intangible heritage taken by other entities, including local government and state administrative bodies.[230] One cannot rule out a situation in which everyone having skills important to their intangible heritage decides not to cultivate it. The law provides no element of force in this respect, so the only remedy would be to use archival documentation concerning a given dance or ceremony to be able to recreate it.

In this last example, a dilemma arises over how to proceed further, and concerning the danger of "restoring something that has been dead for a long time,"[231] since the definition of intangible heritage in the convention covers heritage passed from generation to generation, which is continuously recreated by communities or groups in response to their environment (Article 2 pt. 1 of the convention). Another danger related to any restoration of intangible heritage is that of its becoming shallow and losing value.[232] Numerous risks are mentioned, including "the danger of the diversity and wealth of tradition becoming blurred and pop-culturised, understood as a loss of social awareness of the depth of meanings in the intangible heritage" and "a rite transformed ceases to be a 'living' element of the intangible heritage and becomes a theatrical spectacle."[233]

The situation is different in the case of material cultural heritage since an object has a defined legal status and keeper. The Polish legal system does not foresee any admissible legal circumstances in which the owner of a historical object may abandon the object and transfer it to an authorized entity representing the public interest. Keeping the above in mind, it is easier to free oneself from intangible heritage than from material heritage, for in the former case there is a greater chance that a given tradition will continue to be handed down by other members of the group. The problem of abandoning a historical object came up in the case *Potomska*

[228] Nemateriālā kultūras mantojuma likums, Latvijas Vēstnesis [Latvian Official Journal] No. 204 (5776), 29 Oct 2016. https://likumi.lv/ta/en/id/285526-intangible-cultural-heritage-law. Accessed 1 June 2022.

[229] Schreiber (2017), p. 493.

[230] Vaivade (2017), p. 406.

[231] Brzezińska (2013), p. 126.

[232] Francioni (2020).

[233] Skaldawski (2013), p. 112.

and Potomski v Poland.[234] In its ruling, the European Court of Human Rights (ECHR) found that there should be a mechanism in the Polish legal system by which the keeper of a historical object may decide to abandon the object in a lasting manner that guarantees no property damage will later ensue. The ECHR held that Polish law lacks a solution allowing a historical object to be purchased from its owner other than in the manner provided for security, and—as a last resort—by expropriation. Leaving the holder of a historical object with all the consequences of a change in the status of a real property – in this case, from a plot of land zoned for the construction of a house and workshop to the location of a former Jewish cemetery—resulted in restrictions on the scope of the available use for the property.[235]

The use of intellectual property rights to protect intangible heritage does not seem to be sufficient, and moreover, as shown above, it is not the main goal of those norms. After making a detailed diagnosis of Poland's intangible heritage, work should begin on a future legal framework for managing it. The increasing importance of intangible values, including those which are part of intangible heritage, in economic activities (i.e., their commercial exploitation) requires a search for new legal instruments. Those instruments should prevent elements of intangible heritage from being used in an inappropriate context or in a way that raises doubts; in the case of their use by entities outside of the entitled entities, the right holders should be given specific consideration in the form of remuneration, or a charge paid to a national intangible heritage fund. Further work on conventions protecting traditional knowledge and traditional forms of cultural expression suggest that, in years to come, two new international instruments will be established in this field.

The discussion on intangible heritage and a right to certain components thereof that will be effective *erga omnes* is similar to the process of establishing an intellectual property right. Intangible heritage, or at least part of it, could be the subject of a right similar to that of ownership, although it does not constitute material property. The construction of such a law would have to consider how the holders of that right would be determined, and a legal relationship similar to that of property rights would need to be created. The starting point will be the work of WIPO and UNESCO. The scope of concerned entities in the case of intangible heritage will be based on to persons—the transmitters or bearers of that heritage.

The potential commercialization of intangible heritage may pose a threat to it—or may foster its cultivation, because it can provide opportunities for the right holders to reap material benefits from that heritage. Taking account of commercialization is important in the process of working out protective mechanisms. After all, cultural heritage is a driver of social development, and economic growth as well. Making a division between entities that have ties with a specific part of cultural heritage and private entities (pharmaceutical companies and others) that exploit that heritage for

---

[234] European Court of Human Rights (33,949/05), Judgement of 4 November 2014, case of *Potomska and Potomski v. Poland.*

[235] About new legal solution see Sect. 2.6.

profit-making purposes makes it possible to determine permissible areas of use for intangible heritage.

The first step could be to appoint a national organization to manage intangible heritage, which would work alongside the bearers of that heritage. Such an organization could supervise the use of intangible cultural heritage for commercial purposes. Its status could be similar to that of a collective management organization, and it could act as an association under a ministerial permit. Another model to consider would the creation of a specialized cultural institution similar to the Chopin Institute, discussed further on. A solution not involving the establishment of a new entity would be the creation of a new department within the National Institute of Cultural Heritage. Currently, under Article 5 pt. 15 of its statute, the institute's tasks include implementing agreements, conventions and other documents ratified by Poland connected with protecting and caring for material and intangible cultural heritage entrusted to it by the minister. It seems, though, that the best solution would be an entity similar to a collective management organization.

Where the right to exploit components of intangible heritage commercially cannot be based on existing mechanisms, agreements similar to license agreements could be concluded. This could be done after verifying the purpose of the agreement and determining that it will not lead to a distortion, trivialization or deformation of how the heritage is perceived. The organization would be approached in tandem with the heritage's application for registration in the national list of intangible heritage. The organization could also support entities in preparing applications. At present, this most often takes place with the participation of a museum from a given region, or at their initiative with support of regional offices of National Institute of Cultural Heritage. Having a single institution able to gather experts together within this scope would certainly shorten the process of gathering the necessary documentation and preparing an application. I anticipate it would also lead to considerable savings of costs.

Before such an institution is established, it may be worth planning a project as referred to in Article 18 of the Convention and submitting it to the Committee. Under Article 18 of the Convention,[236]

> On the basis of proposals submitted by States Parties, and in accordance with criteria to be defined by the Committee and approved by the General Assembly, the Committee shall periodically select and promote national, subregional and regional programmes, projects and activities for the safeguarding of the heritage which it considers best reflect the principles and objectives of this Convention, taking into account the special needs of developing countries.

The goal is for the Committee to promote such programs as best practice. Nothing stands in the way of a proposal including tasks related to the Polish legislator seeking ways to strengthen the protection of intangible heritage.

To expand the scope of this potential project, I suggest it could encompass several elements entered on the national list of intangible heritage, such as, for example,

---

[236] Criteria and timetable for selection of Register of Best Safeguarding Practice. https://ich.unesco.org/en/select-for-the-register-00300. Accessed 1 June 2022.

Opole Silesia. A noticeable intensification in Poland in the protection of intangible heritage, including the first Polish entry on the representative list of the intangible cultural heritage of humanity—the nativity scene tradition in Krakow[237]—is conducive to such activities. At the same time, one result of the project would be to set out strategic goals allowing organizations to manage rights connected with intangible heritage and cooperating with depositaries. A discussion on increasing the legal protection for entities that are bearers of intangible heritage could form part of the proposed program, leading to greater input from communities and spurring active engagement.

3.5 Artificial Intelligence, Art, and the Protection of Historical Objects

Machines, which up to now were meant to serve people and carry out tasks after receiving orders, are now capable of preparing an object/project whose final effect humans are not able to foresee or plan. This is something different from computer activities that assist the creative process or permit creative modification. Recently, the question has arisen in discussions concerning the art market of whether things created based on algorithms written by people can be defined as works of art and sold on that market. Researchers involved in artificial intelligence say that how that question is answered is up to the public.[238] Yet, whatever the answer, artificial intelligence has encroached upon the art market, and is here to stay. What remains to be considered are issues of copyright[239] and the future of such products in the context of components of cultural heritage; these problems are discussed below.

It is worth considering the placement of artificial intelligence in the development of culture and progress in civilization. Artificial intelligence (AI) is currently one of the driving forces in economic growth nationally, regionally, and internationally, which is why it is being analyzed in terms of its possible effects on the growth of societies. As AI is increasingly applied multidimensionally, questions concerning legal provisions and ethical dilemmas require the preparation of in-depth analyses.[240] The emergence of AI is also affecting human rights in relation to data

[237] 13.COM 10.b.29,

[238] Audry and Ippolito (2019).

[239] Summary of proposals Szpyt (2020), pp. 161–162.

[240] Azoulay A, Towards Ethics of Artificial Intelligence, UN Chronicle. https://www.un.org/en/chronicle/article/towards-ethics-artificial-intelligence. Accessed 1 June 2022; Założenia do strategii AI w Polsce. Plan działań Ministerstwa Cyfryzacji. Warszawa 9 listopada 2018. https://www.gov.pl/documents/31305/436699/Za%C5%82o%C5%BCenia_do_strategii_AI_w_Polsce_-_raport.pdf. Accessed 1 June 2022; Report of the World Commission on the Ethics of Scientific Knowledge and Technology (COMEST) on Robotics Ethics, SHS/YES/COMEST-10/17/2 REV. Paris, 14 September 2017, https://unesdoc.unesco.org/ark:/48223/pf0000253952. Accessed 1 June 2022; Statement on Artificial Intelligence, Robotics and 'Autonomous' Systems. European Group

processing and its effects,[241] the right to privacy, free and aware access to the latest technologies, and non-discrimination on the basis of gender.[242] The use of AI is considered in the goals for sustainable development as set out in the 2030 Agenda for Sustainable Development.[243] AI is also being used effectively to protect cultural heritage. For example, when creating images of objects before reconstruction or mapping historical areas destroyed during armed conflicts; specialized programs are also able to predict the effects of climate change or tectonic movements that could lead to the destruction of heritage components.

On a global scale, there is a noticeable trend towards adopting national strategies that define risk areas and challenges faced by legislators.[244] Poland adopted *Theses for an AI Strategy in Poland* in 2018.[245] AI is an important element of development in the European Union. On 10 April 2018, a declaration was signed on EU cooperation pertaining to artificial intelligence.[246] However, in a communication of the Commission of the European Parliament, the European Council, the European Economic and Social Committee and the Committee of Regions: Artificial Intelligence for Europe[247] (COM(2018) 237 final), there is no explicit reference to role played by artificial intelligence in the sphere of culture. Here, artificial intelligence is merely viewed as a stimulant of economic growth, streamlining processes, and supporting the health, transport, and food sectors.

In the communication, reference is made to the issue of the culture of states, in part concerning the situation in the EU, pointing out that most developed economies have already laid down assumptions concerning AI that reflect their political,

---

on Ethics in Science and New Technologies. European Commission. Brussels, 9 March 2018. https://op.europa.eu/en/publication-detail/-/publication/dfebe62e-4ce9-11e8-be1d-01aa75ed71a1/language-en/format-PDF/source-78120382. Accessed 1 June 2022.

[241] The Committee of Experts on Internet Intermediaries (MSI-NET). Algorithms and Human Rights, Study on the human rights dimension of automated data processing techniques and possible regulatory implications. Council of Europe study DGI (2017) 112, Strasbourg 2018. https://edoc.coe.int/fr/internet/7589-algorithms-and-human-rights-study-on-the-human-rights-dimensions-of-automated-data-processing-techniques-and-possible-regulatory-implications.html. Accessed 1 June 2022.

[242] West et al. (2019).

[243] Artificial Intelligence for Sustainable Development: challenges and opportunities for UNESCO's science and engineering programmes. Working paper. UNESCO, May 2019. https://unesdoc.unesco.org/ark:/48223/pf0000368028.locale=en. Accessed 1 June 2022.

[244] Artificial Intelligence for Sustainable Development: challenges and opportunities for UNESCO's science and engineering programmes. Working paper. UNESCO, May 2019, p. 48. https://unesdoc.unesco.org/ark:/48223/pf0000368028.locale=en. Accessed 1 June 2022.

[245] Założenia do strategii AI w Polsce. Plan działań Ministerstwa Cyfryzacji. Warszawa, 9 listopada 2018. https://www.gov.pl/documents/31305/436699/Za%C5%82o%C5%BCenia_do_strategii_AI_w_Polsce_-_raport.pdf. Accessed 1 June 2022.

[246] https://ec.europa.eu/digital-single-market/en/artificial-intelligence#Declaration-of-cooperation-on-Artificial-Intelligence. Accessed 1 June 2022.

[247] Communication from the Commission to the European Parliament, the European Council, the Council, the European Economic and Social Committee and the Committee of the Regions Artificial Intelligence for Europe. 25.4.2018 COM (2018) 237 final.

economic, cultural, and social systems, and have incurred significant outlays on developing AI. Within the European Union, reference is made to various programs aimed at supporting innovation and the search for practical applications of artificial intelligence. In the Communication from the Commission to the European Parliament, the European Council, the Council, the European Economic and Social Committee and the Committee of the Regions, Coordinated Plan on Artificial Intelligence, AI's role in improving efficiency is emphasized, since it "improves products, processes and business models in all economic sectors"[248] and should be used to solve key global problems.

In turn, in the Communication from the Commission to the European Parliament, the European Council, the Council, the European Economic and Social Committee and the Committee of the Regions, Building Trust in Human-Centric Artificial Intelligence (COM (2019) 168),[249] AI is treated as a technological strategy. Unfortunately, in this communication as well there is no reference to the role of AI in the culture sector. While it follows from the declaration that the European Union "has a strong regulatory framework that will set the global standard for human-centric AI," one can also assume that cultural needs will also be considered. One of the values of the European Union is respect for human rights, which include cultural rights. Culture, however, is not mentioned in the Commission's white paper on AI, although it is mentioned in a recent European Parliament resolution of 19 May 2021 on artificial intelligence in education, culture and the audiovisual sector.[250] There, AI is indicated as an enabler for the promotion and protection of cultural heritage

> AI technologies can play a significant role in preserving, restoring, documenting, analyzing, promoting and managing tangible and intangible cultural heritage, including by monitoring and analyzing changes to cultural heritage sites caused by threats such as climate change, natural disasters and armed conflicts (Para 51)

and as a response to the needs of the cultural sector if effectively applied. Mention is made of AI's role in creative activities and as a driver in developing cultural and creative sectors and industries (CCSI), and of the need for an in-depth assessment of the relationship between AI and copyright concerning cultural outputs (par. 61), which will lead to activities by Member States in their national strategies. In 2021, the European Parliament adopted resolutions on AI, including within the scope of

---

[248] Communication from the Commission to the European Parliament, the European Council, the Council, the European Economic and Social Committee and the Committee of the Regions Coordinated Plan on Artificial Intelligence. 7.12.2018. COM/2018/795 Final.

[249] Communication from the Commission to the European Parliament, the Council, the European Economic and Social Committee and the Committee of the Regions – Building Trust in Human Centric Artificial Intelligence. 8.04.2019. COM(2019)168.

[250] European Parliament resolution of 19 May 2021 on artificial intelligence in education, culture and the audiovisual sector. 2020/2017(INI). P9_TA(2021)0238.

ethics[251] and civil responsibility,[252] concerning intellectual property rights in the area of developing artificial intelligence technologies.[253]

Regarding the significance of works of art generated by means of AI, as introduced above, this is no longer a marginal issue, but one that decision-makers will need to grapple with in the near future. Algorithms have been extremely important in the cultural sector for a long time and are present in such initiatives as #DigitalYou—Digital Culture, which promotes a uniform digital market, accessibility to services and resources (Europeana), securing cultural heritage resources, and above all development through stimulation of the cultural sector and creative industries. The uniform digital market and digitization are the top priorities, however, while the issue of AI-derived cultural products comes up in the debate on future AI regulations, including those concerning copyright.

Regardless of the EU's strategy and goals for sustainable development, for some time now AI has been present in the cultural sector in the form of works of art created using it. The first sales of works created without an artist's direct participation but using technologies and self-learning algorithms designed by a human being in renowned auction houses will go down in history as a milestone on the international art market. It should be added that such works first appeared in the 1970s, although they made little impact on the international art market at the time.[254] In 2018, auction house Christie's organized a sale of works created by the collective Obvious, or more precisely, generated by the Generative Adversarial Network algorithm prepared for the collective.[255] A picture entitled *Edmond de Belamy*, originally appraised at $7000–$10,000, sold for $442,500. This one-off phenomenon not only confirmed that there are no certainties in the art market, but also showed that selling an atypical or completely unique object whets investors' appetites. The picture is a portrait of a man who does not exist in reality, whose features were created by means of the GAN algorithm.

Another similar example is the project "The Next Rembrandt," in which a portrait of Rembrandt van Rijn was produced.[256] The idea for the project was to verify the technological capabilities of computer programs. In 2016, using a computer program that "learned" the painting techniques of the master from a database of existing portraits of him, an image was produced—a portrait of a man. The project participants wanted to find out whether a computer could be programmed to make use of painting materials in a masterful way. The interdisciplinary approach used to carry

[251] European Parliament resolution of 20 October 2020 on a framework of ethical aspects of artificial intelligence, robotics and related technologies, 2020/2012(INL).

[252] European Parliament resolution of 20 October 2020 on a civil liability regime for artificial intelligence, 2020/2014(INL).

[253] European Parliament resolution of 20 October 2020 on intellectual property rights for the development of artificial intelligence technologies, 2020/2015(INI).

[254] Romo (2018).

[255] Quiñones Vilá (2019).

[256] https://www.nextrembrandt.com/. Accessed 1 June 2022.

out the task was particularly interesting, given that the project involved the cooperation of museums, scientists, art historians and IT experts. The resulting image shows all the typical qualities and features of Rembrandt's art, but was created using a computer program and printed on a 3D printer.[257]

The initiative was a joint venture of Microsoft and ING Group.[258] The project, commissioned by ING, is one of its activities in the area of corporate social responsibility. On the other hand, judging from statements issued by the company managing the project on behalf of ING, it is also a unique marketing campaign. On the project's official website, one learns that "The Next Rembrandt" was intended to bring ING Group's modern spirit and uniqueness into the cultural sector, including art and icons of culture.[259] The involvement of Dutch universities and other institutions, that is, those from the artist's homeland, adds further dimensions to the project—those of building national identity and popularizing culture. The very fact that such institutions take an interest in such projects attests to the inevitable—and already ongoing—connection between the worlds of technology and art. Moreover, the results of that interaction in the future will add to the cultural heritage.

As when generating answers submitted for evaluation in a literary competition,[260] here the computer used data from 346 paintings of Rembrandt;[261] in the case of *Edmond de Belamy* the computer used a database of 15,000 portraits painted from the fourteenth to the twentieth centuries as uploaded by the collective.[262] For copyright, it is vital to establish whether the use of data from those resources, and the way in which they were modified and processed by a machine, resulted in an original work. In the case of the artists from Obvious who ordered their algorithm, they introduced several changes to it. The algorithm was working on the final version so long that the computer system itself was not able to distinguish the generated portrait from the one painted by the human hand.

As a result, the following question has entered the legal debate: Can something that arose by means of a computer be considered a creative work? It has been considered whether we are confronted in a certain sense with a manifestation of creativity and whether it is not "crucial to discuss an extension of the definition of a 'work' (and the protection granted thereto) in the meaning of copyright law."[263] In seeking to answer these questions, it should be emphasized that the need for in-depth research into algorithms, art and artificial intelligence is an urgent one. We must find

---

[257] The 3D printing technology also has important applications in preserving cultural heritage, by printing out missing fragments, printing out smaller copies for research purposes, or printing out copies of sculptures to make them accessible to visually impaired people so that they can familiarize themselves with the sculpture.

[258] tt (2016).

[259] https://www.nextrembrandt.com/. Accessed 1 June 2022.

[260] Hughes (2016).

[261] Dutch Digital Design (2018).

[262] Romo (2018).

[263] tt (2016).

new ways of looking at copyright that consider the products of artificial intelligence. Ontological disputes over the subjectivity of artificial intelligence[264] have practical consequences concerning the scope in which the authorship of such works can be attributed. Yet it is difficult to accept that, in its present form, AI could be the subject of a personal copyright grounded in the connection between an author and a work. In this case, it will be much easier to accept authorship and the consequences it entails in the form of the protection granted by intellectual property rights. The history of the Internet provides an example of how technology evolves rapidly and steadily makes its way into new areas of life.[265] Thus, the dynamic development of AI may lead to unexpected changes that will once again put current solutions to the test.

The discussion on the subjectivity of AI in no way prevents lawyers from classifying products appearing on the art market that were created using artificial intelligence as works.[266] Three positions concerning art co-created by AI can be identified. The first, and the most progressive, permits the acknowledgement that we are dealing with an author and a work subject to legal protection in connection with an expanded circle of potential authors that includes AI and animals. The second is based on the position that we cannot speak of a work in such instances, because the object arose without human participation. The third solution posits the legal fiction that AI operates as a purely subordinate employee or subcontracting entity.[267] In this variant, two situations can be distinguished: one where the algorithm is used by its author to print an image, and the other where the algorithm is used by a user. The user is not necessarily the same person or entity who is entitled to copyright in the resulting works. In the case of "The New Rembrandt," an enterprise in which many experts took part, the copyright holder would be ING, who commissioned the project.[268]

The primary purpose of copyright regulations is to protect the interests of the author. Currently, in the meaning of copyright law, an author can be virtually anyone, as the scope of protection has been extended over the years.[269] On the other hand, certain works of art, while unique and resulting from exceptional concepts and ideas, do not benefit from such protection. This is due to the absence of copyright protection for certain works of modern art,[270] deriving directly from Article 2^1 par. 1 CRRA, which stipulates that only means of expression are subject to protection. Protection does not apply to discoveries, ideas, procedures, methods and rules of operation, or mathematical concepts. Given the rapid developments in art, as well as art co-created or created with the participation of artificial intelligence, there is a growing need for changes to this area of law. In the ongoing discussion, a

[264] Bar (2020), pp. 35–39.

[265] Balkin (2015), p. 48.

[266] Cf. Yanisky-Ravid (2017), p. 726; Yanisky-Ravid and Velez-Hernandez (2018), pp. 50–51.

[267] Yanisky-Ravid (2017), pp. 712–714.

[268] Yanisky-Ravid (2017), pp. 712–714.

[269] Yanisky-Ravid and Velez-Hernandez (2018), p. 51.

[270] Barta and Markiewicz (2019), p. 33.

solution that is likely already functional in the art market, namely that of a natural person applying for authorship, is also mentioned.[271] Some researchers note that, in the case of AI, the problem of making a distinction in new copyright regulations between strong and weak AI is but one of many problems connected with copyright today.[272]

There is much to indicate that it will soon be necessary to reassess the current system of copyright protection, and the AI regulations appearing on the horizon further justify that need. Signals on the need to change how a work is defined can be found in numerous statements by copyright experts.[273] Ryszard Markiewicz has considered a departure from the present concentration on the creative element, pointing instead to "a result that is objectively new (rather than, up to now, subjectively new), non-obvious or significantly creative (culturally meaningful)."[274] It should be added that, in the context of the future of the cultural heritage, the attribute of the significance of a given result to culture, as well as its acceptance by a social group, is important. Shlomit Yanisky-Ravid and Luis Antonio Velez-Hernandez argue in a similar vein that leaving the originality of a work to be defined at the level of national regulations gives domestic legislators plenty of scope to adapt to technological progress.[275] Facing scientific progress head on and utilizing its achievements, Aleksandra Nowak-Gruca proposes using neuroaesthetics when evaluating the creative element, assessing how a given product acts on the minds of its audience, and then using those findings to help create new framework definitions of what constitutes a work.[276] To a large extent, this solution meets the demand to shift emphasis away from the creative entity and the process of how a work arises towards how it is accepted by the public, evaluated based on how audiences respond to it. My view is that the legal solutions planned for the future should consider the interests of the creators of programs and algorithms, the essence of self-learning algorithms, the interests of participants in the art market and, in the long term, the interests of future generations.

From the above description of the work of the collective Obvious, one can conclude that the work they put up for auction was created in connection with human activity. But that could change if we were dealing with AI as an acknowledged, autonomous being, or if the work were not subject to any intervention by the artist's group during the production process. The question of the subjectivity of artificial intelligence comes up in discussions taking place at the level of the theory

[271] Markiewicz (2018b), p. 53.

[272] Chłopecki (2018), pp. 109–112; Uliasz (2019), pp. 23–38.

[273] Markiewicz (2018b), pp. 55–57; Sokołowska (2010), pp. 4–5; Bieda and Okoń (2019), pp. 171–175.

[274] Bieda and Okoń (2019), p. 173; Markiewicz (2018b), p. 56.

[275] Yanisky-Ravid and Velez-Hernandez (2018), pp. 50–51.

[276] Nowak-Gruca (2015), p. 101.

and philosophy of law.[277] It is no secret that attributing subjectivity to AI would shorten the road to placing artificial intelligence within the compass of copyright and the law on the protection of the cultural heritage.

It may be that the result of the debate over the possibility of treating animals as creators will stimulate the search for new solutions, or even determine the direction of change. Where the application of binding law does not allow economic interests to be protected, the only way forward is to change existing legal regulations.[278] Media outlets all over the world covered the famous case of the "monkey selfies" (*Naruto v. Slater*), a dispute over whether the status of an author can be attributed to a non-human; specifically, a monkey. The case was heard under American law, although Polish academics also commented on it, pointing out that the creative contribution to the composition and the processing of a picture could cause it to be covered by copyright protection. Ryszard Markiewicz did not rule out the future possibility of animals being deemed authors within the meaning of copyright law as a result of significant changes being introduced to legal regimes and animals being granted the status of legal subjects (rather than objects).[279] In the *Naruto* case, the court's refusal to acknowledge an animal's rights as an author were criticized for creating yet another obstacle for the development of AI and the expansion of the catalogue of non-human authors. It was suggested that there is a need to adapt the law to new challenges, shifting emphasis in the search for originality in a work from the author to the work itself.[280]

In light of Polish law, a work created by AI, like a photo taken by a monkey, does not benefit from copyright protection. Nor does an image printed using a 3D printing method, or the *Edmond de Belamy* portrait put up for auction at Christie's auction house. Further, one cannot apply the capacious legal instrument which is often sought as an additional remedy—the protection of personal rights. We cannot assume that AI has any personal rights that could be violated by the use of a work. However, observing the debate on the possibility of products of AI being classified as works in the meaning of copyright law permits the conclusion that the application of the law is undergoing a certain change. Today, technological progress is being made in many areas of civilization, and this is forcing us to pay attention to the complexity of AI's place in the legal system.

Unlike conceptual art, such as Christo's famous series of wrapped objects (one of which—the Reichstag—was classified as a work under German law),[281] AI has a much broader reach. In documents pertaining to AI, it appears as a tool to achieve societal developmental goals within the EU and beyond. This is why changes in the

---

[277] During the 29th World Congress of the International Association for Philosophy of Law and Social Philosophy University of Lucerne, Switzerland 7–13 July 2019 several panels were devoted to AI.

[278] Cubert and Bone (2018), p. 425 about Naruto case.

[279] Markiewicz (2018a), pp. 36–37.

[280] Tucker Arensberg Attorneys (2018); Yanisky-Ravid and Velez-Hernandez (2018), pp. 49–50.

[281] BGH 24/1/2002 I ZR 102/99.

law brought on by technological progress involve so many areas, including civil law and criminal law, within the scope of liability for damage that may be caused by the use of AI. Reflections on AI in art and its place in the system of cultural heritage protection as an object subject to such protection comprises only a fragment of the global debate. Keeping the products of AI unprotected may seriously hinder the development of creativity in the field of artificial intelligence. If products of AI in the form of music, texts and images are deprived of protection, this will cause a slowdown in technological development in this area.

One current problem is that of classifying art created with the participation of an algorithm; another is making a legal classification of who is the "author" and "owner" of a given product. It is also important to consider the element of economic growth when considering various proposals. Solutions put forward at the theoretical level will not necessarily correspond to economic or social needs, or be feasible in practice.[282] Given the fact that self-learning algorithms are able to change themselves in a way that is independent of their creators, and then produce objects that no human was able to foresee, the question arises of what the relationship is between the algorithm and the object created.

Concerning the rights to such products, it will be difficult to defend the position that such "works" should belong to the public domain immediately upon their creation.[283] Then again, given the large number of entities participating in the creation of a work—the entity that commissioned the algorithm and established its basic principles and purpose, the programmer, the person who started up the program, the person who fed it with a specific task, and the person who provided the material for the database or the material for 3D printing—it will not be practically feasible to propose an effective model of co-authorship. Also, regarding co-authorship, one cannot speak of cooperation between the algorithm and a human being or, at this stage of technological development, the algorithm's consent to co-creation.[284] Copyright may be acquired through commissioning or ordering a work when this is accompanied by an assignment of economic copyrights. If we wish to treat an algorithm's involvement in the creative process in this way, we will have to determine which entity has the dominant position. Upon analysis, the doctrine of "work made for hire" does not seem fully suited to the needs of art created using AI.[285]

In the context of the Polish provisions concerning works made for hire, an analysis of the solutions proposed in the foreign literature shows that none of them could be introduced into Polish law without amendment. For example, the takeover of rights by an employer would require several changes. Under Article 12 CRRA,

---

[282] Chłopecki (2018), pp. 109–112.

[283] Brown (2018), p. 38; cf. Chłopecki (2018, pp. 109–112) on distinction AI produced outputs and outputs with human involvement.

[284] Cf. Brown (2018), pp. 34–35; Yanisky-Ravid (2017), pp. 691–693.

[285] Yanisky-Ravid (2017), p. 707 et seq.

> unless an act or employment contract states otherwise, an employer whose employee creates a work as a result of performing their duties under the employment relationship acquires economic copyright to the work at the moment it is created within the limits resulting from the purpose of the employment contract and the worthy intentions of the parties.

No doubt, in the case of works generated by an algorithm, there will be no worthy intention of that party and no employment agreement; however, there will exist a dependence similar to that between an employer and employee, at least within the scope of subordination and taking on the risks associated with the end product. Where a work produced by an algorithm is treated as a work made for hire, the tools for protecting the "author's" personal rights will still apply to the holder of those rights. In the literature, the view has been expressed that the solution of a "work made for hire" will not be valid in the Polish legal system because of the difference between the two systems.[286]

It is economically justifiable to introduce a model that will not hamper creativity—the ideas of those persons responsible for creating the algorithm and selecting appropriate data for the database it draws on. On the other hand, consideration must be given to how quickly the regulations dealing with artificial intelligence will develop. As to liability for artificial intelligence, proposals have been made that it should be borne by the state. In a case where the scope of activities is confined to creating a work of art, liability for the end product could be borne by the entity that commissioned and started up the algorithm. This is in partial agreement with Ryszard Markiewicz's view on "an agreement that can be rescinded or modified, commonality in fragmentary parts of an exclusive right attributed to the author of the AI program and its legal user."[287] Markiewicz proposes locating this right among related rights.[288] He raises important arguments—that it may be impossible to distinguish between products of AI and those created by a human being, and that there is a risk that the authorship of a product of artificial intelligence will be attributed to human beings.

It is certainly true that, if no rights holder can be established, creators will think twice about using artificial intelligence to produce works of art.[289] On the other hand, given the experience of creators of conceptual art, protection of an artist's rights may be exercised, for example, under Articles 23 and 24 of the Polish Civil Code in relation to the protection of personal interests. The matter considered here differs from such a situation in that we are faced with a "new" product that arose based on a data set, where the end product could not be foreseen by the entity responsible for gathering and providing the data. For example, the museums that coordinated the process of gathering Rembrandt objects for the New Rembrandt project were unable to define or determine the end result, and the same is true of the

[286] Juściński (2019), p. 40.
[287] Markiewicz (2018a), p. 86.
[288] Markiewicz (2018a), p. 86.
[289] Brown (2018), p. 38.

authors of the program. In this sense, the very idea behind the project, and the person who is the author of that idea, is of new and decisive importance.

Certain possibilities for adaptation are also provided by the Polish provisions on audiovisual works. Under Article 69 CRRA,

> the co-creators of an audio-visual work are the persons who made a creative contribution to it, particularly: the director, the cinematographer, the author of the adaptation of a literary work, the author of musical verbal-musical works created for the audio-visual work, and the author of the script.

While many people are involved in the production of an audiovisual work, their contributions differ, and the law has a supposition of the acquisition of rights by the producer under an agreement on the creation of the work or the use of an existing exclusive right to exploit those works within the new audiovisual work as a whole. In our case, then, the equivalent of the producer would be the entity whose idea is brought to fruition, which incurs the costs of the project and manages the production process. It is worth pointing out that a producer's role is a particular one. For example, in the case of art films, "there can be a situation in which, in accordance with the will of the parties, the economic copyrights remain with the creators. This is possible in the case of amateur and low-budget art film productions."[290]

Applying the above to the arts and artificial intelligence, we can try to determine who is the equivalent of a producer. Certainly, in the case of the image titled *Edmond de Belamy*, this was the collective Obvious. Even on their website, the artists refer to artificial intelligence as a source of inspiration. They "wish to demonstrate that algorithms help us complete our understanding of how we function as humans, and push us to outsmart our current level of creativity."[291] Here, there is no question of their attributing authorship to themselves or falsifying information about the work. To date, works of art created using artificial intelligence have aroused interest precisely because of that circumstance. There will always be, therefore, a group of artists who will want to "share" their authorship with artificial intelligence.

In still seeking other solutions aimed at supporting artificial intelligence, one can consider adapting the institution of *droit de suite* for the needs of art involving AI. Under the act, the right holder of a *droit de suite* is the author of the work and their legal successors. One could agree that the holder of a *droit de coopération avec l'intelligence artificielle* could be an entity managing the interests and development of artificial intelligence in the form of an arts and artificial intelligence fund. Under such a law, 5% of the price of every end product created using AI could be collected from the entity enjoying the copyright at the moment when the object is introduced to trade. Such a solution could supplement the attribution of copyright to the originator of the work because this would support the arts and artificial intelligence fund.

---

[290] Ślęzak (2012), p. 314.

[291] Obvious Art Manifesto, wish to demonstrate that algorithms help us complete our understanding of how we function as humans, and push us to outsmart our current level of creativity. http://obvious-art.com/wp-content/uploads/2020/04/MANIFESTO-V2.pdf. Accessed 1 June 2022.

To return to the relationship between AI and cultural heritage, it must be considered whether products of AI could be deemed historical objects in domestic law, or cultural property under conventions of international law. Works created using AI can fall within the Polish definition of historical objects, since they can only be created by human beings or in connection with human activity. Without doubt, such objects will possess at least one of the values specified in the definition of a historical object: artistic, historical, or scientific value. It seems that, at the time when parliamentary members were defining what a historical object is during the legislative procedure, they were not aware that the doubts they had over human participation in the creation of a historical object were to have broader significance.[292] Those doubts concerned historical parks and gardens, whose final form is not solely dependent on humans. Currently, such a structure makes it possible to protect material objects generated using AI. It does not cover, however, works of art created with the involvement of AI that exist only in digital form, which shall be discussed later. Certainly, when working on a new act on the protection of cultural heritage, even at the stage of laying down the groundwork for the future act, the phenomenon of art created based on an algorithm should be analyzed and considered.

There is less reason to be optimistic about the possibility of protecting products of AI under international conventions on the protection of movable cultural heritage. For example, in the UNESCO 1970 Convention on the Means of Prohibiting and Preventing the Illicit Import, Export and Transfer of Ownership of Cultural Property, cultural property is defined as property belonging to the categories listed in its Article 1. One of those categories is property of artistic interest.[293] The question of whether the convention applies to the portrait created in The New Rembrandt, or more precisely, whether the picture can be deemed as property having artistic interest, must certainly be answered in the negative. The image cannot be classified as "pictures, paintings and drawings produced entirely by hand on any support and in any material (excluding industrial designs and manufactured articles decorated by hand)." It could possibly be treated as "property relating to history, including the history of science and technology and military and social history, to the life of national leaders, thinkers, scientists and artists and to events of national importance" in the future, but this is hypothetical. Unfortunately, it will not fit in the category of objects of artistic interest, although critics have found declared it to have artistic value. The situation is similar when we look at the UNIDROIT Convention on

---

[292] Jagielska-Burduk (2011), p. 69.

[293] Article 1

(g) property of artistic interest, such as:

(i) pictures, paintings and drawings produced entirely by hand on any support and in any material (excluding industrial designs and manu-factured articles decorated by hand);
(ii) original works of statuary art and sculpture in any material;
(iii) original engravings, prints and lithographs;
(iv) original artistic assemblages and montages in any material.

Stolen or Illegally Exported Cultural Property of 1995, whose catalogue of cultural property, contained in an annex, employs similar solutions, or at the Nicosia Convention on Offences Relating to Cultural Property of 2017.

However, there is a very broad definition of cultural heritage in the 1972 Convention concerning the Protection of the World Cultural and Natural Heritage. Cultural heritage here includes monuments, groups of buildings, and sites. Monuments includes

> architectural works, works of monumental sculpture and painting, elements or structures of an archaeological nature, inscriptions, cave dwellings and combinations of features, which are of outstanding universal value from the point of view of history, art or science.

This definition has not yet been amended, although since the convention came into force there has been a change in approach to heritage, towards including its intangible values and means of expression.

The Global Strategy adopted in 1994 influenced how heritage is perceived, and contained an element related to scientific progress. A group of experts pointed to technological evolution as one of the elements that should be considered in the process of achieving a balance between the existing World Heritage List and the creation of a globally representative list of heritage sites.[294] It is also worth mentioning the solutions contained in the Operational Guidelines, which correspond to the essence of future cultural heritage that will arise with the participation of AI. Property that meets the criteria set out in the Operational Guidelines[295] for the Implementation of the World Heritage Convention may be inscribed on the World Heritage List. Certainly, it will be difficult to deem objects created using AI as the fruits of human genius, although they may

> exhibit an important interchange of human values, over a span of time or within a cultural area of the world, on developments in architecture or technology, monumental arts, town planning or landscape design" (criterion ii), or "be an outstanding example of a type of

---

[294] Expert Meeting on the "Global Strategy" and thematic studies for a representative World Heritage List (UNESCO Headquarters, 20–22 June 1994), WHC-94/CONF.003/INF.6. In order to redress the imbalances in the current List, some areas have been identified as having high potential to complete gaps in representation. Areas such as these should be considered in their broad anthropological context through time:

HUMAN COEXISTENCE WITH THE LAND

- Movement of peoples (nomadism, migration)
- Settlement
- Modes of subsistence
- Technological evolution

HUMAN BEINGS IN SOCIETY

- Human interaction
- Cultural coexistence
- Spirituality and creative expression.

[295] Operational Guidelines for the Implementation of the World Heritage Convention, WHC.19/01, 10 July 2019.

building, architectural or technological ensemble or landscape which illustrates (a) significant stage(s) in human history (criterion iv).

The regional system of protection may have an opportunity to deal with the problem of protection based on European Union legislation, at least partially, specifically on Directive of the European Parliament and of the Council 2014/60/EU of 15 May 2014 on the return of cultural objects unlawfully removed from the territory of a Member State and amending Regulation (EU) No. 1024/2012 (Recast). In that directive, the previous solution in the form of an annex was abandoned in favor of leaving Member States free to determine what constitutes their national treasures. In this way, the model approved by a given state will or will not grant protection to products created with the use of artificial intelligence. As provided in Article 2 of the Directive, "cultural object" means an object which is classified or defined by a Member State, before or after its unlawful removal from the territory of that Member State, as being among the "national treasures possessing artistic, historic or archaeological value" under national legislation or administrative procedures within the meaning of Article 36 TFEU." Thus, how cultural objects are defined will depend on individual Member States and their relevant legislation.

In Council Regulation (EC) No. 116/2009 of 18 December 2008 on the export of cultural goods, the phrase "cultural goods" means all objects having significance for archaeology, prehistory, history, literature, art, or science which belong to the categories listed in the table contained in an annex to the regulation and which meet the relevant minimum age threshold stipulated therein. An analysis of the annex leads to the conclusion that objects created with the aid of AI will be eligible to be classified as cultural goods in the meaning of the regulation in the future, under point 15 (b) "Any other antique items not included in categories A.1 to A.14 more than 100 years old" whose value exceeds EUR 50,000. It should be pointed out that, in the case of pictures, paintings, watercolors, gouaches and mosaics made entirely by hand, the age criterion is only half as much. In turn, Regulation (EU) 2019/880 of the European Parliament and of the Council of 17 April 2019 on the introduction and the import of cultural goods lays down, in an annex, a minimum age of more than 250 years for all categories of cultural goods. It is difficult to imagine now how the criterion of 250 years can be applied here, since the first works/works of art involving artificial intelligence arose about 60 years ago; nevertheless, it is worth being aware of the problem now.

Products of AI could not arise without technological progress, which is driven by humans. While for now the creation of Artificial Superintelligence,[296] totally independent of human input, may be confined to the realm of fiction, it will certainly force a re-evaluation of how we define the human heritage eventually. Like copyright law, the law regulating the protection of cultural heritage will need to contend with the new challenges posed by AI's encroachment. No doubt, the solutions adopted after a revision of copyright law, if such a revision occurs, will also affect the protection of cultural heritage. As to conventions, they are definitely more

[296] Bar (2020), p. 42.

difficult to change; solutions will need to be sought in the documents such as Operational Guidelines, and will rely on a change in interpretation of the same.

In the literature, voices are calling for a separation of robotic heritage as such. Dirk H. R. Spennemann analyzes the culture of robots and the products they produce, and discusses products that arise by means of algorithms. He also reflects on the future of "robot culture," pointing out that the problem is a real one, as are the problems that managers of cultural heritage will have to deal with.[297] As to regional systems, in the European Union it seems that the debate, and eventually the revision of legal acts pertaining to the protection of the culture heritage, will take place parallel to the creation of a cohesive policy for the use of AI in the cultural sector. As we move into the future, however, products of AI may be acknowledged as historical objects under the APGM where they are works of human beings and connected with human activity. Computer programs and data will also be protected. This, however, will not affect the continued existence of images or sculptures, which may successfully be admitted to trade and should be safely passed on to future generations.

Once again, in the sphere of what constitutes a "work," a confrontation arises between copyright law and ownership. Consider a material product made by or with the participation of AI. If we ask whether collectors or the public will be more interested in the object's outer form or the legal basis on which it is disposed of, surely the answer will be in favor of the outer form. Just as in certain ways a collector can be creative when putting a collection together, the case of art created using artificial intelligence is also one of certain activities being performed based on an existing source database. Whereas a collector has an open-ended base, for new objects can always be acquired, AI "works" operate according to a defined amount of data provided by humans, but those humans are not able to foresee the end result. There is also an element of estimating the risks involved in collecting such works in terms of the acquirer being able to manage them, for example, by using images of those works in marketing activities. This applies when looking for copyright solutions that consider the results of the debate.[298] That debate, it seems, should also include the place of products of AI as objects introduced on the market. This could have far-reaching consequences. For example, recognizing the authorship of AI would mean that the provisions governing the export of cultural goods laid down in Article 59 par. 1 pt. 6 and 6a APGM would need be revised, for such goods would be deemed works of living authors. The 1995 UNIDROIT Convention also refers to the author of a cultural object. The provisions of Article 7 of the convention regarding the return of illegally exported cultural objects do not apply to an object that was exported during the lifetime of the person who created it or within a period of 50 years following the death of that person. Co-authorship with AI may appear in the future application of this provision. Therefore, it is necessary to flag this issue now rather than later. With this in mind, the discussion should be a broad one, and open to a wide range of legal theorists, not only to experts in copyright law.

[297] Spennemann (2007), pp. 248, 255.

[298] Szpyt (2020), p. 171.

3.6 Contemporary Works of Art, e-Heritage, and Cultural Heritage

Another challenge for private law in the area of cultural heritage is works of modern art that incorporate new forms of expression and the presence of art in cyberspace. Since some of these works will eventually become part of widely accepted cultural heritage, it is worth taking a closer look at their place in the legal system, with particular focus on private law and potential models of protection. Art in cyberspace creates new problems concerning collections' record-keeping, securing property, and changes on the art market relating to the trade in works of an intangible nature. Recently, the attention of the media was caught by the sale at auction of a gif known as the Nyan Cat. After half an hour of bidding, the winner purchased the work using the cryptocurrency Ethereum for an amount equal to USD 561,000 (after conversion).[299] This was an interesting event for collectors because, as a non-fungible token (NFT), the gif can have its authenticity, ownership history and price verified at any time using a blockchain. To what extent this is simply a novelty, like products created by or using AI, and to what extent it represents a new area of the art market that is here to stay, will only become clear in the future.[300] Without a doubt, COVID-19 will help pique investors' interest in this segment of the market. On the other hand, what is occurring marks a kind of merger of the old and new markets, as expressed by Christie's sale of the work *Everydays: The First 5000 Days.*[301] This work by Beeple (Mike Winkelmann), a jpg collage of 5000 images, was sold for 69.4 million dollars and was the first work to have an NFT sold at auction.[302]

The history of art is characterized by continuous change and new stages in artistic activity, as attested to by the information given earlier in the introduction. While some of those stages fit within the existing framework of thinking about art and the creator of a work, there have also been significant turnarounds and sudden breakthroughs. Such a change was that brought about by Marcel Duchamp's famous "ready-made" work of art, *Fountain*, which has even been described as a revolution.[303] Another turning point is the recent use of new technologies in the creative process. And so, an important part of modern art will be new works solely available online, which is why they have been presented together.

Concerning the protection of copyright, one can say at the outset that not all works of modern art will be considered works within the meaning of the CRRA, and consequently they will not be protected, even during the period established for works. From a cultural heritage perspective, even that time-limited protection does not achieve the desired objective. What is more, in the long term, after protection

---

[299] Kinsella (2021a).

[300] Schneider (2021).

[301] Kinsella (2021b).

[302] Elliot (2021).

[303] Broeckmann (2019), p. 2.

expires, at least some of those works should be covered by the protection given to cultural heritage. Before determining the scope and basis of such protection, consideration must be given to the place such objects occupy in the private law system.

The revolution connected with a departure from creative activity in favor of conceptual art has affected the art market. In conceptual works, emphasis shifted from a work of art as the result of creativity towards the artist's creative intentions. Conceptual works were perceived essentially in terms of the artist's intentions and the idea of setting them in a new context. The quest to discover the artist's intentions now takes place with the participation of the public, critics, and curators,[304] while in many cases the creative act itself foresees public participation.

The mechanically manufactured sculptures of Jeff Koons, which are not handmade by the artist himself, show just how far the inclusion of new technologies in the creative process can change how such works are perceived as components of cultural heritage. Often, the artist would be physically incapable of completing a work due to its size or the number of parts in an art installation, or the time, materials or technique employed. For example, the works prepared in the studio of Joanna Vasconcelos in Lisbon could never be put together by one person because of their size and the materials used.[305]

To sum up, the provisions governing the protection of a work will apply only to certain objects. Ready-made works will not be subject to copyright. The idea of putting something in a new context itself is not protected by copyright. This does not automatically mean that such an object does not constitute the result of artistic activity and cannot meet with a favorable response from viewers or alternative means of protection. Ultimately, the object may be protected as a historical object. The relationship between copyright law and the regulations governing the protection of historical objects has been discussed many times, including with reference to works of fine art.[306] There are indications that the protection of the artist's right will eventually give way to the right of future generations to cultural heritage.

As to the protection of authors' personal rights, it has been suggested that "as time passes, it will endure further 'erosion' towards the protection of certain public and universal interests connected with respect for cultural achievements (heritage)."[307] Such an erosion in favor of protecting the public interest will not always be possible using the system of legal regulations for the protection of historical objects. For example, there is a provision that permits a copy of a work to be made in the event that the person in possession of the work wishes to destroy it; this appears as an element of the artist's rights and does not serve to preserve the object, but it does serve the artist (Article 32 par. 2 CRRA).[308] With the awareness that the primary purpose of the provisions of copyright law is to protect authors' rights, this area of

[304] Mazzone and Elgammal (2019), p. 1.

[305] http://joanavasconcelos.com/obras_en.aspx. Accessed 1 June 2022.

[306] Kopff (1961).

[307] Barta and Markiewicz (2005), p. 229.

[308] Cf. Jagielska-Burduk (2011), p. 69.

the law is not the place to look for a future model for the protection of works of modern art. Copyright can only play a supporting role in the use of instruments of private law to protect cultural heritage.

The innovations taking place in new works of art are automatically affecting cultural heritage even now. Furthermore, the new components of that heritage may pose a challenge in the areas of conservation, preservation and record keeping. The use of new media, video, light, and products subject to degradation certainly make the process of preserving such works more difficult. Some artists use their own body to create stagings or artistic provocations. As an example, Marina Abramowić's performance involves allowing the public, with her full consent, to inflict pain upon her body. In 2019, in her "Marina Abramowić. The Cleaner – a Retrospective Exhibition" at the Centre of Contemporary Art in Toruń, volunteers took part in her works, playing out scenes from happenings and performances the artist had done before.[309] A work by Abramowić using the technique of virtual reality (VR) was sold at Christie's in October 2020.[310] The form of the performance of the work *The Life* was not captured on film or still photographs, but can be played back by one viewer at a time using VR technology.[311] This example shows how, over the years, forms of artistic expression change due to the use of new technologies, although the artist remains at the center of the work.

Unconventional artistic creations of a temporary, ephemeral nature that go undocumented do not remain in the memory of societies. For this reason, it is important to document the creative process and its results, especially where the latter are not lasting. It is certain that changes in art will also bring about new ways of looking at cultural heritage. The very statement that only a part of available heritage will be passed on to future generations, just as we only have access to a part of what arose and was created in previous centuries, is inadequate. It is necessary to go beyond the period of copyright protection and consider what the future of "modern art" will be as our cultural heritage.

The developments taking place in art and in the elements used by artists mean that many well-known artistic creations will be difficult to classify as historical objects, and will therefore not be subject to the protection established in the APGM. Historical objects exist in material form. Under the statutory definition, a historical object is material property that constitutes a movable or immovable thing. The question arises, then, of whether the strategy for protecting cultural heritage can apply to modern art and the multitude of forms now available to artists thanks to technological progress. For example, in the case of works in the form of video installations projected on a wall, or works completely based on the projection of light or holograms, it may be difficult to decide whether to categorize a whole installation

[309] https://csw.torun.pl/wystawy-2/wystawa-marina-abramovic-czysta-the-cleaner-wystawa-retrospektywna-26519/. Accessed 1 June 2022.

[310] Brady (2020).

[311] https://www.christies.com/features/Marina-Abramovic-The-Life-10193-3.aspx. Accessed 1 June 2022.

as one thing, or its component parts separately (such as the remote control used to start up a water-light installation, VR goggles, or an application with a hologram of Marina Abramović). When an installation is composed not only of light elements, but also the steel structure connecting them, it will be easier for the entity making the classification to acknowledge that the work constitutes a historical object in the meaning of the APGM.

Yet it is worth noting the important argument that projectors and mechanical devices should be treated only as technical devices that permit a given work to be displayed publicly. A contract between an artist and a museum may include additional provisions concerning technical devices. These may provide for the artist to exchange one such device for a newer one if the old one malfunctions, or may include operating instructions if such changes are to be carried out by someone other than the artist, such as a museum curator. We can imagine a situation where projections from a disk on which an artist recorded his or her work are displayed using lasers on movable mechanical arms, but one arm becomes damaged and must be repaired.

A copy of the contents of the disk might then be made to secure the work for future generations and fulfil the museum's mission of caring for the property entrusted to it. A consequence of this is that, in practice, entries in museum records (inventories) also concern digital content. Alongside information on that content, the relevant carrier is listed (e.g., a projector). In museum inventories, however, what is checked is not the carrier, but the file containing the work. In this way, technical devices are not treated as historical objects. One can imagine a situation where a technical device entered in museum inventory records becomes completely destroyed. The device would then have to be struck off the records; in Poland, this involves a formal procedure requiring the consent of the minister responsible for culture and national heritage.

Including a technical device in the museum records is not out of the question, however, if, according to the artist's intentions, it forms part of a whole work. A device may also be decorated or painted by the artist, or have a large frame that the artist intended to cast a shadow on the wall, or serve to present only one particular work. It would then seem reasonable to enter such a technical device in the museum inventory records provided the set fits the definition of historical object. The conservator of a given museum is responsible for taking care of both material and intangible property. In accordance with best museum practice, a digital file is also recorded on another server to protect the contents of the file from being lost.

There is no material form of a work created solely in digital form and saved online. While works that exist only as electronic files can certainly constitute works (such as computer graphics), it will be difficult to locate their *corporis mechanicum*. There is no compulsion for the author of such a work to print the image in the form of a board or printout; it can be simply stored on disk or in the cloud. Further, the option of storing a work in a carrier is not always available, for example, if the artist decides that the work should exist only in the virtual cloud.

When data is stored on external servers in this way, widespread public access to the information is much easier. Yet, if we look at storing files in the cloud as an activity related to the security of cultural heritage, things get complicated. There is no doubt that some such works should eventually become subject to protection. Given the existing assumptions in respect of the protection of historical objects, and how these are defined, the legal instruments provided by the APGM will certainly be inadequate. Moreover, the definition of intangible heritage, given its rather specific character, does not cover works of modern art.

As discussed above, museums do include digital content in their records, and it also seems justifiable that, in certain situations, both digital content and technical devices can be so recorded. Yet we cannot rule out a situation in which an artist stores their works in the cloud only and sells them to collectors. In accordance with the artist's intentions, the collector in this situation would not save the files on any other server or carrier. We can also imagine that the collector, wishing to benefit from a subsidy granted by a local government unit, approaches a provincial conservator to have his virtual collection entered in the register of historical objects. This will not be possible, because the APGM only covers movable and immovable things, as well as the property set out in its Article 6 par. 2. On the other hand, consultations with the museum community have shown that, in practice, inventory departments encounter such problems frequently; furthermore, one can even speak of certain practices in this regard having arisen.[312]

For example, in the case where a collector bequeathed a collection to a museum, the institution could decide to create an additional copy of it. If, however, a living artist sold works in the cloud to a museum, but upon the condition that no copies be made, then it is probable that the museum would not consider the digital content as part of the museum's inventory and would resort to auxiliary records. The argument used to justify the above model of dealing with artworks and caring for heritage is that it is necessary to protect digital content from being damaged or destroyed in a cyberattack. And the argument is a sound one, for museum inventory records are considered the heart of protection for objects stored in a museum, and must include the most valuable objects in its possession. Further, where goods have not been donated and the museum is not the recipient, but rather the purchaser, the problem of whether the expenditure should be accounted for as a special subsidy (e.g., from an organizer for the purchase) or as a subject annual subsidy arises.

Another challenge in this age of technological progress is that of determining whether we are dealing with a work that was actually created by the artist's own hand. This circumstance has real consequences pertaining to taxation. Whether an object can be classified as a work of art under the meaning of the Value Added Tax Act (VAT Act) depends on whether the work was made entirely by the artist.[313] This

---

[312] I would like to acknowledge consultations and support offered by Ms. Anna Pruss-Świątek.

[313] Article 120(1)

(a) paintings, collages and similar decorative panels, drawings and pastels, executed entirely by the artist, excluding plans and drawings for architectural, engineering, industrial, commercial, topographical or similar purposes, hand-decorated manufactured articles, theatrical scenery, studio backdrops or the like (CN 9701) complicates the modern art scene even further. Works of art in the meaning of the VAT Act are taxed at a lower rate of 7%. It seems necessary to point out that, in the context of the creative process as practised today, the issue of whether the artist created a work entirely on his or her own seems ill-suited to reality. The expression "was made entirely" includes not only the artist's creative contribution, but also the manner of the work's execution. For example, if an artist has a work executed by a 3D printing house, the lower VAT rate will not apply. To demonstrate the inadequacy of the current provisions, it is worth citing the response of an Italian tax official when questioned by an artist.

The case concerned a sculpture printed in 3D, whose surfaces were then smoothed by the artist to give them their final form. The artist reported that he had sold 50 or 200 items of such sculptures. The Italian tax office stated that, to qualify for the lower VAT rate, a work must be an original work of monumental or sculptural art, of any subject, provided that it was made entirely by the artist.[314] Without going into the numerical restrictions in detail, the authority also stated that things not made entirely by the artist, but which involve the use of mechanical procedures, in whole or in part, do not qualify as works of art. Those procedures include 3D printing, FDM 3D modelling software, or even the outsourcing of printing to a third party. In this case, the artist's contribution was deemed only partial, essentially limited to painting the final coat on the figures or, in some cases, smoothing and cleaning the forms.[315] Even assuming that works are individual, but created using 3D printing, this will be reflected in how the delivery of such a work is taxed. It is evident that the provisions of tax law, which are amended frequently, have not been changed with regard to artistic creation. The use of new technologies and techniques should also be given appropriate consideration in the provisions of law concerning their introduction to trade. The condition of being made by the artist's own hand, although somewhat different from the requirements for a work,

(b) original engravings, prints and lithographs, executed in limited numbers, in black and white or in color, of one or more sheets, executed entirely by the artist, regardless of the process or material used, excluding all mechanical or photomechanical processes (CN 9702 00 00)
(c) original sculptures and statuary of any material, provided they were executed entirely by the artist; casts of sculpture limited to eight copies, the execution of which was supervised by the artist or his heirs (CN 9703 00 00)
(d) tapestries (CN 5805 00 00) and wall textiles (CN 6304) made by hand on the basis of original patterns supplied by the artist, provided that there are not more than eight copies,
(e) photographs taken by the artist, published by him or under his supervision, signed and numbered, limited to 30 copies, in all sizes and in all frames;

[314]""Oggettid'arte", le "opere originali dell'arte statuaria o dell'arte scultoria, di qualsiasimateria, purché siano eseguite interamente dall'artista; fusioni di sculture a tiraturalimitata ad otto esemplari, controllata dall'artista o dagli aventi diritto; a titoloeccezionale in casi determinati dagli Stati membri, per fusioni di sculture antecedent il 1° gennaio 1989, è possibile superare il limite degli otto esemplari"" (Agenzia Entrate Divisione Contribuenti, Direzione Centrale Piccole e medie imprese, Risposta n. 303. https://www.agenziaentrate.gov.it/portale/documents/20143/2665720/Risposta+all%27interpello+n.+303+del+2020.pdf/907a73a3-a850-4849-8907-4630065901b5. Accessed 1 June 2022).

[315]Including printing waste.

requires the artist's individual engagement at every stage, and has a technical dimension.

Artists are encouraged to use new means of expression by using existing, accessible online exhibition platforms allowing them to present objects in 3D and to quickly reach their audience, as well as potential buyers.[316] The next step is the acquisition of works of art in an online version, and the inevitable problem of keeping records of these collections[317] in the case of virtual collections and virtual museums. Private collections encounter fewer legal issues. Museologists, though, immediately ask whether it is possible to enter files in the inventory of museum objects. Given that such works do not possess the attribute of materiality, it seems this is not possible.

It is highly likely that what will be recorded in an inventory is the file with the location attributed to it. Taking a cautious approach to the second solution, it is certain that a museum can use another list or breakdown, not specified in the MA, consisting solely of electronic files. Under Article 21 par. 1 of the MA, museum objects are movable or immovable things that constitute the property of the museum and are entered in the inventory of museum exhibits, where these constitute national property; thus, they cannot be works that exist only virtually. This is why an organizer's duty of keeping an inventory of museum objects only concerns that category of property.

Virtual museums, on the other hand—that is, those that in the future may function as museums but whose collections exist solely in electronic form—pose a puzzle that is systemic in nature. This issue will affect the future management of museum objects, and it can be shown that electronic collections already feature in the purchasing policy of some museums. It is inevitable that the acts of law regulating the functioning of museums will need to be changed, for new forms of current and future components of the cultural heritage are constantly appearing.

At the organizational level, a museum's first encounter with the new dimension of culture "in the web," that is, with virtual culture, will be how to interpret the provisions of law concerning the opening of its first permanent exhibition. Many virtual museum websites already exist on the Internet. It is worth noting that not all of them are actual museums within the meaning of Article 1 MA.[318] Establishing a museum entails a series of obligations on the part of the organizer. Museum organizers who are not state or local government museums should consult the statute with the ministry under the procedure of Article 6 par. 6 MA.[319]

[316] https://artspaces.kunstmatrix.com/en. Accessed 1 June 2022.

[317] Gwardzińska (2020), p. 438 et seq.

[318] According to this provision, a museum is a non-profit organization whose objective is to collect and preserve the natural and cultural heritage of humanity, both tangible and intangible, to inform about the values and contents of the collections, to disseminate the fundamental values of Polish and world history, science and culture, to shape cognitive and aesthetic sensitivity and to enable the use of the collections. About virtual exhibitions: Góral (2012), pp. 89–90.

[319] According to article 6 (3) AM the day of completion of organizing a museum is the day of opening a permanent exhibition. Thus a museum moves from the status of a museum in

The need to resolve this issue legislatively will only increase as new areas of creative activity appear and develop, and as some cultural activities for the dissemination of culture, including exhibition activities, move to the Internet. At the same time, the advanced work on digitization already made on certain collection has accustomed Internet users to the possibility of accessing many images of artworks on the web. Further, the appearance of COVID-19 in 2020 forced cultural institutions and other organizations involved in cultural activities to alter and intensify their use of online activities. Alongside scientific, educational, and social activities, artistic activity has also increasingly turned towards the Internet. It seems that the online verification of objects introduced by the largest auction houses during the COVID-19 era is here to stay, although some hold that art auctions transmitted online do not create the proper atmosphere.[320] They may, however, be conducive to a democratization of the art market, and to a heightened awareness of the value of culture and art among a wider audience.

The existing laws on the protection of cultural heritage do not consider how artists actually use cyberspace, that is, of the new face of the cultural heritage. Similarly, new forms of art that involve the use of technology may also pose a challenge concerning the protection of cultural heritage and whether such works can be classified as works of art. It seems that it will be necessary to draft amendments to both the MA and the APGM to accommodate this situation. One possible solution would be to apply a level protection similar to that granted in the APGM, for instance to names of buildings, as discussed above in Sect. 2.4.1. Such objects also do not meet the definition of a historical object, but can nonetheless be entered in the register. Such a solution could serve as a kind of bridge between the existing system of heritage protection and its new dimension.

In view of the findings presented above, where the new problem is faced in practice before it reaches the attention of the legislator, it is advisable to examine museum practice and listen to what the museum community is saying to introduce a solution that meets the expectations of those involved in protecting heritage in specialized institutions. Under Article 11 APGM, a historical object entered in an inventory of museum objects cannot be entered in the register of historical objects. The practice, then, of entering digital- objects in an inventory is mainly of a symbolic nature and is useful from the museums organizational perspective but has no connection with the protection in APGM.

We must not forget that under Article 21 MA, "museum objects are movable or immovable things that constitute the property of the museum and are entered in the inventory of museum exhibits." As a result, there is a clear need to regulate this phenomenon at the normative level. It is worth pointing out that an indirect solution

---

organization to a functioning museum. It seems that in this case the interpretation of the provisions may be adjusted to the challenges of modern times, and the opening of a permanent exhibition will be regarded as making the objects permanently available on the Internet. In the absence of a legal definition of an exhibition, it is possible to accept the view that the moment access to files is granted is the moment when a permanent exhibition is opened.

[320] Reyburn (2020).

would be to create a separate list of multimedia works. To my knowledge, this solution has been used in the case of interviews with witnesses to historical events recorded for exhibition purposes. Such interviews are entered on a list identified as a multimedia inventory, and for security, copies of the files are prepared and located on an independent server. Additionally, transcripts of the interviews are prepared; these provide additional security and are important for making the contents available for academic purposes.

Another solution might be to prepare an additional section of an inventory for components of cultural heritage that exist solely in digital form. First, it must be determined whether the forms of protection that exist in the APGM, and presumably the register of historical objects, could be of use. Intuitively, it would seem that the institution of the register of historical objects is a closer solution, and therefore more appropriate for maintaining records and combining entry in the register with an enhanced regime of protection. It would also be necessary to determine what instruments of protection could apply, and for this purpose assemble the protection foreseen for movable historical objects.

Certainly, the mobility of digital heritage will require a different approach. In the case of a permanent export, or export for an exhibition that includes technical devices, the provisions on exports will apply. One can also imagine access to the cloud, where works from several museums around the world are located and people visiting those institutions can view the files at the same time. In this situation, the problem of mobility does not arise. Nevertheless, the keeper of a given work should continue to exercise care over it. In this context, an issue arises that museums have partially resolved in practice: that of making multiple copies of a file and storing them on different servers. Even if this is contrary to what an artist wishes when they are alive, if after their death their works become classified as items subject to protection, there will be a shift towards securing their works for future generations. That security may involve creating backup copies or replacing outdated technical devices. A further element of the protection regime would be a system of permits covering conservation work, changes in purpose or other activities that could threaten the virtual substance of a work.

Components of digital heritage may also be granted temporary protection, to be commenced when news is received of a decision to delete files. There is little sense in waiting until the idea of deleting files reaches a point similar to that of the case of the well-known collector who planned to have himself cremated along with his favorite paintings.[321] This is why the above outline of the means of protection available under the register of historical objects and the APGM may provide a useful point of reference for developing an effective protection regime for digital works.

In the effort to create a market in cyberspace, it may be helpful to look at the existing case law concerning the rental of eBooks.[322] This can be a starting point for

[321] Sax (2001), p. 7.

[322] The term “copy” of a work also refers to its intangible form (if the work has been reproduced and made available to the public in that form): A “copy” of a work within the meaning of this provision

considering what constitutes the essence of online galleries and art that exists only digitally. Like Jeff Koons, perhaps artists working in cyberspace will begin gaining success by offering a limited number of copies of their works. The issue of provenance then comes up, of some kind of certification of a work by which its importance increases and which must be provided on every occasion where the work is subject to a transaction or changes hands.

Nonetheless, within the scope of the challenges presented by blockchain technology, two important observations should be made. First, for the time being, purchasers will be collectors and private investors. If access to this technology remains only partial for most people, there will be no democratization of the market or universal access. The new model, however, does allow for profits to be shared with entities engaged in the process of creating and promoting works of culture. At present, such transactions are recorded only digitally. This shows that, just as when the first museums and art collections were created in the form of trusts, private entities were the pioneers. A similar process may also be taking place in the case of NFT works, otherwise known as CryptoArt. Close observation of market players will make it possible to identify best practices related to both protection and trade. Already, doubts are being raised in the media as to what will happen if a work admitted to trade is incorrectly attributed to another artist—for example deliberately – and how it will be possible to verify a work.[323] Another problem is that of dispute resolution, since such cases will concern another type of property containing an artistic or cultural element. And in respect of the protection of the cultural heritage, the issues of record keeping and storage come up. In this regard, at the present time such property falls through the cracks of the laws governing cultural heritage. At the same time, these issues are both a challenge and an opportunity for museums, which could sell digital single versions of individual works or series of works in their possession assigned to a blockchain to fund their activities and continue their mission of safeguarding cultural heritage for future generations.[324]

---

is to be understood as any result of the reproduction of the work in the sense referred to in e.g. 6(1)(1) of the copyright law. Thus, the term covers not only material (physical) copies of a work, but also copies made available to the public in electronic form (e.g. via a computer network). This presumption therefore also applies to electronic copies of a work on which the author's name is displayed (Judgment of the Court of Appeal in Łódź of 5 January 2017, I Aca 830/16).

[323] Schneider (2021).

[324] Ciecko (2021).

3.7 Detailed Regulation of the Protection of Cultural Heritage Based on the Example of the Heritage of Fryderyk Chopin

An unusual example of a "fragmentary" regulation of cultural heritage is the normative protection given to the heritage of Fryderyk Chopin.[325] That heritage is treated as a component part of Poland's national heritage.[326] The related legislation is also a unique formula for protecting an artist's legacy in both its material and intangible forms. In an artificial manner, the legislator created a protection regime, identified the property over which protection was to be exercised, and organized a form of guardianship. The protection of property associated with the person and creative achievements of Fryderyk Chopin demonstrates a combination of legislative solutions drawn from intellectual property law, industrial property law, and the laws on the protection of the cultural heritage. The Act on the Protection of the Heritage of Fryderyk Chopin (Chopin Act) does not create new protective mechanisms, but rather creates the possibility to apply existing ones within the scope necessary to achieve the act's main purpose. It covers the works of Fryderyk Chopin, objects connected with him, as well as his name and likeness. The Chopin Act serves as an example of certain opportunities and benefits, but also threats, that may arise when similar laws are adopted in other countries.

The drafting[327] and adoption of the Act of 3 February 2001 on the Protection of the Heritage of Fryderyk Chopin[328] coincided with important anniversaries, namely 1999, the 150th anniversary of Chopin's death, and 2000, the 190th anniversary of his birth. It is worth noting that the Council of Ministers criticized the first draft of the act, including because it provided for funds to be administered annually to the Fryderyk Chopin Society, which is not a public finances sector entity.[329] Another important thing was also pointed out, namely, the commercial value of the heritage of Fryderyk Chopin, including the profits earned by the Fryderyk Chopin Society. It was argued that "the problem of State obligations [obligations relating to guardianship over the composer's heritage – author] and commercial activity requires precise

[325] Kowalski (2004), p. 120.

[326] Zeidler (2004), p. 349.

[327] The parliamentary draft of the act on the protection of Chopin's heritage, Print 1414. Warsaw, 7 May 1999. https://orka.sejm.gov.pl/Rejestrd.nsf/wgdruku/1414/$file/1414.pdf. Accessed 1 June 2022.

[328] Act of 3 February 2001 on the Protection of the Heritage of Fryderyk Chopin. Polish Official Journal (Dz. U.) 2001, No. 16, item 168, as amended.

[329] The opinion of the Polish Government on the parliamentary draft of the act on the protection of Chopin's heritage (Prints no. 1414 i 1414-A), sygn. DSPR-140-138 (2)99 to Prints no. 1414 i 1414a. Warsaw, 23 November 1999. http://orka.sejm.gov.pl/Rejestrd.nsf/8af70e7fca8ea6b3c125658e0038e26c/03bd190888520309c12568340047d4c5/file/1414-1414-A-x.pdf. Accessed 1 June 2022.

regulation."[330] Ultimately, the Chopin Act established a state cultural institution, the Narodowy Instytut Fryderyka Chopina (the Chopin Institute) (Article 4 of the Chopin Act), where the duties of the institute include protecting values associated with Fryderyk Chopin.[331]

The Chopin Act combines two independent models of protection: material and intangible property. Here we must note Article 1 par. 2 of the draft act, pursuant to which "all objects and items associated with Fryderyk Chopin constitute the inalienable property of the Polish Nation, covered by a total prohibition on their being taken outside of the borders of Poland." This was an extraordinary solution, since it covers only certain material objects connected with the composer, and introduced a restriction on their trade. This provision did not make it through to the final version of the law; nevertheless, its appearance in the draft is evidence of an attempt to treat selected property—the legacy of a famous person—in a highly unusual way, with reference to the concept of *res extra commercium*. For the criterion was not the keeper as subject (museum), but tangible property ("objects and items") whose value is assessed according to its association with Fryderyk Chopin. The problem of establishing that connection will be addressed below during the discussion of the management of the Chopin Institute's collection.

The act grants the Minister of Culture and National Heritage a special position as a kind of "guardian" of Chopin's heritage. It also provides for the minister's

---

[330]The opinion of the Polish Government on the parliamentary draft of the act on the protection of Chopin's heritage (Prints no. 1414 i 1414-A), sygn. DSPR-140-138 (2)99 to Prints no. 1414 i 1414a. Warsaw, 23 November 1999. http://orka.sejm.gov.pl/Rejestrd.nsf/8af70e7fca8ea6b3c125658e0038e26c/03bd190888520309c12568340047d4c5/file/1414-1414-A-x.pdf. Accessed 1 June 2022.

[331]Article 3

(1) to cultivate knowledge and memory of him,
(2) conducting research and collaborating in the development of knowledge of the works and person of Fryderyk Chopin
(3) popularising his works, in particular by:
    (a) undertaking or co-financing the release of recordings, scores and other publications,
    (b) organising or co-financing concerts
    (c) taking up or providing financial support for competitions or other initiatives aimed at presenting works and popularising knowledge of Fryderyk Chopin,
    (d) co-participating in the promotion and development of the performance of Fryderyk Chopin's works in Poland and abroad,
(4) to acquire, collect, preserve and make available objects and places connected with his life and works
(5) protection of the personal rights mentioned in Article 1(1) and action aimed at preserving the integrity of the creative work of Fryderyk Chopin

The opinion of the Polish Government on the parliamentary draft of the act on the protection of Chopin's heritage (Prints no. 1414 i 1414-A), sygn. DSPR-140-138 (2)99 to Prints no. 1414 i 1414a. Warsaw, 23 November 1999. http://orka.sejm.gov.pl/Rejestrd.nsf/8af70e7fca8ea6b3c125658e0038e26c/03bd190888520309c12568340047d4c5/$file/1414-1414-A-x.pdf. Accessed 1 June 2022.

procedural entitlement to pursue the protection of property (the composer's name and likeness) where these are used in a prejudicial manner. All amounts awarded as a result of any infringements are transferred to the Chopin Institute. The minister may entrust the above tasks to be carried out by the Institute.

In the context of the protection of cultural heritage, what is striking is the connection of the regulation of Fryderyk Chopin's personal rights as part of the national heritage, and the creation of separate solutions to protect them. Under Article 83 CRRA, claims concerning a person's likeness cannot be pursued after the lapse of 20 years following the person's death. The Chopin Act excludes that provision from being applied to Fryderyk Chopin, and is the only such case concerning a historical person. It is also worthy of note that no such solution is widely applied in other legal systems.[332] The Chopin Act also refers to trademarks, including the use of Fryderyk Chopin's likeness and signature. Under Article 10 par. 2,

> With reference to the registered trademarks using the name or likeness of Fryderyk Chopin, the Law shall come into force after the lapse of 6 months of the date of its promulgation and shall refer also to the trademarks used on its effective date.

Currently, the Chopin Institute has two EU Fryderyk Chopin trademarks registered in a total of 43 classes of goods or services, and almost certainly intends to extend their validity.[333]

The Chopin Institute manages the use of Fryderyk Chopin's likeness in various commercial endeavors (chocolates, watches, pens). The rules for using that likeness are contained in a regulation issued by the director of the institute on the protection of the name and likeness of Fryderyk Chopin.[334] Under par. 3 of that regulation, a license must be concluded with the institute to use "the Chopin mark within the scope that it constitutes a registered or submitted trademark of the Institute." The consulting body in such cases is the Council for the Protection of the Name and Likeness of Fryderyk Chopin, although final decisions on granting licenses are taken by the director of the institute. In discussions on the activities of the Chopin Institute, its having been granted the right to manage Chopin's heritage, particularly the right to grant licenses and the absence of an appeal procedure, has been questioned.[335]

The Chopin Institute is also involved in protecting the memory of Chopin, his birthplace in Żelazowa Wola, and numerous academic and knowledge disseminating projects. Under Clause 8 of its statute, "within the organisational structure of the

[332] No such restrictions appear in case of Amadesu Mozart image Rzążewska (2017), pp. 74–75.

[333] Two classes remain registered with another entity and concern alcoholic beverages. The word and figurative trademark in class 33 is registered by Podlaska Wytwórnia Wódek "Polmos" S.A. On the subject of the "Chopin" trademark, the Supreme Audit Office, Department for Economy, Treasury and Privatisation, Information on results of privatisation control of enterprises operating in the spirit industry, P/04/055 KGP/41016/04 no. 163/2005/P04055/KGP, pp. 52–53.

[334] Regulation issued by the director of the institute on the protection of the name and likeness of Fryderyk Chopin 5/2014 from 27 May 2004.

[335] Sewerynik (2017).

Institute, the Chopin Museum and a library operate."[336] In Clause 15 par. 3 of the statute, the status of the collection is emphasized: "The Institute cannot sell or pledge museum or library objects connected with Fryderyk Chopin, or interests in real estate." If, however, the auxiliary provisions of the Museum Act are applied to the Chopin Museum as an element of the organizational structure of the Institute, then the issue of deaccession of museum objects is regulated by Article 23 MA.[337] This means that certain property cannot be sold or pledged, which is a very far-reaching limitation. Interestingly, that limitation does not apply to objects (movable or immovable) other than those associated with Fryderyk Chopin.

In such cases, then, the provisions on the management of property by a cultural institute and on the disposal of fixed assets apply (Article 27 of the Act on the Organisation and Conduct of Cultural Activity[338] (AOCCA). It is difficult to find a model way of determining what "connected with Fryderyk Chopin" means in respect of material property. Does it mean property with which Chopin had direct contact, or does it also include his family/friends/collaborators? It may be that objects created during the composer's lifetime will also be added to this category, although it seems likely that a separate evaluation will be made in each case when deciding whether to sell or pledge a given exhibit. The best solution would be for the Chopin Institute to publish a document on the method it uses to determine whether an object "is connected" with Fryderyk Chopin. Here, it might be helpful to apply a uniform test. This could be the kind of test used when determining whether the export of an object will cause damage in the national cultural heritage[339] and whether a given object is particularly valuable to the cultural heritage (Article 52 APGM). If such a circumstance is confirmed, "the minister responsible for cultural affairs and the protection of the national heritage may refuse to issue a one-off permit for the permanent export." It seems that the year 2022, over 20 years of the existence of the Chopin Institute, is a good moment to undertake such a project, or at least to revise the existing model of operation.

---

[336] Order of the Minister of Culture and National Heritage of 16 February 2017 on granting the statute to the Fryderyk Chopin National Institute. Annex to the Order of the Minister of Culture and National Heritage of 16 February 2017. Official Journal of the Minister of Culture and National Heritage of 16 February 2017, item 6.

[337] Article 23 AM

(1) State and local government museums may swap, sell or donate museum collections after obtaining permission from the minister responsible for culture and national heritage protection. Permission for the swap, sale or donation of museum collections may be granted only in justified cases. The funds obtained from the sale of museum collections may be used only to supplement the collections of the museum.
(2) The minister in charge of culture and national heritage protection, after consultation with the Museum Affairs Council, may grant permission for the swap, sale or donation of museum collections upon the request of the museum director after consultation with the Museum Council.

[338] Act of 15 October 1991 on Organising and Conducting Cultural Activities, consolidated text. Polish Official Journal (Dz. U.) 2020, item 194.

[339] Szafrański and Jagielska-Burduk (2019), pp. 69–96.

The collection of the Chopin Institute may be added to through purchases or donations. In the years 2015–2020, the institute acquired a total of 150 objects constituting material property (defined as "memorabilia or property connected with the life of Fryderyk Chopin or persons close to him"), 39 of which were donations. Of those 150 items, 41 were manuscripts, and 56 objects listed in the category of painting and graphics.[340] Without examining the value of the acquisitions, it is worth noting that 26% of them came in as donations. Their number would seem to indicate that, given the specific policy and focus on the person of Fryderyk Chopin, the institute tends to be chosen as the first potential recipient of donations.

It is worth adding that, in 1999, exhibits resulting from the composer's creative activity, manuscripts located in the collections of the National Library and the Chopin Society (currently located at the Chopin Institute) were entered in the UNESCO "Memory of the World" International Register. As part of protecting memory, the institute is expanding its collection and holds exhibits from the Chopin Society in Warsaw in deposit. Those exhibited were transferred to the Chopin Institute based on an agreement concluded in 2005, in a clear shift of the entity managing Chopin's legacy—from a non-governmental organization to a new state cultural institution.[341]

In the literature, a detailed analysis of the Chopin Act has been made in terms of the protection of the personal rights of Fryderyk Chopin.[342] The act constitutes a radical departure from the previous legal protection concerning reverence for the dead and their personal rights. Further, its scope encompasses the protection of both the personal rights and the heritage of Fryderyk Chopin.[343] It has been pointed out that the act created a subjective right previously unknown, in that it introduced protection of the likeness and name of Chopin that is unlimited in time.[344] Jacek Mazurkiewicz takes a somewhat different view, that the protection is of an institutional character, "which does not make it impossible at all to protect them [Chopin property – author] based on the concept of subjective rights."[345] What is more, doubts have been raised over the Chopin Institute having a monopoly on the likeness of Chopin, where "this solution is difficult to fit within the tradition of Polish civil law."[346] Tomasz Grzeszczak states explicitly that

[340] Information obtained because of request for access to public information. The author would like to thank the Fryderyk Chopin Museum and the Fryderyk Chopin Institute for providing the information.

[341] An example of a shift could be an acquisition of the Czartoryski collection previously managed by the XX Czartoryski Foundation, by the State Treasury.

[342] Mazurkiewicz (2010), pp. 718–775.

[343] Mazurkiewicz (2010), p. 727.

[344] Barta and Markiewicz (2005), p. 638.

[345] Mazurkiewicz (2010), p. 725.

[346] Grzeszak (2007), pp. 568–569.

> this purpose would definitely be better achieved through the use of solutions that are purely administrative and legal, where the Ministry of Culture and National Heritage would protect the public interest, not the personal rights of Fryderyk Chopin.[347]

In other words, the goal set in the Chopin Act could be achieved by using administrative (public) law. In such a situation, however, it would be more difficult to justify the Chopin Institute's exclusive right to register trademarks. And again, a debate ensues on the extent to which private law methods are able to ensure protection mechanisms and the extent to which they should be replaced by public law norms. It seems, though, that the Chopin Act is a perfect example of a hybrid regulation, where elements of private law—such as granting licenses—intertwine with elements of public law, namely a cultural institution and its scope of activity.

While on the subject of the care given to the heritage of Fryderyk Chopin, it is worth mentioning the Year of Chopin in 2011 and the publication of the comic book *Chopin New Romantic*, which was to be used to promote Polish culture abroad. The publication, which consisted of several stories relating to Chopin, was financed out of funds from the Ministry of Foreign Affairs and the Polish embassy in Berlin. In the story, written by Krzysztof Ostrowski, the character of a musician who looks like Chopin appears, and uses vulgar language. The comic book caught the eye of the media[348] and politicians,[349] and sparked a debate over freedom of artistic expression. The idea of destroying all the copies of the publication set off a protest in social media,[350] and eventually the ministry gave up on that idea. Instead, changes were made: the state emblem and information on who commissioned the book were removed by the publisher, Kultura Gniewu [Anger Culture].[351] During the controversy over the book, a number of issues were raised concerning which embassy employee was responsible for the fiasco, who the publisher was, and the limits of artistic license. No reference was made, however, to the Chopin Act, already in force for 10 years, or to the scope of protection it created.

This, of course, does not rule out the possibility of the Chopin Act being used in the future as a model for similar legislation concerning particularly important elements of cultural heritage. The scope of the act already in force suggests that, in the future, further acts could be adopted concerning people or events of profound historical importance to the nation. Although the procedure has been criticized as a conspicuous intervention in the laws governing copyright and the protection of personal rights, the Chopin Act does prove that the protection granted to property classified as part of the cultural heritage can also encompass other types of property

[347] Grzeszak (2007), p. 834.

[348] MJ/PAP (2011).

[349] Request no 21650 VI to the Minister of Foreign Affairs on the financing by the Ministry of Foreign Affairs of the anthology of the Polish comic book "Chopin New Romantic." http://orka2.sejm.gov.pl/IZ6.nsf/main/7E88AF3E. Accessed 1 June 2022.

[350] Ochronić nakład "Chopin New Romantic." https://www.facebook.com/OchronicNakladChopinNewRomantic/. Accessed 1 June 2022.

[351] MJ/PAP (2011).

that are not protected in the current legal system or are no longer protected due to the passage of time. Furthermore, the adoption of the Chopin Act shows that specific protective solutions can be imposed at the national level, including those concerning cultural heritage.

Unfortunately, the creation of a new cultural institution for each case entails additional financial costs. It is possible that such duties could be carried out by a single specialized organization. For example, separating tasks has proved effective to some extent in the case of shared service centers used by local governments to cut operational costs (services are responsible of finance, human resources, IT services of several institutions). As to introducing such acts to the legal system in the future and connecting them at least on the general level with the APGM or a heritage code, one could consider establishing a specialized institution to act as a cultural institution, or creating a separate unit within the National Institute of Museology and the Protection of Collections or the National Institute of Cultural Heritage that would be responsible for agreements with external entities.

3.8 Conclusions

With regard to the challenges concerning private law and the protection of the cultural heritage, two situations can be distinguished. The first entails a practical problem, already known for a long time, that has been caused by developments in civilization and legal culture and is forcing a search for new legal solutions. This is reflected perfectly by human remains being perceived as part of cultural heritage and the demands being made that those who possess them should return them to their place of origin. The second situation concerns technological progress, that is, the use of new technologies in the creation of new works and in exploring new spaces (including outer space). This entails an automatic expansion of the components of cultural heritage (digital heritage, CryptoArt). In this way, either such property is classified within the system as we know it, or a new legal regime must be created.

In view of those two situations, they both require an action to be taken, with the difference that in the last case it is possible to create or co-create solutions because the process is ongoing. Nevertheless, it is important for legislators and participants in the cultural sector to remain vigilant and jointly diagnose potential problems to propose new solutions in a timely manner. One example connecting the past with the challenges of the future is the status of the space heritage and the need to distinguish various types of these internally distinct resources and where they are to be protected (in situ in outer space, in museums?). On the one hand, there is the old problem of meteorites; on the other, the increasing presence of human beings in space and the appearance of private entities—confined, for the moment, to taking part in space programs.

The division into tangible and intangible heritage does not exhaust the multiple forms that cultural heritage can have. In my opinion, works of art that exist only in electronic or digital form stand apart from that division. Nor can the civil law

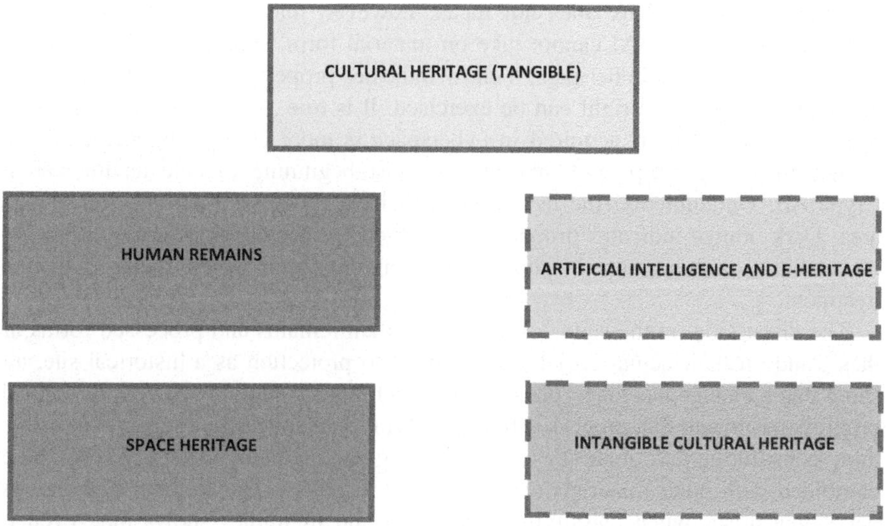

Fig. 3.1 Cultural heritage in private law

distinction between movables and immovables be directly applied to cultural heritage, since some of its components are material, but others are not. A more far-reaching conclusion can be drawn, that such a division cannot be maintained either when defining a historical object or cultural property. One cannot help noticing that certain solutions already applied, and others that are appearing, do not fit in with the civil law tradition, as is evident from the challenges they pose.

As shown above, certain elements of cultural heritage (human remains, space heritage, art created using AI, e-heritage, CryptoArt) are bursting through the legal framework, but still have not caught the undivided attention of decision-makers or the interest of the Polish legislator. They are also at odds with legal regulations concerning things and copyright, which up to now have provided important protection during the period when an author's intellectual property rights can be enforced. The situation is identical to the use of industrial property rights to protect elements of the intangible cultural heritage, which has been under discussion for years.

The diagram shows the segmentation of the subjects of private law regulation in the area of cultural heritage (see Fig. 3.1). To date, the basic model has been ownership of material cultural heritage. It can be decided to exclude part of that heritage from trade, as in the example of public collections in France. This, though, does not alter the need to search for new solutions and adapt to the new challenges posed by the heritagization of new types of property.

The position of (tangible) cultural heritage in the middle of the diagram is intended to show that here we are dealing with material property which, in the case of heritage, sets out the basic model in a certain sense. The broken line next to intangible heritage, artificial intelligence and e-heritage refers to the partly "intangible" dimension of these areas; how they are created or preserved endows them with a particular character. This does not mean, however, that components of cultural heritage created using AI cannot take on material form, similar to some forms of expression of intangible heritage. Yellow indicates property over which ownership or some other absolute right can be exercised. It is true, however, that it has been recently argued that art acquired in cyberspace is more closely connected with a licence than ownership, and investors are just beginning to take an interest in CryptoArt. Undoubtedly, the next stage will be a further normativization of this area. Dark orange indicates property over which we can speak of control, but not ownership (space heritage in situ, human remains), and which require separate treatment.

The discussion on the status of corpses, human remains and processed forms of these, and on their actual burial place subject to protection as a historical site, all show that a change has taken place in how such objects are viewed. Technological progress has meant that processed human remains can appear as a separate movable thing constituting part of another movable thing (e.g., a diamond set in a ring) or be combined with other materials (e.g., a record of music). The element of religious belief that arises when classifying sarcophagi and mummies shows that, even if representatives of science consider the human body to be a thing after death, the conduct permissible with regard to remains, bodies and organs should be regulated based on special rules, including that of museums keeping records and protecting such property based on the laws on the protection of cultural heritage.

Interest in space heritage was first shown by heritage researchers and archaeologists, and only later, after a partial "reconnaissance" of what was at stake had been made, was the subject taken up in legal debates. The legal status of meteorites should be regulated based on special domestic provisions; a general application of the institution of the acquisition of title to ownerless property does not consider the public interest, given the importance of such items for space research and scientific progress. This does not mean that there should be no trade in meteorites, but that the legislator should have the right to record objects found in the country, and to determine which will become the property of the State Treasury. The legal status of components of space heritage located outside Earth's orbit remains undetermined, although it cannot be ruled out that at some point states will return to this subject at the level of an international agreement. In the meantime, it is vital and urgent to include Polish researchers of the law on the protection of cultural heritage in the activities carried out by the Manfred Lachs Polish Centre for Space Law. A similar verification should be made in the legal systems of other states.

Cultural heritage is protected under different legal systems at the national and international levels. The international discussion concerns the place of and right to intangible heritage, while the discourse over the significance of the division into *res corporales* and *res incorporales* in modern legal systems seeks a law that could be effective *erga omnes*. The lengthy work on conventions for protecting traditional knowledge and traditional forms of cultural expression confirms the complexity and complications of the process. Adopting a solution must be preceded by the establishment of a single model that corresponds with different domestic legal systems. The search for a national variant could begin with a project concerning one part of the intangible heritage that has already been documented and within whose framework a discussion could begin on a potential legal model. Once again, as in the case of intellectual property, the issue arises of how to create an effective right to components of the cultural heritage that would be an absolute right.

The importance of artificial intelligence is perceived mainly in terms of future progress. This is resulting in attempts to create legal constructs connected with the rights to a product, while also placing this in the conceptual framework known, for example, from international instruments for protecting cultural property. An additional problem is that of the period of protection; in the case of works or industrial property, that period is limited, which is completely contrary to the idea of the protection of cultural heritage. That cultural heritage is expanding is also a result of technological process. As shown above, the issue of culture and art, although discussed little in strategic documents, constitutes an important part of the global debate on the limits and role of artificial intelligence. Art created using an algorithm is already forcing its way into the discussion at the level of the legal protection of the cultural heritage. By adapting a solution applied to audiovisual works and by creating a certain legal fiction, it may be possible to protect authors' copyright over works now, before more specific legal solutions from the area of the legal protection of cultural heritage are introduced. The models being proposed for determining who the copyright holder is, modifying the institution of *droit de suite* to *a droit de coopération avec l'intelligence artificielle*, and creating a fund for art and artificial intelligence may constitute just one of many voices heard in a debate which should catch legislators' attention very soon.

Modern art poses challenges concerning cultural heritage in terms of its status in private law and its protection in public law. Future digital heritage is not considered in the MA or APGM. Digital files containing virtual works can be secured by being copied, yet because a carrier does not fit the typical definition of a museum exhibit, it cannot be officially entered in museum records. Nor is it possible in light of the APGM to apply a form of protection designated for historical objects to such property. Even the copyright protection enjoyed by some works of modern art does not achieve the purpose of securing heritage for future generations. The digital content of some works of art, cloud computing and bio art all necessitate a thorough review of the system for the legal protection of the cultural heritage, while methods and principles of conservation should be worked out at the same time. Perhaps this problem should be addressed internationally, as part of the museum standards developed, for example, by ICOM in cooperation with UNESCO.

One attempt to go beyond the protection of cultural heritage that encompasses heritage as a broadly understood concept, and the legacy of a natural person, is the Chopin Act. Within the scope of the legacy of people whose destiny, history and achievements are crucial to national identity, this is an acceptable solution. It must not be abused, however, and should be implemented only by way of exception. An analysis of the Chopin Act and the experience of the functioning of the Chopin Institute would seem to allow for the creation of similar acts governing the heritage of other persons. The Chopin Act contains an unusual mechanism for disposing of the heritage of Chopin. Without assessing any specific solutions, it should be noted once again that, in that act, the taken legal solution went against the regime of copyright due to a public interest. The Chopin Act can be seen as a hybrid piece of legislation that combines various elements from industrial property law, copyright, the commercial use of a name, and the likeness of the composer. This hybrid nature also arises in its combination of elements of private and public law, and constitutes one of many solutions that could be used in the future.

References

Audry S, Ippolito J (2019) Can artificial intelligence make art without artists? Ask the viewer. Arts 8(1),35:1–8. https://doi.org/10.3390/arts8010035

Balkin JB (2015) The path of robotics law. California Law Rev Circ 6:45–60

Baniukiewicz E (1994) Pojęcie cmentarza. Działania konserwatorskie. In: Michałowski A (ed) Ochrona cmentarzy zabytkowych: materiały szkoleniowe pracowników Państwowej Służby Ochrony Zabytków oraz materiały z konferencji Organizacja Lapidariów Cmentarnych, Żagań – Kożuchów, 20–23 czerwca 1993. Ośrodek Ochrony Zabytkowego Krajobrazu Narodowa Instytucja Kultury, Warszawa

Bar G (2020) Robot personhood czyli po co nam antropocentryczna sztuczna inteligencja. In: Lai L, Świerczyński M (eds) Prawo sztucznej inteligencji. C.H. Beck, Warszawa, pp 29–44

Barta J, Markiewicz R (2005). In: Barta J, Czajkowska-Dąbrowska M, Ćwiąkalski Z, Markiewicz R, Traple E., Prawo autorskie i prawa pokrewne. Komentarz, 4th edn. Wolters Kluwer, Kraków

Barta J, Markiewicz R (2019) Prawo autorskie i prawa pokrewne. Przepisy z wprowadzeniem. Wolters Kluwer, Warszawa

Bednarek M (1997) Mienie. Komentarz do art. 44–55 Kodeksu cywilnego. Zakamycze, Kraków

Bieczyński MM (2011) Prawne granice wolności twórczości artystycznej w zakresie sztuk wizualnych. Wolter Kluwer Polska, Warszawa

Bieda R, Okoń Z (2019) Prawo własności intelektualnej. In: Założenia do strategii AI w Polsce. Plan działań Ministerstwa Cyfryzacji. Warszawa 9 listopada 2018, pp 173–179. https://www.gov.pl/documents/31305/436699/Za%C5%82o%C5%BCenia_do_strategii_AI_w_Polsce_-_raport.pdf. Accessed 1 June 2022

Blake J (2015) International cultural heritage law. Oxford Scholarship, Oxford. https://doi.org/10.1093/acprof:oso/9780198723516.001.0001

Blake J (2017) From traditional culture and folklore to intangible cultural heritage: evolution of a treaty. SAACLR 2(3):41–60. https://doi.org/10.4467/2450050XSNR.17.021.8422

Brady A (2020, 23 Oct) The Royal Opera House's David Hockney painting sells for £12.8m at Christie's amid deaccessioning debate. The Art Newspaper. https://www.theartnewspaper.com/2020/10/23/the-royal-opera-houses-david-hockney-painting-sells-for-pound128m-at-christies-amid-deaccessioning-debate. Accessed 1 June 2022

Broeckmann A (2019) The machine as artist as myth. Arts 8(1), 25, 1–10. https://doi.org/10.3390/arts8010025

Brown MF, Bruchac M (2006) NAGPRA from the middle distance. Legal puzzles and unintended consequences. In: Merryman JH (ed) Imperialism, art and restitution. University of Cambridge Press, Cambridge, pp 193–217

Brown NI (2018) Artificial authors: a case for copyright in computer-generated works. Columbia Sci Technol Law Rev 20(1):1–41

Brzezińska AW (2013) Reifikacja dziedzictwa kulturowego w świetle Konwencji UNESCO z 2003. Nauka 1:109–128

Budyn-Kulik M (2017) Komentarz do niektórych przepisów ustawy o pobieraniu, przechowywaniu i przeszczepianiu komórek, tkanek i narządów. In: Mozgawa M (ed) Pozakodeksowe przestępstwa przeciwko zdrowiu. Komentarz. Wolters Kluwer Polska, LEX, pp 63–110

Butler DA (2017) Who owns the moon, mars, and other celestial bodies: lunar jurisprudence in corpus juris Spatialis. J Air Law Com 82(3):505–517

Cascone S (2021, 23 April), Oscar Nominee 'The Man Who Sold His Skin' Is Based on a Real Work of Art by Belgian Provocateur Wim Delvoye, https://news.artnet.com/art-world/oscar-nominee-the-man-who-sold-his-skin-1961334. Accessed 1 June 2022

Chłopecki A (2018) Twórczość artystyczna SI. In: Chłopecki A, Sztuczna inteligencja – szkice prawnicze i futurologiczne. C.H. Beck, Warszawa, pp 109–112

Ciecko B (2021, 10 March) The Surging Demand for Digital Collectibles Could Offer a Lifeline for Cash-Strapped Museums – Here's How. Artnet. https://news.artnet.com/opinion/op-ed-digital-collectables-museums-1950808. Accessed 1 June 2022

Cornu M, Vaivade A (2020) Introduction: dialogues between international and national laws relating to intangible cultural heritage. In: Cornu M, Vaivade A, Martinet L, Hance C (eds) Intangible Cultural Heritage Under National and International Law. Going Beyond the 2003 UNESCO Convention. Edward Elgar Publishing, Cheltenham–Northampton, pp 1–11. doi: https://doi.org/10.4337/9781839100031.00008

Cotte M, Ruggles C (2010) Astronomical heritage in the context of the UNESCO world heritage convention: developing a professional and rational approach. In: Heritage sites of astronomy and Archaeoastronomy in the context of the world heritage convention. A thematic study. ICOMOS–IAU, Paris, pp 260–272

Cubert JA, Bone RGA (2018) The law of intellectual property created by artificial intelligence. In: Barfield W, Pagallo U (eds) Research handbook on the law of artificial intelligence. Edward Elgar Publishing, Cheltenham–Northampton, pp 411–427

Czajkowska-Dąbrowska M (2007) Prawa artystów wykonawców. In: Barta J (ed) Prawo autorskie. System Prawa Prywatnego, vol 13. Warszawa, C.H. Beck, pp 319–348

Daszkiewicz W (1989) Karnoprawna ochrona nekropolii. RPEIS 1(51):51–78

Dębowska AS (2014, 17 September) Odkrycia naukowców: serce Chopina jest białe i ma ślady gruźlicy. Wyborcza. https://warszawa.wyborcza.pl/warszawa/7,34862,16656019,odkrycia-naukowcow-serce-chopina-jest-biale-i-ma-slady-gruzlicy.html. Accessed 1 June 2022

Dobosz P (1998) Problemy prawne ochrony zabytków cmentarnych w Polsce. Ochrona Zabytków 51(3):210–217

Doyle SE (2009) International space community and space law. In: Darrin AG, O'Leary BL (eds) Handbook of space engineering, archaeology, and heritage. CRC Press, pp 749–750

Drela M (2017) Zabytkowe części składowe i przynależności a przedmiot wpisu do rejestru zabytków: uwagi de lege lata i de lege ferenda. Roczniki Nauk Prawnych 27(3):27–46

Dutch Digital Design (2018, 14 Jan) The Next Rembrandt: bringing the Old Master back to life, Case study: behind the scenes of digital design. https://medium.com/@DutchDigital/the-next-rembrandt-bringing-the-old-master-back-to-life-35dfb1653597. Accessed 1 June 2022

Elliot JK (2021, 11 March) An 'NFT' digital image just sold for US$69 million – but what is it? Global News. https://globalnews.ca/news/7690676/what-is-nft-beeple-auction-first-5000-days/. Accessed 1 June 2022

Fewer G (2007) Conserving space heritage: the case of tranquillity base. J Br Interplanet Soc 60(1): 3–8

Fincham D (2011) The distinctiveness of property and heritage. Penn State Law Review 115(3): 641–684

Fiskesjö M (2014) Universal museums. In: Smith C (ed) Encyclopedia of global archaeology. Springer, New York. https://doi.org/10.1007/978-1-4419-0465-2_2434

Forrest C (2010) International law and the protection of cultural heritage. Routledge, London–New York

Francioni F (2020) Part II commentary, art.2(1) defining intangible cultural heritage. In: Blake J, Lixinski L (eds) The 2003 UNESCO intangible heritage convention: a commentary. Oxford University Press, Oxford, pp 48–56

Frankiewicz-Bodynek A (2014) O pojęciu i znaczeniu dziedzictwa niematerialnego oraz o zjawiskach świata współczesnego, które mu zagrażają. Przegląd Prawa Konstytucyjnego 2(18):101–117. https://doi.org/10.15804/ppk.2014.02.07

Gallagher S (2010) Museum and the return of human remains: an equitable solution? IJCP 17(1): 65–86. https://doi.org/10.1017/S0940739110000019

Golat R (2004) Ustawa o ochronie zabytków i opiece nad zabytkami. Komentarz, Zakamycze, Kraków

Góral A (2012) E-dziedzictwo – potencjał cyfryzacji w zakresie zachowania ciągłości przekazu niematerialnego dziedzictwa kulturowego. Zarządzanie w Kulturze 13(1):87–100. https://doi.org/10.4467/20843976ZK.12.011.0625

Gorman A (2005a) The archaeology of orbital space. In: Australian space science conference 2005. RMIT University, Melbourne, pp 338–357

Gorman A (2005b) The cultural landscape of interplanetary space. J Soc Archaeol 5:103–104. https://doi.org/10.1177/1469605305050148

Gorman A (2009) Heritage of earth orbit: orbital debris – its CONTENTS mitigation and cultural heritage. In: Darrin AG, O'Leary BL (eds) Handbook of space engineering, archaeology, and heritage. CRC Press, pp 391–392

Gorman A (2016) Culture on the moon: bodies in time and space. Archaeol J World Archaeol Congr 12(1):110–128. https://doi.org/10.1007/s11759-015-9286-7

Gorman A (2019) Dr Space Junk vs the Universe. Archaeology and the Future. The MIT Press, Cambridge

Gounelle M, Gounelle M (2019) Meteorites: international law and regulations. Meteorit Planet Sci 54(12):2887–2901. https://doi.org/10.1111/maps.13396

Grajewski A (2017) Meteoryty i kolekcjonerstwo w świetle prawa. Acta Societatis Metheoriticae Polonorum Rocznik Polskiego Towarzystwa Meteorytowego 8:52–62

Grochalski SM (2019) Rozwój (dynamika) prawa kosmicznego. Od monopolu reżimu międzynarodowego do współczesnych regulacji w systemach prawa wewnętrznego. Zarys problemu. In: Dynia E, Pączek M (eds) Prawo lotnicze i kosmiczne oraz technologie – nowe wyzwania. Wydawnictwo Uniwersytetu Rzeszowskiego, Rzeszów, pp 214–226

Gruszecki K (2020), Art. 121 [Commentary]. Ustawa o ochronie przyrody. Komentarz, 2nd ed., LEX/el

Grygiel B (2019, 4 November) Po śmierci staniesz się... dźwiękiem. Prochy zmarłych w płytach winylowych. Focus. https://www.focus.pl/artykul/po-smierci-staniesz-sie-dzwiekiem-prochy-zmarlych-w-plytach-winylowych-170906105817?fbclid=IwAR3VZYyUkTyI3wDaqeJp52blCqesBOa_U8Al_LrQPfVLg8ZtHpQDSYh4Bzw. Accessed 1 June 2022

Grzeszak T (2007) Prawo do wizerunku i prawo adresata do korespondencji po śmierci pierwotnie uprawnionych. In: Barta J (ed) Prawo autorskie. System Prawa Prywatnego, vol 13. C.H. Beck, Warszawa, pp 567–569

Grzybowski S (ed) (1985) System prawa cywilnego, vol 1: Część ogólna. Zakład Narodowy im. Ossolińskich, Wydawnictwo Polskiej Akademii Nauk, Wrocław–Warszawa

Guzowski B (2011) Status prawny meteorytów w kontekście prawa własności. Przegląd Sądowy 3: 77–88

Gwardzińska Ż (2020) Prawo wobec ochrony e-dziedzictwa, czyli jak teraźniejszość wpływa na ewolucję współczesnego muzealnictwa. In: Jankowska M, Gwoździewicz-Matan P, Stec P (eds) Własność intelektualna a dziedzictwo kulturowe. Księga jubileuszowa dedykowana Profesorowi Wojciechowi Kowalskiemu. Wydawnictwo Ius Publicum, Warszawa, pp 460–471

Herzog K (2015, 10 March) A greener afterlife: is human composting the future for funerals. The Guardian. https://www.theguardian.com/environment/2015/mar/10/a-greener-afterlife-is-human-composting-the-future-for-funerals. Accessed 1 June 2022

Hughes O (2016, 25 March) Japanese AI software co-writes short story that makes it into national literary competition. International Business Times https://www.ibtimes.co.uk/japanese-ai-software-co-writes-short-story-that-makes-it-into-national-literary-competition-1551491. Accessed 1 June 2022

Ignatowicz J (2000) Prawo rzeczowe. Wydawnictwa Prawnicze PWN, Warszawa

Ikram S (2011) Collecting and repatriating Egypt's past: toward a new nationalism. In: Silverman H (ed) Contested cultural heritage. Springer, New York

Jagielska-Burduk A (2011) Zabytek ruchomy. Wolters Kluwer Polska, Warszawa

Jagielska-Burduk A (2014) Koncepcja świadomego dysponenta zabytków w polskim prawie ochrony zabytków. In: Zeidler K (ed) Prawo ochrony zabytków. Wolters Kluwer, Wydawnictwo Uniwersytetu Gdańskiego, Warszawa–Gdańsk, pp 311–318

Jagielska-Burduk A, Mularski K (2015) Problematyka reprywatyzacji zabytków ruchomych. Uwagi na marginesie wyroku Sądu Najwyższego z 12 lutego 2012 r. (III CSK 208/11). In: Stec P, Maniurka P (eds) Kolekcje i zbiory muzealne. Problematyka prawna. Redakcja Wydawnictw Wydziału Teologicznego Uniwersytetu Opolskiego, Opole, pp 201–216

Jastrzębska E (2015) Prawne aspekty eksponowania szczątków ludzkich w muzeach polskich. Muzealnictwo 56:183–189

Jodełka H (2005) Międzynarodowa ochrona niematerialnego dziedzictwa kulturowego. Stosunki Międzynarodowe 3–4:169–187

Juściński PP (2019) Prawo autorskie w obliczu rozwoju sztucznej inteligencji. Zeszyty Naukowe Uniwersytetu Jagiellońskiego 1:5–44

Kapelańska-Pręgowska J, Chrzczonowicz P (2015) Handel organami z perspektywy prawa międzynarodowego oraz polskiego prawa karnego. Przegląd Sejmowy 6(31):71–101

Katner W (2012) Statki powietrze, lotniska i urządzenia naziemne. Pojazdy kosmiczne. In: Safjan M (ed) Prawo cywilne – część ogólna. System Prawa Prywatnego, vol 1. C.H. Beck, Warszawa, pp 1331–1335

Katner W (2014) Art. 45 [Commentary]. In: Księżak P, Pyziak-Szafnicka M (eds) Kodeks cywilny. Komentarz. Część ogólna, 2nd edn. Lex

Kersten P (1910) Bucheinbände in Menschenhaut. Zeitschrift für Bücherfreunde 8:263–264

Kinsella E (2021a, 22 Feb) Is This the Next Art-Market Bubble? A Unique NFT for the Popular 'Nyan Cat' GIF Just Sold for a Whopping $560,000. Artnet. https://news.artnet.com/market/nyan-cat-nft-sells-for-560000-1945679. Accessed 1 June 2022

Kinsella E (2021b, 16 Feb) Christie's Hopes to Open a New Frontier of the Art Market with the First-Ever Major Auction of a Wholly Digital Blockchain Artwork. The starting price for the work is just $100. Artnet. https://news.artnet.com/market/christies-nft-blockchain-art-auction-1943697. Accessed 1 June 2022

Klepczarek R (2012, 21 Dec) Mennica Polska przyznaje, że naruszono prawo. Łowicz Nasze Miasto. https://lowicz.naszemiasto.pl/mennica-polska-przyznaje-ze-naruszono-prawo/ar/c1-1664409. Accessed 1 June 2022

Kobiałka D (2018) Kreatywność za drutem kolczastym: Archeologia i sztuka okopowa z pierwszowojennego obozu jenieckiego w Czersku (woj. pomorskie). Folia Praehistorica Posnaniensia 23:105–136. https://doi.org/10.14746/fpp.2018.23.06

Kobiałka D (2019) Drzewa, okopy, sztuka okopowa – materialne pozostałości po drugiej wojnie światowej wokół Chyciny. Archeologia Historica Polona 27:267–286. https://doi.org/10.12775/AHP.2019.013

Konach T (2014) Problematyka prawnej ochrony dziedzictwa niematerialnego na przykładzie przejawów folkloru. Zarządzanie w Kulturze 15(1):29–38

Kopff A (1961) Dzieło sztuk plastycznych i jego twórca w świetle przepisów prawa autorskiego. PWN, Kraków

Kotowiecki A (2006) Status prawny meteorytów znajdowanych na obszarach polarnych. Biuletyn Polarny 11:76–84

Kotowiecki A, Skórka M (2002) Prawo własności meteorytów. PiP 11:97–111

Kowalski K (2017, 9 November) Naukowcy obejrzeli serce Fryderyka Chopina, Rzeczpospolita. https://www.rp.pl/nauka/art10111461-naukowcy-obejrzeli-serce-fryderyka-chopina. Accessed 1 June 2022

Kowalski W (2004) Nabycie własności dzieła sztuki od nieuprawnionego. Zakamycze, Kraków

Kowalski W (2014) Konwencja UNESCO o ochronie podwodnego dziedzictwa kulturowego przyjętej dnia 2 listopada 2001 roku, na 31 Konferencji Generalnej UNESCO w Paryżu. In: Zalasińska K (ed) Konwencje UNESCO w dziedzinie kultury. Wolters Kluwer, Warszawa, pp 312–391

Kraskowska D (2019, 27 December) Kompostowanie ludzkich zwłok legalne w USA. Czy to możliwe w Polsce? Dziennik Prawny.pl. https://www.prawokonsumenckie.pl/pl/a/kompostowanie-ludzkich-zwlok-legalne-w-usa-czy-to-mozliwe-w-polsce. Accessed 1 June 2022

Księżak P (2005) Rzeczy niczyje. Rejent 4:59–82

Kuźniar D (2019) Ochrona środowiska przestrzeni kosmicznej i ciał niebieskich. Studium prawnomiędzynarodowe. Wydawnictwo Uniwersytetu Rzeszowskiego, Rzeszów

Lewis T (2002) Human remains as 'artistic expression' and the common law offence of outraging public decency: 'human earrings', Human Rights and R. v. Gibson Revisited. J Entertain Law 1(2):83–99

Lixinski L (2013) Intangible cultural heritage in international law. Oxford University Press, Oxford

Lixinski L (2020) Part II commentary, art.3(a) relationship to other international heritage instruments. In: Blake J, Lixinski L (eds) The 2003 UNESCO intangible heritage convention: a commentary. Oxford University Press, Oxford, pp 100–116

Lixinski L, Blake J (2020), Part II Commentary, Art.3(b) Relationship to Intellectual Property and Environmental Instruments. In: Blake J, Lixinski L (eds) The 2003 UNESCO Intangible Heritage Convention: A Commentary. Oxford University Press, Oxford, pp 117–133

Lixinski L, Losier MM, Schreiber H (2021) Envisioning a legal framework for outer space cultural heritage. J Space Law 45:1–45

Low H (2017, 1 February) The man who sold his back to an art dealer. https://www.bbc.com/news/magazine-38601603. Accessed 1 June 2022

Lyall F, Larsen PB (2018) Space law: a treatise, 2nd edn. Routledge, New York

Markiewicz R (2018a) Ilustrowane prawo autorskie. Wolters Kluwer, Warszawa

Markiewicz R (2018b) Sztuczna inteligencja i własność intelektualna. Inauguracja roku akademickiego 2018/2019. Uniwersytet Jagielloński w Krakowie. https://www.uj.edu.pl/documents/10172/140821974/SI_prof_Markiewicz.pdf/35aa8d83-c295-44d4-b470-5e13888f09ea. Accessed 1 June 2022

Marov M (2010) Space achievements as world heritage. In: Heritage sites of astronomy and archaeoastronomy in the context of the world heritage convention. A thematic study. ICOMOS–IAU, Paris, pp 233–237

Mazurkiewicz J (2010) Non omnis moriar. Ochrona dóbr osobistych zmarłego w prawie polskim. Wydział Prawa, Administracji i Ekonomii Uniwersytetu Wrocławskiego, Wrocław

Mazzone M, Elgammal A (2019)1. Art, creativity, and the potential of artificial intelligence, Arts 8(1), 26, pp 1–9. https://doi.org/10.3390/arts8010026

Miligan T (2015) Asteroid mining, integrity and containment. In: Galliott J (ed) Commercial space exploration. Ethics, policy and governance. Routledge, New York, pp 123–133

Misiuk Z, Wrzosek J, Oniszczuk A, Sekuła M, Sabaciński M, Czajkowski K (2019) Wytyczne do prowadzenia badań archeologicznych, part 2. Badania inwazyjne. NID, Warszawa

MJ/PAP (2011, 2 March) Komiks "Chopin. New Romantic" nie będzie zniszczony. Newsweek. https://www.newsweek.pl/komiks-chopin-new-romantic-nie-bedzie-zniszczony/cr3slkz. Accessed 1 June 2022

Mozgawa M (ed) (2020) Kodeks karny. Komentarz aktualizowany. LEX/el

Musonda FB (2013) Decolonising the Broken Hill skull: cultural loss and a pathway to Zambian archaeological sovereignty. Afr Archaeol Rev 30:195–220. https://doi.org/10.1007/s10437-013-9134-3

Nieroba E (2012) Między poznaniem rozumowym a doświadczeniem afektywnym. Eksponowanie szczątków ludzkich w przestrzeni muzealnej. Kultura Popularna 4(34):150–157

Nowak-Gruca A (2015) Konieczne cechy utworu. Uwagi po 20 latach obowiązywania ustawy o prawie autorskim i prawach pokrewnych. RPEiS 77(2):91–103. https://doi.org/10.14746/rpeis.2015.77.2.7

O'Keefe PJ, Prott LV (eds) (2011) Cultural Heritage Conventions and other Instruments. A Compendium with Commentaries. Institute of Art and Law, United Kingdom

O'Leary BL (2009a) The evolution of space archaeology and heritage. In: Darrin AG, O'Leary BL (eds) Handbook of space engineering, archaeology, and heritage. CRC Press, pp 30–49

O'Leary BL (2009b) One Giant leap: preserving cultural CONTENTS resources on the moon. In: Darrin AG, O'Leary BL (eds) Handbook of space engineering, archaeology, and heritage. CRC Press, pp 757–780

O'Leary BL (2015) "To boldly go where no man [sic] has gone before": approaches in space archaeology and heritage. In: O'Leary BL, Capelotti PJ (eds) Archaeology and heritage of the human movement into space. Springer, pp 1–12

Paterson RK (2010) Heading home: French law enables return of Maori heads to New Zealand. IJCP 17(4):643–652. https://doi.org/10.1017/S0940739110000408

Pazdan M (2012) Przegląd dóbr osobistych. In: Safjan M (ed) Prawo cywilne – część ogólna. System Prawa Prywatnego, vol 1. C.H. Beck, Warszawa, pp 1235–1268

Piasecki K (1989) [Commentary]. In: Winiarz J (ed) Kodeks cywilny z komentarzem. Wydawnictwo Prawnicze. Warszawa

Pietrzykowski T (2015) Problem podmiotowości prawnej zwierząt z perspektywy filozofii prawa. Przegląd Filozoficzny – Nowa Seria 2(49):247–259

Polkowska M (2020) Space diplomacy – future perspective. Humanit Soc Sci 27(3):121–128

Polkowska M, Toumi M (2020) Prawo, prywatyzacja i bezpieczeństwo – szczególne wyzwania nowej ery kosmicznej (Newspace). Teka Komisji Prawniczej PAN Oddział w Lublinie 13(2): 435–450. https://doi.org/10.32084/tekapr.2020.13.2-33

Przyborowska-Klimczak A (2011) Rozwój ochrony dziedzictwa kulturalnego w prawie międzynarodowym na przełomie XX i XXI wieku. Wydawnictwo Uniwersytetu Marii Curie-Skłodowskiej, Lublin

Quiñones Vilá CS (2019, 29 May) Creativity is Human, but Technology Helps to Sell – The Impact of AI Art and Blockchain on the Art Market, TIAMSA blog. https://www.artmarketstudies.org/tiamsa-blog-creativity-is-human-but-technology-helps-to-sell-the-impact-of-ai-art-and-blockchain-on-the-art-market-by-claudia-s-quinones-vila/. Accessed 1 June 2022

Radwański Z (ed) (2002) Prawo cywilne – część ogólna. System prawa prywatnego, vol 2. C.H. Beck, Warszawa

Red. (2015, 31 March) Pasmo włosów i kropla krwi. Czesi mają nowy relikwiarz Jana Pawła II. Newsweek. https://www.newsweek.pl/styl-zycia/relikwia-jana-pawla-ii-co-jest-w-srodku/3fjkxn2. Accessed 1 June 2022

Reyburn S (2020, 6 Oct) Livestreamed auctions make gameshows of art, but where is the glamour? The Art Newspaper. https://www.theartnewspaper.com/2020/10/06/livestreamed-auctions-make-gameshows-of-art-but-where-is-the-glamour. Accessed 1 June 2022

Reynolds J (2015) Legal implications of protecting historic sites in space. In: O'Leary BL, Capelotti PJ (eds) Archaeology and heritage of the human movement into space. Springer, pp 111–130

Romo V (2018, 22 Oct) A.I. Produced 'Portrait' Will Go Up For Auction At Christie's. NPR. https://www.npr.org/2018/10/22/659680894/a-i-produced-portrait-will-go-up-for-auction-at-christie-s?t=1562256430215. Accessed 1 June 2022

Rudnicki J (2014) Gdzie szukać rzeczy niczyich, czyli do czego służy kodeks cywilny. Forum Prawnicze 5(25):16–27

Rudnicki S (1987) Zagadnienia cywilistyczne ustawy o cmentarzach i chowaniu zmarłych. Palestra 10–11:104–117

Rudnicki S (2011) Art. 181 [commentary]. In: Gudowski J (ed) Kodeks cywilny. Komentarz, vol 2: Własność i inne prawa rzeczowe. Wolters Kluwer, Warszawa, pp 363–365

Rudnicki S, Dmowski S (2001) Komentarz do kodeksu cywilnego. Księga pierwsza. Część ogólna. Wydawnictwo Prawnicze, Warszawa
Rudnicki S, Trzaskowski R (2014) Art. 45 [Commentary]. In: Gudowski J (ed), Kodeks cywilny. Komentarz, Księga pierwsza. Część ogólna. Lexis Nexis, LEX
Ruggles C (2017) Discussion. In: Ruggles C (ed) Heritage Sites of Astronomy and Archaeoastronomy in the Context of the World Heritage Convention. Thematic Study no. 2. ICOMOS–IAU, Paris, pp 291–304
Ruggles C, Cotte M (2017) Introduction. In: Ruggles C (ed) Heritage Sites of Astronomy and Archaeoastronomy in the Context of the World Heritage Convention. Thematic Study no. 2. ICOMOS–IAU, Paris, pp 1–6
Rutkowska KW (2018) Muzeum Guzików w Łowiczu z perspektywy 20 lat. Zbiór Wiadomości do Antropologii Muzealnej 5:349–356. https://doi.org/10.12775/18913
Rzążewska D (2017) Wizerunek Chopina w biznesie. Kwartalnik Urzędu Patentowego RP 2:73–75
Saunders NJ (2000) Bodies of metal, shells of memory: 'trench art', and the great war recycled. J Mater Cult 5(1):43–67. https://doi.org/10.1177/135918350000500103
Saunders NJ (2011) Trench art: a brief history & guide, 1914–1939, 2rd edn. Pen & Sword Books Ltd., South Yorkshire 2011
Sax JL (2001) Playing darts with Rembrandt. Public and private rights in cultural treasures. The University of Michigan Press 2001
Schmitt DG (2002) The law of ownership and control of meteorites. Meteorit Planet Sci 37(S12): B5–B11. https://doi.org/10.1111/j.1945-5100.2002.tb00897.x
Schneider T (2021, 11 March) Will NFTs Revolutionize the Art Market or Repeat Its Greatest Failures? These 4 Factors Will Determine Their Fate. Artnet. https://news.artnet.com/market/nft-revolution-four-factors-1950645. Accessed 1 June 2022
Schreiber H (2014) Konwencja UNESCO w sprawie ochrony niematerialnego dziedzictwa kulturowego sporządzona w Paryżu dnia 17 października 2003 r. In: Zalasińska K (ed) Konwencje UNESCO w dziedzinie kultury. Wolters Kluwer, Warszawa, pp 392–463
Schreiber H (2017) Dziesięć spostrzeżeń z okazji 10-lecia wejścia w życie Konwencji UNESCO w sprawie ochrony niematerialnego dziedzictwa kulturowego z 2003 roku. In: Schreiber H (ed) Niematerialne dziedzictwo kulturowe: doświadczenia w ochronie krajów Europy Środkowej i Wschodniej oraz Chin. 10-lecie wejścia w życie Konwencji UNESCO z 2003 roku w perspektywie zrównoważonego rozwoju. Narodowy Instytut Dziedzictwa, Warszawa, pp 464–503
Scovazzi T (2012) The definition of intangible cultural heritage. In: Borelli S, Lenzerini F (eds) Cultural heritage, cultural rights, cultural diversity. New developments in international law. Martinus Nijhof, Leiden Boston, pp 179–200
Seddon R (2015) Exploring the heavens and the heritage of mankind. In: Galliott J (ed) Commercial space exploration. Ethics, policy and governance. Routledge, London, pp 149–160
Sewerynik A (2017, 14 May) Korzystanie z marki "Chopin." Rzeczpospolita. https://www.rp.pl/Rzecz-o-prawie/305149976-Korzystanie-z-marki-Chopin.html. Accessed 1 June 2022
Skaldawski B (2013) Krajowy Program Ochrony Dziedzictwa Niematerialnego – propozycja wdrożenia. In: Adamowski J, Smyk K (eds) Niematerialne dziedzictwo kulturowe: źródła – wartości – ochrona. Wydawnictwo Uniwersytetu Marii Curie-Skłodowskiej, Narodowy Instytut Dziedzictwa, Lublin–Warszawa, pp. 111–121
Ślęzak P (2012) Umowy w zakresie współczesnych sztuk wizualnych. Wolters Kluwer Polska, Warszawa
Sokołowska D (2010) "Omnis definitio periculosa" czyli kilka uwag o zmianie paradygmatu utworu. In: Kępiński J, Klafkowska-Wiśniowska K, Sikorski R (eds) Granice prawa autorskiego. Zarys Prawa Własności Intelektualnej vol 1. C.H. Beck, Warszawa, pp. 1–24
Spennemann DHR (2007) A line in the sand? Explorations of the cultural heritage value of hominid, Pongid, and Robotid Artifacts. IJCP 14(2):241–266. https://doi.org/10.1017/S0940739107070075

Szafrański W, Jagielska-Burduk A (2019) Jednorazowe pozwolenie na stały wywóz zabytku za granicę z perspektywy kategorii wieku i wartości – ochrona dziedzictwa kulturowego a rynek sztuki w Polsce. SAACLR 1(5):69–96. https://doi.org/10.4467/2450050XSNR.19.004.10805

Szpyt K (2020) Wykorzystanie sztucznej inteligencji w twórczości *post mortem* a prawa autorskie zmarłego twórcy. In: Lai L, Świerczyński M (eds) Prawo sztucznej inteligencji. C.H. Beck, Warszawa, pp 157–172

Trzciński M (2016) Ochrona ruchomych zabytków archeologicznych. In: Zeidler K (ed) Raport dotyczący stanu ochrony prawnej oraz kierunków zmian w zakresie prawnej ochrony zabytków ruchomych w Polsce przygotowany w ramach realizacji Krajowego Programu Ochrony Zabytków i Opieki nad Zabytkami na lata 2014–2017 dla Narodowego Instytutu Muzealnictwa i Ochrony Zbiorów. Gdańsk

Trzciński M (2017) Praktyczne problemy realizacji badań archeologicznych w związku z prowadzeniem poszukiwań ofiar zbrodni komunistycznych. Kurier Konserwatorski 14:7–17

tt (2016, 12 May) Inżynierowie, programiści i historycy sztuki drukarką 3D "namalowali" obraz Rembrandta. Forbes. https://www.forbes.pl/innogy/gadzety/obraz-rembrandta-w-3d-stworzony-przez-inzynierow/ee4c9dw. Accessed 1 June 2022

Tucker Arensberg Attorneys (2018, 25 April) No Monkeying Around with this Opinion – Naruto v. Slater, No. 16-15469, 2018 WL 1902414 (9th Cir. Apr. 23, 2018). https://www.tuckerlaw.com/2018/04/25/no-monkeying-around-opinion-naruto-v-slater-no-16-15469-2018-wl-1902414-9th-cir-apr-23-2018/. Accessed 1 June 2022

Turrini P (2019) The Sky's not the limit: legal bonds and boundaries in claiming sovereignty over celestial bodies. In: Natoli T, Riccardi A (eds) Borders, legal spaces and territories in contemporary international law. Within and beyond. Springer, pp 173–210

Uliasz M (2019), Sztuczna inteligencja jako sztuczna osoba prawna. In: Flaga-Gieruszyńska K, Gołaczyński J, Szostek D (eds) Sztuczna inteligencja, blockchain, cyberbezpieczeństwo oraz dane osobowe. Zagadnienia wybrane. C.H. Beck, Warszawa, pp 23–38

Vaivade A (2017) Niematerialne dziedzictwo kulturowe i zrównoważony rozwój: studium przypadku przestrzeni kulturowej Suiti na Łotwie. In: Schreiber H (ed) Niematerialne dziedzictwo kulturowe: doświadczenia w ochronie krajów Europy Środkowej i Wschodniej oraz Chin. 10-lecie wejścia w życie Konwencji UNESCO z 2003 roku w perspektywie zrównoważonego rozwoju. Narodowy Instytut Dziedzictwa, Warszawa, pp 398–407

Vaivade A, Wagener N (2017) National laws related to intangible cultural heritage: determining the object of a comparative study. SAACLR 2(3):91–108. https://doi.org/10.4467/2450050XSNR.17.024.8425

Verheyen PD (2016) Die Collins: W. Collin, Hofbuchbinder & Ernst Collin, der Autor des Pressbengels. Libraries' and Librarians' Publication

Vigneron S (2020) The repatriation of human remains in France: 20 years of (mal)practice. SAACLR 2(6):313–338. https://doi.org/10.4467/2450050XSNR.20.022.13025

West M, Kraut R, Chew HE (2019) I'd blush if I could. Closing Gender Divides in Digital Skills through Education. EQUALS, UNESCO

Wysocki T (2019, 31 Oct) Uniwersytet Medyczny pokaże zbiory Muzeum Medycyny Sądowej. https://www.wroclaw.pl/portal/uniwersytet-medyczny-pokaze-zbiory-muzeum-medycyny-sadowej?fbclid=IwAR1YAgAFD6Wm44aY8sr2UpRedE-t4gPzEdyd984smbgPMWg-hz7agsKAtm8. Accessed 1 June 2022

Yanisky-Ravid S (2017) Generating Rembrandt: artificial intelligence, copyright, and accountability in the 3a era – the human-like authors are already here – a new model. Mich St Law Rev 659–726. https://doi.org/10.2139/ssrn.2957722

Yanisky-Ravid S, Velez-Hernandez LA (2018) Copyrightability of artworks produced by creative robots and originality: the formality-objective model. Minn J Law Sci Technol 19(1):1–53
Z (1930) Skóra ludzka oprawą do książek. Polska Gazeta Introligatorska 1:8–19
Zalasińska K (2017) Niematerialne dziedzictwo w systemie ochrony dziedzictwa kulturowego w Polsce. In: Schreiber H (ed) Niematerialne dziedzictwo kulturowe: doświadczenia w ochronie krajów Europy Środkowej i Wschodniej oraz Chin. 10-lecie wejścia w życie Konwencji UNESCO z 2003 roku w perspektywie zrównoważonego rozwoju. Narodowy Instytut Dziedzictwa, Warszawa, pp 316–323
Zeidler K (2004) Pojęcie "dziedzictwa narodowego" w Konstytucji RP i jego ochrona prawna. Gdańskie Studia Prawnicze 12:343–353

Chapter 4
A New Approach to Cultural Heritage and the Legal Regime of Common Resources in Poland

4.1 Introduction

This chapter discusses the "ownership" of items of material property that are not considered things (rights to waters, mineral deposits, animals) in order to show the process by which such property is classified, the legislative decisions referring to how it is to be separated from other property and the criterion accepted for its designation. Further, this chapter addresses the model for the use of such resources, taking into account the participation of private entities, and how the legislator creates mechanisms through which public interest can be protected.

The protection of cultural heritage under civil law (Chap. 5) is deliberately preceded by examples of regulations concerning the "ownership" of waters, mineral deposits and animals within the scope in which they point towards the direction of the changes taking place in this area, and to a definition of the property subject to that law. In the context of the components of cultural heritage, which are at the centre of these reflections, it is vital to determine in what situations the legislator can use a legal construction similar to that of ownership. Based on the examples analysed, a certain framework for legislative activities will be set out, with reference to how the laws governing the components of cultural heritage are structured.

Cultural heritage is perceived as resources that cannot be replaced if destroyed. While this does not rule out restorations and reconstructions, these cannot actually bring back the original substance of the property.[1] The items of material property not constituting things that are analysed below are of a similar, unique nature and constitute natural resources important for human survival, including waters, minerals and animals. The process for protecting natural resources is connected with the process for protecting cultural heritage. An example at the level of international law

The chapter was translated from Polish into English by Anthony Sloan and the author.

[1] Marcinkowska and Lipska (2018).

A. Jagielska-Burduk, *Cultural Heritage as a Legal Hybrid*,
https://doi.org/10.1007/978-3-031-04946-0_4

is the Convention Concerning the Protection of the World Cultural and Natural Heritage, in which the protection of natural and cultural heritage is combined, along with the cultural significance of natural property, for example in the form of the cultural landscape. It is thus all the more important to study how the legislator regulates the "ownership" of certain property at the level of domestic law, particularly if preserving that property is important to public interest. An analysis of how property is categorised abroad and the legal model used to regulate it can be applied to the need for protecting domestic cultural heritage in law.

Regardless of how property is classified, changes in which the protection of cultural heritage and natural heritage is perceived are imminent. A holistic approach to protecting cultural and natural heritage is a consequence of the changes taking place in how the world and human environment are perceived. A holistic conception of heritage that combines cultural and natural elements is a starting point for building protective mechanisms. In seeking to take this into account, I will also look at whether the upcoming changes in the ownership of material property that does not constitute things are reflected in a holistic approach to cultural heritage, based on selected examples from both Polish and international laws. Including a natural component in cultural heritage is a consequence of shifting the protection of natural heritage towards cultural heritage. On the other hand, the protection of the components of cultural heritage in Polish private law, as discussed in Sect. 4.3.1, does not take this cultural element into account.

Defining rights to material property that does not constitute things within the meaning of civil law usually occurs through secondary legislation. In every case, the pivotal point is the right of ownership as the most important right *in rem*. The Roman triad of ownership constitutes the fundamental starting point for analysing rights to material property. Regarding the ownership of waters, animals and mineral deposits, in the Polish scholarship, it was mentioned that the legislator constructs the right to material things in a way that is more or less anchored to ownership. In the case of mineral deposits, the provisions of the Civil Code are invoked. When it comes to animals, the law refers to general provisions on material things. Last but not the least, in the case of water rights, the very word "ownership" is used in a new meaning. Referring to binding acts of law allows the legislator to create rights to material property that does not constitute things. How rights to such property have been formed was supported by the pre-war legal concept of rights similar to property rights.

On rights similar to property rights[2] and their place in the legal system, Fryderyk Zoll wrote that "while in private law, especially recently, their function is quite momentous, they still do not possess full citizenship in the system of subjective rights".[3] Zoll showed that the absence of a joint classification of such items and their dispersion in secondary legislation have an impact on how the provisions are applied. Among those areas particularly affected, he mentioned the provisions on

[2]Zoll (1931), p. VIII, footnote 1.

[3]Zoll (1920), p. 25.

hunting, fishing and intangible property.[4] In his later writings concerning rights similar to property rights under the Property Law Decree of 1946,[5] he stated that the decree, to a certain extent, established their "res" character in relation to mining law and water law. Unfortunately, no "right similar to property rights" appears in the decree,[6] just as it is absent from today's Polish Civil Code.

Granting protection similar to that granted to things, and extending the right of ownership to other types of property, took place by applying detailed provisions when, due to the type of property involved, the traditional construction of a right of ownership could not be applied.[7] That protection was meant for property other than things, that is, property that did not constitute intrinsic material parts of nature that had been separated either naturally or artificially. It was assumed that not all rights similar to property rights should be included in the Civil Code. Therefore, a proposal was raised to include "ownership elements" of the rights to waters and mineral deposits, as well as of electrical and atomic energy, in the Civil Code. The idea was to keep the detailed provisions that fulfilled public interest outside civil law regulations. However, its central part dealing with the subject of the right should be mentioned in the general part of civil law.[8] Cultural property was never mentioned in this debate and also failed to appear in the draft general section of the Civil Code.

Certain ideas, though, were partially reflected in the draft general section of the Civil Code. Property that does not constitute things appeared in this section in the open catalogue of legally protected property.[9] The draft was prepared by the Civil Law Codification Commission at the Ministry of Justice and was presented in 2008. While the Commission's work was discontinued, the draft marks an important stage in assessing the future of civil law and the issues related to cultural heritage. The catalogue of protected property is an open one, but the inclusion of material property that does not constitute things, and intangible property such as works, is an important step in including "ownership elements" over such property in the Civil Code.

Given the place occupied by cultural heritage in the provisions of civil law today, the demand that cultural property be included in that catalogue seems fully justifiable. Considering the form of the Civil Code, the changes concerning the protection of cultural property and the publicisation of private law concerning the protection of cultural heritage, the catalogue could be successfully expanded to include cultural

---

[4] Zoll (1920), p. 25.

[5] Decree on Property Law of 11 October 1946. Polish Official Journal (Dz. U.) No. 57, item 319.

[6] Zoll (1947), p. 25.

[7] Stelmachowski (1969), p. 199.

[8] Stelmachowski (1994), p. 111.

[9] Commission for the Codification of Civil Law acting under the Minister of Justice Book One of the Civil Code Draft with Explanatory Memorandum Article 2 Legally protected goods include, in particular: "(1) personal property; (2) property; (3) animals; (4) things; (5) premises; (6) businesses; (7) farms; (8) money; (9) securities; (10) works; (11) inventions; (12) utility and industrial designs; (13) rationalisation projects; (14) trade and service marks; (15) geographical indications; (16) topographies of integrated circuits; (17) minerals; (18) flowing waters, underground springs and underground water reservoirs; (19) energy."

property (a concept that now appears in the Civil Code). In view of the variety of the components of cultural heritage and the strong differences in the scope of rights to particular components, we must resolve whether legally protected property should consist only of cultural property or whether it should also include components of cultural heritage as understood more broadly.

4.2 Public Ownership and Distribution Models: Between Public and Private Rights

4.2.1 Mineral Rights

Since the regulation of this type of property began, mineral deposits have not been treated as things in the civil sense but have been subject to a special legal regime. It should be noted, though, that differing views have been expressed towards this situation. For example, it was argued that separate mineral deposits have intrinsic properties.[10] This was supported by the view that mineral deposits, being part of nature, may be extracted in an artificial or natural manner.[11] As mineral deposits are not real estate, it was considered subject to a similar right.[12] In this last case, the author referred to an interesting construction: a thing that is neither real estate nor movable property but structurally similar to the former. In this way, the dichotomy between movable things and immovable things was broken, and a third category was added. Unfortunately, to the great detriment of the study of civil law, these considerations were not developed further. Such a qualification would mean that mineral deposits are immovable, and only their extraction through a disruption of the integrity of a deposit, or their use, has economic sense. In the currently binding law, the relationship between a mineral deposit and extracted minerals is understood as the whole of the minerals separated from the deposit.

It seems that, due to the specific nature of mineral deposits and their strategic importance for development, the legislator wanted to create a separate subjective right attributed to the State Treasury. That intention may also be derived from the justification to the draft of the Act.[13] Further, since in mining matters that have not been normalised the binding law calls for the application of the relevant provisions

[10] Agopszowicz (1966), p. 26.

[11] Agopszowicz (1965), p. 86; Agopszowicz (1966), p. 29; Agopszowicz (1968), p. 165; Grajner (1977), p. 26.

[12] Agopszowicz (1965), pp. 86–87.

[13] Works of the Sejm of the 6th term, Print no. 1696, pp. 4–5: "The essence of this solution is to "break the legal bond" between the landed property and the mineral deposit. It consists in assuming that some of these deposits are not components of the real estate, and thus they are not included in the land ownership. Instead, they are the subject of a separate property right vested exclusively in the State Treasury."

of the Civil Code concerning land property (Article 11 of the Geology and Mining Law Act (GMLA 2011)[14]), the legislator points out that the subject of the right is not identical to the right of ownership and the right of mining ownership. It is difficult to accept that the provisions on real property will be applied to mineral deposits treated as movable property. It would be more appropriate to follow the concept that mineral deposits are "things similar to real property", as discussed above.

The importance of mines for safeguarding public interest forced the legislator to build a legal construction that was separate from ownership under civil law. At the same time, a "bridge" was created between the right to deposits and the right of an owner of real property, between whom those rights may come into conflict. The legal situation of mines is regulated in GMLA 2011. In accordance with its legal definition, a mineral deposit "constitutes a natural agglomeration of minerals, rocks or other substances whose extraction may bring economic benefits". Mining ownership extends to those deposits enumerated in Article 10 par. 1 GMLA 2011,[15] that is, not to all existing mines. Mining ownership covers deposits regardless of their location. The legislator extended to include mining ownership to deposits of curative waters, thermal waters and brines. In this way, the subject of mining ownership is internally heterogeneous and isolated formally on the basis of the criterion of function, not the properties of deposits. The right to mines covered by a right of mining ownership belongs to the State Treasury. Additionally, the right of mining ownership covers parts of rock mass situated outside the spatial limits of land (real property), in particular when located within the maritime borders of the Republic of Poland. Mineral deposits not mentioned by the legislator in Article 10 par. 1 GMLA 2011 are covered by the right of ownership over the land where they are located.

Wojciech Szydło expressed the opinion that

> mineral deposits mentioned in Article 10 par. 1 and 2 GMLA 2011 are therefore separate things (movables) that constitute the subject of ownership by the State Treasury. In addition, in the case of mineral deposits located within real property owned by the State Treasury, it must be held that those deposits do not comprise component parts of that real property (even if they are situated within the borders set out in Article 143 Civil Code), but are simply separate things owned by the State Treasury. This is the new conception of mining ownership of the State Treasury, where a certain group of things is separated whose ownership is attributed to the State Treasury.[16]

Accepting this view allows us to consider that we are dealing with a thing, and from this conception, there follows a right of ownership over all deposits, as referred to in Articlc 140 of the Civil Code.

---

[14] Geology and Mining Law Act of 9 June 2011, consolidated text. Polish Official Journal (Dz. U.) 2019, item 868.

[15] These are deposits of hydrocarbons, hard coal, methane occurring as an associated mineral, lignite, metal ores with the exception of bog iron ores, metals in their native state, ores of radioactive elements, native sulphur, rock salt, potassium salt, potassium-magnesium salt, gypsum and anhydrite, precious stones, rare earth elements and precious gases.

[16] Szydło (2014), p. 316.

The history of the legal regulation of mining ownership is a history of legally determining who is the owner of deposits and of a debate over the scope of that ownership. First, we should look at the key elements of that right, including the definitions of deposits, internal divisions of deposits made by the legislator and how the legal relationship between deposits and land (real property) is formed. This division of deposits made by the legislator was accompanied by problems involving deposits located within the borders of land (real property) and how to define the scope of such ownership. In the regulations, emphasis has shifted over time between the subject and the object of mining ownership. In each case, the right to mining ownership has constituted a right separate from civil law ownership.

The concept of mining ownership appeared in a regulation by the President of the Republic of Poland of 1930 on the Mining Law.[17] The legislator pointed out that minerals occurring in natural deposits "are subject to mining will, that is, may be the object of mining ownership, granted to anyone under the conditions set out in this law (Article 1 of the Regulation)". The Act identified deposits "reserved for the benefit of the State" that could be the object of mining ownership granted solely to the state. The ownership of minerals located in natural deposits was separated from the right of ownership over the land. Pursuant to Article 15 of the Regulation, mining ownership arose through the issuance or approval of a consolidation, division or exchange of mining fields. After a deposit was discovered and the discovery was reported, an application for ownership had to be made to the regional mining authority.

It is worth noting the fact that mining ownership could be granted to anyone who, within the meaning of the Act, was capable of acquiring that ownership; it was not confined solely to the state. And the moment ownership arose did not occur *ex lege* but only after the completion of a certain procedure. The scope of ownership of a mining field was regulated by Article 29 of the Regulation, which stipulated that the borders in the horizontal dimension were straight lines on the surface[18] and in the vertical dimension were vertical planes intersecting the horizontal lines to an unlimited depth. The law of mining ownership was connected with the obligation to exercise it,[19] including to conduct operations connected with extracting the mineral specified in the mining concession. Where the right of mining ownership was not exercised in this way, the right could be revoked (Article 172 et seq. of the Regulation). The public interest was also taken into account when an owner or holder of land transferred the land for the benefit of the owner of a mining field. The right of mining ownership over different minerals could overlap (Article 57 of the Regulation), and in a situation where several owners of fields applied for the same land, priority was given to the one whose purpose was most in favour of public

[17] President of the Republic of Poland of 29 November 1930 on the Mining Law. Polish Official Journal (Dz. U.) 1930, No. 85, item 654.

[18] However, it is stipulated that the horizontal boundary is determined by straight lines if possible due to the local conditions.

[19] Zoll (1947), p. 25.

interest (Article 84 of the Regulation). Even though the right of mining ownership was aimed at bringing specific, important benefits for the public good, it gave way to a competing public interest: that of preserving cultural heritage. Pursuant to Article 71 of the Regulation, on the basis of a decision, it was possible to exclude certain parts of a mining field from exploitation if it had a "particular value for scientific or historical research", whereas the right to explore for minerals, granted prior to mining ownership, was excluded in areas of "immovable objects regarded as of historical value"[20] (Article 5 pt. 1 of the Regulation).

In a subsequent legal act, the Mining Law Decree of 1953 (MLD 1953),[21] the legislator named the State Treasury as the entity that enjoyed a right to extract minerals where it is not otherwise provided under the Mining Law (Article 4). The right set out in Article 4 of MLD 1953 was analysed in the early years after the entry into force of the Civil Code. The research concluded that there is

> no basis for accepting that mineral deposits – with the exception of waters – located within the borders of non-state land real property are the property of the state. No provision of the law so stipulates, and only the exception of ground water has been expressly regulated in a separate manner.[22]

Nor was there any agreement on how to qualify the right to deposits; it was perceived as a right *in rem*, similar to a right *in rem* or solely having the character of an administrative right.[23] The legal analyses conducted at that time led to two variants: first, that "Article 4 of the Mining Law invokes an intrinsic right similar to mining ownership or regulated only the exclusivity of entitlements resulting from ownership of land (second variant - note by the author)."[24] It was asserted that what is under the ground remains the property of the state, and the provisions on ownerless property do not apply, whereas mineral deposits were seen not only as material property not constituting things but also through the prism of their function as a means of production in the socialist state.[25] This conclusion was one of several put forward in academic publications of the time.[26] Considering the number and variety of views on mineral rights, others argued that "the legal situation of the interior of the earth is very vague *de lege lata*. None of the binding provisions defines what that space is or determines whose property it is."[27]

---

[20] At that time, cultural heritage protection was regulated in the Regulation of the President of the Republic of Poland of 6 March 1928 on the Care of Monuments. Polish Official Journal (Dz. U.) 1928, No. 29, item 265.

[21] Mining Law Decree of 6 May 1953. Polish Official Journal (Dz. U.) 1953, No. 29, item 113.

[22] Agopszowicz (1966), p. 29.

[23] Grajner (1977), p. 29.

[24] Grajner (1977), p. 27.

[25] Agopszowicz (1965), p. 87.

[26] Lipiński (1979), pp. 108–109.

[27] Mikosz (1991) p. 128.

The amendment of 9 March 1991[28] introduced the provision of Article 5 par. 1 MLD 1953, specifying the State Treasury as the owner of mineral deposits, though adding at the same time that this does not infringe the rights of owners of land (real property).[29] As a result, the State Treasury had the right to exploit deposits to the exclusion of other persons. The act also invoked the socio-economic purpose of that right as determining the scope within which it could be exercised. In its disposition of the law, the State Treasury could give mining usufruct rights by granting concessions. That amendment, however, did not dispel all doubts over the ownership of deposits located within the borders of real property, and in less than 3 years a new act was adopted.[30] The direction proposed in the amendment was taken further in the new act.

In the Act of 4 February 1994 (Geology and Mining Law Act, GMLA 1994),[31] a legislative effort was made to define the subject of mining ownership, and a corresponding title was given to Chapter 2 of the Act: "Mining Ownership and Use". Pursuant to Article 7 of GMLA 1994, "mineral deposits not constituting component parts of land real property are the property of the State Treasury". In this way, a division was introduced between deposits that constitute property of the State Treasury and those that are component parts of real property. During the life of the previous act, the problem of deposits as component parts was also analysed in the scope affecting the status of mineral deposits. It was shown that separating deposits from the ground does not, in principle, cause damage to or an essential change in the whole.[32] In the Act of 1994, however, a different construction was accepted based on the recognition that some deposits will constitute a component part of real property.

Article 7 par. 2 of GMLA 1994, in turn, provided for the possibility of the State Treasury exploiting deposits and mines and disposing of that right by way of establishing a mining usufruct.[33] What is striking is that in the previous act, emphasis was placed on legal entities, including the State Treasury. Regarding the issue of mining ownership, the term "component part" is of key importance, as are the provisions on land (real property). Practically, the greatest difficulty posed is how to define the borders of real property and thereby define what mines are covered by the ownership of real property. Some commentators pointed out that only a legislator's intervention can bring about a proper solution. This should be introduced into

[28] Act amending the Mining Law of 9 March 1991. Polish Official Journal (Dz. U.) 1991, No. 31, item 128.

[29] Article 5.1 State Treasury is the owner of mineral deposits. This provision does not infringe the rights of owners of land (real property).

[30] Lipiński and Mikosz (2003), Art. 7 [Commentary].

[31] Geology and Mining Law Act of 4 February 1994. Polish Official Journal (Dz. U.) 1994, No. 27, item 96.

[32] Agopszowicz (1966), p. 24.

[33] Lipiński and Mikosz (2003), Art. 7 [Commentary].

the Civil Code or, perhaps because of the specificity and meaning of the resource, into the Constitution.[34]

In terms of mining ownership, Article 143 of the Civil Code on the borders of land property is of critical importance; it stipulates that, within the borders determined by the socio-economic designation of land, the ownership of land extends to the space both above and below the surface of the land. This provision, though, does not infringe the provisions normalising water rights. It need only be added that, up to the adoption of GMLA 1994, this provision referred not just to water rights but also to minerals. Thus, there is an observable intervention by the legislator in the Civil Code, in this case in order to introduce changes that form and define the right to mineral deposits, along with the development of legal thought and the construction of mining ownership. That provision referred not to a specific act but to legal regulations concerning water and mining rights. The history of the regulation of mining rights confirms that, since the Civil Code entered into force, three acts of law have been in force within the scope of mining rights, which means that the construction of the reference was proper and raised no doubts. What continued to raise doubts was the manner in which the lower limit of real property was defined.

The manner of defining borders under the Decree on Property Law and the Civil Code has been analysed in response to the reference in Article 143 of the Civil Code to water and mining rights.[35] Given the varying socio-economic conditions involved, the borders of real property will not be uniform. In each case, the interests of the owner and the designation of the land must be taken into account. To the extent that public interest determines the State Treasury's ownership over waters and mineral deposits, the exercise of ownership over real property within those borders is not possible. Alfred Klein, considering real property as a legal construct,[36] has stated that "in the case of a specific legal ownership relationship, a specific real property can be defined within sufficient precision for practical needs."[37] According to the model accepted in GMLA 2011, regardless of whether they are located within or without the space of a given real property, mineral deposits constitute the subject of a separate law. In this way, mineral deposits thus located determine the limits of a given land real property, as does water.

The Act largely set the issue of mineral rights in order. The structure of those rights was based on a division of minerals into those specified by the legislator as constituting property of the State Treasury and other minerals. A closed catalogue of minerals constituting the subject of mining ownership made it easier to separate this from the subject of land (real property) ownership.[38] In this way, minerals are divided into those subject to mining ownership and those covered by land (real property) ownership. Mines constituting the subject of mining ownership were

[34] Lipiński and Mikosz (2003), Art. 7 [Commentary].

[35] Lipiński (1979), p. 115.

[36] Klein (1985), p. 97.

[37] Klein (1985), p. 98.

[38] Cf. Szuma (2012), p. 50.

selected for their economic significance. Or, to put it in a different way, whether a given deposit of minerals is or is not subject to mining ownership depends on its value. A hierarchy of property was introduced that led to a legal regime. This division is a deliberate solution aimed at maintaining a strong regime governing the use of certain property.

The exercise of a mining ownership right may lead to significant restrictions affecting the owner of the real property involved. An interesting example would be where an entire real property is filled with minerals—this could result in the real property losing all value for the owner. Moreover, the owner could also use the right of access to a significant part of the property due to mining ownership. This problem has been analysed in terms of the possible expropriation of land (real property) from its owner, possible compensation paid to the owner and the spatial borders of real property.[39] Here, mention should be made of the concept of indirect expropriation, which leads to the impossibility of an owner using or reaping the benefits of his ownership right as a result of taxes imposed upon the property.[40] This finding also refers to mining rights, arguing that this concept does not apply in the legal dimension, though economically such a conclusion may seem legitimate.[41] The concept closest to that of indirect expropriation in the cultural property context is the protection granted to historical objects in the form of a register of immovable and movable historical objects. In the first case, it often happens that an owner of real property cannot go ahead with their investment plans because this would adversely affect the substance of the historical objects on their property.[42] In turn, the owner of a movable historical object entered in the register cannot bring it permanently out of the country, offer it for sale there or sell it for an amount higher than it would obtain in Poland.[43] In both cases, there is no system for compensating owners; further, in contrast to what can be said about indirect expropriation, here, there is little chance of these problems being eliminated or alleviated.

Compared with the "ownership" of other material property not constituting things, the subject of mining ownership, and that subject's internal heterogeneity, is atypical. The basic criterion of separation is the subject, while the object of the right is only of secondary importance. One of the answers given to the question of why the legislator separated mining ownership is that

> in this type of ownership, the typical instruments of civil law are unreliable, though at the same time the conviction exists that this problem cannot entirely be divorced from civil law. This type of ownership, therefore, is to combine certain typical elements from civil law with atypical elements that rule out of the possibility of civil law categories being applied.[44]

[39] Agopszowicz (1965), p. 94; Mikosz (2008), pp. 177–179; Mikosz (2013), p. 459.

[40] Stelmachowski (1969), pp. 214–215 gives an example of real estate and revenues from rental agreements.

[41] Lipiński (1979), p. 117.

[42] Cf. Sługocki (2014b), pp. 103–105 and 117–112.

[43] Jakubowski and Jakubowski (2014), pp. 224–233.

[44] Rakoczy (2015b), Art. 10 [Commentary].

The essence of mining ownership justifying a separate regulation is its object, whose properties are important to the public interest. Consequently, the State Treasury is identified as the ownership subject, who can dispose of its right (mining ownership) solely by establishing a mining usufruct. That right is even more special in that it is an inalienable right attributed to just one entity. Minerals not listed by the legislator in Article 10 GMLA 2011 share the legal fate of the land (real property) in which they are located, the object of ownership remaining, within civil law meaning, with the owner of the real property.

The changes presented above concerning mining ownership, and the many stages it has undergone, confirm that rights to material property not constituting things are subject to change as a result of the intervention by the legislator. Public interest, expressed in how mining ownership has been formed and attributed to the State Treasury, also permeates the form of the law and, for example, the limitations on how it can be exercised. Two constructions in the binding act clearly demonstrate a hierarchy of property. In relation to property having high importance to the public interest, the legislator decided on the construction of mining ownership enjoyed solely by the State Treasury, the disposal of which entails the involvement of a special administrative apparatus. The legislator was certainly guided by similar thinking when it appointed the State Treasury as the owner of archaeological artefacts found in the ground or extracted from it.

The changes that have taken place in how mineral rights have been defined or constructed reflect the social and political system of the day. At the same time, they are the result of years of academic debate and case law—certainly important drivers of successive legislation. The variety of views expressed by representatives of the doctrine, and the classification of minerals outside the dichotomy of movable and immovable things, shows how certain property is "susceptible" to new proposals aimed at strengthening the regimes under which it is managed, not only because of its inherent properties but also because of its strategic importance.

4.2.2 *Water Rights*

Another type of material property that is not a thing and to which an "ownership right" is contained outside the Civil Code is water resources. Water resources take on many forms. Apart from those forms found occurring in nature (standing and flowing water), water can also exist in a separate form (e.g. in a bottle or other types of closed containers). This allows water to be traded, for it has the attribute of self-existence.[45] Water is not only a vital part of the human body and of human and animal organisms; its natural reservoirs are also places where flora and fauna abound and where property connected with human existence can be found, including archaeological artefacts (underwater archaeological heritage). The legal regulations

[45] Mikosz (2013), p. 476.

on waters are internally diverse due to the many forms in which water exists (standing, flowing, surface, ground, public, non-public). These divisions result not only in different constructions of ownership; they also determine the owner as a subject. Among those owners, the State Treasury dominates the field in Poland.

In water rights, elements of state and private ownership appear, as does the concept of the common good. In domestic law, different states classify rights in different ways. At the same time, the approach connected with managing natural resources and always attending to their public function is increasing in importance.[46] The structure of water rights has changed in Polish law over the years. In the literature, attention has been drawn to the blurriness of the borders between states in which water constitutes a thing and when it does not, as in, for example, the issue of seepage or precipitation altering the volume of water in closed reservoirs. This problem of "fuzzy borders" did not pose an important obstacle to the practical classification of waters.[47] There is no doubt that changes in the political system of a country had an impact on research into civil law and water ownership. Studies prepared over the years have certainly contributed largely to forming a civil law concept of water and creating a modern model for its legal classification.[48]

The Water Act of 19 September 1922 reflected the principle of the public "ownership" of water to the extent that, on the basis of the Act or specific legal titles, it did not constitute private property (Articles 1 and 2).[49] Pursuant to Article 1 of the Act, "waters are either public or private. The first constitute public property (part of the common good), the second are private property." Water rights were from the beginning regulated in acts on water resources and therefore distinct from the civil law concept of ownership. The crux of the subsequent Water Law of 1962[50] was state ownership over water (Article 1). An exception was foreseen, however, for stagnant water on the surface of land and water in wells and ditches. This structure of ownership was maintained in the subsequent Water Law of 1974.[51] Pursuant to Article 2 of that act, standing surface water and water in wells and ditches constituted property of the owner of the land on which it was located. Here, a construction was applied based on the concept of a component part, where it was shown that such water constitutes a part (but not a component part) of the land. All other water was subject to state "ownership", which constituted "a particular, absolute subjective property right".[52]

46 Schorr (2017), pp. 281–282.

47 Cf. Grzybowski (1985), p. 435.

48 Dybowski et al. (1957).

49 Water Law of 19 September 1922. Polish Official Journal (Dz. U.) 1922, No. 101, item 936.

50 Water Law of 30 May 1962. Polish Official Journal (Dz. U.) 1962, No. 34, item 158.

51 Water Law of 24 October 1974. Polish Official Journal (Dz. U.) 1974, No. 38, item 230.

52 Grzybowski (1985), p. 435.

The Supreme Court commented on the nationalising character of the provisions of the 1962 Water Law.[53] In response to a question from the Public Prosecutor General, the court passed a resolution laying down a legal principle as follows:

> water and land which, pursuant to the Water Law of 19 September 1922 (Polish Official Journal [Dz. U.] 1928 No. 62 item 574 as amended) constituted private property but which, pursuant to the Water Law of 30 May 1962 (Polish Official Journal [Dz. U.] No. 34 item 158) were counted among the property belonging to the State, became State property on the day the Water Law entered into force.[54]

In that resolution, reference was made to the content of the draft and its justification, applying a historical interpretation. It was also indicated that the common courts have jurisdiction over resolving ownership disputes over water rights. Intervention by the legislator causing a legal transfer of ownership to the State Treasury constituted a radical change in the ownership structure of water.

In the Water Law of 2001, the ownership of water became based on a division into public and non-public waters.[55] The definition of the subject of the act in Article 1 and the reference to "water management" without regard for the criterion of "owner" are especially noteworthy. Public waters are defined as waters constituting property of the State Treasury or a local government unit (Article 10 par. 2 WL 2001). It is also assumed that public flowing waters are not subject to trade under civil law, apart from statutory exceptions (given to fishing) and that they constitute *res omnium communes* (Article 10 par. 3 WL 2001). In the opinion of some, water ownership was "(in reference to water ownership) signalled (for it would be hard to maintain that it was regulated)".[56] An amendment to the Water Law in 2005 made the regulatory scope of the law more precise. Pursuant to the additional provision of Article 1a, "the act regulates matters of the ownership of water and land covered in water, as well as the principles of managing these components in relation to the property of the State Treasury". The legislator's intention was not to hamper water managers or prevent water from being disposed of because water could still be traded in the cases specified in the act.

In the act, in force since 2017,[57] the scope of regulation extended to matters of ownership of water and land covered in water, as well as the principles of managing these components in relation to the property of the State Treasury (Article 2 WL 2017). The problem of water ownership is dealt with in Chapter I (Ownership of water and obligations of owners), Section VI (Management of State Treasury

---

[53] Supreme Court, Resolution of a panel of seven judges of the Supreme Court—Civil Chamber of 8 November 1971, III CZP 28/71. OSNCP 1972 No 3, item 43, OSPiKA 1973, No. 1, item 1.

[54] Supreme Court, Resolution of a panel of seven judges of the Supreme Court—Civil Chamber of 8 November 1971, III CZP 28/71. OSNCP 1972 No 3, item 43, OSPiKA 1973, No. 1, item 1.

[55] Water Law of 18 July 2001. Polish Official Journal (Dz. U.) 2001, No. 115, item 1229.

[56] Radecki (2005), p. 56.

[57] Water Law of 20 July 2017, consolidated version. Polish Official Journal (Dz. U.) 2018, item 2268.

property).[58] In Article 211 par. 1 of the Water Law, the following are indicated as owners of water: the State Treasury, other legal persons and natural persons.[59] Pursuant to Article 211 par. 2, ownership by the State Treasury extends to maritime territorial waters, internal sea waters, inland flowing waters and groundwater.

The act contains a repetition, after WL 2001, concerning categories of public water. In turn, the issue of exclusion from civil law trading applies to inland flowing waters. The exceptions in the act concerning trade relate to fisheries rights and the right to use land covered with water (Article 261 WL 2017). There was continuity from the previous act regarding the regulation of standing inland waters and water in ditches, which share the fate of the real property where they are located and constitute property of the owner of the real property. The scope of application of that provision was expanded to include water in ponds, provided that the pond is filled not using water services but by rainwater, snowmelt or groundwater.[60] When classifying the above-indicated types of water, some authors accept that we are dealing with a component part and with the ownership of those waters in the meaning of civil law,[61] while the rest favour a law that is separate from the ownership of real estate.[62] It seems that the latter position is also a continuation of the case law dividing the right of ownership of land and the "ownership" of water.[63]

The act's focus on the mechanisms for managing water resources means that the object of the right—water—is presented through its function and importance to society.[64] The new act introduced changes in the competencies of public administrative bodies in matters concerning water management, and in place of the National Water Management Authority, it appoints an organisational unit in the form of a state legal entity—Państwowe Gospodarstwo Wodne Wody Polskie ("Wody Polskie", Article 239 WL 2017). Wody Polskie was established to create a new water management system. It replaced the National Water Management Authority and regional water management authorities and acts on the basis of a statute handed

[58] Ownership of waters was included in further provisions of the Act in relation to the systematics of the previous Act.

[59] Organizational units without legal personality, which are granted legal capacity by the law were not mentioned in the regulation. In the course of the interpretation, it was concluded that these entities may also act as owners (cf. Kościelak et al. (2019), Art. 211 [Commentary]).

[60] Kościelak et al. (2019), Art. 214 [Commentary].

[61] Some scholars approve the component part concept cf. Kościelak et al. (2019), Art. 214 [Commentary]. Similarly, under WL 2001: Golat (2014); Rakoczy (2013), p. 24.

[62] Gurgul (2019); see also Agopszowicz (1973), pp. 31–32 under the APCP 1962.

[63] Supreme Court, Civil Chamber, Judgement of 19 November 2004, II CK 146/04, Legalis 83608. The judgement recalled the resolution of a panel of seven judges of the Supreme Court—Civil Chamber of 8 November 1971, III CZP 28/71.

[64] Article 10 of the Act states that the management of water resources shall serve to meet the needs of the community and economy and to protect the waters and environment associated with these resources.

down by the Minister of the Environment.[65] Wody Polskie exercises ownership entitlements in relation to water and real property connected with water management that are property of the State Treasury or so far have been handed over for permanent management by regional water management authorities that are state budget units.[66] The legislator's intention was to centralise the entities exercising the ownership entitlements of the State Treasury and to manage these in accordance with the Act of 16 December 2016 on the Rules for Managing State Property, which, for example, restricts the authority solely to the minister responsible for water management affairs.[67]

This model relates to the public trust doctrine.[68] The public trust doctrine, in turn, arose as a result of treating certain (natural) property as non-renewable and important to society. This conception assumes that the state is not the owner of such property, but rather it manages it for the benefit of current and future generations.[69] Joseph L. Sax proposed the use of this conception beyond its initial scope concerning water and pointed to the possibility of extending it to other areas, including the natural environment.[70] He also referred to public trust in the context of the protection of cultural heritage.[71] Though this construction provides many possibilities because of its flexibility, the experience gained in other countries has not yet been widely applied in Poland.

The importance of water certainly goes beyond the subject of the owner or the subject of water law, as is confirmed by a variety of informative and inspection instruments for managing water resources, including water rationing. Water is perceived as an integral part of the environment, natural habitat or a multitude of

---

[65] Regulation of the Minister of the Environment of 28 December 2017 on granting the statute to the State Water Management Company Wody Polskie. Polish Official Journal (Dz. U.) 2017, item 2506.

[66] Article 528: "1. From the date of entry into force of this Act Wody Polskie represents the State Treasury and exercises the property rights of the State Treasury in relation to the following waters being the property of the State Treasury; (1) waters referred to in Art. 11 (1) (2)–(4) of the Act repealed in Art. 573, or parts thereof, and land covered by these waters, excluding land covered by waters referred to in Art. 11 (1) (3) of the Act repealed in Art. 573; (2) land properties located in the embankments, properties under flood embankments and flood banks with water facilities functionally connected with them, adjacent to the waters referred to in Art. 11, section 1, items 2 and 4 of the Act repealed in Art. 573, as well as buildings and other facilities located on these properties; (3) real estates other than specified in item 2, hitherto left in permanent management of Regional Water Management Boards being state budgetary units and the buildings and other equipment and premises located on those real estates; 2. If the properties referred above or parts thereof were before the date of entry into force of this Act leased, rented, let out or lent, the rights and obligations of the lessor, lessee, lessor or lender shall be assumed by the Waters of Poland as of the date of entry into force of this Act."

[67] Government draft law—Water law, Explanatory report, Print no. 1529, pp. 19–23. http://www.sejm.gov.pl/Sejm8.nsf/druk.xsp?nr=1529. Accessed 1 June 2022.

[68] About public trusts Zacharasiewicz (2016), p. 366, footnote 54.

[69] Resta (2017), p. 240.

[70] Sax (1970), pp. 475–566.

[71] Rose (1998), pp. 352–353.

organisms and is subject to protection regardless of who owns it (Article 50 WL 2017). There are a number of separate rules for managing water; one in particular stands out—the norm stipulating that

> the principle of common interests is taken into account, the cooperation between public administration, water users and representatives of local communities is required within the scope that allows the maximum social benefits to be obtained (Article 9 par. 2 WL 2017).

Concerning water management, an element arises as to how a given property can be used by a given unit. Article 32 provides for a common right to use public inland surface waters, internal sea waters and maritime territorial waters unless provisions stipulate otherwise. Pursuant to Article 33 of WL 2017, an owner of land may use water constituting the owner's property, as well as ground water located beneath that land. The use of water, however, has a defined purpose connected with satisfying one's own economic needs and is limited to collecting groundwater or surface water in amounts that do not exceed 5 m^3 per day averaged annually. All other activities involving the use of water law devices require appropriate consent. In turn, exceeding the water collection limit is governed by the provisions on water services. What is interesting is the position of an owner of real property, who may use water within the limits imposed by the act but may become a recipient of water services if those limits are exceeded. Water services as such are addressed to a broader group of entities.

The element of local community participation and cooperation is similar in the case of managing cultural heritage, with a difference that in the latter case, this constitutes an additional expression of the exercise of cultural rights. A holistic element (Article 9 WL 2017 used the term "comprehensive") also appears in the treatment of surface waters and groundwater resources that takes account of their amounts and quality; this is also very close to the protection of cultural heritage. One can expressly state that, to a great extent, the new Water Law considers global trends in the management of certain property that exists in limited amounts.

The right to water is conceived quite differently in the Water Law than in civil law. Rights to flowing water under the Decree on Property Law[72] were treated similarly to property rights. In relation to standing water (in wells, vessels, ponds), the construction of ownership was applied.[73] The absence of the self-existence of water meant that, in and of itself, it was not treated as a thing and therefore could not be an object of ownership. This view still exists today and affects what kinds of water rights are established; it also "leads to the conclusion that it's all about a right whose content can at least be compared with the content of ownership".[74] The legislator decided to name this right to property that is not a thing "ownership", bearing in mind historical regulations in this scope. But it did not manage to prepare a solution that would put an end to the doctrinal discussion. Indirectly, the absence of

[72] Decree of 11 October 1946, on Property Law. Polish Official Journal (Dz. U.) No. 57, item 319.
[73] Zoll (1931), p. 117.
[74] Mikosz (2013), p. 485.

any radical changes in the act pertaining to civil law means that, for effective water management, certain solutions may not go beyond the level of statements by the representatives of legal doctrine and jurisprudence.

The internal variety of water resources is confirmed by the status of groundwater, which is not a component part of land. Here, one cannot help but notice the exceptional treatment of certain types of property and their exclusion from the regulations of the Water Law—in particular, I am thinking of groundwater, which in certain situations is subject to the law governing minerals (Article 7 GMLA). This deep intervention on the part of the legislator and the artificial divisions made in a single category confirm that, apart from the criterion of physical properties (e.g. liquid or solid state), a material's importance for society is also of key importance. This latter criterion, which the legislator considers, is based on water's economic and social function. It is highly likely that the results of the discussion being conducted on this subject will effectively fuel the debate on cultural heritage.

Ownership of water has been formed as an absolute subjective right, which is not the type of ownership defined in the Civil Code. Given the incompatibility of the object of the law—water—with the definition of a thing, the legislator constructs an absolute subjective right whose content is close to that of ownership.[75] Within the scope of material property not having the attributes of a thing, the legislator creates absolute rights similar to ownership.[76] This approach is similar to existing constructions that create ownership over intangible property, such as intellectual property and industrial property, where these last cases involve a separate subjective right. While the ownership of water does not constitute ownership as defined in civil law, there are several arguments in favour of using the concept of ownership contained in the act. The argument made to date that this construction is proper, as is the use of the concept of "ownership", refers to the connection between an owner of water and water[77] in the context of the acquisition or exercise of a right, full control over the property and the possibility of using its resources—organisms and plants living in it.

It has been rightly pointed out that "the problem of water as an object of a civil law relationship must be approached practically".[78] This is key with respect to the scope in which water in its various forms can be traded and used rationally in accordance with people's needs. The observation of the emergence of another right similar to a right *in rem* is particularly important for further studies on cultural heritage, for in the case of archaeological artefacts that are found or discovered, the legislator also stipulates that their owner is the State Treasury. Such an internal differentiation of a resource can also be made regarding heritage, with the difference

[75] On the right to water resources and the classification of this right among rights in rem, see Agopszowicz (1973), p. 36. The author points out that the assumption that we are dealing with an "object" is determined by law and not by the object's features. He gives a building as an example, which may be a component part of real estate or constitute a separate object of ownership. Only in the latter case is it an object in the legal sense.

[76] Grzybowski (1985), p. 237.

[77] Rakoczy (2013), p. 26.

[78] Katner (2012), p. 1325.

that in the case of cultural heritage, its forms are continuously evolving (e-heritage, art created using algorithms).

In some legal systems, nature is granted legal subjectivity, and parts of it may even be treated as living persons. The idea of vesting rights in nature so that it can "look after its own interests" was initiated by Christofer Stone.[79] The development of legal thought on the protection of the natural environment has given rise to the first changes in legal systems during the twenty-first century. A theory from the 1970s has influenced how our surrounding reality is being shaped.[80] Granting rights to nature is not for the purpose of regulating nature's internal relations but for the objective of reforming relations between nature and humanity. As to the regulation of water, reference must be made to several relatively new and certainly innovative water regulations in Australia, New Zealand and India.

The earliest creation of a separate entity possessing its own water took place in Australia. The Victorian Environmental Water Holder, established in 2010, has ownership rights and decision-making power over the resources transferred to it. It was created as a legal person close in form to an association, though not subject to the particular provisions applicable to associations. It is recognised as a public entity within the meaning of Victoria's Public Administration Act of 2004 and spends public monies.[81] It represents an attempt to solve the particular problems involved in managing Victoria's water resources. Before the regulatory change, water was owned by the government, and water management had a political dimension that the new act sought to weaken.

In turn, a change in the status of the Te Awa Tupua river in New Zealand came about based on a legislative act from 2017.[82] The granting of legal personality to this water source connects two elements: it resolves the problem of the relationship between the Maori people and the river, which for them has religious and cultural significance, and it introduces a new model of managing the river and protecting its rights. Interestingly, there is no reference in the act to a legal person and its possible types as a corporation or foundation, but only to a person, a living being. This is confirmed by the content of Article 12 of the act. This shift is based on the acknowledgement of Te Awa Tupua as constituting an indivisible whole consisting of the river (over its entire length from the mountains to the sea), along with all of its physical and metaphysical elements.[83] In terms of legal theory, this is a highly controversial move because the river has no capacity to perceive, think rationally or endure suffering.[84]

---

[79] Stone (1972).

[80] Such changes have been introduced in the constitutions of Bolivia and Ecuador. Most likely, these changes have provoked new approaches to the problem of natural resources in the countries.

[81] O'Donnell and Talbot-Jones (2018), p. 3.

[82] Te Awa Tupua (Whanganui River Claims Settlement), Public Act 2017, no. 7.

[83] Art. 12 Te Awa Tupua is an indivisible and living whole, comprising the Whanganui River from the mountains to the sea, incorporating all its physical and metaphysical elements.

[84] Argyrou and Hummels (2019), pp. 755–756.

The final form of this solution was influenced by two key things. Firstly, the Maori people consider the river to be their ancestor. The sentence "I am the river and the river is me" (Article 13 letter c) of the act) illustrates the connection between the Whanganui Maori and the river and demonstrates the unity of their interests with the river and the protection and security of the river.[85] Secondly, previous negotiation processes concerning the ownership of land and rivers confirmed the existence of a dispute on this plane, while the act itself was the culmination of a process in which the indigenous people pursued their rights and implemented the suggestions of the Waitangi Tribunal.[86] Granting the river legal personality made it possible to avoid the problem of ownership since by acknowledging the river as a person, no transfer of ownership was necessary. This new legal formula is intended to protect the river, care for the legacy of the Maori ancestors and ensure that the river is used properly. The model of representing the interests of a river is a rejection of the popular trust system in favour of care provided by two wardens appointed by local authorities and the Maori people.

A final example worth examining is that of the Ganges and Yamuna rivers in India. Several days after the adoption of the act in New Zealand, on 20 March 2017, a court in Uttarakhand ruled that the rivers Ganges and Yamuna are recognised as living persons having the rights and obligations of a living person.[87] Both rivers are considered holy in Hindu mythology and are culturally important. The main aims of this solution were to combat the pollution of the rivers as a result of the existing water management policy and the waters' use for irrigation and generating hydro-electric energy.[88] In the Indian model, wardens are appointed by the court, as they sometimes are for minors.[89] It should be added that the very idea of portraying holy, divine rivers as beings in need of protection has not gained full acceptance as it violates the essence of divinity.[90]

The fact that the new status of the rivers was granted by a court, without any changes in the binding acts of law, caused the practical application of the ruling to be questioned and appeal proceedings to be initiated.[91] The Supreme Court, however, did not agree with the reservations of the government and upheld the previous ruling on 7 July 2017. The Ganges and Yamuna are therefore now treated as living

[85] Original: Ko au te awa, ko te awa ko au.

[86] The Whanganui River Report. Waitangi Tribunal 1999. GP Publications, Wellington. https://forms.justice.govt.nz/search/Documents/WT/wt_DOC_68450539/Whanganui%20River%20Report%201999.pdf. Accessed 1 June 2022.

[87] On granting legal personality to icebergs the High Court of Uttarakhand Gangotri and Yamunotri, Lalit Miglani v. State of Uttarakhand and others.

[88] O'Donnell (2019), pp. 165 et seq.

[89] The High Court of Uttarakhand, Judgement of 20 March 2017 Ganges and Yamuna Case, Mohd. Salim v State of Uttarakhand & others, WPPIL 126/2014.

[90] Alley (2019), p. 14.

[91] Issue of rivers' liability for losses caused by potential flooding was raised (Rivers do not have same rights as humans: India's top court (2017, 7 July). https://phys.org/news/2017-07-rivers-rights-humans-india-court.html. Accessed 1 June 2022.

beings,[92] though they are not natural persons. Unlike the Te Awa Tupua river, the Ganges and Yamuna have not been provided with the funds needed to represent their interests.[93] Their cultural and spiritual value and their importance to religion and culture are not the same as the care for the natural dimension of their condition. There is also a clearly observable political context to these decisions, which may not necessarily translate into the real protection of the rivers in practice.[94]

The basic assumption is to grant nature a right to protection in view of the historical, political and cultural context in which it is situated. Rather than having non-governmental organisations fighting over environmental protection, guardians can be appointed in a dispute to represent the interests in question. The formula of giving the rivers representatives and of including experts, advisory bodies and communities in river management (thereby detaching the rivers from state policy, which is dependent on political authorities) may be conducive to protecting the interests of the rivers in the future. The search for new categories of legal entities is ongoing and relates not only to technological progress but also to changes taking place in how we perceive the world around us. In each of the examples above, a river was granted a legal personality in a different way.

There is observable hybridity in these solutions. In each case, a new entity was called to life, whose form is related to that of a legal person or natural person. The law was used as a protective mechanism but was not a typical environmental protection public law; instead, it established a new entity and granted that entity rights to property that does not constitute a thing—in the case at hand, a river. The noticeable flexibility of this construction suggests that it may have a wider application. This makes it possible to bring about changes in the structure of ownership—to detach certain property from state ownership and create a new management framework that is beneficial to society and takes account of the interest of the property that has been legally separated.

This focus on solutions concerning water resources is an indication of how awareness is growing as to the importance of water. On the one hand, a river is granted legal personality; on the other hand, it remains a resource that is necessary for human life and that people exploit. No elements of the doctrine of public trust are present, in accordance with which everyone is entitled to a given property; instead, a new, independent legal entity is created. This subject is often granted financial resources (public), and its task is not only to protect its property but also to act in the interests of future generations. Its central task, therefore, is to care for the property and to be responsible for its relations with its surroundings. In turn, the interest of the community, that is, the broader interest of today's generations, is given a back seat and taken into consideration only insofar as it does not clash with the "interest" of the resource and future generations.

---

[92] Kukreti (2017).

[93] O'Donnell and Talbot-Jones (2018), p. 5.

[94] Alley (2019), p. 17.

This solution seems culturally far removed from the Polish system of law; nevertheless, it is worth examining some main assumptions that, due to their flexibility, may be drawn on later. The focus on the transparency of representing the interests of waters is intended to obtain independence from political decision-makers. The financial resources for protecting the interests of a given type of property and how it may be used are allocated to an organisation that is independent of public administration. Separating the interest of contemporary entities from that of future generations and granting protection to property as a living organism that, at the level of legal fiction, can feel do strengthen its position as property requiring guardianship.

4.2.3 *The Legal Status of Animals*

In the Polish Civil Code, the legislator makes several references to animals, for example by describing the responsibility for an animal or the rules under which the ownership of a swarm of bees or of a lost animal is to be determined. Apart from the many provisions in the Civil Code, however, the status of animals is essentially established by supplementary normative acts concerning how animals are to be treated. These stipulate the scope of animal protection and the manner of conduct with regard to animals, and these affect the situation in private law. The main purposes of such provisions are to protect animals and create a framework of control that makes it possible to verify whether the provisions of the law are being applied and whether animals are treated humanely.[95] Alongside this dereification, the issue of the personification of animals comes up more and more frequently. Granting animals legal subjectivity and the possibility of pursuing their rights is not unimaginable, but it does require the creation of an appropriate legal framework for this new status. The case of the monkey selfie described above and the legal regulations governing things confirm that there are many ways to protect property and that these may also encompass changes in civil law status.

The evolution in how animals are perceived has led to a change in their situation as subjects of civil law relations. The dereification of animals took place on the basis of the Animal Protection Act (APA) of 21 August 1997.[96] Animals, previously considered things, are no longer considered as such under the APA.[97] This dereification in Polish law is an example of the important changes taking place in how the subjects of civil law relations are classified. Certainly, even prior to the normative change on animals, this was not a "typical" thing. One may wonder, though, if the initial definition of a thing was proper to animals. If we trace the

[95] About animals Pazdan (2012), pp. 1043–1044.

[96] Animal Protection Act of 21 August 1997, consolidated text. Polish Official Journal (Dz. U.) 2019, item 122.

[97] For instance, free living animals.

different solutions applied to the ownership of wild and domestic animals, what emerges is a model of control based on legal fiction and a connection with real property (animals in the wild as component parts of real property). For this reason, before tackling the issue of the dereification of animals, I will present some legal constructions concerning animals living in the wild that cannot be taken into possession within the meaning of civil law.

From the very beginning of the Polish discussion on the status of animals, a division has been made between animals subject to the will of humans and those living in the wild. With regard to the former, there was no doubt about their specific nature, which is incompatible with that of things. It was more difficult, however, to classify wild animals, that is, those living free,[98] for such animals were considered incapable of being subject to a property relationship. The key element was to determine whether animals not subject to human control can be objects of possession, and it was found that what only makes an animal an object of possession is being subject to such control. Ever since animals have been legally regulated, the issue of an animal's value has been present, initially in connection with a ruler's interest in hunting and the animals obtained therefrom (hunting privileges or regalia). The institution of regalias foresaw the existence of areas of economic activity solely available to the monarch. They encompassed all larger animals, as well as all animals in a selected territory, resulting in their exclusion from hunting. At the same time, hunting small game was available to all.[99]

It should be added that constructions based on the acceptance of a certain legal fiction have been present from the beginning. During the work on a draft property law, it was assumed that a game animal constitutes a component part of a domain (real estate) while alive but a movable thing when dead. This was humorously presented by Fryderyk Zoll: "the above concept of a thing is sometimes ridiculed in the words that a hare on the run is immovable property, while a hare that has been shot is movable property".[100] This shows that, in the case of animals, the formal construction chosen by the respective legislation is very significant. Similar constructions for civil law needs have been made in respect of water and minerals, where their goal was to define the right holder and thereby fit the law to a given type of material property.

In accordance with the binding provision of Article 21 par. 1 APA, animals living free were deemed national goods. Such animals also include game animals living in the wild. Pursuant to Article 2 of the Hunting Law Act (HLA) of 13 October 1995,[101] game animals in the wild are the property of the State Treasury. All other animals living in the wild, though, are not covered by this regulation.[102] Nowadays,

[98] Polish Supreme Court, Judgement of 9 March 1973, ICR 58/73, NP. 1974, no. 9, item 1211.

[99] Bardach et al. (1993), pp. 71–72.

[100] Zoll (1938), p. 216.

[101] Hunting Law Act of 13 October 1995, consolidated text. Polish Official Journal (Dz. U.) 2018, item 2033.

[102] Mikosz (2013), p. 497; Pązik (2015), p. 25.

treating game animals as national goods refers, to a certain extent, to the historical place of animals in the hierarchy of property. The discussion on the right to game animals living free, as discussed below, is largely based on the public element of that right, defined as ownership by the State Treasury (Article 2 HLA). The Act also regulates the acquisition of ownership over an animal that has been hunted and the right to the body of the animal after its death.[103]

In the analyses of the ownership right of the State Treasury to hunted animals, three main threads appear. The first states that as long as an animal is free, it is not subject to ownership and cannot be the subject of a civil law relation.[104] The second thread concerns the treatment of the right of the State Treasury as a public law right. Supporters of the third viewpoint argue that the provision creates a law that "is a civil law, . . . though one marked heavily by elements of public law".[105] This evolution in the right of ownership shows that it is possible to make a distinction for animals (whereby they are granted autonomy) and to manage hunting breeding plans.[106] Some authors are not in favour of any of those conceptions and emphasise that whatever the character of the law is, up to the moment a game animal is taken into possession, it belongs to the State Treasury.[107]

Alongside the issue of determining who is a right holder and calling a right to an animal "ownership", it is equally important to determine the specific nature of animals as sentient beings. Pursuant to Article 1 HLA, "as a living being capable of suffering, an animal is not a thing". In the second sentence of the same article, the legislator adds that people ought to respect, protect and take care of animals. This is a very broad formulation of the relationship between humans and animals. Notably, the act only covers vertebrate animals (Article 2). The legislator distinguished various categories of animals according to their various functions and habitats (wild vs domestic animals). A regulation contained in the Animal Protection Act has serious legal consequences.[108] The existence of different types of relations between people and animals should also fit the directive on conduct contained in Article 1 APA. In every situation, regardless of whether we are dealing with a domestic animal, a farm animal, a laboratory animal used for specific purposes or an animal living in the wild, the notion of humane treatment should be taken into consideration.

At the beginning of the act, there is already a reference to a thing in the meaning of civil law since the legislator refers to matters not regulated by the act for the

[103] Three subjects could potentially acquire ownership of the animal that has been hunted. Provided Article 15 of the Hunting Law Act, the State Treasury will own the animal only if it is not located in the hunting districts. When the animal is acquired in the hunting districts, the property belongs to the lessee or operator of the hunting district. The two latter entities may give the game to persons performing the hunt.

[104] Katner (2012), p. 1337.

[105] Radecki and Danecka (2019), p. 71.

[106] Stec (2014), Art. 2 [Commentary].

[107] Pązik (2015), p. 25.

[108] About animals Pazdan (2012), pp. 1043–1044.

appropriate application of the provisions concerning things. The reference in Article 1 APA to an animal as a living being that experiences pain and suffering can be treated as a declaration by the legislator. It is argued that the reference to the appropriate application of the provisions does not solve the problem since the legislator simply shifts the verification of the provision, and thus the strengthening of animal protection, to those entities that apply the law. Agnieszka Bielska-Brodziak et al. refer expressly to the ongoing discussion between citizens and entities enforcing the law.[109] The legislator's intention was to achieve a state where an entity applying the law, aware of the directive contained in Article 1 APA, will apply its provisions cautiously and in consideration of the specific nature of the subject of protection. Stepping beyond the formal dimension, the dereification of animals is only possible when there are adequate instruments available that guarantee animal protection. This means that a statutory dereification of animals can have a real impact on animal protection only if provisions exist that establish mechanisms of protection and if there is a threat of punishment for entities that do not comply with the rules for dealing with animals.

Pursuant to Article 1 par. 3 APA, animal protection activities should be carried out by public administration bodies. It is crucial that these do not operate in an organisational vacuum but rather cooperate with other entities. Article 1 par. 3 stipulates that animal protection activities should be taken in cooperation with domestic and international institutions and organisations. Cooperation by public administration bodies is also mentioned in Article 3 APA, where the legislator focused solely on implementing the provisions and specified what entities should cooperate for the benefit of animals.[110] One of the tasks of such entities is to engage in activities that raise societal awareness and change how animals are perceived; the importance of educational campaigns cannot be overstated,[111] just as in the case of environmental protection and cultural heritage protection.

Despite the active role played by animal welfare organisations, the dereification of animals is not taking place at an even tempo, and problems are appearing in both statutory and common law systems.[112] Even under pressure from international organisations, domestic legislators approach the protection of animals as living beings in different ways. The Polish Act was a consequence of a change in how people perceive animals, while earlier a similar legislative change was approved in Austria.[113] At this stage of the legislative process, whether animals would no longer

---

[109] Bielska-Brodziak et al. (2019), p. 111.

[110] The Veterinary Inspection, as well as other relevant government and local government authorities, in order to achieve the goals set by the act, should cooperate with the following groups: the veterinary professionals association, institutions and non-governmental organizations that have animal protection as their statutory goal.

[111] About community, social attitude and education in the dereification process: Shyam (2019), pp. 78–79.

[112] Bradshaw (2018), pp. 812–814.

[113] Katner (2012), p. 1335.

be deemed things was not a foregone conclusion.[114] Nevertheless, the absence of a decision to dereify animals does not mean that in a given legal system, they are less protected. Dereification may be treated as an expression of a legal revision of the existing system governing material property and as an argument in support of the legal protection of animals.

For example, in 2019, a draft bill was proposed in Spain to amend the Civil Code and the Mortgage Act in relation to a change in the regulations covering animals.[115] In 2021, the act was introduced and constitutes unique legal development. Apart from adapting legal provisions to the greater social sensitivity towards animals that exist, it introduced solutions regarding rules relating to divorces and the regime of cohabitation and care of pets, an issue that has already been the subject of court deliberations. Additionally, the new law includes provisions on inheritance and the fate of an animal in the event of the owner's death.[116]

Legislative progress in acts related to animal protection has stood as a confirmation that a certain stage in the debate on the status of animals has come to an end, though doubts over the status of animals also concern the issue of legal subjectivity. That legal debate is being fuelled by the results of the discussion on artificial intelligence. Hence, the changes taking place can now be associated with technological progress. Seemingly independent problems have a common element—that of how property is to be located in the legal system. In the case of animals, the key element is that they can suffer, whereas the subjectivity of artificial intelligence results from its ability to create property "autonomously" in a way that is impossible for human beings to foresee and to engage in highly complex activities based on many variables.[117] With animals, there is an additional problem of how to determine which species are to be recognised as being capable of experiencing pain and suffering. Nor should we omit the conception that subjectivity should be granted to all species or, even more broadly, to inanimate parts of nature, such as forests and streams,[118] as has been partially illustrated above using the example of the legal status of rivers.

It is often noted that progress in legal thought tends to be reflected in legislation with a certain delay.[119] Often, the response of the legislator is not groundbreaking

---

[114]Paliwoda and Bąk (2015), p. 113.

[115]Proposición de Ley de modificación del Código Civil, la Ley Hipotecaria y la Ley de Enjuiciamiento Civil, sobre el régimen jurídico de los animals. Boletín Oficial de Las Cortes Generales, Serie B: Proposiciones de Ley, 1 de marzo de 2019, Núm. 167-5. http://www.congreso.es/public_oficiales/L12/CONG/BOCG/B/BOCG-12-B-167-5.PDF. Accessed 1 June 2022.

[116]Ley 17/2021, de 15 de diciembre, de modificación del Código Civil, la Ley Hipotecaria y la Ley de Enjuiciamiento Civil, sobre el régimen jurídico de los animales. "BOE" núm. 300, de 16 de diciembre de 2021, páginas 154134 a 154143. https://www.boe.es/boe/dias/2021/12/16/pdfs/BOE-A-2021-20727.pdf. Accessed 1 June 2022.

[117]Michalczak (2017), pp. 95 and 97.

[118]More Michalczak (2017), p. 93.

[119]Pietrzykowski (2018), p. 3.

but merely satisfies a practical need. In the case of statutory legal systems, it may be justifiable to carry out legislative work "in installments". For example, a new legal regulation may be preparatory in nature if the changes to be introduced are highly controversial or considered too radical. A legal regulation may also be symbolic in nature and never applied. In examining the effects of dereification, some authors invoke the concept of "symbolic" laws. These include killing fish at points of sale during the pre-Christmas period and the ban on circus events involving animals.[120] The dereification of animals does not in itself guarantee animal protection but may be treated as the core or central point around which legislative solutions aimed at implementing the basic principles expressed in Article 1 APA are gathered.

Discussions on the subject of animals are developing in many different directions, including granting animals legal subjectivity and the right to own the land they inhabit.[121] In Polish legal thought, animals are not considered legal entities. In the awareness that they are living organisms, they are situated in a set of property having special characteristics. While further research in this area has not been carried out, the idea of whether a separate conceptual category could not be created for animals, somewhere between subject and object, has arisen.[122] From the perspective of legal philosophy, the subjectivity of animals has been analysed by Tomasz Pietrzykowski.[123] He describes the concept of an impersonal subject and how it might be applied not only to animals[124] and draws attention to the pace of legislative change. He points to an element related to animals' capacity to feel and the "right of a given being to have its interests taken into account when the law is resolving conflicts between those and the interests or entitlements of other entities".[125]

This change in the general perception of animals as property not belonging to the category of things has been brought about by changes in the law, which in turn have resulted from advanced discussions on the subject. Other questions arise, namely whether groundbreaking legislative changes are a solution in themselves, whether the goal of animal protection and animal welfare can be achieved solely through regulation or whether the proper driving force for change is people's mentality.[126] Moreover, implementing changes also requires a reflection on how they will affect the entire legal system and how new legislation will confront other acts of law.[127] In a certain sense, the foundation of strengthening animal protection regulations is the

[120]Bielska-Brodziak et al. (2019), p. 111.

[121]Bradshaw (2018), pp. 812–814.

[122]Cf. Goettel (2013), pp. 15–16. Goettel expresses the opinion that in the practical dimension, such a solution would not be operational.

[123]Pietrzykowski (2015), pp. 247 et seq.

[124]To show the dynamics of change, he refers to the change in the legal approach to homosexuality and the recognition in some jurisdictions of the equality of same-sex marriages.

[125]Pietrzykowski (2015), p. 247; on the constitutional basis for animal protection, see Pietrzykowski (2019), pp. 8–13.

[126]Katner (2012), p. 1338.

[127]Pietrzykowski (2018), pp. 3–4; Pietrzykowski (2019), pp. 21–22.

recognition that animals can experience pain and fear, and therefore they do not belong to the civil law category of things. This does not change the fact that only a legislative decision ended the debate over the status of animals, which attests to the force of legislative action, including when doctrinal experts hold widely different views.

The dereification of animals has taken place only in relation to some animals. The criterion used was not the status of the entitled subject but its particular characteristics, including the capacity to experience suffering. On the other hand, such particular characteristics can also apply to the animal world as part of the natural environment. In the Act, animals living free are defined as national goods. Yet in Article 4 par. 1 of the Nature Protection Act of 16 April 2004,[128] it is stated that bodies of public administration, legal entities, other organisational units and natural persons are obliged to be stewards of nature, which is part of the national heritage and wealth. The act refers to both animate nature (including animals) and inanimate nature as national wealth. Within that heritage and wealth, which is subject to protection, APA also distinguishes property that does not constitute things. In this way, apart from the criterion of importance to the public interest, the specific characteristics of the types of property are also taken into account. In the long term, given the ongoing theoretical discussion on the legal status of animals, dereification itself may prove to be only a transitional solution.

One can safely say that this process will only concern a small section of the animal world. Nevertheless, the act granting legal personality to the Urewera forest in Australia shows that animals constitute only a part of a greater whole, such as a forest, river or wetland.[129] Pursuant to Article 11 of the Te Urewera Act, the Urewera forest is a legal entity represented by the Urewera Council. Granting legal subjectivity to a forest, as has been done in Australia, will involve a need to determine whether animals living free within the forest constitute parts of it. In Poland, the practical problem of assigning wild animals to a defined territory could be resolved by reverting to a legal fiction known to be used during the interbellum.

The problem of how the interests of animals can be represented other than by animal welfare organisations taking part in proceedings concerning their protection remains unresolved. Further modifications will certainly draw on legislative achievements in other countries, including granting legal subjectivity to animals and creating a mechanism for representing them. The first step could be impersonal subjectivity. In the context of animal protection, such a solution in criminal proceedings has been proposed by Paweł Mazur.[130] One way would be to create the possibility to defend animals and their rights; this would also strengthen their position as living beings.

---

[128] The Nature Protection Act of 16 April 2004, consolidated text. Polish Official Journal (Dz. U.) 2018, item 142 as amended.

[129] Te Urewera Act 2014, Public Act, 2014 No 51. http://www.legislation.govt.nz/act/public/2014/0051/latest/whole.html#DLM6183705. Accessed 1 June 2022.

[130] Mazur (2018), p. 136.

The defence of those rights, however, would be confined to relations between animals and people and actions by the latter that harm the former. The concept would not be applied to relations between animals themselves. The real purpose of this type of empowerment is for animals to be perceived not as beings that are destined to suffer from human activities but as ones with defined rights connected to their safe development and the maintenance of their habitats in a condition that does not threaten them with extinction. This does not change the fact that in the case of farm animals held for the purpose of satisfying people's need for food, the burden of respecting their rights will shift to the conditions in which they are kept.

4.3 A Holistic Approach to Cultural Heritage and the Process of Classifying Property

4.3.1 A Holistic Approach to Cultural Heritage in Polish Law and the Process of Classifying Property

A holistic approach to protecting cultural and natural heritage is a consequence of changes in how the world and human environment are perceived. As a result, there is a departure from having only fragmentary mechanisms in place for protecting cultural heritage. This can be illustrated using the example of a historical building, where the scope of protection takes into account the building's interaction with adjacent buildings (architectural complexes), natural elements, people and the function of the building in the local community (cultural landscape). Its protection must also be considered during the construction of new investments; spatial planning constitutes an important tool for protecting the natural and cultural value of the landscape.[131]

In other words, a holistic approach means striving to perceive resources collectively, considering their specific characteristics and the overriding goal of creating solutions to manage and protect those resources effectively. A holistic conception of cultural heritage arises when intangible heritage is taken into account, as well as—in this age of technological progress—digital heritage. This approach of addressing material, intangible and digital heritage is particularly important for conservation practice.[132] Here, I will only deal with the element of nature to the extent that it is directly connected with material property not constituting things.

A holistic conception of cultural heritage in its natural and cultural dimensions can be linked with an integrated approach to cultural heritage. This posits an acceptance of the coexistence of a natural component in cultural value and therefore in cultural heritage. Attention is drawn to the gradual inclusion of a natural component in cultural heritage. There are two reasons for this. The first concerns the

[131] Gawin (2018), p. 7.

[132] Szmelter (2018), p. 33.

creation of additional mechanisms of protection, apart from those foreseen in environmental protection law. The second stems from the long-standing, mistaken idea that natural resources are renewable and inexhaustible. This phenomenon is all the more interesting in that the above-discussed property not constituting things is natural property whose creation depended not on human beings and their evolution but on nature itself. Their importance for society has caused the legislator to grant "ownership" over some of this property to the State Treasury. The foreign regulations discussed above demonstrate that there is a cultural dimension to the natural environment and that new, unique regimes can be created to protect the environment, including those based on granting certain property (e.g. rivers) legal subjectivity.

To a certain degree, the debate on a holistic approach to natural and cultural heritage completes the domestic discussion separating certain branches of the law on the protection of historical objects.[133] Cultural heritage is of fundamental importance for human development—in terms not only of spiritual growth but also of economic growth. In turn, the assumptions of environmental protection law, a branch of law already recognised in Polish law, posit maintaining the environment in a state that permits the healthy functioning of society. At the level of international law, there is a view that cultural heritage law constitutes a small part of a greater whole—international environmental protection law.[134] Yet it seems that even at the international level, heritage protection law stands out due to the large number of legal instruments used to regulate this issue. It is my hope that the findings resulting from this analysis may, to some extent, complement the already extensive arguments that exist for the emergence of a new field of law.

Essentially, the resources of cultural heritage and natural heritage are non-renewable and irreplaceable. Their importance is confirmed by the many mechanisms protecting them, which are contained in international and domestic acts of law. Heritage is an object of care and interest that is supranational and of vital importance to both current and future generations. Perceiving each such resource as something important for humanity has been analysed in terms of their particular relationship with people: cultural heritage as a creative force and natural heritage as an element forming the environment. In uninhabited natural areas having exceptional conditions, there is little or no human activity.[135] Globally, the concept of shared natural resources has run into fewer problems than does cultural heritage in terms of ownership, how to determine entitled entities or even whether there is a need to protect resources.[136]

In analysing the specific characteristics of these two types of resources, it is worth looking at the important differences between them. Cultural heritage resources accumulate, and their total number will always increase (despite obvious reductions due to ageing and destruction); natural resources do not increase at the same rate, if at

[133]Zeidler (2014), pp. 23–33.

[134]Blake (2015), p. 117.

[135]Blake (2015), p. 117.

[136]Kowalska (2018), pp. 21–22.

all. In the case of natural heritage, we are also faced with the possibility of protecting animals and breeding sites, as well as restricting or banning fishing, that is, protecting types of animate nature. Within cultural heritage, one can distinguish objects connected with beliefs and rituals that have been returned to the representatives of the population concerned or their descendants, as well as the problem of human remains.[137] Cultural heritage is heterogeneous due to the variety of cultures that exist, as well as the differences at local, regional and national levels. This diversity can be considered in the context of how cultures interpenetrate each other on material and intangible levels. Natural heritage, on the other hand, results from nature and its laws, with humanity contributing little to its creation. There is also less interpenetration in natural heritage, and where this does occur, it is usually due to human intervention in the material components of that heritage. Examples of this process are valuable objects brought to Poland from abroad by members of aristocratic families in the nineteenth century or the arboretum in Kórnik, which contains plants originating in various corners of the world and which still delights visitors today.[138]

There are also differences in the measures taken to preserve different components of heritage. Human intervention in natural resources does not facilitate protection activities, while fostering the development of natural heritage "artificially" is not always widely supported. Most often, what best protects natural heritage is not interfering with how it functions and not engaging in activities that could disturb it. In the case of cultural heritage, though, as well as non-interference, numerous activities are conducted aimed at conservation, which involves intervention in the "cultural fabric". It is indisputable that the physical survival of humanity primarily depends on the role played by natural heritage. Nevertheless, in the long run, a lack of attention to culture could adversely affect the quality of life and security of societies. Culture, heritage, the acceptance of cultural diversity and intercultural dialogue are vital to building the future, while education through heritage supports activities aimed at maintaining world peace, which is the foundation for the sustainable development of societies. Furthermore, culture is included in COVID-19 recovery plans. Hence, determining what stage domestic and international legislators have reached in perceiving cultural heritage and natural heritage jointly, as well as perceiving the existence of a natural component in cultural heritage, is of fundamental importance to build legal mechanisms of protection in the future and to evaluate whether a holistic conception of cultural heritage may help or hinder the process of identifying property of special importance.

Pursuant to Article 5 of the Polish Constitution,

> The Republic of Poland shall safeguard the independence and integrity of its territory and ensure the freedoms and rights of persons and citizens, the security of the citizens, safeguard the national heritage and shall ensure the protection of the natural environment pursuant to the principles of sustainable development.

---

[137] Paterson (2010), pp. 643 et seq.

[138] The spread of natural elements through natural forces (water, wind) cannot be ignored.

Alongside territorial integrity and the security of members of society, national heritage and environmental protection are mentioned.[139] This demonstrates the importance of the two elements that are the main focus of this chapter and makes their inviolability and protection one of the main duties of the state. It should be added that some scholars of constitutional law argue for a very narrow interpretation of national heritage, as contained in Article 5, since it refers only to national heritage connected with Poland.[140] The prevailing view is that cultural heritage is part of the national heritage, while in Article 6 of the Constitution on national heritage, the broad scope of this norm and as the nation itself is not a culturally uniform category.[141] Cultural goods whose preservation lies in the interest of future generations may then be seen as components of the national cultural heritage.[142]

Does the joint reference to environmental protection and national heritage permit a holistic approach to them? It would seem not, for this article of the Constitution is only a proclamation of the highest goals and duties of the state. The Polish Constitutional Tribunal has ruled that

> a linguistic and functional interpretation of the provisions of the Constitution shows that the constitutional legislator used both the word 'safeguard' and its synonym 'ensure' (used interchangeably) in a broad sense, encompassing all forms of state activity.[143]

In that ruling, the concept of safeguarding was interpreted to mean that the state at least co-participates in protection. In my view, the use of the phrase "ensure the protection of the natural environment" implies a greater amount of state responsibility and a broader impact therefrom.[144] A legal norm obligating the state to ensure the protection of the natural environment forces the state to engage in activities whose results are beneficial for a wider group of recipients (for example, the inhabitants of neighbouring countries) and for adjoining natural areas located beyond the country's borders. Examples include the Tatra National Parks in Poland and Slovakia. Certainly, a lack of action could have adverse consequences for natural heritage in Poland and in the neighbouring park in Slovakia.

If a state withdraws from environmental protection, this brings about adverse consequences much faster than in the area of cultural heritage; those effects may include the poisoning of animals and water intakes, epidemic diseases or the destruction of recreation and leisure sites. In the long term, however, the effects in both areas are comparably harmful since if safeguarding the cultural heritage is neglected, future generations will be materially and culturally poorer—deprived of the ties culture provides. Abandoning activities that strengthen cultural heritage

---

[139] Drela (2006), p. 21.

[140] Frankiewicz-Bodynek (2019), pp. 112–154.

[141] Florczak-Wątor (2016), p. 289.

[142] Florczak-Wątor (2016), p. 288.

[143] Polish Constitutional Court, Judgement of 8 October 2007, K 20/07, OTK-A 2007/9/102. Polish Official Journal (Dz. U.) 2007, No. 192, item 1394.

[144] Cf. Florczak-Wątor (2016), p. 288.

resources would also be detrimental to cultural development and artistic activities—whose results are to add to that heritage in the future.

One can attempt to conceive cultural heritage and natural heritage jointly based on the provision of Article 5 of the Constitution, stating that the Republic will safeguard the national heritage. It is worth invoking Article 4 par. 1 of the Nature Protection Act of 16 April 2004,[145] which states that bodies of public administration, legal persons, other organisational units and natural persons are obliged to be stewards of nature, which is part of the national heritage and wealth. Nature—defined as national heritage and wealth—complements the national cultural heritage. In this respect, it can be acknowledged that the national heritage referred to in the Constitution has two dimensions, one natural and one cultural. Environmental protection encompasses the protection of not only the natural heritage but also, pursuant to Article 1 of the Environmental Protection Act (EPA) of 27 April 2001,[146] the principles of environmental protection and the conditions for the use of natural resources, taking into account the sustainable development requirements that go beyond the issue of protecting natural assets.

The current fragmentation makes the system for protecting cultural heritage weaker than could be achieved by a single act modelled after the French *Code du patrimoine*. It cannot but be noticed that the lack of cohesion in the protection of natural monuments and landscape degradation are two weaknesses in a SWOT (strengths, weaknesses, opportunities and strengths) analysis of the state of cultural heritage and current trends in its protection. This finding, made within a SWOT analysis, was published in the National Programme for the Protection and Guardianship of Monuments 2014–2017.[147] Several years have passed since that diagnosis, yet it is difficult to avoid the impression that the Polish legislator is only halfway down the road from transforming this weakness into a strength.

Among the acts of law that complement the Environmental Protection Act, the following should be noted: the Nature Protection Act (NPA) of 16 April 2004,[148] the Act on Making Available Information on the Environment and Its Protection and on Societal Participation in Environmental Protection and on Environmental Impact Assessments of 3 October 2008[149] and the Forest Act (FA) of 28 August 1991.[150]

[145] The Nature Protection Act of 16 April 2004, consolidated text. Polish Official Journal (Dz. U.) 2018, item 142 as amended.

[146] The Environmental Protection Act of 27 April 2001, consolidated text. Polish Official Journal (Dz. U.) 2018, item 799.

[147] Resolution No. 125/2014 of the Council of Ministers of 24 June 2014 on the "National Programme for the Protection and Care of Monuments", p. 42.

[148] The Nature Protection Act of 16 April 2004, consolidated text. Polish Official Journal (Dz. U.) 2018, item 142 as amended.

[149] Act on Making Available Information on the Environment and Its Protection and on Societal Participation in Environmental Protection and on Environmental Impact Assessments of 3 October 2008, consolidated text. Polish Official Journal (Dz. U.) 2017, item 1405 as amended.

[150] The Forest Act of 28 August 1991, consolidated text. Polish Official Journal (Dz. U.) 2014, item 1153 as amended.

Similarly, matters of culture, including issues related to cultural heritage protection, appear as a leading element in a number of acts, including the MA, the National Archival Resources and Archives Act[151] (ANARA), the Library Act and the ARNCP. The expansiveness of these acts, however, cannot be compared with that of the legislation on environmental protection.

Historical sites subject to protection include parks, gardens and other forms of designed greenery (Article 5 par. 1 pt. 1 letter g APGM). Such other forms can include, for example, an orchard that, together with a park, forms part of the grounds of a manor house.[152] No doubt, the key to identifying such historical sites is their form, which is an expression of a human idea expressed in a design. When determining whether a park, garden or other form of designed greenery has the status of a historical site, what counts most is that the vegetation was prepared and arranged in accordance with a creative concept. It seems that the absence of precise design documentation over time does not determine whether we are dealing with a form of designed greenery. When entering a historical site in the register, however, it is important to precisely determine the borders of a garden or park[153] and when these are being entered along with a historical building, such as a manor house; its position and other architectural elements (fountains, sculptures, arches, decorative walls) should also be included.

In practice, such sites usually appear in the vicinity of historical buildings or other building objects that form part of a historical complex. In the register of historical monuments, there may be an entry of a historical site comprising a historical palace and a historical garden or park. One can imagine, for example, a historical park with an architectural component in the form of a historical mausoleum or observation tower in relation to which court administrative proceedings were brought to verify whether there were any infringements by the site's holder, which excluded the possibility of a tax exemption.[154] It should be emphasised that, given the nature of a historical site, the presence of plants and other natural elements only extends the duties of the administrator of the site.

Historical value is not determined in the same way as for historical monuments that do not contain a natural element. The need to make changes, for example replacing plants or stands of trees, is treated differently.[155] To maintain a site's historical value, it is important that the composition of the whole remain legible and capable of being accurately recreated. The historical sites analysed combine natural and cultural elements. It may even seem that these elements are interwoven, but the

[151] Act of 14 July 1983 on the National Archival Resource and Archives, consolidated text. Polish Official Journal (Dz. U.) 2020, item 164.

[152] Voivodship Administrative Court in Warsaw, Judgement of 1 January 2018, VII SA/Wa 1841/17, LEX no. 2557394.

[153] Sikora (2010), p. 16.

[154] Supreme Administrative Court in Warsaw, Judgement of 6 June 2018, II FSK 1441/16, LEX no. 2550496.

[155] Voivodship Administrative Court in Warsaw, Judgement of 1 January 2018, VII SA/Wa 1841/17, LEX no. 2557394.

cultural value prevails over the fact that the creation of the site was dependent on a natural element. The compositional and aesthetic element comes to the fore,[156] though it is permissible to protect a site due to its historical and natural attributes.

Such an integration of cultural and natural elements occurs in cultural parks. A cultural park is established

> on the basis of a resolution for the purpose of protecting the cultural landscape and preserving distinctive landscaped areas with immovable historical objects characteristic of the local building and settlement tradition (Article 16 par. 1 APGM).

The establishment in the resolution of prohibitions and restrictions on the grounds of a cultural park may limit the use of the property, in this case as a compensatory mechanism, as indicated in the EPA. While it is worth noting this reference to environmental protection law, this does not imply a specific connection between legislative acts, only the legislator's rational effort to avoid duplicating legal solutions. The reference is important to follow the rules of legislative technique, but it shows clear similarities, the specific characteristics of the protection and a recurrent obligation to compensate for the restrictions associated with them.

The reference to Cracow for the purposes of publication seems further justified by the fact that the city was entered on the World Cultural Heritage List as having universal value for all humankind. In seeking, then, to demonstrate how these elements are integrated in practice, it is worth noting that the resolution establishing the Kraków Old Town Cultural Park[157] contains a reference to green areas. It also states that the cultural park is created in order to protect the functionality and composition of the Cracow Planty and other greenery, gardens and squares of historical value, as well as the green slopes of Wawel Castle Hill, and foresees the possibility of these being revalorised. In the introduction to the "Plan for the Protection of the Old Town Cultural Park in Cracow", reference is made to the value of the cultural and natural elements that coexist there and to the role of the cultural park as a means of "implementing the principles of integrated protection".[158]

The plan involves protecting and preserving the landscape of Kraków's Old Town, where the

> landscape, understood as the cultural physiognomy and natural environment of the Old Town, is treated as a very literal synthesis of all the processes taking place in the area from a historical perspective that form its present and future.[159]

A basic goal of the sustainable development of the park is to protect its cultural heritage; this is to be accomplished in a way that is integrated with protecting the

---

[156] Voivodship Administrative Court in Warsaw, Judgement of 25 April 2018, II OSK 2382/17, LEX no. 2499014.

[157] Annex to the Resolution No. R XLII/544/12 of the Krakow City Council of 4 April 2012 on the approval of the "Protection Plan of the Old Town Cultural Park in Krakow", p. 2.

[158] Annex to the Resolution No. R XLII/544/12 of the Krakow City Council of 4 April 2012 on the approval of the "Protection Plan of the Old Town Cultural Park in Krakow", p. 2.

[159] Annex to the Resolution No. R XLII/544/12 of the Krakow City Council of 4 April 2012 on the approval of the "Protection Plan of the Old Town Cultural Park in Krakow", p. 2.

natural environment. Another goal directly concerns the natural environment and involves protecting biological diversity and natural assets, in addition to improving the state of the natural environment and preventing it from degradation.[160]

A cultural park is a form of protection of the cultural landscape, which takes two elements into consideration. Distinguishing landscape issues from the protection of historical heritage and from the definition of a historical site has been postulated in the literature on the subject, referencing the United Nations Educational, Scientific and Cultural Organization (UNESCO) recommendation concerning the Safeguarding of Beauty and Character of Landscapes and Sites.[161] Accordingly, a direction for change was indicated.[162] In accordance with a revised legal definition from 2015, a cultural landscape is an area identified by people, which contains both natural elements and products of civilisation, historically formed by natural factors and human activity (Article 3 pt. 14 APGM).[163] In this case, a holistic approach is less evident, though integrated protection—and therefore integrated management—remains in the foreground. Managing a park necessitates the creation of interdisciplinary expert advisory bodies, an interdisciplinary steering group,[164] and, when developing programmes, drawing on documents connected with natural protection, including the Regulation of the Minister of the Environment of 12 May 2005 on preparing draft plans for the protection of national parks, nature reserves and landscape parks, modifying such plans and on the protection of natural resources, products and components.[165]

In practice, attention should be paid to the competing nature of the forms of protection provided in the APGM and NPA and to the consequences of any conflict between them pertaining to the proper implementation of a protection model. For example, this may arise when applying additional protection in the form of a nature reserve as

> nature protection resulting from the status of a reserve (acceptance of natural succession) may be contrary to preserving the historical purity of spatial forms (compositional axes, viewing openings and directions, structure of stands of trees).[166]

Pursuant to Article 13 NPA,

> nature reserves include areas maintained in a natural or little altered state, ecosystems, natural refuges and habitats, plant habitats, animal habitats, mushroom habitats, and products and components or inanimate nature distinguished by particular natural, scientific, cultural or landscape values.

---

[160] Annex to the Resolution No. R XLII/544/12 of the Krakow City Council of 4 April 2012 on the approval of the "Protection Plan of the Old Town Cultural Park in Krakow", p. 7.

[161] Recommendation concerning the Safeguarding of the Beauty and Character of Landscapes and Sites adopted by the General Conference of UNESCO at its 12th session, Paris, 11 December 1962.

[162] Zalasińska (2010), p. 265.

[163] About definition of cultural landscape Jagielska-Burduk (2016a), pp. 204–205.

[164] Böhm et al. (2005), p. 11.

[165] Böhm et al. (2005), p. 8. Polish Official Journal (Dz. U.) 2005, item 794.

[166] Fortuna-Antoszkiewicz and Łukaszkiewicz (2015), p. 25.

The same may also be subject to protection as a historical monument under the legal definition contained in the APGM. There is a close interaction between the "natural, scientific, cultural or landscape values" attributed to reserves and the "historical, artistic or scientific" values attributed to historical monuments. But the means of protection are different, being based on different assumptions; for example, in the case of a historical garden, it involves maintaining its aesthetic value and caring for and replacing plants. A reserve established on a historical site needs no such intervention. Potentially, this may lead to conflicts between, for example, an aesthetic need to replace a stand of trees and the natural process of changes in vegetation that take place in reserves undisturbed.

It is also worth noting that, by a decision of the legislator, the legal definition of a forest in FA includes a criterion that relates to historical value. Pursuant to Article 3 pt. 1 letter c FA, a forest is land of an area of at least 0.10 ha covered in forest vegetation (forest crops)—trees, shrubs and undergrowth—or temporarily devoid of such vegetation that is entered in the register of historical monuments. This is a special situation within the system of cultural heritage protection (Article 3 pt. 1 letter c FA). This construction is all the more unique in that, generally speaking, forests develop without human participation. Yet we cannot ignore forestry activities, such as planting new forests and establishing tree nurseries; these human activities lead to the growth of forests that would not otherwise exist. As a result, not every forest will qualify as a historical monument under the definition in the APGM. Without a doubt, the accent on human activity is different in the case of historical monuments than in the case of forests.[167]

In the first case, the emphasis is on people's creative input in cultural heritage; in the second case, human activity is only an additional circumstance that does not substantially affect the value of a forest as such. What is more, in the case of a forest treated as an immovable historical monument, its potential use for production, attributed automatically in the FA, is eliminated. Here, the intention was for a forest to be subject to a form of protection granted to historical objects without being a historical monument.[168] One can see how the combination of the types of protection resulting from the provisions on protecting nature, forests and historical monuments indicates that heritage is perceived holistically, through the prism not only of the dependence of regulations but also of their coexistence. This example shows the importance of the legislator's intention when aligning regulations not only in terms of practice and cooperation among entities but, above all, in order to send signals to researchers, commentators and experts on how certain phenomena are to be perceived on the basis of a particular legislative solution. The shift towards cultural heritage would pose no theoretical problem under Japanese law, for instance, nor would the perception of culture and natural elements by indigenous peoples.

Finally, it is worth considering the presence of natural elements in museums. In accordance with the definition found in Article 1 of MA, a museum is a non-profit

[167] Rakoczy (2015a), pp. 4–6.

[168] Rakoczy (2015a), p. 9.

organisational unit whose purpose is to collect and protect material and intangible property belonging to the natural or cultural heritage of humanity. Thus, collecting and protecting the natural heritage of humanity is part of a museum's activities. Among the examples of museum tasks mentioned in the MA, one can find tasks that expressly concern natural heritage, such as Article 2 pt. 4 MA: "securing and conserving collections and, to the extent possible, securing immovable archaeological artefacts and other immovable objects and material culture and nature".

The wide range of museum activities includes a natural component that is also emphasised in Article 3 MA, pursuant to which museums may be created for one or more areas of human activity and creations of nature. This is also reflected in attempts to systematise and identify types of museums.[169] Every occurrence of a natural element draws attention to itself, such as in the connection between natural history museums and natural science museums, in the distinct category of natural history museums and in the inclusion of open-air museums in the conceptual apparatus. This does not change the fact that the scope of activities for different types of museums overlap, while this segment of museums stands out from others.

Pursuant to Article 21 par. 1 MA, "museum objects are movable or immovable things that constitute the property of the museum and are entered in the inventory of museum exhibits". The relationship between MA and APGM and the question of whether only historical objects can be museum objects have been the subject of many analyses.[170] Unfortunately, these issues met with no reaction from the legislator and remained unsolved for some time.[171] Today, one can structure a museum collection based on the binding provisions concerning museum inventories. Pursuant to Article 24 par. 3 MA,

> in the case of a museum exhibit that is a historical monument, a permit to delete it from the inventory may be issued provided that it has been entered in the register of historical objects. The deletion occurs at the moment of the exhibit is entered in the register of historical monuments.

Additionally, the heterogeneous content of museum collections (consisting of historical and non-historical objects) is determined by the definition of "national cultural property of the Republic of Poland" pursuant to ARNCP. In accordance with that legal definition, the national cultural property of the Republic of Poland is also a thing that is not a historical object, provided that it is entered in an inventory of museum exhibits in a museum and meeting the criteria for a cultural institution within the meaning of Article 10 par. 2 of AOCCA. In this situation, not only historical objects within the meaning of the APGM constitute museum exhibits—but also specimens of plants and insects or butterfly collections can be museum exhibits.

---

[169] Antoniak (2012) Art. 3 [Commentary]. Folga-Januszewska (2006), p. 11 indicates that museums can be specified as follows: art museums, museums of antiquity and archaeology, museums of natural history and natural science, and history museums. Żygulski Jr (1982), pp. 81–106 distinguishes art, historical, archaeological, natural history, technical-scientific and economic museums.

[170] Zalasińska (2008), pp. 22–30.

[171] Jagielska-Burduk (2016c), pp. 113–154.

In this situation, one could also assume that a forest, as referred to in Article 3 pt. 1 letter c MA, is also a museum exhibit if it constitutes museum property and is entered in the museum inventory.

The thread of natural collections is connected to soft law related to museum activities. The ICOM Code of Ethics for Museums[172] is often attached to the code of ethics issued by the director of an individual museum. Regulations on natural collections are found in the section dealing with expanding collections and addressing issues of collections of living organisms, as well as collecting biological or geological specimens. Particular care should be exercised when acquiring objects relating to Article 2.4 of the Code of Ethics if there is any suspicion that "the acquisition of an object involved arbitrary, unscientific or deliberate destruction of or damage to ... the natural environment". Pursuant to Article 2.6 of the Code of Ethics, museums expanding their collection

> should not acquire biological or geological specimens that have been collected, sold, or otherwise transferred in contravention of local, national, regional or international law or treaty relating to wildlife protection or natural history conservation.

In turn, Article 2.7 of the Code of Ethics refers to collections of living organisms and stipulates:

> When the collections include live botanical or zoological specimens, special consideration should be given to the natural and social environment from which they are derived as well as any local, national, regional or international law or treaty relating to wildlife protection.

As a side note, it is worth observing that concerning open-air museums, the Polish legal system is not conducive to their development; in fact, in certain situations, such as those concerning animate nature, the regulations hinder museums from fulfilling their mission.[173] One can assume that in any new act on museums, should one appear, the element of nature will be taken into account, including the practical functioning of open-air museums. Good opportunities and good platforms for reflecting on this subject are all the thought-provoking meetings of representatives of open-air museums and the activities of the Association of Open Air Museums in Poland[174] and, Europe-wide, the Association of European Open Air Museums affiliated with the International Council of Museums.[175]

The link between legal regulations on cultural and natural heritage in Poland still need in-depth analysis. It appears in the forms of protection, specific regulations to a certain component of cultural heritage and diverse structures of cultural property. In terms of future regulations, the idea of including some parts of natural protection provisions in cultural-heritage-related acts is recommended. The same applies when

[172] Kodeks Etyki ICOM dla Muzeów. Translated from English, French and Spanish version by S. Waltoś. https://icom.museum/wp-content/uploads/2018/07/poland.pdf. Accessed 1 June 2022.

[173] Gwardzińska (2018), p. 250.

[174] www.muzeaskansenowskie.eu. Accessed 1 June 2022.

[175] The Association of European Open Air Museums (AEOM), https://uia.org/s/or/en/1100034651. Accessed 1 June 2022.

it comes to dealing with problems regarding heritage, where two ministries responsible for culture and cultural heritage and nature are involved. The organisational silos and management will not fuel a holistic approach to cultural heritage, therefore the horizontal cooperation should complement the existing legal protection framework. At the operational level, the cooperation that goes beyond is an inevitable part of an existing policy.

4.3.2 A Holistic Approach to Cultural Heritage in Selected Acts of International Law

One example of the joint regulation of natural and cultural heritage is the UNESCO Convention concerning the Protection of the World Cultural and Natural Heritage of 1972. Not only does it foresee the joint protection of these areas, but it also creates an international model of cooperation within the scope of heritage protection, which includes a system of financial aid. During the period when the Convention was being drafted, its conception of cultural and natural heritage was pioneering and constituted an important step forward in thinking about heritage as a whole. While the definitions of cultural heritage and natural heritage describe resources accepted as such within the meaning of the Convention, their significance goes beyond that act. It should be added that the Convention arose on the basis of two separate drafts prepared with the participation of the International Council on Monuments and Sites (ICOMOS) and the International Union for Conservation of Nature (IUCN)[176] and was the first marriage of cultural and natural heritage in international law.

The preamble, which acts as a solemn introduction and sets out the assumptions and needs lying at the heart of the Convention, states that damage to or destruction of any property belonging to the cultural or natural heritage constitutes an irreversible impoverishment of the heritage of all the peoples of the world and draws the attention of the international community to the issue of heritage protection. In this context, heritage means all natural and cultural property in the world.[177] In addition, reference is made to ownership, with emphasis on "the importance, for all the peoples of the world, of safeguarding this unique and irreplaceable property, to whatever people it may belong".

As an example of effective, integrated protection, a Japanese act[178] that connected the issues of natural heritage and cultural heritage is provided. That act provides for cooperation among ministers responsible for the environment and

[176] O'Keefe and Prott (2011), p. 77.

[177] O'Keefe (2004), p. 189, footnote 4.

[178] Law for the Protection of Cultural Property of 30 May 1950, Law no. 21. https://en.unesco.org/sites/default/files/japan_law_protectionproperty_entno.pdf. Accessed 1 June 2022.

cultural heritage. For example, when registering a natural site, it is necessary to verify whether the mechanisms foreseen for environmental protection must be implemented (Article 109 par. 5). This legislative connection was made in Japan in 1950, when the new act was adopted.[179] This is why the Japanese joint approach was raised during the work on the Convention Concerning the Protection of the World Cultural and Natural Heritage. In the Convention, cultural heritage and natural heritage are regulated jointly, while their co-dependence is confirmed by the entries made on the World Heritage List.[180]

The World Heritage List, created pursuant to Article 11 par. 2 of the Convention, constitutes a list of cultural and natural heritage property that the World Heritage Committee acknowledges as having exceptional universal value. The list is an open list. At present, it contains 1154 entries, though for the purposes of this chapter, the most important are those that jointly include natural and cultural values, that is, cases of "a mix of cultural heritage and natural heritage". This results from the ideas and goals of the Convention, expressed in the preamble, and from the provisions of the Operational Guidelines for the Convention. The importance of world natural heritage is confirmed by the number of successful entries to the list.[181] Geographically, the largest number of mixed entries are in Africa, East Asia, Oceania and Southwest Europe (Albania, Greece). The number of mixed entries (39) is far lower than the number of entries concerning natural heritage (218). Nevertheless, most entries by far continue to include cultural heritage (897).[182]

The entry criteria to be used by States Parties, and later for determining what features of the cultural and natural heritage constitute outstanding universal value, are set out in the Operational Guidelines.[183] The World Heritage Committee was entrusted with the task of preparing this document, the contents of which have been amended several times. From the introduction of the Guidelines in 1977 to the

---

[179] Scott (2003), p. 386.

[180] Pursuant to Article 1 of the convention, the cultural heritage consists of: "architectural works, works of monumental sculpture and painting, elements or structures of an archaeological nature, inscriptions, cave dwellings and combinations of features, which are of outstanding universal value from the point of view of history, art or science; groups of buildings: groups of separate or connected buildings which, because of their architecture, their homogeneity or their place in the landscape, are of outstanding universal value from the point of view of history, art or science; sites: works of man or the combined works of nature and man, and areas including archaeological sites which are of outstanding universal value from the historical, aesthetic, ethnological or anthropological point of view". Whereas, in the meaning of the convention, natural heritage consists of "natural features consisting of physical and biological formations or groups of such formations, which are of outstanding universal value from the aesthetic or scientific point of view; geological and physiographical formations and precisely delineated areas which constitute the habitat of threatened species of animals and plants of outstanding universal value from the point of view of science or conservation; natural sites or precisely delineated natural areas of outstanding universal value from the point of view of science, conservation or natural beauty".

[181] Piotrowska-Nosek (2014), p. 236.

[182] https://whc.unesco.org/en/list/. Accessed 1 June 2022.

[183] WHC.17/01 of 12 July 2017.

present, there have also been changes concerning the interaction of cultural heritage and natural heritage; these reflect the growing need for an integrated approach, which has evolved since the Convention came into force. Even in the first version of the Guidelines, it was stated that states should, as soon as possible, include in their proposals heritage whose outstanding universal value results from a specific combination of natural and cultural values.[184] This passage was located in the last (fourth) part of the document entitled "Recommendations for State Parties". In the version from 1980, this information was moved to the principal part of the Guidelines, par. 13.[185] Here, reference was made to the spirit of the Convention and the will of the States Parties to propose World Heritage List property whose outstanding universal value derives from a particularly clear connection/arrangement of natural and cultural features.

Until 2005, separate criteria were in place to assess natural heritage and cultural heritage. In the version of the Guidelines from 2005, in the section containing the definitions of world heritage, a category of "Mixed Cultural and Natural Heritage" appeared for the first time, with joint criteria for outstanding universal value[186] presented. These were defined as partially or wholly fitting the definition of both natural and cultural heritage set out in Articles 1 and 2 of the Convention. The procedure for nominated mixed heritage was elaborated by the World Heritage Committee and advisory bodies.[187] The fate of the cultural landscape has been even more complicated; initially, it was treated as natural heritage and later on as cultural heritage.[188] The problem has now been resolved, and the issue of how property is to be assigned has been systematised, at least at the level of the UNESCO Convention. In practice, problems continue to crop up, with the most noticeable being the divide between how the cultural landscape is understood in international and domestic laws and how the concept is to be applied in practice.[189] This is why it is so important for experts to take part in forming procedures and developing methodologies for evaluating the cultural landscape and for the results of their work to be implemented at the domestic level.[190]

This is not to suggest, however, that people's perceptions of the landscape dimension of the natural and cultural heritage, or of humanity's role in forming it, are always shared and equal.[191] The cultural landscape is defined in Article 1 of the

[184]CC 77/Conf.001/8, par. 28. As far as possible, Member States should include, in their submissions, properties that combine in a significant way cultural and natural features of outstanding value.

[185]WHC 05/1 of 2 February 2005.

[186]Operational Guidelines, WHC 05/1 of 2 February 2005, Para. 49–53.

[187]World Heritage Committee: 39 COM 9B, Progress report on the reflection on processes for mixed nominations, https://whc.unesco.org/en/decisions/6207/. Accessed 1 June 2022.

[188]Whitby-Last (2008), pp. 52–57.

[189]Dailoo and Pannekoek (2008), pp. 41–42.

[190]Rössler (2002).

[191]Blake (2015), p. 131.

Convention as cultural property representing "works of man or the combined works of nature and man". Such works illustrate the evolution of human society and settlement over time, as affected by the physical limitations and/or possibilities provided by the natural environment and affected by interacting social, economic and cultural forces, both external and internal. This explanation of issues in connection with the landscape arose due to the difficulties encountered in classifying property and evaluating whether the entry criteria had been met.[192] For practical reasons, the cultural landscape was defined as the cultural heritage where there is a simultaneous, explicit and resonant natural element.[193] In light of the Convention and the Guidelines, the status of the cultural landscape is confirmed by the overlapping of the natural and cultural heritage.[194]

In five decades since the Convention was signed, there have been many changes in its interpretation, to keep in step with the spirit of the Convention and the spirit of the times. Such changes have been supported by the Operational Guidelines. These affect practice and are the most important tool of the Convention, allowing it to evolve. One of the decisions contained in the Guidelines is that a balance should be maintained between the entries of cultural heritage and natural heritage.[195] That balance has not yet been achieved. Perhaps this is a result of States Parties paying more attention to cultural heritage when making entries to the World Heritage List. Attempts to steer the number of entries in another direction have met with disapproval from experts because such artificial coordination is not in line with the fundamental assumptions underlying the Convention.[196] There is also a lack of balance geographically, in the sense that some regions are more heavily represented than others. This problem was noticed many years ago and led to decisions by the UNESCO World Heritage Committee.[197] The situation is due to the absence not of natural or cultural resources but of organisational possibilities and teams of qualified people.[198] Thus, practice continues to fall short of achieving the basic goals of the Convention.

The use of the term "cultural heritage" in the Convention confirms that there has been an evolution of the concept and a gradual departure from strictly material heritage with an ownership aspect: "cultural property". Indirectly, the connection made between culture and the environment is confirmed by the shortened name of

[192] Whitby-Last (2008), p. 57.

[193] Whitby-Last (2008), p. 62.

[194] Cf. Strecker (2018), pp. 62–66.

[195] Operational Guidelines for the Implementation of the World Heritage Convention, WHC.02/2, 2002 Par. 15.

[196] Scovazzi (2008), p. 167.

[197] World Heritage Committee, Decision 28 COM 13.1, 2004, Global Strategy for a representative, balanced and credible World Heritage List, https://whc.unesco.org/en/decisions/33/. Accessed 1 June 2022. Earlier Decision: CONF 202.9, 2002, Budapest Declaration On World Heritage. https://whc.unesco.org/en/decisions/1217/. Accessed 1 June 2022.

[198] Musitelli (2002), pp. 328–329.

the Convention—"World Heritage Convention".[199] This does not mean, however, that the Convention is devoid of references to ownership issues. Article 6 par. 1 refers to rights *in rem*. In accordance with the Convention, the States Parties recognise that such heritage constitutes a heritage of significance to the world, whose protection is the duty of the international community as a whole, which must make efforts to cooperate, in full respect for the sovereignty of states on whose territory cultural and natural heritage is located and without violating the rights *in rem* to that heritage resulting from domestic legislation. Since the Convention entered into force, this article has been said to raise doubts or even to contain hidden contradictions.[200] In the context of the universal value of heritage and its treatment as a common good, this issue of rights *in rem* can be difficult to reconcile with the interests of the state in which a given heritage item is located, with those of the international community and with an evaluation of what is beneficial for the heritage.

Moreover, given the various forms of world heritage, this provision refers not only to property rights but to similar rights as well. An outstanding example of the different legal regimes that apply to material property is the historical silver mine in Tarnowskie Góry,[201] entered on the World Heritage List. This case involves both ownership of real estate and ownership by the State Treasury of mines and minerals. In other words, in relation to one property protected by the Convention, different rights to particular parts of it are enjoyed by different right holders. Also worthy of note are the relations between particular types of cultural heritage that complement each other, thus forming a whole, and their place in the world heritage. For example, the World Heritage List contains entries for both the Old Town of Warsaw[202] and the Archives of the Capital Reconstruction Bureau, entered on the Memory of the World List in 2011.[203] Note that the Memory of the World Programme supplements, in a certain sense, the much older entry on the World Heritage List. The creation of new forms of protection or mechanisms for managing heritage, which not only coexist but have common roots, makes it possible to compile a complete picture of that heritage, without artificial divisions. The legal regulations and ways of dealing with a particular type of cultural heritage will in each case be applied, while new regulations should be developed for new types of heritage, keeping their specific nature in mind.

The Convention's position among other acts of international law demonstrates its importance as a pioneering act that proposed a new approach to heritage. This international act for the protection of cultural and natural heritage initiated new trends and a new way of thinking about heritage, making it accessible to multiple states. As a regulation that unifies the natural and cultural heritage, the Convention can also be viewed as an organism that is evolving—not only in terms of how it is

[199] Piotrowska-Nosek (2014), p. 236.

[200] Francioni (2008), p. 5.

[201] Decision: 41 COM 8B.25.

[202] Decision: CONF 016 V.12.

[203] Komorowski (2018), p. 51.

interpreted or the changes made to the Operational Guidelines but also in terms of new challenges and threats to heritage that are arising. Perceiving heritage as a complex process[204] is in line with the spirit of the Convention since it is evident from the Convention that the natural heritage and cultural heritage form a harmonious whole.

This connection between the natural environment and cultural heritage comes across somewhat differently in the conventions of the Council of Europe. In the European Cultural Convention adopted on 9 December 1954 in Paris,[205] it is difficult to find a holistic view of cultural heritage that contains a natural component. That Convention does speak, however, of the need for states to cooperate in heritage protection and in supporting research concerning culture. Pursuant to Article 1, states undertake to take appropriate measures to safeguard and encourage the development of their national contribution to the common cultural heritage of Europe. In the Convention on the Value of Cultural Heritage for Society of 13 October 2005 (also known as the Faro Convention), the issues of culture and heritage are treated quite differently.[206] This is a framework convention that depicts the relationship between cultural heritage and society. A broad understanding of heritage, its interaction with people and their surroundings, and the place of heritage in the broader context were the key elements discussed during the work on this Convention.[207] The definition of cultural heritage contained in it emphasises the multi-dimensional significance of resources for humanity, while the document refers to cultural rights (the right to heritage, the right to take part in cultural life).[208] Cultural heritage emerges as a reflection or expression of changing values, beliefs, knowledge and traditions. Heritage includes all elements of the environment that have resulted from the interaction between human beings and a given place over time. This mutual interaction between people and their surroundings also includes the natural environment.

The emphasis placed on an integrated approach to policies on cultural heritage and other resources varies. Pursuant to Article 8 of the Convention, states undertake to utilise all heritage aspects of the cultural environment to promote an integrated approach to policies concerning cultural, biological, geological and landscape diversities. The goal of these activities is to achieve a balance between those components (pt. b).[209] Furthermore, states are given the task of promoting qualitative changes in

---

[204] Purchla (2012), p. 63.

[205] European Cultural Convention signed in Paris on *19th December* 1954 (ETS No. 018), convention was ratified by Poland. Polish Official Journal (Dz. U.) 1990, No. 8, item 44.

[206] Council of Europe Framework Convention on the Value of Cultural Heritage for Society signed on the 13 October 2005, ETS No. 199. The legislative procedure to ratify the convention is launched in Poland: Government Draft to ratify the Council of Europe Framework Convention on the Value of Cultural Heritage for Society, done at Faro on 27 October 2005, Print no. 1571. https://www.sejm.gov.pl/Sejm9.nsf/druk.xsp?nr=1571. Accessed 1 June 2022.

[207] Fojut (2009), p. 19.

[208] Jakubowski (2016), p. 163.

[209] Przyborowska-Klimczak (2011), p. 188.

the environment that will not threaten its cultural value (pt. d). The Convention also proposed a new, holistic way of looking at heritage and culture. Although the categories of cultural heritage were not expanded, they were placed in a context that includes the natural context. In the Explanatory Report to the Convention, consideration is given to the most recent trends relating to cultural values, the landscape and the environment, taking into account the idea of a cultural environment.[210] The Convention thus proposes a new vision of cultural heritage that includes its use for the development of humanity, as well as joint and individual responsibility for cultural heritage.[211] At the same time, it marks an important step towards a new dimension of cultural heritage as a resource, which combines both cultural and natural elements.

Moving the borders of cultural heritage in a conscious way and including a natural component in the legal regulation on culture constitute a further step in defining heritage and creating a legal framework for protecting it. Similar changes have been made concerning the protection of species of animals—that is, nature—followed by a shift in emphasis towards the protection of their habitats.[212] Currently, habitat protection, as indicated earlier, is a difficult area to regulate for it does not fit in squarely with property law. Evidently, though, placing the accent on people's interaction with nature is a natural consequence of the changes taking place in how we perceive our surroundings and affects the system for environmental protection, planning and management.

It is also worth mentioning the European Landscape Convention adopted in Florence on 20 October 2000,[213] which grew out of an idea to create a convention on this subject matter dating back to 1994.[214] Earlier, the concept of a cultural landscape appeared in the Operational Guidelines to the World Heritage Convention of 1972. The European Landscape Convention was preceded by, for example, Recommendation No. R (79) 9 of 20 April 1979 concerning the identification and evaluation card for the protection of natural landscapes,[215] Recommendation No. R (89) 6 of 13 April 1989 on the protection and enhancement of the rural architectural heritage[216] and Recommendation No. R (95) 9 of 11 September 1995 on the

[210] Explanatory Report to the Council of Europe Framework Convention on the Value of Cultural Heritage for Society, ETS No. 199, par 5.

[211] About new image of cultural heritage Jagielska-Burduk (2016b), p. 49.

[212] Fojut (2009), p. 15.

[213] Council of Europe Landscape Convention of 20 October 2000, (ETS No. 176), Poland ratified the convention. Polish Official Journal (Dz. U.) 2004, No. 14, item 98.

[214] Explanatory Report to the European Landscape Convention, ETS No. 176, par. 1.

[215] Recommendation No R (79)9 concerning the identification and evaluation card for the protection of natural landscapes adopted by the Committee of Ministers on 20 April 1979. https://rm.coe.int/CoERMPublicCommonSearchServices/DisplayDCTMContent?documentId=09000016804e1985. Accessed 1 June 2022.

[216] Recommendation No. R (89) 6 on the protection and enhancement of the rural architectural heritage adopted by the Committee of Ministers on 13 April 1989. https://rm.coe.int/

integrated conservation of cultural landscape areas as part of landscape policies adopted by the Committee of Ministers of the Council of Europe.[217]

In the European Landscape Convention, emphasis on cultural and natural components is placed quite differently than in the World Heritage Convention. Pursuant to Article 1 pt. a of the European Landscape Convention, landscape means "an area, as perceived by people, whose character is the result of the action and interaction of natural and/or human factors". In the literature, attention is drawn to the position that, in the case of natural factors, without human interaction, there can be no talk of cultural landscape.[218] Yet the most widespread view is that there are no "pure" natural landscapes, for humans have always had an impact on their environment; there is no place completely devoid of any trace of human presence.[219] This is well illustrated by the example of a mountain or hill where there is no human activity on a daily basis but whose importance derives from knowledge and beliefs and which therefore constitutes an element of the culture of the people living in the area and a part of the landscape having a cultural dimension. An example of how the concept of landscape has evolved globally is the case of Uluru, the sacred mountain of the Anangu in Australia, which was initially entered on the World Heritage List under natural heritage but was later changed to cultural heritage.[220] A similar interpretation can be drawn from the Explanatory Report to the Convention.[221]

The subjective scope of the Convention encompasses a variety of areas: rural, urban, suburban and natural. The cultural value of a landscape is not an aesthetic one, for the Convention refers to ordinary, common and degraded landscapes, as well as exceptional ones. The preamble emphasises: "Acknowledging that the quality and diversity of European landscapes constitute a common resource, and that it is important to co-operate towards its protection, management and planning." The cultural and natural values of European landscapes thus form part of the common European heritage.[222] Article 5 of the Convention sets out certain activities of states, including

> to recognise landscapes in law as an essential component of people's surroundings, an expression of the diversity of their shared cultural and natural heritage, and a foundation of their identity.

CoERMPublicCommonSearchServices/DisplayDCTMContent?documentId=09000016804cc8c2. Accessed 1 June 2022.

[217] Recommendation No. R (95) 9 on the integrated conservation of cultural landscape areas as part of landscape policies adopted by the Committee of Ministers on 11 September 1995. https://rm.coe.int/CoERMPublicCommonSearchServices/DisplayDCTMContent?documentId=09000016804fd025. Accessed 1 June 2022.

[218] Cf. Sługocki (2014a).

[219] Dailoo and Pannekoek (2008), p. 27.

[220] Strecker (2018), p. 67.

[221] Explanatory Report to the European Landscape Convention, 20 października 2000 r., ETS No. 176 par. 26, 38.

[222] Explanatory Report to the European Landscape Convention, 20 October 2000, ETS No. 176 par. 30.

The landscape is perceived in terms of human rights. The connection between the landscape and human rights was emphasised in the Recommendation of the Committee of Ministers on the contribution of the European Landscape Convention in the exercise of human rights and democracy, with a view towards sustainable development.[223] The goals of the Convention focus on the right of everyone to use the landscape[224] and further state that the right to the landscape should be a human right in the twenty-first century.[225]

Following the adoption of the Convention, the Council of Europe approved new recommendations aimed at facilitating and streamlining the process of Member States ratifying and implementing the Convention. The recommendation on guidelines concerning the implementation of the European Landscape Convention contains theoretical, methodological and practical guidelines for states. It also indicates that the adoption of the Convention is often the turning point in how states perceive the environment, while the Convention itself constitutes a unique instrument for helping states manage the environment.[226] Landscape is defined differently than from a heritage perspective; it is treated as "capital" or a "resource", understood as a physical place containing elements of culture or nature. The Convention proposes viewing the landscape from the point of view of people and their relationship with the external world, whose quality is a condition for further development.

Elements of nature are also referred to in other conventions concerning moveable cultural property, intangible heritage and underwater heritage. For example, the UNESCO Convention on the Means of Prohibiting and Preventing the Illicit Import, Export and Transfer of Ownership of Cultural Property of 17 November 1970 defines cultural property in Article 1 letter a) as "Rare collections and specimens of fauna, flora, minerals and anatomy, and objects of palaeontological interest". This is the only passage on the application of the Convention that refers to natural elements; the other categories in pts. b–k encompass objects whose cultural value is intuitively obvious, all of which are deemed to be cultural property.[227] Ridha Fraoua has commented on the inclusion of a natural element in Article 1, pointing out that the objects included in letter a) are important because of their scientific value. The others are important for archaeology, prehistory, literature and the arts, where their value can be cumulative.[228] Patrick O'Keefe sees this definition

[223] Recommendation CM/Rec(2017)7 of the Committee of Ministers to Member States on the contribution of the European Landscape Convention to the exercise of human rights and democracy with a view to sustainable development (adopted on 27 September 2017). https://rm.coe.int/1680750d64. Accessed 1 June 2022.

[224] Prieur and Luginbühl (2018), p. 18.

[225] Prieur and Luginbühl (2018), p. 19.

[226] Recommendation CM/Rec(2008)3 of the Committee of Ministers to Member States on the guidelines for the implementation of the European Landscape Convention (adopted on 6 February 2008). https://search.coe.int/cm/Pages/result_details.aspx?ObjectID=09000016805d3e6c. Accessed 1 June 2022.

[227] Cf. Zalasińska (2014), p. 186.

[228] Fraoua (1986), p. 53.

differently; he does not recognise the relationship noted by Fraoua between the definition and the categories set out in Attachment No. 1.[229] He proposes fossils as an example. A fossil may have scientific value in the field of prehistory or archaeology, or for science as broadly understood, including the natural sciences.[230]

In accordance with the Convention, states are to determine which objects should be deemed cultural property themselves, where they belong to one of the categories set out in Article 1 letters a)–k), though in practice this has not led to a harmonisation of domestic regulations.[231] During the debate over the content of Article 1, it was argued that the definition, which encompasses natural objects and works of art, was imprecise and could therefore require different legal solutions.[232] Nonetheless, this did not lead to any change in the content of Article 1, and natural elements remained among the categories of cultural property in the meaning of the Convention. In a report on the strengths and weaknesses of the Convention after 40 years of its enactment, no mention was made of Article 1 letter a). One may therefore assume that other problems connected with the implementation of the Convention, the achievement of its goals, prospects for changes or an additional protocol proved more important.[233] Or it may be that the definition in Article 1 has not posed a practical problem for the parties to the Convention.[234]

In the Operational Guidelines to the Convention, there is no indication that natural elements are difficult for the States Parties to identify cultural property. What has proven difficult are objects acquired from illegal archaeological and paleontological excavations, elements deriving from dismantled artistic or historical objects or archaeological sites, and ethnological objects or those derived from indigenous people. An example of the latter is human remains, which do not constitute cultural property within the meaning of the Convention. Indigenous peoples frequently seek their return to the country of origin and in order to provide proper burial. It is said that states should fully recognise such claims and, where necessary, introduce special legal regulations in accordance with the principles expressed in such documents as the United Nations Declaration on the Rights of Indigenous Peoples (UNDRIP) of 2007[235] and the earlier Principles and Guidelines for the Protection of the Heritage of Indigenous People, which was prepared by an

---

[229] O'Keefe (2007), p. 36.

[230] O'Keefe (2007), p. 36.

[231] Cf. Przyborowska-Klimczak (2011), pp. 25–26.

[232] Analysis of general observation and comments made by the Member States, which involve proposals to amend the preliminary draft convention: Means of prohibiting and preventing the illicit import, export and transfer of ownership of cultural property. Paris, 27 February 1970, Doc. UNESCO/SHC/MD/5, Add II, pp. 1–2. http://unesdoc.unesco.org/images/0006/000686/068690eo.pdf. Accessed 1 June 2022. Cf. Przyborowska-Klimczak (2011), p. 26.

[233] Prott (2011).

[234] In the report Fraoua (2012) refers to objects ID and division into "natural" and "cultural."

[235] United Nations Declaration on the Rights of Indigenous Peoples (A/RES/61/295). The United Nations Declaration on the Rights of Indigenous Peoples (UNDRIP) was adopted by the General Assembly on Thursday, 13 September 2007.

expert and the leader of the UN Working Group on Indigenous People, Erica-Irene A. Daes, in 1995.[236]

Here, it is worth pointing out that indigenous people could not pursue claims for returns under the procedure of the Convention. The Principles and Guidelines proposed in the year 2000, in a revised version,[237] not only refer to people's rights to human remains and objects related to cultural or religious practices but also show that entities (academics, academic institutions and museums) should take steps to return such goods. States and international institutions should support indigenous representatives in the process of recovering such property.[238] In short, apart from objects of culture and nature, an additional element appears that necessitates comprehensive protection and consideration of both culture and the legal status of human remains, as discussed in Sect. 3.2.[239] While this problem does not relate directly to the integration and division of property into natural and cultural, the important place it holds in the discussion on the point of contact between cultural heritage and natural heritage is indisputable.

A complementary international legal instrument is the UNIDROIT Convention on Stolen or Illegally Exported Cultural Objects of 24 June 1995,[240] which is a private international law instrument and a self-executing treaty.[241] Both conventions are recognised as being the most important international legal instruments for combating illegal trade in cultural property during peacetime.[242] The definition of cultural property accepted for the needs of the Convention refers to the definition in the UNESCO 1970 Convention and is the result of the discussion among the working group members who worked on that text.[243] Pursuant to Article 2 of the UNIDROIT Convention, cultural objects are those that, on religious or secular grounds, are of importance to archaeology, prehistory, history, literature, the arts or sciences and belong to one of the categories listed in the Annex to this

---

[236] Principles and Guidelines for the Protection of the Heritage of Indigenous People, E/CN.4/Sub.2/1995/26/Annex.1. https://www.cwis.org/document/ecn-4sub-2199526annex-1-principles-and-guidelines-for-the-protection-of-the-heritage-of-indigenous-people/. Accessed 1 June 2022; Operational Guidelines for the Implementation of the Convention on the Means of Prohibiting and Preventing the Illicit Import, Export and Transfer of Ownership of Cultural Property (UNESCO, Paris, 1970), Resolution 3.MSP 11, pp. 6–7. https://en.unesco.org/fighttrafficking/operational-guidelines. Accessed 1 June 2022.

[237] Report of the seminar on the draft principles and guidelines for the protection of the heritage of indigenous people (Geneva, 28 February–1 March 2000), E/CN.4/Sub.2/2000/26, Annex I, pp. 12–18. http://hrlibrary.umn.edu/demo/HeritageofIndigenous_Daes.pdf. Accessed 1 June 2022.

[238] Vrdoljak (2008), pp. 269–273.

[239] About human remains' legal regulation and 1970 UNESCO Convention ratification by the USA Nafziger (2009), pp. 116 et seq.

[240] Polish translation was prepared by Wojciech Kowalski (Konwencja UNIDROIT o skradzionych lub nielegalnie wywiezionych dobrach kultury. Polski Instytut Spraw Międzynarodowych, Warszawa 1996).

[241] Tasdelen (2016), p. 47.

[242] Hauser-Schäublin and Prott (2016), p. 4.

[243] On defining cultural objects Groenen (2018), pp. 49–59.

Convention. Among the categories of objects enumerated in letter a) of the Attachment are rare collections and specimens of fauna, flora, minerals and anatomical objects having paleontological value.[244] In one of the first versions, reference is made to the UNESCO Convention in Article 2,[245] but in the final version, it was decided to delete this provision and include the categories (identical with those in the UNESCO 1970 Convention) in the Attachment to the Convention itself. According to the findings made in the Institute for the Unification of Private Law (UNIDROIT) in Rome, there is no information stating that objects from the categories contained in letter a) of the Attachment have been the subject of legal or administrative proceedings based on the Convention. Nevertheless, the duplication of the solutions from the UNESCO Convention confirms that there has been a conscious expansion of the scope of cultural heritage to include a natural element. The role of the Convention not only is limited to creating a mechanism for return and restitution but also serves to change how cultural heritage is perceived by professionals, including museologists.[246]

Furthermore, the UNESCO Convention on the Protection of the Underwater Cultural Heritage of 2 November 2001[247] is inseparably connected with one of the elements of nature by its very scope. In the definition of underwater cultural heritage, a requirement was included that its components should "have been partially or totally under water, periodically or continuously, for at least 100 years" (Article 1 par. 1). The components of underwater cultural heritage listed in Article 1 par. 1 of the Convention include (i) sites, structures, buildings, artefacts and human remains, together with their archaeological and natural context; (ii) vessels, aircraft, other vehicles or any part thereof, their cargo or other contents, together with their archaeological and natural context; and (iii) objects of prehistoric character. It is worth noting that two of these three points contain a natural element (Article 1 par. 1 (i) and (ii)). This emphasis on the natural context is of considerable significance when evaluating activities in the vicinity of underwater heritage and determining whether they pose a threat. Underwater heritage, and its natural context, is threatened with destruction due to human activities that may accidentally disturb their condition, as well as activities aimed directly at them. The single legal regime created for objects of underwater cultural heritage was indicated as a reason for not including a natural component more broadly. During the work on the Convention, some states

[244] According to information obtained at the UNIDROIT in Rome in November 2018, no information has been provided to the Institute that objects in the categories listed in the Annex under paragraph A were the subject of proceedings under the Convention.

[245] Appendix IV Diplomatic Conference for the Adoption of the Draft UNIDROIT Convention on the International Return of Stole nor Illegally Exported Cultural Objects, Rome 7–24 June 1995 (As approved by the UNIDROIT Committee of governmental experts on the international protection on cultural property on 8 October 1993). In: Prott (1997).

[246] M.V.M. Clarelli during the 20th Anniversary of the UNIDROIT Convention Conference on the 28th May 2015 in Rome Clarelli (2015), p. 493.

[247] Convention on the Protection of the Underwater Cultural Heritage of 3rd November 2001. https://unesdoc.unesco.org/ark:/48223/pf0000124687.page=56. Accessed 1 June 2022.

favoured an expansion of the scope of the Convention to include natural sites or the prehistoric landscape. It was decided, however, that within the proposed protection and management model, such objects could not be given proper care.[248]

In turn, the UNESCO Convention for the Safeguarding of the Intangible Cultural Heritage of 2003 expressly declares the importance of the environment in protecting cultural heritage.[249] In its preamble, mention is made of the far-reaching interdependence between intangible cultural heritage, material cultural heritage and natural heritage. This concerns not only indigenous people but all communities. The impact of humans and their environment, including the natural environment, is confirmed by the broad definition proposed by the authors of the UNESCO 2003 Convention. Pursuant to Article 2 par. 2 of the Convention, intangible cultural heritage is partially manifested in knowledge and practices concerning nature and the universe. Practices concerning nature and the universe appear alongside other fields, including oral traditions and expressions; performing arts; social practices, rituals and festive events; and skills related to traditional craftsmanship. Natural elements can also be found in the background of customs and rituals or in places deemed sacred where such events take place.

A perfect example of the balanced roles of people, nature and culture is the traditional system of Corongo's water judges in Peru, which existed even prior to the Incan civilisation. The role of a judge, appointed for 1 year, is to manage water and improve the region's irrigation system by cleaning the canals since most members of the community are involved in farming. It is worth noting that water is distributed according to the principles of justice and equality. The judges' duties are strictly connected with the community's customs and beliefs and include taking part in ceremonies.[250]

An important part of traditional craftsmanship is obtaining materials from the natural environment in the form of, for example, willow shoots for weaving baskets, both as a skill and as an element of the identity of a given community, which may include running willow plantations, as is the case of the Polish community of Lucimia.[251] Referring once again to national lists of intangible heritage, there is the example of the rafting tradition in Ulanów, inseparably connected with that place and rafting trips, or bee keeping, entered on the Representative List of the Intangible Cultural Heritage of Humanity in 2020 as a set of practices and traditions connected with honeybees, their habits and their relationship with people and nature.[252] Falconry also involves an interaction with nature, where the protection of certain

[248] Dromgoole (2013), p. 89.

[249] Blake (2015), p. 120.

[250] Traditional system of Corongo's water judges Peru Inscribed in 2017 (12.COM) on the Representative List of the Intangible Cultural Heritage of Humanity. https://ich.unesco.org/en/RL/traditional-system-of-corongos-water-judges-01155. Accessed 1 June 2022.

[251] Weaving baskets "kabłącok" in Lucimia. https://nid.pl/dziedzictwo-niematerialne/krajowa-lista-niematerialnego-dziedzictwa-kulturowego/. Accessed 1 June 2022.

[252] Rafting tradition in Ulanów. https://nid.pl/dziedzictwo-niematerialne/krajowa-lista-niematerialnego-dziedzictwa-kulturowego/. Accessed 1 June 2022.

species of birds also comes into play. Falconry is inscribed as an element of intangible heritage at both the national and world levels. It was entered on the Representative List of the Intangible Cultural Heritage of Humanity in 2016 and covers many countries,[253] and since December 2021, Poland has been among them.[254]

4.4 Conclusions

Systematic categorisation of property requires a complex legislative process. Granting rights to property not constituting things may result in the impossibility of their classification as things within the meaning of the Civil Code. Another example is provided by the establishment of intellectual property rights in relation to property that does not fit the definition of a thing but is a creation of the human mind. Yet another case is the recognition that a given resource is of strategic importance, where the legislator therefore decides to separate it and create mechanisms for its management. The importance of the property concerned may be economic, social or political. The basis for separating property may be twofold: with regard to the criterion of being a thing and the importance of a resource, as in the case of water. Moreover, a new formulation of the status of certain property may lead to changes in how people think about and value it, in their affective reactions to it, which may in turn cause changes in how society approaches and perceives the surrounding world. Some of the resulting changes may be purely symbolic, having no practical dimension, but important nonetheless.[255]

In Polish acts of law, phrases concerning the importance of a given type of property stand out, such as recognising animals living in the wild as national property and public waters as public property (part of the common good), or the definition of cultural property as national wealth in the now-defunct APCP. After separating types of property, the legislator distinguishes between property that can be a subject of private ownership and property solely designated for the State Treasury. Property that is "owned" by the State Treasury may be given over for use by third parties (mining use or the use of state land covered with water). In each case, the manner of concluding an agreement is set out in detail in an act of law and requires a relevant concession. We must not ignore, of course, that at the same time, universal access to property may be possible, such as in the case of water, as an expression of a universal right of access and of the entitlements of landowners.

[253] Eleventh session of the Intergovernmental Committee for the Safeguarding of the Intangible Cultural Heritage, Decision 11.COM 10.b.15.

[254] Sixteenth session of the Intergovernmental Committee for the Safeguarding of the Intangible Cultural Heritage, Decision 16.COM 8.b.14. Inscribed in 2021 on the Representative List of the Intangible Cultural Heritage of Humanity. https://ich.unesco.org/en/8b-representative-list-01191. Accessed 1 June 2022.

[255] Cf. Praduroux (2017), p. 68.

The nature of absolute rights to the property described here has not been fixed over the course of time. At various moments, private ownership has been more or less accepted, and possible trade restrictions have been justified with new arguments. The strategic importance of some types of resources precludes them from being treated as ordinary objects of trade. In the Polish legal system, the legislator creates rights similar to rights *in rem* in a manner that is not uniform. This largely depends on the specific nature of a given type of property and, in the case of material property, results from the variety of properties they have and the functions they play in the economy and society. The dynamic results from changes being introduced at different times. Practically, every groundbreaking legal change is preceded by a lively discussion that goes on up to the critical moment when the new legislative solution is introduced. For example, the development of legislation concerning animals is the result of a scientific debate on how animals are perceived as living beings. Amendments to water law, on the other hand, demonstrate how the implementation of EU law can be used to introduce changes, such as by making the concept of the State Treasury's "ownership of water" more precisely defined.[256]

The discussion on ownership or other rights to the types of property described above has been one of the stages in the state's economic development. Historical systems based on regalia focused on the privileged position of the monarch. In the case of minerals and water, the legislation in force at the beginning of the twentieth century permitted a greater share of private ownership, but later, there was a systemic takeover of such property by the state. The ownership of minerals and water now involves a state monopoly, while the establishment of rights to these (such as mining use) does not constitute a limited right *in rem*. The "ownership" of material property not constituting things is always supported by additional protective mechanisms.

The "ownership" of vital and strategic resources is usually assigned only to the State Treasury. In this sense, we can treat water and mineral deposits as an element of the common good, which is managed by the state. The way such resources are used is set out in acts of law and must not cause their total exhaustion—the use must be sustainable. This balancing of interests takes account of the need to hand the resources concerned down to future generations. At the same time, every current generation is entitled to use them. This is similar in a way to the institution of the fee tail, which constitutes a separate estate that cannot be alienated and serves to maintain a family, including its future generations.

The analyses of mineral deposits, water and animals in this chapter attest to the legislator's individual approach to these in treating them as objects of civil law relations. In each of these categories, several particular solutions appear, depending on express criteria, such as animals living in the wild versus domestic animals. There is also a division between mineral deposits situated below the surface of the earth and those already extracted. Such types of property change freely from one form

[256] Draft Act amending the Act—Water Law and some other acts along with draft executive acts, Explanatory report, Sejm of the 6th term, Print no. 3601, p. 5. http://orka.sejm.gov.pl/Druki4ka.nsf/wgdruku/3601/$file/3601.pdf. Accessed 1 June 2022.

(standing water in a lake) to another (bottled water), thereby changing their capacity to be an object of trade.[257] The status of property sometimes depends on its location, its physical discovery by people and its kinetic state (e.g. flowing water).

When creating artificial divisions, the legislator pursues in each case a specific goal, such as granting certain waters the status of minerals. As mentioned above, certain types of property are assumed to be state property. This does not mean, however, that private entities are excluded from using them (fishing entitlements, water law permits). Natural resources, including water, forests, parks and cultural heritage, may also be treated as belonging to the common good. The examples of water and forests exhibit both private ownership and State Treasury ownership, where the State Treasury is granted some of these resources (e.g. flowing waters).

Modifications of the law resulting from changes in the political system, acts of nationalisation and the reorganisation of the structure of ownership led to certain types of property being treated as public property having strategic importance (e.g. the mining industry). Furthermore, the main emphasis was on determining the scope of use of such property; in each case, the state (and thereafter the State Treasury) became the entitled entity, then the manager, until a model was created for resources to be managed by separate state management units (e.g. Wody Polskie). In shaping the ownership of waters, differences in those resources were identified and led to the acceptance of different legal constructions concerning standing waters and flowing waters. Additionally, in the case of both mineral deposits and waters, there arose a need to establish the limits of the law and of the ownership of real estate.

A particular example of this process is the separate legal regulation of animals as living beings capable of experiencing suffering. This places animals outside the classic dichotomy of subject and thing. The dereification of animals has resulted from changes in how people think about animals and from the international debate on the subject; as the examples of Poland and Spain show, that influence does not lead to the adoption of identical domestic regulations. The direction of change is being laid out in case law and by doctrinal experts, while in a certain sense, the legislative process is only the culmination of a prior transformation. The dereification of animals stems from a theoretical discussion and also from a debate in society, which is most frequently set off by an event that is a gross violation of animal rights and basic human values. Such eye-catching or even shocking events make people emotionally ready to support a tightening of the legal regime and confirm the justness of improving animals' legal position. The existing internal diversity of animals and the detailed regulations confirm that a single, universal assumption on dereification will not eliminate the problems that arise concerning animal rights; primarily, such a change stands as a step forward for civilisation.[258]

The outstanding changes in animal protection legislation that are described in this chapter and that could also be applied in other areas are summarised by Ewa Łętowska. She points out that, in a number of cases, by focusing on the success of

---

[257] Different opinion Agopszowicz (1973), p. 36.

[258] Cf. Goettel (2013), pp. 42–49.

specific changes to be introduced, the debate fails to reach the core of the problem. Łetowska argues that

> the way in which civil lawyers argue allows the debate over 'animals in civil law' to be treated as merely an interesting contribution to what is in fact a failure to see one's own 'legal' thinking, inspired by a narrow point of view.[259]

This observation also aptly reflects the discussion on cultural heritage, the multitude of its forms and the successful or unsuccessful attempts to fit these into the frame of civil law or, more broadly, private law.

Certainly, the solution of granting legal personality to some parts of nature, such as rivers or forests, poses a challenge to the typology of civil law subjects. These models are intended to put the interests of such property at the forefront. At present, the "ownership" right over property not constituting things is focused on the public interest and the benefits from responsible management on the part of current and future generations. The foreign models presented here shift the emphasis from the entitled entity or entities to the property itself and "its" interest. This is because the existing systems of protection are inadequate; new solutions must be sought. The new solution that brings to life a new entity that can pursue its rights, has guardians or representatives, and most importantly does not constitute ownerless property, is intended to enable that property to endure.

There is also a noticeable change in how we think about material property and things and how we classify them. The division into movable and immovable things has evolved based on the value of a given type of property. The criterion of mobility was related to the greater value of real estate, though this did not mean that, for example, a herd of animals would not be defined as real estate. In respect of material property not constituting things, in the cases discussed above, their value as part of the common good also arises, as does the need to preserve them for the public interest. In relation to the components of cultural heritage, one can find similar dependencies connected with the criterion of value and the significance of a given part that rises above the interests of the current holder. Making a division based solely on the dichotomy between movable and immovable things is not possible. Yet cultural heritage is perceived through the prism not of material value but of the intangible value incorporated in it.

A holistic approach to cultural heritage should be taken into consideration when seeking new legal regimes. Looking at common heritage as something that humanity should take an interest in and care for reinforces the element contained in the Faro Convention, which puts humanity at the centre of cultural heritage, whereas the document "Model for a National Act on the Protection of Cultural Heritage"[260] includes the protection standards established by the UNESCO 2001 Convention and the UNESCO 1970 Convention. Its introduction contains a sentence concerning

---

[259] Łętowska (1997), p. 73.

[260] Model for a National Act on the Protection of Cultural Heritage. https://docplayer.net/15301881-Model-for-a-national-act-on-the-protection-of-cultural-heritage-please-also-consider-the-inclusion-of-regulations-on-natural-heritage-if-applicable.html. Accessed 1 June 2022.

natural heritage.[261] The authors of the document encourage, to an extent possible, the inclusion of regulations on natural heritage within a given domestic legal system. In the definition of cultural heritage, reference is also made to the natural context of the components of cultural heritage.

A holistic view of heritage found in the World Heritage Convention is confirmed by the constellation of external actors involved, including the institutions that cooperate in evaluating state applications (ICCROM, ICOMOS, IUCN). In addition, the inclusion of the definitions of cultural landscape and mixed heritage is a sign of progress in the discussion and in building principles of cooperation. By treating cultural heritage as a joint category, the goals set out in the Convention are the same, including the most important goal of passing cultural property down to future generations. In the case of the legal regulations concerning real estate outside the World Heritage List, this is less evident. The legal framework covers elements of nature (European Landscape Convention). Regulations are clearly connected at the level of movable property in the UNIDROIT and UNESCO Conventions, which also refer to collections of nature.

There is an observable mirror effect in the interaction between international and domestic laws. One of the factors that strengthen the development of certain areas of domestic law is the experience and achievements made at the international level. The overlapping of certain models of conduct in domestic law and the use of a definition of cultural heritage in the process of interpreting domestic provisions are important for the development of laws on the protection of cultural heritage. The cultural function of natural heritage in international law must be revised and redefined.

The need to prepare an international framework convention similar to the Faro Convention has been pointed out by Ana Vrdoljak.[262] Ultimately, such a convention could become a framework in the area of cultural heritage and serve as a road map for states. It is worth suggesting that this instrument be preceded by the appointment of teams of experts to make legal diagnoses of domestic regulations and to create a model for good solutions (similar to the "best practices" applied in managing cultural heritage). It might be good to start with a declaration, followed by the appointment of teams of experts, who could also employ a holistic approach to heritage.

Here, it is worth mentioning the scope of activities undertaken with regard to cultural and natural heritage. Due to the impossibility of reconstructing or restoring the initial state of the environment, preventive actions and their effectiveness are what guarantee that it remains in good condition. Unfortunately, interfering with natural resources may prove to be irreversible, with protection efforts only resulting in less destruction or a lack of further degradation (e.g. oil spilled from a tanker in coastal waters poisoning, injuring and killing animals). In the case of cultural heritage, restoration and reconstruction are possible. Moreover, reconstruction occasionally has a symbolic dimension. With regard to natural heritage, restoration can

[261] Model for a National Act on the Protection of Cultural Heritage, p. 1: "Please also consider the inclusion of regulations on natural heritage, if applicable".

[262] Vrdoljak (2015), p. 553.

be achieved by replanting forests and rebuilding an ecosystem, for example by stocking a river with fish. Yet we must not ignore the fact that the devastation of natural heritage may have irreversible consequences, while attempts to restore it may go on for decades.

Examples of a joint approach and how synergies can be created are provided by the cultural and natural heritage programmes conducted internationally. The overlapping of cultural heritage and natural heritage, and even to a certain extent the natural element being absorbed by the cultural element, is the result of a shift in emphasis from the property being protected to its role in the daily life of individuals and society. The role of cultural heritage in economic growth is also significant for in this way a resource, in both the material and intangible dimensions, supports growth and leads to the creation of new jobs. All possible ways of using heritage, though, must not pose a risk of destruction or irreversible change.[263]

A complex approach is of vital practical importance. In Australia, this occurs at the national level (Department of the Environment and Energy),[264] while in Great Britain, local departments dealing with both culture and the environment function successfully. In Australia, the situation is further conditioned by the structure of the country's cultural heritage, which combines both cultural and natural elements, as well as the protection of the rights of indigenous people. This practical dimension also involves activities for planning and organising protection within state structures and, equally importantly, the functioning of the financing model.

Certainly, this overlapping of issues presented herein is also conducive to the selection of research areas. Researchers often present findings from their analyses of both cultural heritage and the natural environment.[265] Because the two areas overlap to such an extent, scholars take a broad view of problems that appear *prima facie* to fall within the scope of cultural heritage, taking account of their environmental context and impact.[266] Certainly, when an expert sets a given subject in a broader context and remains sensitive to cultural heritage, their research can only bring benefit.

A holistic approach to heritage does not facilitate classifying cultural heritage as special property. Considerations on the process of classifying property that is vital for the public interest usually refer to property that is homogeneous. By a decision of the legislator, a certain key criterion for making such classifications is accepted. As shown using the examples of water, animals and mineral deposits, these criteria are not fixed but change over time. All of the above types of property, as well as cultural heritage, are part of the common good because of either their importance to society or the intangible value they incorporate.

---

[263] Article 8 The UNESCO Declaration on the Responsibility of the Present Generations Towards Future Generations, adopted 12 November 1997.

[264] http://www.environment.gov.au/about-us. Accessed 1 June 2022.

[265] E.g. Przyborowska-Klimczak (2004, 2011).

[266] Blake (2015).

Conceiving heritage holistically makes it possible to apply a number of legal regimes and to combine the protective mechanisms designated for historical and natural monuments. The need to take several regimes into consideration may lead to a strengthening of protection that considers the complex nature of certain types of property. As in the case of intangible property, it will be possible to use two types of protection, even though these may not always serve the same purpose. For example, up to a certain point, the protection of a historical object may be available under the APGM and under copyright law. Given a holistic approach to heritage, a combined regime will encompass the cultural heritage together with a natural element. Yet one cannot exclude a third element where a certain part of heritage is protected by copyright law. This could be, for example, the design for a park or garden or an art installation that combines metal with plant material.

References

Agopszowicz A (1965) W sprawie ujednolicenia przepisów o gospodarowaniu wnętrzem ziemi. RPEiS 27(1):81–96

Agopszowicz A (1966) Prawo wydobywania kopalin. RPEiS 28(3):21–45

Agopszowicz A (1968) Wody podziemne jako przedmiot stosunków prawnych. Studia Cywilistyczne 11:109–166

Agopszowicz A (1973) Własność wód (jej istota i charakter prawny). Zeszyty Naukowe Uniwersytetu Jagiellońskiego. Prace z Wynalazczości i Ochrony Własności Intelektualnej 1: 25–40

Alley KD (2019) River goddesses, personhood and rights of nature: implications for spiritual ecology. Religions 10(9):502. https://doi.org/10.3390/rel10090502

Antoniak P (2012) Ustawa o muzeach. Komentarz. LEX, Warszawa

Argyrou A, Hummels H (2019) Legal personality and economic livelihood of the Whanganui River: a call for community entrepreneurship. Water Int 44(6–7):752–768. https://doi.org/10.1080/02508060.2019.1643525

Bardach J, Leśnodorski B, Pietrzak M (1993) Historia ustroju i prawa polskiego. Wydawnictwo Naukowe PWN, Warszawa

Bielska-Brodziak A, Drapalska-Grochowicz M, Suska M (2019) Symbolic protection of animals. Soc Register 3(3):103–121. https://doi.org/10.14746/sr.2019.3.3.06

Blake J (2015) International cultural heritage law. Oxford Scholarship, Oxford. https://doi.org/10.1093/acprof:oso/9780198723516.001.0001

Böhm A, Łuczyńska-Bruzda M, Środulska-Wielgus J, Wielgus K, Forczek-Brataniec U, Stokłosa K, Skrzyńska A (2005) Zasady tworzenia Parku Kulturowego, zarządzania nim oraz sporządzania planu jego ochrony. Materiały instruktażowe dla gminnych samorządów terytorialnych, autorów planów ochrony, wojewódzkich i samorządowych konserwatorów zabytków Kraków. Accessed 1 June 2022

Bradshaw K (2018) Animal property rights. Univ Colorado Law Rev 89(3):809–861. https://doi.org/10.2139/ssrn.2837372

Clarelli MVM (2015) Welcome and opening remarks. Uniform Law Rev 20(4):493–494. https://doi.org/10.1093/ulr/unv043

Dailoo SI, Pannekoek F (2008) Nature and culture: a new world heritage context. Int J Cult Prop 15(1):25–47. https://doi.org/10.1017/S0940739108080077

Drela M (2006) Własność zabytków. C.H. Beck, Warszawa

Dromgoole S (2013) Underwater cultural heritage and international law. Cambridge University Press, Cambridge. https://doi.org/10.1017/CBO9781139020503
Dybowski T, Grzybowski S, Nowakowski Z (1957) Zagadnienia cywilistyczne prawa wodnego. PWN, Warszawa
Florczak-Wątor M (2016) Art. 5 [Commentary]. In: Safjan M, Bosek L (eds) Konstytucja RP, vol 1: Komentarz do art. C.H. Beck, Warszawa, pp 1–86
Fojut N (2009) The philosophical, political and pragmatic roots of the convention. In: Thérond D et al (eds) Heritage in beyond. Council of Europe Publishing, Strasbourg, pp 13–21
Folga-Januszewska D (2006) Muzeologia, Muzeografia. Muzealnictwo. Muzealnictwo 47:9–14
Fortuna-Antoszkiewicz B, Łukaszkiewicz J (2015) Konflikty różnych form prawnej ochrony parków zabytkowych. In: Hodor K, Łakomy K (eds) Dziedzictwo zagrożone, ogrody historyczne w Polsce. Politechnika Krakowska im. Tadeusza Kościuszki, Kraków, pp 25–43
Francioni F (2008) Ilie 1972 World Heritage Convention: an introduction. In: Francioni F, Lenzerini F (eds) The 1972 World Heritage Convention. A commentary. Oxford University Press, Oxford, pp 3–8
Frankiewicz-Bodynek A (2019) Konstytucyjna regulacja dziedzictwa narodowego oraz dóbr kultury. Wydawnictwo Adam Marszałek, Toruń
Fraoua R (1986) Convention concernant les mesures à prendre pour interdire et empécher l'importation, l'exportation et le transfert de propriété illicites des biens culturels (Paris, 1970). UNESCO, Paris. http://unesdoc.unesco.org/images/0007/000723/072383fo.pdf. Accessed 1 June 2022
Fraoua R (2012) Legislative and institutional measures to combat trafficking in cultural property in Arab States. Background paper for participants in the Second Meeting of States Parties to the 1970 Convention UNESCO Headquarters, Paris, 20 and 21 June 2012. http://unesdoc.unesco.org/images/0024/002452/245275e.pdf. Accessed 1 June 2022
Gawin M (2018) Przestrzeń jako wartość. Wiadomości Konserwatorskie 56:6–7
Goettel M (2013) Sytuacja zwierzęcia w prawie cywilnym. Wolters Kluwer Polska, Warszawa
Golat R (2014) Własność gruntu a prawa do wód. Nieruchomości 10. https://czasopisma.beck.pl/nieruchomosci/artykul/wlasnosc-gruntu-a-prawa-do-wod/. Accessed 1 June 2022
Grajner M (1977) p. 26, Prawne formy korzystania z wnętrza ziemi. Zagadnienia prawa cywilnego i administracyjnego. Prawne Problemy Górnictwa 1:24–31
Groenen ACC (2018) UNIDROIT 1995: tackling the illicit trafficking of cultural property through private law means: an evaluation of the appropriateness of the 1995 Unidroit Convention on stolen or illegally exported cultural objects to cultural property theft in comparative perspective. Universitaire Pers Maastricht, Maastricht. https://doi.org/10.26481/dis.20181002ag
Grzybowski S (ed) (1985) System prawa cywilnego, vol 1: Część ogólna. Zakład Narodowy im. Ossolińskich, Wydawnictwo Polskiej Akademii Nauk, Wrocław
Gurgul S (2019) Wody jako szczególny przedmiot prawa własności. Nieruchomości 9. https://doi.org/10.32027/NIER.19.9.6. https://czasopisma.beck.pl/nieruchomosci/artykul/wody-jako-szczegolny-przedmiot-prawa-wlasnosci/. Accessed 1 June 2022
Gwardzińska Ż (2018) Jubileusz muzeów w Klukach i Swołowie oraz Seminarium Naukowe "Organizacyjno-prawne uwarunkowania w funkcjonowaniu muzeów na wolnym powietrzu w Polsce. Stan obecny – propozycje zmian" 5–7 czerwca 2018 roku. SAACLR 1(4):247–250
Hauser-Schäublin E, Prott LV (2016) Introduction: changing concepts of ownership, culture and property. In: Hauser-Schäublin E, Prott LV (eds) Cultural property and contested ownership. The trafficing of artefacts and the quest for restitution. Routledge, London, pp 1–20
Jagielska-Burduk A (2016a) Formy ochrony zabytków jako mechanizm zarządzania dziedzictwem kultury. In: Jagielska-Burduk A (ed) Mechanizmy prawne zarządzania dziedzictwem kultury. Wolters Kluwer Polska, Wydawnictwo Uniwersytetu Gdańskiego, Gdańsk–Warszawa, pp 171–212
Jagielska-Burduk A (2016b) Nowy wizerunek dziedzictwa – między ochroną a zarządzaniem. In: Jagielska-Burduk A (ed) Mechanizmy prawne zarządzania dziedzictwem kultury. Wolters Kluwer Polska, Wydawnictwo Uniwersytetu Gdańskiego, Gdańsk–Warszawa, pp 44–65

Jagielska-Burduk A (2016c) Problematyka muzealiów – ochrona zabytków w muzeach i kolekcjach prywatnych. In: Zeidler K (ed) Raport dotyczący stanu ochrony prawnej oraz kierunków zmian w zakresie prawnej ochrony zabytków ruchomych w Polsce przygotowywany w ramach realizacji Krajowego Programu Ochrony Zabytków i Opieki nad Zabytkami na lata 2014–2017 dla Narodowego Instytutu Muzealnictwa i Ochrony Zbiorów. Gdańsk, pp 107–146

Jakubowski A (2016) Cultural heritage and the collective dimension of cultural rights in the jurisprudence of the European Court of Human Rights. In: Jakubowski A (ed) Cultural rights as collective rights: an international law perspective. Brill, Leiden, pp 157–179

Jakubowski A, Jakubowski O (2014) Pierwokup przy wywozie dóbr kultury za granicę – analiza kierunkowych zmian w prawie polskim. In: Jagielska-Burduk A, Szafrański W (eds) Kultura w praktyce. Zagadnienia prawne, vol 3: Muzea a rynek sztuki. Aspekty prawne. Wydawnictwo Poznańskiego Towarzystwa Przyjaciół Nauk, Poznań, pp 205–234

Katner WJ (2012) Wody i urządzenia wodne. In: Safjan M (ed) Prawo cywilne – część ogólna, System Prawa Prywatnego, vol 1. C.H. Beck, Warszawa

Klein A (1985) Ewolucja pojęcia nieruchomości w polskim prawie cywilnym. In: Kordasiewicz B, Łętowska E (eds) Prace z prawa cywilnego: wydane dla uczczenia pracy naukowej profesora Józefa Stanisława Piątowskiego. Ossolineum, Wrocław, pp 85–100

Komorowski T (2018) Pamięć świata – polska aktywność. Biuletyn Informacyjny PKN ICOMOS 1–2(40–41):43–51

Kościelak M, Michalski P, Tarkowski P (2019) Prawo wodne – gospodarowanie mieniem Skarbu Państwa. Własność wód i obowiązki ich właścicieli. Komentarz. Legalis

Kowalska E (2018) Własność zabytku a dyskrecjonalna władza konserwatorska. Wydawnictwo Uniwersytetu Gdańskiego, Gdańsk

Kukreti I (2017, 7 July) SC stays Uttarakhand HC order declaring Ganga, Yamuna living entities. https://www.downtoearth.org.in/news/water/sc-stays-uk-hc-order-declaring-ganga-yamuna-living-entities-58245. Accessed 1 June 2022

Łętowska E (1997) Dwa cywilnoprawne aspekty praw zwierząt: derefikacja i personifikacja. In: Szpunar A (ed) Studia z prawa prywatnego. Księga pamiątkowa ku czci Profesor Biruty Lewaszkiewicz-Petrykowskiej. Wydawnictwo Uniwersytetu Łódzkiego, Łódź, pp 71–91

Lipiński A (1979) Uprawnienie do wydobywania kopalin. Prawne Problemy Górnictwa 3:107–130

Lipiński A, Mikosz R (2003) Ustawa Prawo geologiczne i górnicze. Komentarz, 2nd edn. Dom Wydawniczy ABC, Warszawa

Marcinkowska M, Lipska D (eds) (2018) Warsaw recommendation on recovery and reconstruction of cultural heritage. UNESCO. World Heritage Centre, Warsaw. https://whc.unesco.org/document/168799. Accessed 1 June 2022

Mazur P (2018) Uwagi o sytuacji prawnej zwierzęcia pokrzywdzonego czynem zabronionym w polskim procesie karnym. Ethics in Progress 9(1):128–139

Michalczak R (2017) Animals race against the machines. In: Kurki VAJ, Pietrzykowski T (eds) Legal personhood: animals, artificial intelligence and the unborn, Law and Philosophy Library, vol 119. Springer, Cham, pp 91–101. https://doi.org/10.1007/978-3-319-53462-6_6

Mikosz R (1991) Własność i dysponowanie zasobami naturalnymi wnętrza ziemi (Uwagi de lege ferenda). Prawne Problemy Górnictwa 14:126–148

Mikosz R (2008) Uprawnienia górnicze de lege ferenda (uwagi na tle projektu nowego prawa geologicznego i górniczego). In: Lisicka H (ed) Prawo ochrony środowiska i prawo karne. Książka jubileuszowa z okazji 40-lecia pracy naukowej Profesora Wojciecha Radeckiego. Wydawnictwo Uniwersytetu Wrocławskiego, Wrocław, pp 173–184

Mikosz R (2013) Prawa do złóż kopalin oraz innych fragmentów górotworu. In: Gniewek E (ed) Prawo rzeczowe. System Prawa Prywatnego, vol 3. C.H. Beck, Warszawa

Musitelli J (2002) World heritage, between universalism and globalisation. Int J Cult Prop 11(2): 323–336. https://doi.org/10.1017/S0940739102771464

Nafziger J (2009) The protection and repatriation of indigenous cultural heritage in the United States. In: Pue WW (ed) Protection of first nations cultural heritage. Laws, policy, and reform. UBC Press, Vancouver, pp 110–152

O'Donnell E (2019) Legal rights for rivers. competition, collaboration and water governance. Routledge, London
O'Donnell EL, Talbot-Jones J (2018) Creating legal rights for rivers: lessons from Australia, New Zealand, and India. Ecol Soc 23(1):7. https://doi.org/10.5751/ES-09854-230107
O'Keefe R (2004) World Cultural Heritage: obligations to the international community as a whole? Int Comp Law Q 53(1):189–209. https://doi.org/10.1093/iclq/53.1.189
O'Keefe P (2007) Commentary on the 1970 UNESCO Convention on the means of prohibiting and preventing the illicit import, export and transfer of ownership of cultural property, 2nd edn. Institute of Art and Law, Leicester
O'Keefe PJ, Prott LV (eds) (2011) Cultural Heritage Conventions and other instruments. A compendium with commentaries. Builth Wells, Brecknockshire
Paliwoda P, Bąk B (2015) Legal dereification of animals – the Polish perspective. Sci J Bielsko-Biala Sch Finance Law 6(2):110–120. https://doi.org/10.5604/01.3001.0012.2671
Paterson R (2010) Heading home: French law enables return of Maori Heads to New Zealand. Int J Cult Prop 17(4):643–652. https://doi.org/10.1017/S0940739110000408
Pazdan M (2012) Pozycja prawna zwierząt. In: Safjan M (ed) Prawo cywilne – część ogólna. System Prawa Prywatnego, vol 1. C.H. Beck, Warszawa
Pązik A (2015) Art. 10 [Commentary]. In: Pązik A, Słomski M (eds) Prawo łowieckie. Komentarz. Wolters Kluwer, Warszawa
Pietrzykowski T (2015) Problem podmiotowości prawnej zwierząt z perspektywy filozofii prawa. Przegląd Filozoficzny – Nowa Seria 2(94):247–259
Pietrzykowski T (2018) Personhood beyond humanism, animals. Chimeras, autonomous agents and the law. Springer, Cham
Pietrzykowski T (2019) Moralność publiczna a konstytucyjne podstawy ochrony zwierząt. Studia Prawnicze 1(217):5–26. https://doi.org/10.37232/sp.2019.1.1
Piotrowska-Nosek K (2014) Konwencja w sprawie ochrony światowego dziedzictwa kulturalnego i naturalnego, przyjęta w Paryżu dnia 16 listopada 1972 r. przez Konferencję Generalną Organizacji Narodów Zjednoczonych dla Wychowania, Nauki i Kultury na jej siedemnastej sesji. In: Zalasińska K (ed) Konwencje UNESCO w dziedzinie kultury. Komentarz. Wolters Kluwer Polska, Warszawa, pp 236–311
Praduroux S (2017) Objects of property rights: old and new. In: Graziadei M, Smith L (eds) Comparative property law. Global perspectives. Edward Elgar, Cheltenham, pp 51–70
Prieur M, Luginbühl Y (2018) Conceptual report. In: Déjeant-Pons M (ed) Council of Europe Landscape Convention. Contribution to human rights, democracy and sustainable development. Council of Europe Publishing, Strasbourg, pp 15–23. https://rm.coe.int/council-of-europe-landscape-convention-contribution-to-human-rights-de/16807bffda. Accessed 1 June 2022
Prott LV (1997) Commentary on the UNIDROIT Convention on Stolen and Illegally Exported Cultural Objects 1995. Institute of Art and Law, Leicester
Prott LV (2011) Strengths and weaknesses of the 1970 Convention: an evaluation 40 years after its adoption. Background paper for participants in the meeting the fight against the illicit trafficking of cultural objects The 1970 convention: past and future. Paris, UNESCO Headquarters, 15–16 March 2011. https://unesdoc.unesco.org/ark:/48223/pf0000191880. Accessed 1 June 2022
Przyborowska-Klimczak A (2004) Ochrona przyrody. Studium prawno-międzynarodowe. Wydawnictwo Uniwersytetu Marii Curie-Skłodowskiej, Lublin
Przyborowska-Klimczak A (2011) Rozwój ochrony dziedzictwa kulturalnego w prawie międzynarodowym na przełomie XX i XXI wieku. Wydawnictwo Uniwersytetu Marii Curie-Skłodowskiej, Lublin
Purchla J (2012) Naród – Dziedzictwo – Pamięć. Zagadnienia Sądownictwa Konstytucyjnego 2(4): 59–68
Radecki W (2005) Ustawa o rybactwie śródlądowym. Komentarz. Difin, Warszawa
Radecki W, Danecka D (2019) Prawo łowieckie. Komentarz, 4th edn. Difin, Warszawa

Rakoczy B (2013) Własność wód w prawie polskim. Przegląd Prawa Ochrony Środowiska 1:928. https://doi.org/10.12775/PPOS.2013.001
Rakoczy B (2015a) Ochrona lasu jako zabytku w prawie polskim. In: Pływaczewski W, Gadecki B (eds) Ochrona dziedzictwa kulturalnego i naturalnego. Perspektywa prawna i kryminologiczna. C.H. Beck, Warszawa, pp 1–10
Rakoczy B (ed) (2015b) Art. 10 [Commentary]. Prawo geologiczne i górnicze. Komentarz, LEX
Resta G (2017) Systems of public ownership. In: Graziadei M, Smith L (eds) Comparative property law. Global perspectives. Edward Elgar, Cheltenham, pp 216–257
Rose CM (1998) Joseph Sax and the idea of the public trust. Ecol Law Q 25:351–362
Rössler M (2002, 5–7 Aug) UNESCO World Heritage Centre Background Document on UNESCO World Heritage Cultural Landscapes. Prepared for the FAO Workshop and Steering Committee Meeting of the GIAHS (project: Globally Important Ingenious Agricultural Heritage Systems). Rome. https://www.fao.org/fileadmin/user_upload/giahs/docs/WorldHeritage_CulturalLandscapes_MechtildRoessler.pdf. Accessed 1 June 2022
Sax JL (1970) The public trust doctrine in natural resource law: effective judicial intervention. Mich Law Rev 68(3):471–566
Schorr DB (2017) Water rights. In: Graziadei M, Smith L (eds) Comparative property law. Global perspectives. Edward Elgar, Cheltenham, pp 280–289
Scott GR (2003) The cultural property laws of Japan: social, political and legal influences. Pac Rim Law Policy J 12(2):315–402. https://core.ac.uk/download/pdf/267981625.pdf. Accessed 1 June 2022
Scovazzi T (2008) Articles 8-11. World Heritage Committee and World Heritage List. In: Francioni F, Lenzerini F (eds) The 1972 World Heritage Convention. A Commentary. Oxford University Press, Oxford, pp 147–174
Shyam G (2019) How community attitudes can strengthen arguments for changing the legal status of animals. Soc Register 3(3):67–82
Sikora D (2010) Parki historyczne w rejestrze zabytków – ustalenie przedmiotu i zakresu ochrony, problemy weryfikacji rejestru, granice ochrony konserwatorskiej. Kurier Konserwatorski 7:11–16
Sługocki J (2014a) Dylematy ochrony prawnej krajobrazu kulturowego. Samorząd Terytorialny 12: 55–64
Sługocki J (2014b) Opieka nad zabytkiem nieruchomym. Problemy administracyjnoprawne. Wolters Kluwer Polska, Warszawa
Stec R (2014) Art. 2 [Commentary]. In: Rakoczy B, Stec R, Woźniak A (eds) Prawo łowieckie. Komentarz. LEX
Stelmachowski A (1969) Wstęp do teorii prawa cywilnego. PWN, Warszawa
Stelmachowski A (1994) Przedmiot własności w prawie cywilnym. Studia Iuridica 21:105–111
Stone CD (1972) Should trees have standing? Toward legal rights for natural objects. South Calif Law Rev 45:450–501
Strecker A (2018) Landscape protection in international law. Oxford University Press, Oxford
Szmelter I (2018) Holizm to przyszłość? Całościowa perspektywa ochrony dziedzictwa kultury materialnego, niematerialnego i cyfrowego. Wiadomości Konserwatorskie 56:33–52
Szuma K (2012) Własność górnicza, użytkowanie górnicze i inne uprawnienia górnicze według ustawy z dnia 9 czerwca 2011 r. Prawo geologiczne i górnicze. Przegląd Prawa Ochrony Środowiska 2:29–53. https://doi.org/10.12775/PPOS.2012.008
Szydło W (2014) Art. 143 [Commentary]. In: Gniewek E (ed) Kodeks cywilny. Komentarz. C.H. Beck, Warszawa
Tasdelen A (2016) Cambodia's struggle to protect its cultural property. In: Hauser-Schäublin E, Prott LV (eds) Cultural property and contested ownership. The trafficing of artefacts and the quest for restitution. Routledge, London, pp 45–63
Vrdoljak AF (2008) International law, museums and the return of cultural objects. Cambridge University Press, Cambridge

Vrdoljak AF (2015) Challenges for international cultural heritage law. In: Logan W, Nic Craith M, Kockel U (eds) A companion to heritage studies. Wiley, New York, pp 541–556. https://doi.org/10.1002/9781118486634.ch36

Whitby-Last K (2008) Article 1. Cultural landscape. In: Francioni F, Lenzerini F (eds) The 1972 World Heritage Convention. A commentary. Oxford University Press, Oxford, pp 51–62

Zacharasiewicz M (2016) Trust i inne stosunki powiernicze w prawie porównawczym i prawie prywatnym międzynarodowym. Wydawnictwo Uniwersytetu Śląskiego, Katowice

Zalasińska K (2008) Pojęcie muzealiów w prawie ochrony dziedzictwa kultury. In: Włodarski JA, Zeidler K (eds) Prawo muzeów. Wolters Kluwer Polska, Warszawa, pp 22–30

Zalasińska K (2010) Prawna ochrona zabytków nieruchomych w Polsce. Wolters Kluwer Polska, Warszawa

Zalasińska K (2014) Konwencja dotycząca środków zmierzających do zakazu i zapobiegania nielegalnemu przywozowi i wywozowi i przenoszeniu własności dóbr kultury. In: Zalasińska K (ed) Konwencje UNESCO w dziedzinie kultury. Komentarz. Wolters Kluwer Polska, Warszawa, pp 174–235

Zeidler K (2014) Prawo ochrony dziedzictwa kultury jako nowa gałąź prawa. In: Zeidler K (ed) Prawo ochrony zabytków. Wolters Kluwer, Wydawnictwo Uniwersytetu Gdańskiego, Warszawa–Gdańsk, pp 23–33

Zoll F (1920) Prawa rzeczowe na ziemiach polskich, Part 1. Księgarnia J. Czarneckiego, Warszawa

Zoll F (1931) Prawo cywilne, vol 2: Prawa rzeczowe i rzeczowym podobne. Wojewódzki Instytut Wydawniczy, Poznań

Zoll F (1938) Przedmiot praw rzeczowych. Kwartalnik Prawa Prywatnego 3:203–242

Zoll F (1947) Prawo cywilne w zarysie, vol 2: Prawo rzeczowe, issue 1. Księgarnia Powszechna, Kraków

Żygulski Z Jr (1982) Muzea na świecie. Wstęp do muzealnictwa. PWN, Warszawa

Chapter 5
Polish Private Law and Cultural Heritage

5.1 Introduction

The search for an ideal model to manage cultural heritage occurs simultaneously with the evolution of laws governing cultural heritage and the particular components thereof.[1] Instruments that have future potential in this respect include trusts, *res extra commercium*, the historical *fideicommissum* and shared property.[2] Most of these institutions are anchored in civil law. For years, private law mechanisms have been used to manage cultural heritage, with a basic model of protection established in public law. While property is protected regardless of its ownership status, how a right to it is exercised and the scope of that right do play an important role in how protection is implemented in practice.

In the case of material property not constituting things, as discussed in Sect. 4.2, the process of recognising such property and arriving at the regulations now in force took many years. With regard to cultural heritage in Poland, during the first stage of building legal structures for protecting historical objects, the discussion focused on what types of property should be designated for protection. The issues of defining cultural property and changes in the terminology used in successive acts of law also led to a certain fluidity in how cultural heritage components were regarded. New trends deriving from international standards or the need to implement EU law acted as springboards for introducing broader changes. Yet material heritage remains at the centre of Polish law, though, as shown in Chap. 2, this state has already undergone a number of changes, which are forcing an expansion of what is meant by cultural heritage. Ownership remains a key right to the components of cultural heritage,

The chapter was translated from Polish into English by Anthony Sloan and the author.

[1] Jakubowski (2016).

[2] About foundation and *fideicommissum* Jagielska-Burduk (2016a), pp. 238–253; on trust: Jagielska-Burduk and Szafrański (2016), pp. 254–284; Kowalski (2010), pp. 227–242.

A. Jagielska-Burduk, *Cultural Heritage as a Legal Hybrid*,
https://doi.org/10.1007/978-3-031-04946-0_5

though it does not rule out other absolute rights to certain types of property. In each case, building new legal regimes that apply solely to property owned by the State Treasury or public law entities is the safest option. As will be shown below, at this stage of the law's development, certain legal institutions already take into account the property of private entities (for example, the institutions of public collections).

In this part, I present the "ownership" of cultural heritage components, that is, law of a broader scope that goes beyond the strictly understood ownership of historical objects to the extent it constitutes the centre of interest in civil law. I recall certain civil law institutions connected with the acquisition of ownership of cultural heritage components and trace the path that legislative intervention has taken in connection with the new place occupied by cultural heritage in private law. Recently, regulations in civil law have broken or extended the principle of certainty in trading in favour of protecting cultural heritage, excluding certain property from provisions on the acquisition of ownership of movable things in good faith or though acquisitive prescription.

Civil law constitutes an important pillar of movable cultural property protection, alongside administrative and criminal laws. Here, it is worth pointing out that it is often worth making a separate evaluation of the structure of a given legal institution and how that institution functions in practice. With regard to the National Register of Lost Cultural Property, the ineffectiveness of the register is one of the most important factors in the debate over private law and cultural heritage. In observing these changes, a need to analyse the currently binding solutions in civil law arises, considering existing regulations on cultural heritage both domestically and internationally. This allows us to determine what direction the legislator is heading and to examine the extent to which civil law can still be used "to serve the protection of the cultural heritage" and to create or strengthen protection at the national level.

An analysis of the long-established legal institutions related to the acquisition of ownership of cultural heritage components, and of the evolution, timing and purpose of introducing new institutions, should lead to a determination of whether there are any signs of a new perception of cultural heritage at the level of law creation, application and interpretation. A new approach to cultural heritage results from the challenges the legislator faces as new types of cultural property emerge (technological development), as existing property is viewed in new ways (the human body) and as changes in this area are initiated in international law. Given the broad range of cultural heritage components, in every case, the question arises as to who is the keeper, owner or otherwise authorised entity of such property. Various definitions of cultural heritage and its components, prepared for the needs of specific acts of law at the domestic and international levels, attest to the relationships and connections that exist between those components, which increase their value.

The problem of how to create a system of legal protection that ensures that at least some of those components are passed on to future generations arises in this context. Mechanisms of protection are created after a determination is made of the type of material or intangible property involved. Polish law focuses primarily on material property, though protection is also granted to intangible property constituting components of cultural heritage by means of provisions on the protection of intellectual property. Those provisions, however, were not originally created with that function in mind. Yet this does not diminish their importance; in fact, one can envisage adapting some of them for these institutions to protect cultural heritage in the future, as discussed in Sect. 3.4.

5.2 Between Property and "Property"

Cultural heritage is treated as a process[3] consisting of memory and how resources are interpreted and selected. It also includes changes taking place in legal protection regulations, including cultural heritage becoming situated in private law. By creating legal foundations of protection, the important task of recognising and interpreting cultural heritage as "one's own" and worthy of being preserved is performed. It may seem that, given the wide scope of cultural heritage, private law should give way to administrative law mechanisms for selecting which property should be preserved. In order to avoid the trap of deeming public law as paramount in managing or protecting cultural heritage, it is important to determine the status of such property in civil law. Such a determination constitutes the foundation of protection. In relation to the normalisation of other types of property that are certainly more useful and important economically, including water and minerals, the normalisation of cultural heritage is moving at a slower pace and seems not to be treated as an integral part of protective regimes. At the same time, the function of cultural heritage is evolving; it is no longer only about the past but also about building links with other cultural heritage elements. Cultural heritage should facilitate and accelerate achieving the goals of the Sustainable Development Agenda, of peacekeeping and of rebuilding communities that have suffered from wars or natural disasters.[4] In short, heritage is viewed not only as a catalyst for development and as a connector between diverse communities and nations but also as a tool for rebuilding and reinforcing resilience. It seems, then, that cultural heritage can be seen as a strategic resource needed for more than guaranteeing access to cultural property.

In the past, cultural heritage components were mainly examined through the lens of private law as historical objects within the meaning of the Act of 23 July 2003 on the Protection and Guardianship of Monuments (APGM).[5] In systemic studies of private law, when making a functional distinction between different types of ownership, reference was made to the "ownership of cultural property constituting the national heritage (ownership of historical objects)".[6] A distinction can be found in the Polish legal scholarship between the ownership of cultural property and the ownership of agricultural land, forests, natural resources, residential resources,

[3] Purchla (2010), p. 70; Purchla (2012).

[4] Kono (2019).

[5] Dobosz (1997), Drela (2006), Zalasińska (2010), Zeidler (2007), and Zeidler (2014).

[6] Stelmachowski (2003), pp. 197 et seq.; Stelmachowski and Zaradkiewicz (2013), pp. 331 et seq.

intellectual property and industrial property. Rights to natural resources include the ownership of water and minerals. These are distinguished by their designation, substantive complexity and the fact that they do not constitute things. When describing the ownership of cultural property, reference was made only to material heritage, that is, artefacts and immovable historical objects.[7] This does not include cultural heritage components that are material property but do not fit the definition of a historical object (certain space heritage components or those sometimes falsely considered historical objects, such as graves or relics).

Private law constitutes an important pillar for protecting and managing cultural heritage. The elements of the discussion on absolute rights to material objects not constituting things presented in Sect. 4.2 are important drivers of solutions for protecting cultural heritage in the private law system. Certain tendencies demonstrated by the legislator can already be identified in the law on cultural heritage. When cultural heritage is viewed in both the material and intangible dimensions, holistically and with the inclusion of natural elements, the legal regime for protecting it necessarily becomes complex. The same category of cultural heritage can cover both movable things and real estate, as well as intangible property (intangible heritage). In Chap. 2, it was shown that while not all types of cultural property are historical objects, they should still remain at the centre of attention in private law. It seems that, up to now, the legislator has avoided seeing the whole mosaic of cultural heritage and its consequences in private law.

Already at this stage, one can state that the law cannot treat all components of cultural heritage in a uniform manner. The wide variety in cultural heritage requires the legislator to consider both its material and intangible dimensions. It is not possible to unequivocally categorise all heritage components as material property or things subject to ownership within the meaning of Article 140 of the Civil Code (CC) ("Within the limit set by the law and the principles of community life, an owner may, to the exclusion of other persons, use a think in accordance with the social and economic purpose of his right, and may, in particular, collect the profits and other revenues from the said thing. Within the same limits, he may dispose of the thing"). Regarding material cultural heritage constituting things, and particularly historical objects, much thought has been given to the possible forms of ownership.[8] In case of cultural heritage components not constituting things, it is possible to identify an "ownership" right closer to that of water rights, which results in a model for managing a particular resource.

Changes in how cultural property is perceived are noticeable, for example in how heritage is presented in the justifications to draft acts of law aimed at establishing a new place for cultural heritage in civil law. In the justification to an act, reference is made to cultural property as property at the point of contact between the present and the future:

[7] Stelmachowski (2003), pp. 197 et seq.; Stelmachowski and Zaradkiewicz (2013), pp. 331 et seq.
[8] Drela (2006) and Jagielska-Burduk (2011).

> cultural objects, while being the property of individual private and public entities, are in the social sense common goods. For they contribute to the formation of the historical and cultural awareness of the nation. The owner of an item of cultural property possesses it not only for themselves, but also for future generations. The owner is obliged to deal with a historical object in a manner that ensures it will be preserved for as long as possible in the best possible condition. In this sense, the owner possesses the historical object based on the principle of trusteeship. He is the guarantor towards society that the object will not be destroyed.[9]

At the societal level, the document emphasises the common good as important for everyone and, in this context, invokes the idea of the nation. Reference to trusteeship is made in order to emphasise the temporary nature of an individual's rights to a cultural heritage component. At the same time, the owner is given a new function, that of a holder burdened with certain responsibilities.

The goal of this chapter is to examine the extent to which one can diagnose signs of change by analysing legal provisions on the acquisition of ownership and the newest regulations in this area. This should make it possible to assess whether and how clearly the legislator perceives that there is a need for a systemic change. To this end, I present civil law institutions connected with the acquisition of ownership of cultural heritage components and the status of cultural property in the Polish legal system. The chapter's summary is thought to connect the current state, attempts to make changes, and the designated place of cultural heritage components in the private law system. Critical moments can be identified when cultural heritage moved from one state to another in which it was possible to take possession of objects and therefore acquire ownership over them (found archaeological artefacts or treasure). When evaluating cultural heritage as an object of civil law relationships, it is also important to identify a given object and gather information on where it is located (e.g. illegal archaeological excavations). It sometimes happens that there is little information available on the place where an archaeological find is situated. In such cases, the very fact of entry in the register of historical objects ensures that this undefined resource is afforded legal protection. The State Treasury is granted sole ownership over a certain segment of property; in the case of cultural heritage, this concerns archaeological artefacts. In other cases, there is an assumption of the coexistence of private and public administrators, while public interest is strongly present in the exercise of ownership rights.

Concentrating solely on the ownership of a thing is no longer sufficient, given the ways heritage is evolving and the changes taking place in how it is perceived. As a starting point for further reflection, this chapter looks at the regulation for acquiring ownership of cultural heritage components. In the Polish legal system today, ownership applies to the material components of heritage that constitute things and can be taken into possession. In relation to material property not constituting things, we can speak not of an ownership structure but of rights similar to ownership. The

[9] Government Draft on Found Property and Amendments to Certain Other Acts, Explanatory Report, Print no. 2064 p. 3, http://www.sejm.gov.pl/Sejm7.nsf/druk.xsp?nr=2064. Accessed 1 June 2022.

example of human remains permits an examination of how such property is managed by museums and other entities. Whereas with regard to tombstones, there is an element of subjective rights in the form of personal rights.

Space heritage, studied only relatively recently, also involves legal problems on how to classify rights to its components. Where these are left in their original location, we are faced with "managing" them and with the element of joint responsibility for them. The most advantageous way to create rules for such management would be in the form of an international agreement. In the near future, it is difficult to imagine a "museum branch/department" whose collection is scattered in space but subject to human control. Yet technological development allows us to believe that one day, this may be possible. As certain types of property come to be seen as part of the human commonwealth, changes will be made in the rules of trading, state ownership will be extended, provisions will be harmonised and new solutions will be introduced as a joint reaction to or in order to combat undesirable phenomena, such as illegal trade in cultural property. At the same time, public collections will be separated from other types of property due to their need for special protection. However, extending the ownership of the State Treasury is risky in that there is no way to predict the costs this will involve. It should be mentioned that as regards the purchase of an item of cultural property where no permit for the permanent export of the object is obtained, the legislator will have to determine where the funds for such purchases are to come from.[10] This does not apply to situations where the ownership of certain goods is acquired under a procedure set out in the Civil Code, the Act of 20 February 2015 on Found Property[11] (AFP) or the APGM. In the long term, continually expanding the resources of the State Treasury may prove quite burdensome, with the solution to this problem being left to future generations of decision-makers.

5.3 *Res Extra Commercium* and the Polish Cultural Heritage Law

The division into things admitted to trade and those excluded from it is largely a manifestation of the state system that exists at a given moment. In the period of the socialist economy in Poland, for example, that division had no practical significance. It has been pointed out that

> the exclusion of things from civil trading is not a mechanical consequence of particular properties of theirs, but results from a determination of specific goals those things are to serve, and therefore from their socio-economic purpose. Exclusion from civil trading, then, extends only as far as unrestricted civil trading would be contrary to that purpose.[12]

[10] Cf. Jakubowski and Jakubowski (2014).

[11] Act of 20 February 2015 on Found Property, consolidated text. Polish Official Journal (Dz. U.) 2019, item 908.

[12] Grzybowski (1985), p. 426.

According to this view, the function of the institution was updated at the moment the political system changed and private sector ownership was rebuilt. The exclusion of certain types of property from trade means they cannot be privately owned. This division can also have a moral dimension stemming from values universally recognised as worthy of protection. One need only consider generally held views on human tissues and organs, which are treated as *res extra commercium*,[13] as are corpses.[14]

It is worth considering, then, how *res extra commercium* institutions are constructed in Polish law and whether there is a general legal scheme for excluding property from trade. Attempts at such legislative measures are always caused either by the emergence of new phenomena or by increased social awareness of the place of certain property in the system. Medical progress and the possibility of using human cells, tissues and organs in providing medical assistance have created a need to regulate such use, including their exclusion from trade for moral reasons. Pursuant to Article 3 par. 1 of the Act on the Collection, Storage and Transfer of Cells and Tissues, it is unlawful to demand or accept payment, other material benefits or personal gain with respect to the use of cells, tissues or organs taken from a donor. While the goal of the legislator can be inferred, this does not eliminate the interpretive doubts caused by the language in which the provisions are expressed.[15] The justification for this exclusion from trade is based on values, whereas the use of cells, tissues and organs takes place in accordance with the procedure set forth in the Act.[16]

A very different example is that of public roads; the fact that they are used by everyone justifies their status as things excluded from trade. The ownership of national roads is divided between the State Treasury (national roads) and the provincial, county or district governments (provincial, county and district roads) (Article 2a of the Act on Public Roads[17]). It is accepted that public roads cannot be disposed of or subject to enforcement and remain the property of the relevant road management authority.[18] The issue of the status of public roads was not free of problems of a practical nature and was studied with respect to whether real estate constituting a public road could be subject to acquisitive prescription. Opposing

[13] Act of 1 July 2005 on the Collection, Storage and Transfer of Cells and Tissues. Polish Official Journal (Dz. U.) 2015, item 793, 1893, 1991.

[14] Bednarek (1997), p. 63 while recognising that human corpses are excluded from circulation, defines them as things in a "broad sense" alongside res omnium communes (air, sea, flowing water).

[15] Cf. Haberko and Uhrynowska-Tyszkiewicz (2014), Art. 3 [Commentary].

[16] It should be pointed out that the legislator assigns the tasks connected with the implementation of tasks to budgetary entities—the Organisational and Coordination Centre for Transplantation "Poltransplant" and the National Centre for Tissue and Cell Banking. The model of delegating tasks is to some extent similar to the functioning of competence centres at the Ministry of Culture and National Heritage, i.e. NIMOZ and NID, whereas the scope of activity makes the scope of independence of entities different.

[17] Act of 21 March 1985 on Public Roads, consolidated text. Polish Official Journal (Dz. U.) 2018, item 2068.

[18] Rychter (2019), Art. 2a [Commentary].

views appeared in case law over land being designated as a public road in the land register,[19] where some pointed to the need for real, infrastructural use of a given piece of real estate.[20] Without delving too deeply into the problem of public roads, two important findings that are also relevant to historical objects nevertheless arise. Firstly, the reorganisation of the ownership structure, and the creation of legal acts and a model for road management, took years. Secondly, recording real property in the land register and on maps does not constitute a sufficient condition to deem land a public road, with all of the legal consequences that designation entails.

Can the above findings and experience affect the legal situation of cultural heritage? The debate over the meaning of *res extra commercium*, as it may apply to cultural heritage, has been going on for a long time.[21] *Res extra commercium* appears in statements by experts on jurisprudence,[22] in discussions in museum circles[23] and in demands by politicians.[24] Unfortunately, in rulings by Polish courts, the issue of exclusion from trade has never appeared, even as a supporting argument or as starting point for further considerations pertaining to cultural heritage components. *Res extra commercium*, or precisely the arguments in favour of introducing it, also constitutes an element in support of the search for new forms of protection for movable historical objects.

Experience from other countries shows that such solutions are certainly effective within the borders of a single state. In the case of organised theft and "forum shopping", though, without support from international instruments, attempts to effect the return of an object may end in failure. In 1990 an object was stolen from a French museum. It could not be effectively acquired from an unauthorised entity in France but lost protection abroad and could then be treated as an "ordinary thing". Thus, an Italian buyer who purchased the object under Italian law did acquire ownership.[25] It should be added that this case revealed the lack of cohesion in how cultural heritage is protected, as well as the need to weigh the interests of good faith acquirers against the interest of protecting certain heritage components. Since the ruling was issued, additional instruments have appeared that, if applied, might have altered the result of that proceeding.

Without a doubt, the regime of *res extra commercium* holds an important place in the system of international law today, specifically in the United Nations Educational,

---

[19] Polish Supreme Court, Judgement of 6 March 2015, III CSK 196/14, LEX No. 1666022.

[20] Polish Supreme Court, Decision of 15 February 2012, I CSK 293/11, OSNC 2012 r., No. 9, item 104.

[21] On the Polish debate about res extra commercium Szafrański (2016), pp. 127–171.

[22] Drela (2006), pp. 184–189.

[23] Congress of Polish Museum Professionals resolution on the essence of a museum, mausoleums, museum profession and museum organizers.

[24] Reply of the Secretary of State at the Ministry of Culture and National Heritage—under the authority of the Minister—to the interpellation no. 11612 on the status of public collections, Parliamentary of the 7th term. http://www.sejm.gov.pl/sejm7.nsf/InterpelacjaTresc.xsp?key=34230811. Accessed 1 June 2022.

[25] Cf. Stato francese v. Ministero per i beni culturali ed ambientali e De Contessini 1990.

Scientific and Cultural Organization (UNESCO) and the International Institute for the Unification of Private Law (UNIDROIT) conventions. Pursuant to Article 13 pt. d of the UNESCO Convention,

> each State Party to the Convention undertakes to recognise the indefeasible right of each State Party to this Convention to classify and declare certain cultural property as inalienable, which should therefore ipso facto not be exported, and to facilitate recovery of such property by the State concerned in cases where it has been exported.[26]

The right of a state to classify and declare certain property as inalienable cannot be questioned and is of a permanent nature.[27]

When preparing the UNIDROIT Convention, discussions were held on a suitable procedural model for objects covered by the *res extra commercium* regime.[28] In Article 3 (4), the UNIDROIT Convention refers to objects that constitute part of monuments and archaeological sites or belong to public collections and exempt them from time-barring, only indicating a deadline for initiating a procedure—3 years from the moment the rightful owner becomes aware of the location of the object. The level of protection may be reduced at the will of any State Party to the Convention by establishing a 75-year or longer time-barring period in accordance with its domestic law. This weakening of protection was caused by some states taking a strong stance against the solution of time-barring and was enacted as a compromise between them.[29]

Both of the above conventions foresee compensation for good faith acquirers or for an entity that acted with due diligence. Without a doubt, this solution in a way contradicts the idea of *res extra commercium*. Nevertheless, the exclusion or extension of the time-barring period does constitute special treatment of certain resources. The recognition in the conventions of particular regulations for protecting objects in their country of origin means that, when thinking about the future of heritage, domestic legislators should be more inclined to introduce *res extra commercium* in relation to cultural heritage components in their legal systems.

In the Polish legal system, the potential of *res extra commercium* has not been fully exploited. The domestic *res extra commercium* regime results in a privileged position when seeking the return of an object. During the process of preparing the UNESCO-UNIDROIT Model Provisions on State Ownership of Undiscovered Cultural Property in 2008, Patrick O'Keefe encouraged states to take advantage of the possibility of declaring certain objects inalienable in the context of cultural property and components of archaeological heritage, as well as objects yet undiscovered.[30]

---

[26] See about "escape language" Nafziger (2016), p. 188.

[27] O'Keefe (2007), p. 85.

[28] O'Keefe (2017), p. 182.

[29] Prott (1997), pp 38–39; Prott (2021), p. 60.

[30] Expert Committee on State Ownership of Cultural Heritage, Model Provisions on State Ownership of Undiscovered Cultural Objects. Explanatory Report with model provisions and explanatory guidelines, UNESCO, UNIDROIT, 2011, p. 2. https://fr.unesco.org/sites/default/files/unesco-unidroit_model_provisions_en.pdf. Accessed 1 June 2022.

In the European Union, a legislative achievement supplementing the UNESCO and UNIDROIT instruments is Council Directive 93/7/EEC on the return of cultural objects unlawfully removed from the territory of a Member State. In the literature, it is indicated that the adoption of this Directive led to the adoption of an autonomous system for the restitution of cultural property that is regional in character (now Directive 2014/60/EU of the European Parliament and of the Council of 15 May 2014 on the return of cultural objects unlawfully removed from the territory of a Member State).[31] Piotr Stec has emphasised that, apart from its role in supplementing the international conventions, the Directive is significant in terms of the principle of the free movement of goods within the European Union, in that it establishes an exception with regard to national cultural property.[32]

In the first version of this Directive (Council Directive 93/7/EEC of 15 March 1993 on the return of cultural objects unlawfully removed from the territory of a Member State),[33] the time period for initiating a restitution proceeding before the courts was extended with respect to certain property. This concerned objects constituting part of a public collection and ecclesiastical goods, where these were subject to special protective solutions under domestic law. Examples of such special protective solutions are the *res extra commercium* regime and other models limiting trade. In the meaning of Article 7 par. 1 of the Directive, the time period for initiating a restitution proceeding was extended to 75 years, with the exception of the Member States in which such procedures were not limited at all or in the case of bilateral agreements between the Member States in which a time period of greater than 75 years was established. The recast version of the Directive of the European Parliament and of the Council 2014/60/EU[34] maintains this special regime for property subject to special protection in domestic law. States themselves indicate what national treasures are subject to return; these should figure in the set of property contained in Article 36 Treaty on the Functioning of the European Union (TFEU).[35]

The general time period for bringing restitution claims was extended to 3 years as a result of this instrument.[36] Directive 2014/60 also adopts a new way of identifying what property is subject to return and contains provisions that make the model of due diligence more precise. Both versions provide for the return of an object and the possibility of compensation being paid by a Member State in a situation where the entity in possession of the object exercised due diligence when acquiring it. A change from the first version of the Directive benefits a party applying for the return

[31] Zeidler (2011), p. 250.

[32] Stec (2015), p. 104.

[33] Council Directive 93/7/EEC of 15 March 1993 on the return of cultural objects unlawfully removed from the territory of a Member State. OJ L 74, 27.3.1993, pp. 74–79.

[34] Directive 2014/60/EU of the European Parliament and of the Council of 15 May 2014 on the return of cultural objects unlawfully removed from the territory of a Member State and amending Regulation (EU) No 1024/2012 (Recast). OJ L 159, 28.5.2014, pp. 1–10.

[35] Frigo (2016), p. 75.

[36] Górka (2016), pp. 29–31.

of an object. Article 9 93/7/EEC provides that "the burden of proof shall be governed by the legislation of the requested Member State". In the recast version, Article 10 states that "the possessor demonstrates that he exercised due care and attention in acquiring the object". The special treatment that Directive 2014/60 grants to certain types of property also confirms the importance of domestic regulations on cultural property, including *res extra commercium*.

As regards the Polish legal system, the exclusion of cultural property from trade has not been given sufficient attention for a long time, and its application in practice, for example in the Act on National Archive Resources and Archives (ANARA), is far from ideal. The review, presented further on, of the forms of artefacts and their status and of particular regulations based on the types of property they concern (museums, archives) is a starting point for examining the basis for classifying certain objects as *res extra commercium*. The basic selection criteria are an object's purpose and mode of use, followed by its ownership status. Bearing in mind that both public and private entities may possess cultural heritage components, it may be that the criterion of subjectivity will allow appropriate borderlines to be drawn. There exists a greater conviction in society that public collections should be excluded from trade, although, as shown later on, how public collections are defined can also break through the hard division between public and private collections. This results from regimes already in force in France and Italy and from the belief that public collections, usually in the care of museums, constitute the core of the heritage we must pass on to future generations.

The adoption of a *res extra commercium* regime could lead to a strengthening of international protection for objects of Polish origin. The first such regulations introduced with regard to property in public collections were implemented in France and Italy.[37] The protection resulting from the *res extra commercium* regime is effective within the borders of the country concerned. A problem arises, though, at the moment an object is taken out of the country having the strongest protective regime.[38] On a number of occasions, the Polish legislator has noticed the problem of cultural property being transferred elsewhere. This has occurred during the work on the amendments concerning the scope of international private law. Unfortunately, on these occasions, no real changes were made, even though on two of them plans were made for including provisions on claims for the restitution of cultural property.

The first attempt, made in 2008, concerned things subject to legal protection in their state of origin. At that time, the person entitled to demand restitution could choose the applicable law (the law of the state from which the object was removed or the law of the state in which it is located).[39] The draft provision would have

[37] Kowalski (2010), pp. 233–236.

[38] Kowalski (2005), pp. 123–149.

[39] Government draft law—Private International Law, Sejm of the 6th term, Print no. 1277: Art. 43 Where an object regarded by the law of the country in which it is situated as a legally protected cultural object is exported to another country in violation of the law of that country, claims for its recovery shall be governed, at the option of the claimant, by the law of the country from which the object was exported or by the law of the country in which it is situated.

strengthened protection for persons deprived of cultural property.[40] Its stated goal was to expand the legal opportunities of persons seeking protection.[41] Ultimately, though, no provision on cultural property found its way into the draft sent to the Polish parliament for adoption.[42] It is generally thought that the absence of that provision means that the law in the country in which a thing is now located applies.[43] Jacek Górecki, however, notes that the provisions forming the regime for protecting property in the country of origin must be applied (mandatory provisions) and strengthens their significance.[44]

In the Act, however, effective provisions on intellectual property were added. The earlier Act of 12 November 1965 on Private International Law (APIL)[45] did not contain provisions concerning the law applicable to intellectual property.[46] Jurisdiction was determined on the basis of Article 24 APIL. In the draft Act, a link was made in the form of the place where that law is applied (Article 45).[47] The propositions contained in Article 43 (cultural property) and Article 45 (intellectual property) all constituted a kind of innovation. But only the latter ended up in the finally adopted Act. The addition of conflict-of-law provisions confirmed the existing interpretation of this provision as to the law applicable to rights *in rem*. The change regarding cultural property was made in order to afford such property legal protection and, in this way, went beyond traditional solutions.

A renewed attempt concerning changes in private international law was made in 2018.[48] In the draft amendments to the Civil Code, the Code of Civil Procedure and the Act on Private International Law, changes concerning cultural property were again proposed. This time, those framing the law focused on cultural property lost as a result of the Second World War. Pursuant to the draft, Article 41 of the Act on Private International Law was to be supplemented with two new points, 1a and 2a.[49] The draft also contained transitional provisions ordering compliance with

---

[40] Górecki (2009) p. 17.

[41] Government draft law—Private International Law, Sejm of the 6th term, Print No. 1277, pp. 22–23.

[42] Government draft law—Private international law, Sejm of the 6th term, Print No. 3675.

[43] Górecki (2015), p. 1001.

[44] Górecki (2015), p. 1001.

[45] Act of 12 November 1965 on Private International Law. Polish Official Journal (Dz. U.) 1965, No. 46, item 290 as amended.

[46] Nowicka (2005), p. 227.

[47] Government draft law—Private International Law, Sejm of the 6th term, Print No. 1277, p. 23.

[48] Senat Print no. 760.

[49] Article 3 In the Act of 4 February 2011—Private International Law (Polish Official Journal [Dz. U.] of 2015, item 1792) in Article 41: "1) the following paragraph 1a shall be added after paragraph 1: "1a. Ownership of a movable item constituting a work of art seized from the territory of the Republic of Poland during World War II shall be governed by Polish law."; 2) the following sec. 2a shall be added: "2a. In the case referred to in paragraph 1a, it shall not be possible to acquire ownership of a movable property that is a work of art seized from the territory of the Republic of Poland during World War II before its return to the rightful owners or authorities of the Republic of Poland""".

> an assessment of the acquisition of ownership over movable things constituting works of art plundered during World War II, of the ownership right of the acquirer of ownership, and of the jurisdiction of the Polish court in cases of rights in rem and the possession of such things . . . the provisions of acts . . . in the wording given in this act regardless of the date possession of a thing was taken (Article 4 of the draft).

Among the remarks submitted by entities consulting on the draft, mention should be made of those that directly concerned the issue and principles of international private law.[50] In the end, the work on the Act was suspended. One of the reasons for this suspension was the adoption of the Act on the Restitution of Cultural Property and the desire to see how that restitution mechanism would function. To date, no further work on the proposal has been completed.

The lack of an amendment to the Act on Private International Law and the removal of provisions on cultural property during the legislative work do not eliminate the protection that can be granted to such objects by applying the *public order clause* or the mandatory provisions that require its application. It is therefore necessary to consider the selection of applicable law in disputes over cultural property, as well as applicable mandatory provisions. M.A. Zachariasiewicz writes:

> the history of the institution of mandatory provisions shows that, just as one cannot make a clear border between the provisions of public and private law, one cannot separate public from private interests. One of the main benefits of the concept of mandatory provisions is exactly this, that it covers the 'grey area' between public law and private law.[51]

This difficulty concerning separate public and private interests, and the impossibility of drawing a clear line in a legal regime between private and public laws, is particularly noticeable in the laws on the protection of cultural heritage. And so, in this matter, a thread also emerges connected to cultural heritage appearing as a legal hybrid.

The issue of international private law concerning historical objects and works of art was discussed by Wojciech Kowalski in the Polish literature when the previous Act was still in force.[52] Jacek Górecki wrote: "still to be considered is the protection resulting from recognising the material law provisions serving to protect those goods as mandatory provisions", referring to other findings.[53] It is worth pointing out that the character of mandatory provisions can vary. In the case of cultural heritage, two situations are possible. The first concerns the substantive status of an object when it changes location. Provisions connected with protecting the environment, including historical real estate, can also be mandatory provisions.[54]

---

[50] Documents submitted in the consultations by the Ministry of Culture and National Heritage (28 May 2018), Ministry of Justice (7 June 2018), Ministry of Foreign Affairs (17 May 2018), Supreme Court (5 June 2018).

[51] Zachariasiewicz (2010), p. 12.

[52] Kowalski (2005), pp. 123–149.

[53] Górecki (2015), p. 1001; Jakubowski (2006), pp. 414–416.

[54] Zachariasiewicz (2010), p. 40.

Here, to the extent necessary for the further findings presented herein, reference must be made to the mandatory provisions within the legal system. Mandatory provisions are dealt with in Article 8 APIL. The norms it contains refer to the mandatory provisions of Polish law and those of the laws of other states. The provisions of public law concerning cultural property may be considered mandatory provisions. Those provisions, whether part of public or private law, should be directly connected with the legal relationship under evaluation. They apply even when another law is applicable; in each case, this must be preceded by an analysis of the particular facts.[55] In accordance with the division adopted in French and German doctrines, provisions on works of art, as well as certain types of cultural property, constitute provisions protecting the public interest of the state, defined as *lois de police "de direction"* or *Eingriffsnormen*.[56]

The regulations of the mandatory provisions of a third country are aimed at reducing the risk of forum shopping.[57] Forum shopping certainly constitutes a serious threat in the trade of cultural property, and at times, when ruling in such cases, courts do not take into account the provisions regulating the acquisition of an object due to its exceptional status in its country of origin, such as by refusing to order the return of stolen property to its rightful owner. In the foreign literature, this phenomenon is known as "title laundering" or "artwork laundering"—a practice that requires the thief or dealer in the trade to know the laws of the countries involved.[58]

Pursuant to Article 8 par. 2 APIL,

> when applying the applicable law, one can consider the mandatory provisions of another state with which the legal relationship being assessed is strictly connected if, according to the law of that state, those provisions apply regardless of what the applicable law governing that relationship is. When determining whether to take account of such provisions, it is necessary to consider their nature and purpose, as well as what will result from applying them or omitting them.

It is worth noting the view that those provisions need not necessarily be applied each time but need only be considered.[59]

With regard to cultural property, the purpose of the *res extra commercium* regime is to provide protection abroad as well. This is why it is worth citing examples of rulings by foreign courts where such an exceptional status was considered (state property, anti-alienation clause, ban on exports). Trade restrictions, such as an anti-alienation clause or *res extra commercium* status, have not always been taken into account. On some occasions, the law of the state of origin of an object illegally removed from the country has not been considered, with the security of trading being paramount. Today, however, there is an observable trend towards applying the cultural heritage protection regulations of a given country. As the strongest regime, *res extra commercium* should

---

[55] Zachariasiewicz (2010), p. 12.

[56] Zachariasiewicz (2010), p. 21.

[57] Zachariasiewicz (2018).

[58] Francioni (2017), p. 384; Kowalski (2005), p. 147.

[59] Fuchs (2013), p. 76.

be considered first, similar to the way in which ownership by the State Treasury (or by the state) is determined in the case of archaeological artefacts. Provisions restricting trade in property will be of less importance to the court.

In a case often cited in academic works, that is, *Iran v. Bakarat*, the British court applied Iranian law as the law shaping the legal situation of the property concerned. In the literature, it has been pointed out that this ruling took account of the principle of international cooperation in combating illegal trade in cultural property.[60] The proceedings in *Iran v. Bakarat*[61] are quite important for, there, the law of the country of origin of the objects was applied, which broke a series of rulings by the English courts that had been unfavourable for the owner of the objects concerned.[62] The court acknowledged Iran's ownership of the objects and held that cooperation among states in protecting cultural heritage is recognised internationally.[63] The case concerned objects constituting state property acquired during illegal excavations. This additional element makes this case even more complex because the state of origin may have difficulty in documenting the actual origin of objects. In its justification, the court referred to international instruments that undoubtedly set a certain standard for protecting the cultural heritage of particular countries.[64]

Much earlier, a German court ruled on the basis of a very different set of facts concerning an insurance agreement.[65] The case concerned Nigerian cultural property (masks and figures) taken out of the country to Germany and damaged in shipping. It was determined that six bronze figures had been lost. In court, it was found that, firstly, the objects had probably not been included in the shipment and, secondly, that the shipment had been made contrary to Nigerian law, which prohibited the export of such objects. In its ruling, the court also referred to the UNESCO Convention of 1970, even though this was not binding in Germany. The Supreme Court upheld the Appellate Court's position that Article 138 Bürgerliches Gesetzbuch (BGB) should apply in the case, pursuant to which a legal action contrary to good custom is invalid.[66] The justification also stated that the export prohibition in force in the country of origin applied and that the Appellate Court had rightly noted the need to protect countries from having works of art plundered by foreign collectors and dishonest intermediaries in the art trade.[67]

---

[60] Francioni (2017), p. 382.

[61] Government of the Islamic Republic of Iran v The Barakat Galleries Ltd.—EWHC 2007.

[62] Attorney General of New Zealand v. Ortiz, [1984] AC 1.

[63] Chechi et al. (2011).

[64] "[n]one of these instruments directly affects the outcome of this appeal, but they do illustrate the international acceptance of the desirability of protection of the national heritage." Para 163.

[65] Rechtsprechung BGH, 22.06.1972—II ZR 113/70.

[66] Nigerianisches Kulturgut Berücksichtigung drittstaatlicher Eingriffsnormen im internationalen Privatrecht (Art. 3 ff EGBGB) trotz Anwendbarkeit deutschen Sachrechts (hier: über § 138 BGB).

[67] Cf. Zachariasiewicz (2010), p. 34, footnote 83.

Given the existing instruments available at the international level, one must agree that there is a need for harmonisation[68] and, in Poland, for the ratification of the UNIDROIT Convention. The independent global trend towards respecting the protective provisions in force in countries of origin shows that, in such cases, the protection of cultural heritage dominates the element of certainty in trade. Certainly, the courts' assessments above were affected by the norms contained in instruments of international law, including the UNESCO Convention, the UNIDROIT Convention and Directive 2014/60. While these may not apply in a given case, courts still refer to them because they create an international obligation to respect cultural heritage and to protect the interest of a given nation. This is confirmed by the references made to those conventions and the directive in court rulings, and all of this means that the application of the regime of *res extra commercium* or other legal mechanisms for protecting movable heritage components is extremely important for protecting such property internationally, now and in the future.

In the Polish legal system, museum exhibits and archival materials are worthy of attention. The existing regulations mainly concentrate on determining their status and loss (museum exhibits being stricken from the inventory) and regulating how archival resources are to be collected and managed. These two categories are presented below from the perspective of the *res extra commercium* regime.

5.3.1 Museum Exhibits

Pursuant to Article 5 of the Museum Act (MA), museums may be established by both public and private actors. Among them are ministers and heads of central government units, local government units, natural persons, legal persons and organisational units without legal personality. The MA distinguishes between national museums created by government administration bodies and local governmental museums established by local governments. Other entities, when establishing a museum, have to follow a similar procedure; for example, they must consult the museum's statute with the minister of culture and national heritage. But there are differences concerning financial sources and the legal regime governing collections. The legal provisions on public museums are more restrictive, as shown below.

However, the legislator decided to designate all museum exhibits as national property in the sense of their being common goods, regardless of the entity that established the museum (Article 21 MA[69]). This emphasises the importance of these goods and the need to make them publicly available.[70] Wojciech Kowalski and Katarzyna Zalasińska argue that this wording underlines an axiological approach

[68] Kowalski (2005), p. 148.

[69] Mausoleums constitute national goods.

[70] Antoniak (2012), Art. 21 [Commentary].

and can be treated as a value equivalent.[71] In my opinion, nothing stands in the way of deeming all museum exhibits as constituting national property because of the museums' mission, and this extends to exhibits located in museums organised by a body of government administration, a local government unit or another entity (Article 5 par. 1 MA). Even though the wording of Article 21 par. 1 a MA[72] refers to property of the entity that established a museum in the case of a museum without legal personality (museum within the organisational structure of the university), the notion of the common good in my opinion remains valid.

It should be emphasised that in this context, another determination was made, in accordance with which national goods under Article 21 par. 1 MA are limited to museum exhibits located in state and local government museums. In the literature, the view has been expressed that this results in museum exhibits being granted a different status, which may raise doubts.[73] I am convinced that even if we accept that the Museum Act is not perfect as it pertains to other museums and the regulations addressed to objects stored in them,[74] this should not result in their being deprived of having the status of a national good in the sense presented above. That status is a consequence of the mission and activities of a museum as an institution. In my opinion, which entity owns a museum is of little importance when defining museum exhibits as national goods, provided this does not interfere with their property status (publicly or privately owned).

The status of national goods in no way limits the significance of museum collections or their belongingness to world heritage. The link is made to show the universal importance of museum exhibits in the structure of material property. Meanwhile, movable or immovable things that constitute the property of a museum and are entered in the inventory of museum exhibits are deemed museum exhibits (Article 21 MA). These two criteria should be jointly met. If a museum does not have a legal personality, its exhibits constitute the property of the entity that created the museum. The manner in which museum exhibits can be managed is limited; they can be sold, exchanged or donated solely under a procedure set out in the Museum Act. A transfer of ownership, however, is not limited by law to entities from the public finance sector.

With regard to the "rotation of collections", the structure of *res extra commercium* was discussed in an interpellation, which not only completely negated the views expressed that museum exhibits are things excluded from trade but also stated that

> the introduction of the institution of res extra commercium in respect of public collections would restrict the independence of cultural institutions regarding their policy of creating

---

[71] Kowalski and Zalasińska (2013), p. 79.

[72] 21.1a. MA: In the case of a museum without legal personality, museum exhibits are movable and immovable objects owned by the entity which established the museum and recorded in the inventory of museum exhibits, which established the museum and which is registered in the inventory of museum exhibits.

[73] Cf. Frankiewicz-Bodynek (2019), p. 244, footnote 178.

[74] Golat (2008), pp. 11 et seq.

> museum collections. It must be remembered that the collections of institutions are also enriched through exchanges of exhibits with other institutions or private collectors. The objects of such transactions are usually other copies of the same objects, known as doublets. Obviously, such exchanges do not involve unique items or other property of extraordinary value. An undesired consequence of introducing a total ban on the alienation of museum property would be the elimination of the possibility of enriching a collection.[75]

It should be clarified that the category of *res extra commercium* does not rule out the possibility of managing collections through transfers from one museum to another at the same level or between levels of a local government unit or museum organised by the minister or a body of government administration. It is worth considering whether a transfer of ownership can take place from the local government level to the State Treasury. Here, I have in mind a determination of who the owner is of objects located in local government museums.[76] It seems that this problem has been determined by doctrine, such that local government museums are the owners of their collections. Certainly, some collections may be excluded from a museum and transferred to a newly created entity. In each case, this will involve deaccession under the procedure described in the Museum Act. The deaccession of museum exhibits and their sale to private entities, however, are a different issue.

Certain doubts are raised by the wording of Article 21 MA, which makes no distinction regarding the type of museum to which the provisions on museum exhibits apply. May they then also apply to university museums whose regulations were approved by the minister? Certainly, a museum would be interested in such a status for its collections. The issue of university museums comes up increasingly often in discussions on Polish museology, while university museums themselves cooperate in the Association of University Museums.[77] As a unit within the structure of a university, however, a museum is not a separate entity, and its collections are the property of the university. Katarzyna Zalasińska states that

> the criterion of ownership therefore allows a categorical distinction to be made between public museums (state and local government) and private ones. Contrary to the classification employed by the National Institution of Museology and Collection Protection, this also justifies counting museums that function within the structures of public administration bodies and administrative establishments within the group of public museums.[78]

This raises the question of how such a determination would affect how collections are managed. I am convinced that the statutory procedure for the deaccession of museum exhibits does not apply. If it were otherwise, an entry in the inventory of a university museum would be tantamount to an entry in the register of historical objects.

---

[75] Reply of the Secretary of State at the Ministry of Culture and National Heritage—under the authority of the Minister—to the interpellation no. 11612 on the status of public collections, Parliamentary of the 7th term. http://www.sejm.gov.pl/sejm7.nsf/InterpelacjaTresc.xsp?key=34230811. Accessed 1 June 2022.

[76] Drela (2014), pp. 65–81; Kowalski and Zalasińska (2013), p. 81.

[77] https://muzeauczelniane.pl/. Accessed 1 June 2022.

[78] Zalasińska (2013), p. 159.

I believe that the regimes under which such collections are managed will be grounded in the Law on Higher Education and Science (LHES).[79] Article 423 par. 2 LHES applies to components of fixed assets whose market value exceeds 2 million zlotys. This provision invokes Articles 38–41 of the Act of 16 December 2016 on the Principles of Managing State Property. Managing a work of art or museum exhibit as a fixed asset within the meaning of the provisions on accounting will require the consent of the President of the General Prosecutor's Office of the Republic of Poland. An application for such consent must contain an attachment, including the consent of the university council.[80] Thus, there will be a special procedure concerning collections whose value exceeds the above amount, which in today's reality is not out of the question. It seems, though, that the disposal of such a collection is more likely still. For example, the city of Kraków, as the last to do so under the Act, inherited an apartment and an art collection of more than 100 objects, including (according to the media) paintings by Jacek Malczewski, Wlastimil Hoffman and Jerzy Wróblewski.[81] If that collection, however, had been bequeathed instead to Jagiellonian University, the procedure for selling it off, if considered by the university authorities, should be conducted based on Article 423 par. 2 PSW and the provisions of the Act on the Principles of Managing State Property to which it refers.

One cannot therefore rule out a transfer—in the form, for example, of a donation from a cultural institution to a local government unit that is not the organiser of that cultural institution (donor). If the cultural institution has a collection and it is not a museum (e.g. musical instruments in a philharmonic orchestra), then the provisions of the AOCCA apply. Pursuant to Article 27 AOCCA, a cultural institution may dispose of fixed assets. Where fixed assets are being disposed of, the provisions concerning state enterprises apply, specifically those of the Act of 25 September 1981 on State Enterprises.[82] As to donations, a cultural institution should announce its intention of performing a legal transaction concerning fixed assets to its organiser, that is, to the state or local government (Article 46a par. 1). Within 1 month, the organiser may turn down the request. If the institution fails to make such an announcement, the agreement on the disposal is invalid (Article 46b).

In the case of the winding up of a museum, a mechanism to protect its collections is initiated. The winding up of a local government museum takes place under a procedure described in Article 26 MA. There are two options for acquiring museum property. The first involves granting a priority right to acquire museum objects to the relevant executive body of a district, county or province. The second option concerns

[79] Act of 20 July 2018—Law on Higher Education and Science, consolidated text. Polish Official Journal (Dz. U.) 2021, item 478.

[80] Zieliński (2019), Art. 423 [Commentary].

[81] Kto dostał w spadku kolekcję ponad 100 cennych obrazów i mieszkanie? Miasto Kraków, czyli my wszyscy, 5 March 2020. https://krknews.pl/kto-dostal-w-spadku-kolekcje-ponad-100-cennych-obrazow-i-mieszkanie-miasto-krakow-czyli-my-wszyscy/. Accessed 1 June 2022.

[82] Act of 25 September 1981 on State Enterprises, consolidated text. Polish Official Journal (Dz. U.) 2017, item 2152.

museums created in the process of the communalisation of state property and assumes that the property is acquired free of charge by a local government unit. If the priority right is not exercised, the organiser determines what happens to the property in consultation with the provincial governor. On the other hand, if the objects do not become part of another museum collection after being deleted from the museum inventory, they should be entered in the register of historical objects at the request of their new owner. A separate procedure is foreseen for the winding up of a state museum, pursuant to which, in each case, the rules for managing museum exhibits are set out by the competent minister in the form of a decision. The Act imposes a duty on the minister to obtain an opinion from the Council for Museums (Article 27 MA).

An interesting case concerning museum exhibits is the return of cultural property recovered under the Act on the Restitution of National Cultural Property (ARNCP) from

> the winding up of a cultural institution or a state unit in the public finance sector to which the ownership of cultural property has been transferred ... the ownership of that cultural property transfers [back] to the State Treasury, while the minister competent for cultural matters and the protection of the national heritage exercises the entitlement of the State Treasury in the scope of managing that cultural property (Article 13 ARNCP).

This legal norm also concerns objects transferred to "a state cultural institution or other state unit of the public finance sector as referred to in Article 9 pts. 11 and 12 of the Act of 27 August 2009 on Public Finances", that is, entities that do not necessarily have a museum status. This solution is similar to the one used in the Museum Act, described above, during the communalisation of state property. It is worth noting, however, that a free-of-charge transfer may also concern cultural property owned by the State Treasury, including property recovered under restitution proceedings. When choosing the entity to which a given object is to be transferred, consideration is given to the structure of its collections and their connection with the cultural heritage component to be assigned.[83]

In this case, there is a strengthening of the principles protecting an object, namely its automatically becoming property of the State Treasury, for this is not a priority right to a free or paid acquisition but another case of a transfer of ownership or, more precisely, its return to the State Treasury. The word "management" is used to clearly establish what the role of the Minister of Culture and National Heritage is after property is restored to the State Treasury. Management refers to (1) the management of cultural property obtained through restitution conducted by the Republic of Poland (RP) or of national cultural property of the RP forfeited to the State Treasury and (2) donations of cultural property to the State Treasury.

Yet the liquidation of a cultural institution is an exception[84] and is rather unlikely to occur in the case of museums. To my knowledge legal provisions presented above

[83] Only if several entities own the collections in which the object was previously included or there is no such institution, then the decision is made by the minister (Article 13.2 ARNCP).

[84] Jagielska-Burduk and Zajęcki (2013).

are not applied very often. For the principle is to maintain the continuity of collections, or possibly making such a transformation or using the form of a joint institution so that the museum can continue to function. In practice, bridging solutions are also done, such as subsidising an institution without altering the model under which it is managed. This model of proceeding, which is of an incidental nature and is applied in exceptional cases, indirectly confirms the special character of objects collected in museums and highlights the role of non-systemic mechanisms in maintaining the continuity of museums and public collections.

It is odd that, when introducing reinforced legal protection and new legal provisions, the legislator did not introduce a *res extra commercium* regime for both the collections of local government museums and state museums in subsequent amendments of the Act. A good example is the norm contained in Article 30 MA, which only concerns state and local government museums.[85] Museum exhibits in their inventories are not subject to enforcement on the basis of an enforcement order issued in court or administrative enforcement proceedings. This clear difference from other museums organised by, for example, a natural person could serve well as a starting point for new solutions connected with the circulation of museum exhibits. It could also provide a basis for strengthening the protection of local government and state museum collections. Perhaps the legislator's inactivity in this regard results from a change in perspective and a search for models that would also encompass other types of museums.

In the current legal state, it is hard to define museum exhibits as *res extra commercium*, though they can be considered things partially restricted from trade. The current civil law status of museum exhibits does not allow for them to be deemed things excluded from trade. The idea was expressed that, with regard to museum exhibits gathered in state museums, Article 169 CC should have been excluded after the deletion of Article 171 CC;[86] however, that view was not accepted by other researchers. Similarly, the more recent position that "until the minister issues consent, we can assume that museum exhibits are things excluded from trade"[87] also seems to go too far. The permissibility of disposing of museum exhibits is not ruled out but is limited by a procedure in which many entities take part. In the case of public waters, the legislator specifies that these are excluded from civil law trade and can only be handed over for use, e.g. fishing. Such statutory exceptions, however, do not include a change in the owner, who continues to be the State Treasury. No similar solution is in place for museum exhibits.

Given their origin and the types of institutions in which they are located (local government, state), they are dealt with differently when an institution is wound up. They both circulate in the same manner, however, in accordance with a de-accession procedure. It seems reasonable to think that in the case where a museum wishes to dispose of certain objects, such as recovered cultural property,

[85] Antoniak (2012), Art. 30 [Commentary].

[86] Szpunar (1999), p. 33.

[87] Drela (2006), p. 187.

the consent of the minister is unlikely to be obtained. Museum exhibits certainly constitute things that are restricted in trade. At present, the regime governing public collections is also highlighted by the Act on the Restitution of National Cultural Property (ARNCP), which excluded the application of Articles 169 and 173 CC to museum exhibits. The status of public collections is described in 5.4 below.

5.3.2 Archival Materials

The legal definition of archival materials forming part of the national archive collection is very broad (Article 1 of the Act on National Archival Resources and Archives (ANARA)).[88] The national archive collection is divided into state national archive collection and non-state archival collection. Although both belong to the same collection, the regulations that apply to them differ. The status of archival materials created by the legislator is non-uniform and raises many concerns. It foresees different restrictions on trade for registered, non-state materials than for state materials. As a result of this division, there exists a two-level system of protection.[89] Pursuant to Article 7 ANARA, archival materials constituting components of state archives cannot be disposed of, and a transfer of these to another entity is subject to the regime provided by that Act. The Act sets forth special rules for their circulation, whereas pursuant to Article 43 ANARA, archival materials that are part of registered, non-state archival resources cannot be objects of trade and as such are deemed *res extra commercium*. That provision employs the phrase "ownership of archival materials" that cannot be objects of trade. The core of the Polish regulation in this case is to prevent such objects from becoming the property of an entity other than a state archive, but its wording leads to different statuses and blurs the legal regime.

From ANARA, one can track a "life cycle" of archival materials created during the activities of the entities defined in its Article 42. The catalogue contained therein

[88] Archival materials forming part of the national archive stock, the archival materials, hereinafter referred to as "archival materials", include all kinds of files and documents, correspondence, financial, technical and statistical documentation, maps and plans, photographs, films and microfilms, sound and videophone recordings, electronic documents within the meaning of the Act of 17 February 2005 on informatisation of the activity of entities performing public tasks public tasks (Polish Official Journal [Dz. U.] 2019, item 700, 730, 848, 1590 and 2294) and other documentation, regardless of the manner of its creation, which is significant as source of information of historical value on the activities of the Polish State, its individual organs and other state organisational units and about its relations with other states, about the development of social and economic life, about the activities of organisations of a political, social, economic, professional and religious nature The information on the development of social and economic life, on the activities of political, social, economic, professional and religious organisations, on the organisation and development of science, culture and art, as well as on the activity of local self-government units and other self-government organisational local government organisational units—created in the past and created contemporary.

[89] Kowalski (2006), pp. 16–17.

includes political parties, political organisations, cooperatives and other social organisations, churches and religious associations, and non-state organisational units other than those mentioned in Article 42 pt. 2 ANARA. The final stage in the cycle is when an item enters a national archive; exclusion from trade takes place in order to maintain the unity of collections; it is another example of the institution of *res extra commercium*. After a given non-state archival resource ceases to be managed as such, it becomes property of the state and part of the state archival resources. The State Treasury acquires ownership under a procedure set out in Article 44 par. 1 ANARA. Currently, there is no way to determine the intention of the legislator when drafting this provision. One can only suspect that behind this regulation lays the principle of the integrity of archival resources. Non-state archival resources excluded from trade are then transferred to the state's resources.

The Act specifies the moment at which ownership is transferred, which is the day liquidation proceedings are commenced or bankruptcy declared with regard to the organisational unit concerned; this moment is defined in the Act as the moment of the permanent cessation of activity.[90] At that moment, the unit loses its special status. It is assumed that

> the existence of events causing dissolution and liquidation (or bankruptcy) of a 'private' organisational unit sets in motion a procedure for dealing with registered archival materials, which should result in their being taken into the state archival resources.[91]

The legal effect of the above events is described unequivocally, where registered resources "become the property of the State and enter into the state archival resources". It seems that this is an automatic acquisition of ownership that requires no declaration or consent to such disposal. The materials concerned are promptly handed over to the state archive indicated in a decision issued by the General Director of State Archives. This is a rare case of removing enhanced protection in favour of weaker protection. It would be difficult to contend that the protection granted to resources belonging to a registered, non-state archive affects the status given to state archival resources. No longer *res extra commercium*, they become things restricted in trade. One can discern the legislator's intention that some non-state resources may more readily be acquired by an unauthorised entity more quickly than if the same documents or materials are part of a state archive.

It is worth noting the opposite view that components of registered, non-state archives are not *res extra commercium* but fall within the category of things restricted in trade.[92] In support of this idea, reference is made to the possibility of disposing of such materials for the benefit of the State Treasury (Article 15 par. 2 ANARA). Given that civil law agreements are concluded concerning archival materials, e.g. deposits or exhibition loans, it has been argued that such materials are

[90] See more on this legal provision history Konstankiewicz (2015), p. 18.

[91] Niewęgłowski (2014), pp. 51–55.

[92] Konstankiewicz (2016), Art. 43 [Commentary].

indeed objects of trade.[93] In this regard, it must be said that the essence of the institution of *res extra commercium* does not prevent Italian museums from lending or borrowing museum exhibits to or from other institutions.

The interpretation of the provision presented here is not what results from a straightforward linguistic interpretation. Such a departure, though, is only permissible if the linguistic interpretation leads to an absurd result, which is very doubtful in this case. The provision of Article 15 ANARA sets forth what materials comprise state archival resources. The example given here of the acquisition of archival materials through purchase, donation or other means concerns resources from various sources, not only registered, non-state archival resources.[94] It also covers other archival materials, including those arising from the activities of political, social and economic activists; creators in the fields of science, technology, culture and art, as well as other people who have made a historic contribution to the development of the Polish state and its political, social and economic life or to the development of science, technology, culture or art (Article 15 par. 2 pt. 4 ANARA); and families that have had a historic influence on matters of state or political, economic and social relations, as well as materials related to their property, businesses and other economic activities (Article 15 par. 2 pt. 5 ANARA).[95]

Interestingly, Article 44 par. 2 ANARA stipulates that, apart from the situation where a non-state organisational unit is wound up, its archival materials may still become state property by a decision of the competent bodies of that unit. The transfer of ownership to the State Treasury may take place earlier than as a result of the unit's winding up. The transfer of ownership of such materials is specified in a form of an understanding that wrongly suggests MOU (Clause 3 paras. 2 and 3 of the regulation).[96] Commentators have indicated that, despite the ambiguity of the provision, this is a case of a civil law agreement or, more precisely, of a sale or donation where there is no obligation for consent to be granted to a proposal for the transfer of ownership by way of a donation.[97] The original wording of the provision,

[93] Konstankiewicz (2016), Art. 43 [Commentary].

[94] The registered non-state archival resources consist of archival materials that originated and were created as a result of the activity of (1) political parties, (2) political, cooperative and other social organisations, (3) churches and religious associations, (4) non-state organisational units other than those mentioned in item 2 and constituting their property.

[95] These are materials resulting from the activities of: "1) political parties and other organisations of a political, social, professional and economic nature, 2) churches and religious associations 3) other non-state organisations and organisational units, 4) political, social and economic activists, creators in the fields of science and technology, culture and art as well as other persons who have made a historic contribution to the development of the Polish State, political, social and economic life and to the development of science and technology as well as culture and art, 5) Families and families who exerted a historical influence on state affairs, political, economic and social relations, as well as on their estates, enterprises and other economic activities."

[96] Ordinance of the Minister of Culture and National Heritage of 14 October 2015 on the conditions and procedures for transferring to state archives archival materials forming the recorded non-state archival collection. Polish Official Journal (Dz. U.) 2015, item 1733.

[97] Konstankiewicz (2016), Art. 44 [Commentary].

"pursuant to a decision of the competent non-state bodies", was changed to "by a decision of the competent bodies of non-state organisational units".[98] This removed the doubt that this is an administrative decision, which cannot be issued by the entity authorised to hand over the materials.

When interpreting the provision on the permissibility of trading in particular materials originating from the sources mentioned in the Act, it is important, however, to read it alongside Article 43 ANARA. That provision states that archival materials forming registered, non-state archival resources cannot be the objects of trade; moreover, this is also restricted by the provisions of Articles 6[99] and 8 ANARA. To return to Article 15 par. 1 ANARA, which sets out groups of archival materials, it cannot be inferred that Article 15 par. 1 pts. 1–5 ANARA applies to all types of acquisitions (purchase, donation, other manner). When we juxtapose the above with Article 8 ANARA, the result is that archival materials forming part of a registered, non-state archival resource cannot be disposed of, where the only means of transferring them should be in accord with Article 44 ANARA. The transfer of ownership of such materials can occur in one direction only, that is, as a transfer to the State Treasury. It can be argued that the ultimate destination of such archival materials is that they will become part of a state archive.

The reservation in the Act that materials may be transferred to the State Treasury earlier can be read as part of a rescue procedure for the resources of a given entity. It seems unacceptable that an entity could reap some kind of benefit through the early handover of materials that would become the property of a state archive anyway after its liquidation. Such a transfer, therefore, should be in the form of a donation. It seems that an archive may decide not to admit materials if the provisions of law or other provisions have established that those materials are not endangered. Undoubtedly, the costs of storing the materials must be considered; these may justify a refusal.[100]

---

[98] Act of 20 March 2015 amending the Act on the National Archival Resource and Archives. Polish Official Journal (Dz. U.) 2015, item 566.

[99] Article 6 para 1 State authorities and state organizational units, authorities of local government units and local government organizational units local self-government bodies and self-government organizational units shall be obliged to ensure proper recording, storage and protection against damage, destruction or loss of "1) documentation generated in them, in a manner reflecting the course of dealing with and resolving matters; 2) documents sent to them and submitted to them in the manner referred to in item 1."

[100] I would like to thank Prof. Marek Romaniuk from the State Archive in Bydgoszcz for consultation.

5.4 The Legal Status of National Treasures Belonging to Public Collections

The construction of national cultural property is a result of the implementation of EU law and, at the same time, the Polish legislator's use of that opportunity to strengthen the protection granted to certain types of property to combat illicit trade. The ownership of national cultural property belonging to public collections is governed by ARNCP. Pursuant to the provisions of Chapter 5 ARNCP, an object's affiliation with a public collection has specific legal consequences in how it can be managed. The introduction of provisions excluding time-barring, acquisitive prescription and the possibility of acquiring an object from an authorised entity are a direct result of the implementation of Directive 2014/60/EU, which was used to build additional protection for some public collections.

In the justification to the draft Act, the authors referred to the use of an extended time period foreseen for restitution claims with regard to public collections, which is not limited to 75 years,[101] since pursuant to Article 8 of the Directive,

> in the case of objects forming part of public collections, defined in point (8) of Article 2, and objects belonging to inventories of ecclesiastical or other religious institutions in the Member States where they are subject to special protection arrangements under national law, return proceedings shall be subject to a time-limit of 75 years, except in Member States where proceedings are not subject to a time-limit or in the case of bilateral agreements between Member States providing for a period exceeding 75 years.

The possibility of applying special protective measures to public collections was used. In a way, one can argue that the new version of the Directive forced to take more decisive legislative steps in Poland, which, at least in part—as presented above concerning museum objects—had previously only been considered and discussed. For this reason alone, the creation of such a regulation should be seen in a positive light and is deserving of a more detailed analysis.

According to Article 2 pt. 8 of the Directive, "public collections" means

> collections, defined as public in accordance with the legislation of a Member State, which are the property of that Member State, of a local or regional authority within that Member State or of an institution situated in the territory of that Member State, such institution being the property of, or significantly financed by, that Member State or local or regional authority.

As indicated in the justification to the Act,

> Directive 2014/60/EU does not impose on Member States a definition of public collections; it formulates such a definition only for the purposes of interpreting Directive 2014/60/EU internally.[102]

---

[101] Government draft law on restitution of national cultural property, Works of the Sejm of the 8th term, Print No. 1371, pp. 12, 23, 31–32.

[102] Government draft law on restitution of national cultural property, Works of the Sejm of the 8th term, Print No. 1371, p. 12.

The category of public collections first appeared in the Polish legal system prior to the Directive's implementation, along with the provisions on exports. Pursuant to Article 51 par. 1 pt. 3 APGM, historical objects

> in public collections constituting property of the State Treasury, local government units or other organisational units belonging to the public finance sector cannot be permanently exported abroad.

This provision was introduced by the Act of 18 March 2010 on an Amendment of the Act on the Protection and Guardianship of Monuments and Certain Other Acts.[103] The absence of a Polish definition of public collections had been pointed out previously, and it was suggested that there was a need to determine

> which Polish monuments belonging to the State Treasury, local government units or other organisational units belonging to the public finance sector are public collections.[104]

A more direct consequence of the Directive's implementation was the adoption of a legal definition of public collections in Article 2 pt. 6 of ARNCP. The Act defines public collections as

> all historical objects and other cultural property constituting property of entities designated by the legislator. In terms of the criterion of ownership, public collections are collections of the State Treasury, units of the public finance sector, non-governmental organisations, and entities as referred to in Article 3 par. 2 and 3 of the Act of 24 April 2003 on Public Benefit and Volunteer Work, which carry out work for the benefit of the public in the fields of culture, art, and the protection of cultural property and the national heritage. To that catalogue are added other entities that use public funds or manage them while this Act is in force, or which manage historical objects or other cultural property which during that period are or were maintained, directly or indirectly, including securing or studying them from public funds.

In this way, the definition provides what property belongs to public collections as a subject and object. Provided Article 51 par. 1 pt. 3 APGM, as mentioned above, it can be held that, indirectly, that proposal to specify the objects included in public collections was accepted in the definition adopted for the needs of the new Act.

In order to define the semantic scope of public collections, we must examine the key elements of that definition. In the objective criterion adopted, apart from historical objects legally defined in the APGM, mention is also made of "other cultural property". The Act contains a definition of cultural property whose starting point is the evaluative criteria of a historical object. In accordance with that definition, cultural property comprises

> historical objects in the meaning of Article 3 pt. 1 of the Act of 23 July 2003 on the Protection and Guardianship of Monuments, movable things not constituting historical objects, as well as their components parts or sets thereof, whose preservation lies in the interest of society due to their artistic, historical or scientific value, or due to their importance for heritage and cultural development.

---

[103] Act of 18 March 2010 on an amendment of the Act on the Protection and Guardianship of Monuments and certain other Acts. Polish Official Journal (Dz. U.) 2010, No. 75, item 474.

[104] Jakubowski (2010), p. 290.

The novelty in this definition is the addition of the criterion of importance for heritage and cultural development.

It is worth noting that a legal definition of cultural property returned to the legal system after an absence of 18 years. The last definition of cultural property was found in the Act on Protection of Cultural Properties (APCP), which was repealed when the APGM entered into force. Pursuant to Article 2 APCP,

> cultural property in the meaning of the act is every movable or immovable object, from the past or contemporary, that is significant for the heritage and cultural development due to its historical, scientific or artistic value.

The old definition of cultural property from 1962 also encompassed contemporary property and was not limited to movable things not constituting historical objects. It seems that the new definition draws on the APCP, for example by invoking the importance of heritage and cultural development, which is not found in the APGM. The definition refers to historical objects (as cultural property from the past) and to movable things not constituting historical objects (monuments). It is puzzling, though, that cultural property means a historical object (which can be a movable thing or real estate) or a movable thing that is not a historical object if it meets certain criteria, while real estate that is not a historical object is omitted, even if it is important for heritage and cultural development. No doubt, this is because the regulation concerns restitution and the implementation of the Directive, as well as the need to create a legal definition for the purpose of this particular Act. Yet one cannot avoid the impression that this definition of cultural property is a rather unsuccessful result of borrowing the definition of a historical object from the APGM and the definition of cultural property from the APCP.

The special regime is of limited application as it is intended only for national cultural property constituting part of a public collection. The definition of national cultural property[105] refers to the APGM, specifically to those provisions related to historical objects being taken abroad. In this context, this solution is exceptionally inadequate. Firstly, Article 51 par. 1 APGM[106] contains a list of categories of

---

[105] Art. 2 item 4 national cultural property of RP: (a) a monument referred to in art. 51 paragraph 1 of the Act of July 23rd, 2003 on the protection and guardianship of monuments, or (b) a monument referred to in art. 51 paragraph 4 of the Act of July 23rd, 2003 on the protection and guardianship of monuments, not being a monument referred to in letter a, or (c) archival material forming part of the national archival resource referred to in art. 1 of the Act of 14 July 1983 on the national archival resource and archives (Polish Official Journal [Dz. U.] 2019, item 553 and 730), or (d) an object which is not a monument if it is entered in the inventory of museums in museums which are cultural institutions within the meaning of Article 10 (2) of the Act of 25 October 1991 on the organization and management of cultural activities (Polish Official Journal [Dz. U.] 2018, item 1983 and of 2019, item 115 and 730), or (e) library material which is not a historical monument and is included in the national library stock referred to in Article 6 (1) of the Act of 27 June 1997 on libraries (Polish Official Journal [Dz. U.] 2018, item 574 and 1669).

[106] Art. 51.1: "(1) A single permit to permanently export a monument abroad is required for monuments falling into one of the following categories: 1) archaeological monuments that are more than 100 years old and are part of archaeological collections or have been acquired as a result of archaeological research or accidental discoveries; 2) elements forming an integral part of

objects, along with their age and value, upon which the obligation to obtain an export permit depends.[107] Given how much discussion there was over that provision, the dependence on value and age is difficult to accept.[108] The definition also refers to Article 51 par. 4 APGM, that is, to the categories of objects that, regardless of their age and value, cannot be permanently exported.[109]

The fact that an object constitutes national cultural property in a public collection has important consequences as to how it may circulate. A common feature of public collections is that they comprise historical objects and other cultural property, that is, cultural property not constituting historical objects. Such sets are defined using the criterion of ownership. This very broad approach to public collection in the Polish Act, however, gives one cause for consideration, for the EU legislator specified how public collections should be understood while allowing states a certain amount of freedom to also include collections of other institutions. The Act provides a broader scope of collection than is indicated in the Directive. The Directive contains a certain auxiliary criterion containing the reservation that a collection should largely be financed out of public funds.

There is no doubt that collections of the State Treasury and units of the public finance sector are public collections. Doubts arise over non-governmental organisations and other entities supported by public funds. Determining this group is all the more difficult in that it does not specify how to identify collections that are or were

---

architectural monuments, interior decoration, monuments, statues and works of artistic craftsmanship, which are more than 100 years old; 3) works of painting made with the use of any technique and on any material, not included in the categories specified in points 4 and 5, which are more than 50 years old and their value is higher than PLN 40,000; 4) watercolours, gouaches and pastels made on any material, which are more than 50 years old and their value is higher than PLN 16,000; 5) mosaics, not falling into the categories specified in points 1 and 2, and drawings made in any technique and on any material, which are more than 50 years old and their value is higher than PLN 12,000; 6) original graphic works and matrices for their production and original posters, which are more than 50 years old and their value is higher than 16,000 zlotys; 7) original sculptures, statues or their copies made with the same technique as the original, not falling in the category specified in item 1, which are more than 50 years old and their value is higher than PLN 20,000; 8) individual photographs, films and their negatives, which are more than 50 years old and their value is higher than PLN 6000; 9) single or in a collection of manuscripts which are more than 50 years old and their value is higher than 4000 zł; 10) single or in the collection books which are more than 100 years old and their value is higher than PLN 6000; 11) single printed maps and scores which are more than 150 years old and their value is higher than PLN 6000; 12) collections and items from zoological, botanical, mineral or anatomical collections whose value is higher than PLN 16,000; 13) collections of historical, palaeontological, ethnographic or numismatic interest whose value is higher than PLN 16,000; 14) means of transport which are more than 50 years old and their value is higher than PLN 32,000; 15) other categories, not mentioned in points 1–14, covering monuments that are more than 50 years old and their value is higher than PLN 16,000."

[107] Gredka-Ligarska (2019), pp. 107–109.

[108] Cf. Gredka-Ligarska (2019), p. 108.

[109] These are monuments entered in the register, entered on the Heritage Treasures List, included in public collections which are the property of the State Treasury, local government units or other organisational units included in the public finance sector, entered in the inventory of a museum or included in the national library inventory.

"maintained, directly or indirectly, including securing or studying them out of public funds". Public funds are defined in Article 5 par. 1 of the Act on Public Finances.[110] Given that the ARNCP did not introduce a new definition, public funds must be understood as funds, as referred to in the Act on Public Finances. For example, public funds may be funds allocated to subsidise the conservation or study of a collection where the funds are obtained from a local government unit for the implementation of tasks by a non-governmental organisation or private collector.

In the Polish definition, there is no reference to "degree of financing," and so this element can be considered omitted. In the justification to the draft Act, the authors emphasised that this definition is important for how the Directive is to be interpreted internally. This is why an evaluation of what collections constitute public collections is extremely important and should be made on the basis of clear criteria. In view of their absence, it becomes necessary to make as detailed an analysis as possible of the legislator's intentions. In the justification, the "other entities" referred to in Article 2 pt. 6 letter d ARNCP were merely mentioned. However, it is possible to derive certain assumptions from the work on the Act.[111] What catches one's attention are the references to maintaining certain property due to its value and making it available to the public. One may suppose that, here, the authors had in mind objects that were to be entered on the List of Heritage Treasures. Pursuant to Article 78 par. 5 APGM, read together with Article 74 par. 2 APGM, the subsidy of an object entered on the List of Heritage Treasures is made in the full amount, and in accordance with the main aims of this form of protection of historical objects, the objects should be made publicly available.

It is immensely difficult to verify the correctness of this definition in the practical dimension. Nevertheless, one can indicate a number of situations that raise reasonable doubts. For example, we can imagine that a collector receives a grant from a local government for cultural activity by natural persons involving the publication of

---

[110] Act of 27 August 2009 on public finance, consolidated text. Polish Official Journal (Dz. U.) 2021, item 305, 1236, 1535, 1773, 1927, 1981.

Article 5 (1) Public funds are: "1) public revenues; 2) funds from the budget of the European Union and non-refundable funds from the assistance provided by the Member States of the European Free Trade Agreement (EFTA); 2a) funds referred to in Article 3b of the Act of 6 December 2006 on the principles of development policy (Polish Official Journal [Dz. U.] 2018, item 1307 and 1669); 3) funds from non-recoverable foreign sources other than those mentioned in item 2; 4) revenues of the state budget and budgets of local government units and other units of the public finance sector coming from: a) from the sale of securities, b) privatisation of State Treasury assets and assets of local government units, c) from repayment of loans and credits granted from public funds, d) from loans and credits received, e) from other financial operations, 5) revenues of public finance sector entities from activities conducted by them and from other sources."

[111] Government draft law on restitution of national cultural property, Works of the Sejm of the 8th term, Print no. 1371, p. 32: "This way of defining it is justified by the diversity of forms of involvement of the state and local self-governments—both organisational and financial—in the implementation of the constitutional task of enabling the public to access cultural heritage and its protection: starting with direct establishment of own cultural institutions, through joint operation of such institutions with non-governmental entities, financing of the activities of such entities in the field of national heritage, ending with maintenance of cultural assets (in view of their importance and in order to ensure public availability) constituting property of such entities."

a collection catalogue. Indirectly, those objects are worked on using public funds. Does this mean that the collection now comprises a public collection since the grant agreement was concluded with the owner? Here, I have in mind the grants foreseen in Article 7b AOCCA.[112]

Pursuant to that article,

> in relation to the cultural centres and institutions subordinate to them, and in relation to local government units, the minister competent for cultural matters and the protection of national heritage, other ministers, and the heads of central offices may provide grants to persons involved in artistic activity, the dissemination of culture or the guardianship of historical objects.

The conditions and procedures under which grants are provided are determined by the minister through a regulation and by governing bodies in the form of a resolution. To complicate the situation further, one can imagine a completely plausible example where, as part of a scientific activity, a conservator of historical objects obtains funds to renovate and study an object of another private entity, for example a collector known to the conservator. Will that privately owned object then also be privileged, and will acquisition from an unauthorised entity in good faith be excluded?

Given the lack of any clear guidance in this regard, there is great uncertainty as to whether the partial or indirect financing by public funds causes objects to be treated as components of a public collection. Another example of an "indirect" use of public funds for a collection is when a local government museum organises an exhibition and prepares a catalogue describing the collection. Studies are often made using public funds at the disposal of a museum (within their budget or as a subsidy targeted for a specific purpose, in this case it would be organisation of an exhibition). Yet another example is an agreement on a loan to a museum of objects belonging to the private collection of an association. Assuming that the museum has been studying and conserving these objects for years using public funds and certain items are on permanent display, do they comprise a public collection within the meaning of the Act?

All of this confirms that the definition in use raises more questions than it answers. Evaluating and classifying cultural property as belonging to a public collection now requires a precise analysis of every case, and when applying the provisions in practice, the issue of whether objects can be classified as belonging to a public collection will certainly arise. One can ask another question: does every holder of historical objects or other cultural property who obtains even the slightest financial aid thereby alter the status of those objects? Furthermore, there arises the problem of proving the fact of financing by means of subsidy agreements, decisions, agreements on the transfer of an object to a museum for an exhibition, loan agreements and grant agreements. Certainly, the aim was to protect the broadest possible scope of collections that could be treated as public collections. However, it

---

[112] Act of 25 October 1991 on the organization and conduct of cultural activities, consolidated text. Polish Official Journal (Dz. U.) 2020, item 194.

resulted in challenging certainty in trade and the unclear status of at least some types of objects.

It is also puzzling whether public funds that have been obtained should be used to preserve every object. For example, a collector obtains financing for the conservation of certain objects and plans to submit an application concerning other objects in the following year. Will those objects that have not yet been subject to conservation treatment but that can be deemed national cultural property also be covered by a strengthened legal regime? It does not follow from a literal interpretation that it is enough for only some of the components to be maintained out of public funds. Yet it will be even more difficult to prove that funds were allocated to an individual object. Another problem with classification may arise in a situation where financing was granted but the funds were not used and, in the meantime, the object was stolen.

It is therefore important to define categories of public collections so as to eliminate any uncertainty over the status of objects. One of the simplest proposals in this respect would be to establish a threshold amount of public funds that must be allocated for maintaining a public collection owned by a given entity. A somewhat more complex solution would be to establish a certain amount in relation to the value of an object. Unfortunately, this would not be advantageous in the long run because the value of objects and the level of financing can, and in fact should, change due to changes in the economy (conservation costs, studies, etc.). With regard to the provisions governing export, the use of the criteria age and value serves a clearly different purpose as those criteria are verified at the moment of export. In the first version of the Directive, restitution proceedings could be conducted in relation to a historical object considered within one of the categories specified (in the no longer binding Article 64 APGM). Currently, states identify national cultural property according to their own criteria,[113] and the Polish definition again refers to value as a criterion.

With this in mind, it can be said that the goal established through Polish law—and by extension the EU Directive—will not be achieved by setting the amount of financing from public funds. However, it is worth specifying how financing is to be allocated, focusing on the direct flow of subsidies to an owner or other entities holding a title to objects on the basis of a civil law agreement (e.g. a museum in possession of a collection under a loan agreement). In Article 36 par. 5 APGM, a similar solution was employed to determine the circle of entities authorised to apply for a permit to carry out work on historical objects. An application for a permit may be submitted by a natural person or an organisational unit holding a legal title to use a historical object where this results from ownership, perpetual usufruct, permanent administration or a limited right *in rem* or contractual agreement.

In museums, there are objects whose status (i.e. being stored or even exhibited in a state or local government museum) does not result from a contractual agreement. It also happens that the ownership status of certain objects is "undetermined", even though they are stored and possibly conserved using public funds. From the perspective of the ARNCP, it is worth considering whether such objects can be deemed national cultural

[113] Stec (2015), p. 112.

property forming part of a public collection. Such objects are not museum exhibits for they should be entered in other registers kept by a museum or in deposit records. In this scope, part of the definition of national cultural property contained in Article 2 pt. 4 letters b and d and Article 2 pt. 6 letter d ARNCP[114] can be helpful.

The goal of affording protection to objects entered in an inventory of museum exhibits is a laudable goal. It seems, however, that the formulation used definitely extends beyond the scope of the change intended. A literal interpretation of the provision also allows things not constituting historical objects and not constituting museum property to be classified as national cultural property if they appear in a museum inventory. In this way, even objects that are not owned by a museum but are entered in its inventory rather than its deposit records—even by mistake—will benefit from the protection granted in the ARNCP. Objects entered in the inventory that should be registered there will also benefit from such protection. For instance, objects in the collection of the Sanguszko family, whose return was denied by the Supreme Court on the basis that their claim for return in accordance with the rules of museum record keeping had become time-barred, should have been entered not in the inventory of museum exhibits but in a separate register.[115] The same can be said of objects seized and handed over to a museum without a legal basis as a result of the decree on agricultural reform,[116] even though, since that time, the costs of storing and maintaining them have been paid out of public funds.

One can infer that such a group of objects will belong to a set of national cultural property constituting the property of "other entities ... which manage historical objects or other cultural property which during that period are or were maintained, directly or indirectly, including securing or studying them out of public funds". In this way, it could be said that if those objects meet the criteria of age and value, they will be protected by a stronger regime in case they are stolen from the museum. Yet the question arises as to whether the "managing entity" is the owner, who may know nothing about the object and its location or knows about it but has no effective instruments for recovering it and the museum will not consent to a transfer of possession in the absence of legal measures forcing it to do so. I believe this alludes

[114] Art. 2 item 4) National cultural property of the Republic of Poland: "a) a monument referred to in Art. 51.1 of the Act of July 23rd, 2003 on the protection and care of historical monuments, or b) a monument referred to in art. 51 section 4 of the Act of July 23rd, 2003 on the protection and care of historical monuments, not being a monument referred to in point a, or c) archival material constituting a part of the national archival resource referred to in art. 1 of the Act of 14 July 1983 on the national archival resource and archives (Polish Official Journal [Dz. U.] 2019, item 553 and 730), or d) an object that is not a historical monument, provided that it is entered in the inventory of museums in museums that are cultural institutions within the meaning of Article 10(2) of the Act of 25 October 1991 on the organization and conduct of cultural activities (Polish Official Journal [Dz. U.] 2018, item 1983 and of 2019, items 115 and 730), or e) library material which is not a historical monument and is included in the national library stock referred to in Article 6 (1) of the Act of 27 June 1997 on libraries (Polish Official Journal [Dz. U.] 2018, items 574 and 1669)."

[115] Jagielska-Burduk and Mularski (2015), pp. 201–216.

[116] Decree of 6 September 1944 on agricultural reform. Polish Official Journal (Dz. U.) 1944, No. 4, item 17.

to the structure used in Articles 5 and 28 APGM,[117] which impose obligations on the holder of a historical object.[118] The addressees of those norms are owners and possessors of a historical object. One suspects that, in the same context, the same definition was used for entities managing historical objects or other cultural property.

There is no need to employ a double reference to public collections in the definition of national cultural property by referring to Article 51 par. 4 APGM. In pt. 3 of that provision, mention is made of historical objects in public collections, among which are objects constituting property of the State Treasury, local government units or other organisational units belonging to the public finance sector. Yet a much broader definition of public collections is adopted in Article 2 pt. 6 letter d ARNCP. This double use of the category of public collections with a different meaning makes the provision even less clear. To a certain extent, the ARNCP repeats the solution used in the APGM that public collections comprise the total amount of historical objects and other cultural property constituting property of the State Treasury or units of the public finance sector. However, this is not limited solely to historical objects within the meaning of the APGM but extends as well to other cultural property defined in the ARNCP. I am convinced that it would be easier to create a definition of cultural property without invoking Article 51 par. 4 APGM as this has caused a double enumeration in the form of historical objects and non-historical objects in museum inventories (Article 2 pt. 4 letter d ARNCP), as well as library materials constituting and not constituting historical objects (Article 2 pt. 4 letter d ARNCP).

The authors of the draft Act referred, in their justification, to issues relating to combating illegal trade in cultural property. They described proposed solutions

> initially seeking to eliminate the possibility of ownership being lost as a result of acquisitive prescription (Article 174 Civil Code) or acquisition in good faith by a third party (Article 169 Civil Code) (Article 46 of the draft). These are the most common threats to cultural property. They not only exacerbate the harm suffered by an owner who was the victim of a crime, but

[117] Article 5 APMG The care of a monument by its owner or holder consists, in particular, in providing the conditions for: "1) the scientific examination and documentation of a monument; 2) carrying out conservation, restoration and construction works at the monument; 3) securing and maintaining the monument and its surroundings in the best possible condition; 4) using monument in a manner ensuring permanent preservation of its value; 5) popularising and disseminating the knowledge about the monument and its significance for history and culture."

Article 28 APMG "1. Regardless of the obligations arising from the care of monuments specified in Article 5, the owner or the possessor of a monument entered in the register or a monument located in the provincial records of monuments shall notify the provincial monuments conservator about: 1) damage, destruction, loss or theft of the monument, not later than within 14 days from the date of becoming aware of the occurrence of the event; 2) the threat to the monument, not later than within 14 days from the date of becoming aware of the threat; 3) change of the storage place of the movable monument within one month from the date of the change; 4) changes concerning the legal status of the monument, not later than one month from the date of their occurrence or becoming aware of them. 2. The owner or holder of a monument entered on the Heritage Treasures List shall notify the minister competent for the matters of culture and protection of national heritage about the events referred to in par. 1."

[118] About responsible holder Jagielska-Burduk (2014), pp. 311–318.

above all violate the security and integrity of the cultural heritage. For this reason, it is justifiable to encompass at least those heritage resources that are most accessible to society, be it through being made publicly available or because of their religious function (or both), and to grant them special protection that prevails over certainty in trading (rights acquired in good faith).

The ARNCP excludes the application of the provisions on acquisitions from an unauthorised entity and acquisitive prescription in relation to the national cultural property of the Republic of Poland belonging to a public collection (Article 46 ARNCP). Furthermore, claims for the return of such property do not become time-barred (Article 47 ARNCP). An acquirer in good faith may bring a claim against the person from whom he acquired an object or against persons jointly responsible therewith. Pursuant to Article 51 ARNCP, the provisions of the chapter "National Cultural Property of the Republic of Poland belonging to public collections" accordingly apply to the national cultural property of Poland constituting property of churches and other religious associations, church legal persons, church associations and foundations established by church legal persons, and legal persons established by other religious associations.

The Act also introduced the required form for a legal transaction. All legal actions involving the transfer of ownership or an encumbrance should be made in writing, with a specific date. In the justification to the Act, it is stated that "legal actions performed without this form are invalid".[119] Pursuant to Article 73 par. 2 CC, in a situation where a particular form is prescribed for a legal action, a failure to comply with that form gives rise to the invalidity of the action. It seems that the entities specified in Article 2 pt. 6 letter d ARNCP had two obligations imposed on them that are not easy to fulfil in practice—firstly, to determine whether objects constitute national cultural property and, if so, whether the sets concerned are public collections. Placing a provision regarding the form for legal actions in the ARNCP may cause some collectors and foundations to conclude contracts without observing that form. Perhaps placing this provision in the APGM would make this norm clearer for those to whom it is addressed.

Based on the analysis made of categories of public collections, one can say with confidence that not all national cultural property belonging to a public collection will be accessible to society. The possibility of excluding provisions on acquisitive prescription and acquisition in good faith came in "through the back door", as it were regarding movable things and collections owned by private entities. It is a pity that no such solution was introduced for private collectors, tying it to the register of collections or an obligation to provide public access, rather than with the idea of financing out of public funds, which is rather difficult to grasp.

Moreover, the Act introduces provisions that force private entities to apply for public funds if they wish to strengthen the protective regime for their collections. Here, one can assume that such entities will not always desire such funds or may

---

[119] Government draft law on restitution of national cultural property, Works of the Sejm of the 8th term, Print No. 1371, p. 79.

apply for very small amounts of subsidies only to supplement their own large contribution to a project's budget. On the other hand, the National Register of the Lost Cultural Property (NRLCP), which is discussed below, constitutes an optimal solution for owners of historical objects. Unfortunately, the protection afforded by the NRLCP does not extend to works of modern art (defined as other cultural property)[120] belonging to private collectors who decide against or do not receive financing out of public funds.

In such a configuration, the coexistence of the NRLCP and public collection institutions is indicative of an irrational legislative action. Legislative initiatives are not prepared with the idea that a particular solution will last a long time; they instigate discussions whose results may be used in future legal regulations. Here, it should only be stated that the NRLCP only results in a temporary exclusion of the provisions on prescriptive acquisition and acquisition in good faith. Interestingly, the scope of application of the NRLCP does not extend to movable historical objects not entered in the register, while at the same time national cultural property in public collections need not meet this criterion.

The application of the Act must be considered separately for several variants of property described earlier, i.e. archival materials and museum exhibits. Firstly, one must consider whether there was a change in the scope of materials belonging to national archival resources. In line with what was established above, non-state registered resources constitute *res extra commercium*, whereas state-owned, registered resources are things restricted from trade. Here, it seems that the legal status changes only with regard to the latter category. Regarding museum exhibits, the introduction of these provisions is of vital importance for it diametrically alters the position of a museum, which becomes deprived of the possession of objects. The

[120]Government draft law on restitution of national cultural property, Works of the Sejm of the 8th term, Print No. 1371, p. 26: "In addition to the above-mentioned categories, i.e., monuments and archival materials covered by existing export restrictions under Polish law, the proposed law also incorporates into national cultural property categories of objects that are cultural property not previously covered by export restrictions—at the same time, such restrictions, by amending the provisions of the Law on Museums (Article 57.2, which introduces a new Article 29a) and the Law on Libraries (Article 58.1, which introduces a new Article 6a), but covered by other forms of legal protection under specific regulations. These are museum objects, which are not monuments and are entered into the inventory of a museum that is a cultural institution (and thus constitute a public collection within the meaning of the act) and library materials belonging to the national library resource. The extension of the category of national cultural property to include non-historic objects results from European Union regulations, including Directive 2014/60/EU and its predecessor Directive 93/7/EEC, which provide for the protection of the cultural heritage of individual Member States not only with respect to historic monuments, but also to cultural property that is not a monument. It should be emphasized that these categories of objects have not been subject to export restrictions under Polish law so far, which undoubtedly should be regarded as a gap in the system of cultural heritage protection, especially with regard to museum collections of contemporary art, which constitute a significant part of museum collections and very often represent a high market value. Provisions of the proposed act eliminate this loophole and at the same time adjust the system of protection of cultural heritage to the broader framework of protection of this heritage, provided for by the EU regulations, than it has been the case in Polish law so far."

museum will then have two possible courses of action, either to recognise the fact that the protection foreseen for public collections is sufficient or to apply to the NRLCP, whose register, if it operates, will become one of the most visited websites in Poland for collectors and their advisors wishing to exercise due diligence. In the case of library materials, whether they constitute historical objects or not, their status has also changed diametrically. An important question still arises, however. Since the provisions of the NRLCP were introduced into the Civil Code, why similar provisions with regard to public collections were not implemented using this way?

The perception of "event" actions—very selective legal interventions in the area of cultural heritage—remains valid.[121] A recent legal initiative, which was given a lot of media attention, was the introduction of a List of Heritage Treasures, which is not yet operational at the time of writing; in fact, plans are underway to close down the institution altogether.[122] The List of Heritage Treasures is to be removed from the APGM. The authors of the draft amendment argue that this form of protection "has not been applied in practice so far and remained a dead regulation". Today, the legal system for the protection of heritage seems to be going through a crisis, and fragmentary legislative initiatives only make things worse. We are faced with a large number of regulations, some of which do not work. These may lead to claims for compensation, which I discuss further in the section on NRLCP.

A failure to perceive the variety of heritage leads to the creation of solutions that are inflexible and that, despite the best of intentions, do not guarantee the security of heritage or promote a feeling of security among those in charge of it. It is strange that, despite the NRLCP's presence in the legal system, the legislator did not decide to employ the register as a tool for enhancing the security of public collections. It cannot be ruled out that when preparing the draft Act, the legislator was aware that the NRLCP was being spoken of in legal circles as a dead institution that would soon be removed from the legal order. Yet removing the NRLCP in the future will require an amendment of the Civil Code, which will not only challenge the role of cultural heritage protection but will further discourage lawyers specialising in private law from proposing changes.

The notion of public collections in the Directive is an artificial structure. It is not a model developed within the domestic legal order but is dependent on the requirements contained in the Directive. When formulating a definition of public collections, it was not analysed how this would supplement or overlap with other legal institutions already in force. Nor did it make use of comprehensive regulations. One has the impression that we are dealing with a forced solution caused by the obligation to implement the Directive, where no proper consideration was taken of the domestic legal system's needs and the specifics thereof. Thus, apart from the one goal related to the amendment of the Directive and the need to implement it in the

[121] Jagielska-Burduk (2016b), pp. 171–212.

[122] Governmental draft law on amending Act on the Protection and Guardianship of Monuments Act and Certain Other Acts, UD247, Justification to the draft, p. 1. https://legislacja.gov.pl/projekt/12356151. Accessed 1 June 2022.

legal order, no attempt was made to build a strong system of public collections in Poland based on scientific achievements and the opinions of practitioners. Further, given the problems shown above concerning the semantic scope of the concept, it is difficult to distinguish those public collections that are owned by private entities. Given this state of affairs, there is an urgent need to amend the ARNCP and fully integrate the Polish vision of cultural heritage protection into its provisions.

5.5 State Ownership of Archaeological Artefacts

The link between archaeological property and world cultural heritage is seen most vividly against the background of other cultural heritage components.[123] Certainly, what makes it possible to connect archaeological heritage with world heritage is the age of the objects involved and the fact that some objects attest to the history of groups, nations and states that no longer exist. How to define archaeological property is not a new problem, nor is how to structure ownership rights to it. In the APGM, archaeological property is defined as an

> immovable monument constituting surface, underground or underwater remains of human existence or activity, composed of cultural accumulations and works or traces thereof contained in these accumulations, or a movable monument constituting such a work (Article 3 pt. 4 APGM).

In both cases, the object must meet the listed conditions to be considered a monument.

The most controversial element of the above definition is how old an object must be to be deemed archaeological property. This problem was perceived when the previous Act was in force[124] but the dilemma is still present, and there is nothing to indicate that a uniform stance on the issue is likely to emerge among archaeologists.[125] Proposals for introducing a time threshold have therefore been made. This would reduce the potential number of "new" archaeological objects.[126] Alternatively, setting a threshold date closer to the present time will increase the number of archaeological objects that potentially constitute property of the State Treasury.

Each time a discovery is made, the new components must be stored, which creates a complex organisational problem. While commentators write about the privileged position of museums,[127] which obtain deposits in this way, representatives of museums see things somewhat differently; they point to the practical difficulties faced in storing such objects. Furthermore, a faulty application of legal provisions can lead to a depletion of archaeological property constituting property of the State

[123] Jagielska-Burduk (2011), pp. 258–259.
[124] Sieroszewski (1971), pp. 67–68.
[125] Trzciński (2011), pp. 209–213; Trzciński (2014), pp. 116–120.
[126] Trzciński (2011), p. 212.
[127] Golat (2004), p. 61.

Treasury. In the literature, cases mention criminal proceedings being discontinued and archaeological property[128] being returned to the accused rather than being secured. No matter how powerful are the legal mechanisms for protecting archaeological property or all cultural heritage components, what is crucial to their preservation is how the provisions of the law are applied.

Archaeological property may consist of movable or immovable property. The previous Act (APCP) referred to archaeological and palaeontological objects, such as

> ground traces of an initial settlements and human activity, caves, prehistoric mines, fortified settlements, cemeteries, burial mounds and all products of ancient cultures (Article 5 pt. 5 APCP).

From the start of the archaeological heritage legal, it constituted an important part in the protected resources. It should be observed that only in 2000 that archaeological objects were entered in the register of historical objects with the separate designation C.[129] Previously, the register of historical objects contained only books A (immovable historical objects) and B (movable historical objects), with a separate section being kept for archaeological property in each book.[130] As a separate category containing both movable and immovable property, archaeological property constitutes a very difficult subject of regulation since the category should be uniform for archaeological heritage but at the same time take into account the differences between movables and immovables.

The model for how to proceed with an archaeological object that has been found, including the issue of ownership, is deliberately regulated separately in the APGM rather than in the Civil Code. Unfortunately, the existing dispersion of provisions in various acts of law can hinder their application. It is also argued, with some justification, that this fragmentation harms the protection of cultural heritage. Yet one cannot avoid seeing similarities to other regulations, such as those on animals. Provisions on animals appear in private law, where the fundamental provision establishing that an animal is not a thing is found in the APA. In my opinion, it is entirely justifiable to leave these provisions outside of the Civil Code. The provisions on "The management of historical objects, conducting research and other work, as well as other activities relating to historical objects" are contained in Chapter 3 of the APGM. There is no reference at all, though, to the acquisition of ownership in the chapter's title.

[128] Trzciński (2011), p. 206; Trzciński (2013), pp. 234–242.

[129] Ordinance of the Minister of Culture and National Heritage of September 6, 2000 on the maintenance of the register of historical monuments and the central register of cultural goods, Polish Official Journal (Dz. U.) 2000 No. 86, item 965.

[130] Ordinance of the Council of Ministers of 24 November 1986 amending the ordinance on keeping a register of historical monuments and a central register of historical monuments, Polish Official Journal (Dz.U.) 1986, No. 42, item 204. In § 5, section 1, of the ordinance on keeping a register of historical monuments and a central register of historical monuments, the following second sentence was added: "Within section A of the register, a separate book may be kept for archaeological monuments."

In Poland, a solution was adopted in relation to archaeological property whereby the ownership of archaeological artefacts that are found or discovered goes to the State Treasury. This solution makes it possible for the state to pursue the return of archaeological property deriving from illegal excavations and introduced to the market. In order to disseminate the principle of state ownership of archaeological property as an element in combating illegal trade in cultural property, international experts prepared the document UNESCO-UNIDROIT Model Provisions on State Ownership of Undiscovered Cultural Objects.[131]

The document, which is not, however, legally binding, contains provisions that states can use when planning revisions or large changes to the legal regulations concerning archaeological heritage. When seeking the return of an object, a state does not need to show that the object is entered in a national list or inventory but may instead rely on legislation establishing the state ownership of archaeological property and, if such a solution is in place at the domestic level, treat the object as *res extra commercium*.

The UNESCO Convention of 1970 does not cover the question of ownership of objects deriving from illegal excavations. Such objects are discussed, however, in the guidelines to the Convention,[132] which refer to the UNESCO-UNIDROIT Model Provisions on State Ownership of Undiscovered Cultural Objects.[133] It should be added that state ownership is very difficult to demonstrate when objects deriving from illegal archaeological excavations appear on the art market. The state bears the burden of proving the provenance of an object when it brings about a claim for restitution. Objects from illegal excavations do, however, fall within the scope of the UNIDROIT Convention and are subject to the restitution procedure established among the parties to the Convention.

State ownership of archaeological cultural objects was discussed in the case of the history of the famous dinosaur Sue. Joseph L. Sax while presenting this case compared provisions on property rights to found archeological objects and role of the state ownership model. The fossil was found in 1990 and is one of the best-preserved remains of a *Tyrannosaurus rex* in the world. The author compared the regulation in force in the United States on the legal status of an archaeological discovery with the French regulation and came up with two different solutions. One was based on the right to the location of the discovery, with the result that ownership over a find should be granted to the owner of the property. The second solution, in accordance

[131] Expert Committee on State Ownership of Cultural Heritage, Model Provisions on State Ownership of Undiscovered Cultural Objects. Explanatory Report with model provisions and explanatory guidelines, UNESCO, UNIDROIT, 2011. https://fr.unesco.org/sites/default/files/unesco-unidroit_model_provisions_en.pdf. Accessed 1 June 2022.

[132] The Operational Guidelines for the implementation of the 1970 Convention, RESOLUTION 3. MSP 11. https://en.unesco.org/fighttrafficking/operational-guidelines. Accessed 1 June 2022.

[133] Expert Committee on State Ownership of Cultural Heritage, Model Provisions on State Ownership of Undiscovered Cultural Objects. Explanatory Report with model provisions and explanatory guidelines, UNESCO, UNIDROIT, 2011. https://fr.unesco.org/sites/default/files/unesco-unidroit_model_provisions_en.pdf. Accessed 1 June 2022.

with French law, granted ownership to the state.[134] This analysis was conducted after the end of the dispute over who owned Sue. In 1997, the fossil was put up for auction at Sotheby's by the owner of the property on which it had been discovered. It was acquired by the Field Museum of Natural History in Chicago, where it is now on display.[135] Under a different legal system and different legal and political assumptions, the result of the dispute could have been different. Sax found the French model, in which ownership of the archaeological heritage goes to the state, to be more beneficial. It is worth noting that in October 2020, another *T. rex* fossil was sold for over $31 million during the 20th Century Evening Sale at Christie's. As the buyer chose to remain anonymous, it appears that this was a private purchase.

In seeking to investigate how the Polish regulation establishing State Treasury ownership of archaeological monuments has been formed, one must go back to acts prior to the APGM. Proceedings concerning excavations and finds were regulated in the Decree on Guardianship of Artistic and Cultural Artefacts of 1918. Pursuant to Article 27 of the Decree, the government had the right to use or expropriate land for scientific purposes if a discovery was made on that land. Moreover, the government had the right to "pre-purchase" excavations and finds within 3 months after becoming aware of them.[136] In this way, rather than expropriation, there was a limited time period for "pre-purchase" that the government could utilise to exert ownership rights over an archaeological discovery.

In Article 27 of the Regulation of the President of the Republic of Poland of 6 March 1928 on the Care of Monuments, a somewhat different model of ownership was adopted; namely,

> artefacts that are excavations or finds may be expropriated, regardless of the conditions foreseen in Article 18, for the benefit of the State, units of local government or legal persons involved in the guardianship of artefacts, upon their request or with their consent.

The circle of entities for whose benefit a historical object could be expropriated was quite broad. It is noteworthy that this circle extended to legal persons involved in the guardianship of artefacts, including certain museums, as referred to in the Act on Museums of 1933, as well as public law corporations and associations run by other institutions if in the latter case their collections were made available to the public.

The Regulation also provided for the expropriation or temporary seizure of land on which discovery had been made. In both cases, expropriation took place upon submission by entities or with their consent. Article 28 of the Regulation concerned land on which archaeological monuments were discovered. In accordance with that provision, such land could

> be expropriated for scientific purposes or seized temporarily for the benefit of the State, units of local government or legal persons involved in the guardianship of artefacts, upon their request or with their consent.

[134] Sax (2007), pp. 69–72.

[135] *T-Rex* fossil was sold at the Christie's 20th Century Evening Sale for $31 million, the buyer wants to remain anonymous (Small 2020).

[136] Kowalczyk (2017), pp. 208–210.

An exception was made for land owned by the Roman Catholic Church. It is striking that the act provided the possibility for the owner of the land on which an archaeological object was found to later apply for expropriation.

A phrase similar to that contained in the binding act appeared in Article 24 APCP, which unequivocally determined that "archaeological excavations and finds constitute property of the State". There has been an evolution, then, of the regulations on the legal status of archaeological property, with stronger protection created through state ownership. However, it seems that every archaeological object that was obtained before the APCP entered into force does not constitute property of the State Treasury and, as such, may be an object of trade. When the Regulation of 1928 was in force, attention was paid to the procedural model when making investments and securing finds. Information on this was contained, *inter alia*, in a circular by the Minister of Energy dated 14 January 1954.[137] In the case of extensive construction works, a permanent inspector could be assigned by the Ministry of Culture and Art to the relevant site,[138] provided, of course, that land was not expropriated based on the binding provisions of the time. In the case where such an object is traded nowadays, information on it will be crucial in terms of establishing the buyer's due diligence (or lack thereof).

The change of ownership of archaeological objects for the benefit of the state introduced in the APCP coincided with the adoption of the UNESCO Recommendations International Principles Applicable to Archaeological Excavations in 1956.[139] Article 5 pt. 2 letter e of this document stipulates that the Member States should define the status of archaeological artefacts discovered beneath the earth, and where state ownership of such components is foreseen, this should be expressly laid down in an act of law.[140] It may be that the authors of the Polish provision drew inspiration from that recommendation; they certainly acted in line with its guiding spirit.

However, the issue of the relationship between the provisions on treasure in Article 189 CC and those regulating archaeological property in Article 35 APGM remains.[141] In Article 189 CC (the initial version), it was provided that

> (i)f a thing of considerable economic, scientific or artistic value is found in such circumstances that a search for its owner would clearly be futile, the finder is obliged to hand the thing over to the competent authority. A thing found becomes State Treasury property and the finder is entitled to appropriate compensation.

---

[137] Sieroszewski (1960), p. 41.

[138] Sieroszewski (1960), p. 42.

[139] Recommendation on International Principles Applicable to Archaeological Excavations, 5 December 1956.

[140] "Define the legal status of the archaeological sub-soil and, where State ownership of the said sub-soil is recognized, specifically mention the fact in its legislation."

[141] Sieroszewski (1971), pp. 67–68.

Two approaches are evident, both of which, it should be noted, had already been expressed before the amendment of Article 189 CC.[142] The first concerns treating Article 35 APGM as a *lex specialis* in respect of Article 189 CC.[143] According to the second view, we are faced with a double regulation since the norms neither contradict one another nor coincide with each other, while an archaeological object falls within the scope of what is designated as treasure.[144] This problem was eliminated upon a change in the wording of Article 189 CC.[145] The amended Article 189 CC provides:

> (I)f a thing is found in such circumstances that a search for its owner would clearly be futile, it becomes the subject of co-ownership in fractional parts of the finder and the owner of the real estate on which the item was found, however, if the item is an historical object or archival item, it becomes the property of the State Treasury, and the finder is obliged to immediately hand it over to the proper county administrator (starosta).

The norm contained in Article 35 APGM only encompasses archaeological property, while in its new wording, Article 189 CC refers to historical objects and archival materials. In this way, the relationships between the legal norms are formed differently because in both cases, the concept of a historical object (monument) is used. Archaeological objects also fit within the scope of the definition of a historical object used in the Civil Code. In this new arrangement, it is fitting to consider the provision of the APGM a *lex specialis* in relation to how treasure is regulated in the Civil Code. An important remark should be made here concerning archaeological property whose owner cannot be established since this may cause the application of Article 187 CC.[146]

[142] Art. 189—version before amendment: If a thing of considerable economic, scientific or artistic value is found in such circumstances that a search for its owner would clearly be futile, the finder is obliged to hand the thing over to the competent authority. A think found becomes State Treasury property and the finder is entitled to appropriate recompense.

[143] Piątkowski (1977), p. 372.

[144] Drela (2006), p. 199.

[145] Art. 189: If a thing is found in such circumstances that a search for its owner would clearly be futile, it becomes the subject of co-ownership in fractional parts of the finder and the owner of the real estate on which the item was found, however, if the item is an historical object or archival item, it becomes the property of the State Treasury, and the finder is obliged to immediately hand it over to the proper county administrator (starosta).

[146] Art. 187 "§ 1 Found property which is not collected by an authorized person within one year from the date of delivery of a call for collection, and in the case of within two years from the day it was found, it becomes the property of the finder if the finder has fulfilled his obligations. However, if the item was handed over to the starosta, the finder becomes its owner, if he/she the finder collects the item within the time limit specified by the head of district (starosta); § 2 The found object being an item of historical monument or archival material after the expiry of the time limit for its collection by the authorised person it becomes the property of the State Treasury. Other found items become the property of the district upon expiry of the time limit for claiming them by the finder; § 3 Upon the moment of acquiring ownership of the item by the finder, the county or the State Treasury. The moment the finder acquires ownership of the item, the county or the State Treasury expires the limited property rights." Goettel (2019), pp. 24–25; Kaczan (2016), pp. 82–83.

In Article 189 CC, the term "becomes State Treasury property" is used. One can infer that this occurs at the moment it is determined that circumstances have occurred making it obviously pointless to search for the owner of a find. Pursuant to Article 35 par. 1 APGM, "objects being archaeological monuments discovered, accidentally found or obtained as a result of archaeological research constitute property of the State Treasury". Under Article 35 par. 2 APGM, State Treasury property also includes archaeological objects acquired as a result of a search for hidden or abandoned movable historical objects, including archaeological objects, through the use of any type of electronic or technical device or diving equipment on the basis of a valid permit (Article 36 par. 1 pt. 12). In Article 35 paras. 1 and 2, we find a statement that objects constitute property of the State Treasury. Given the construction of the provisions on ownership of archaeological objects and how they are found, it is difficult to identify the exact moment at which ownership is acquired.

By examining how the provisions are worded, one can attempt to answer the question of which archaeological objects do not constitute State Treasury property. Are objects not yet discovered beneath the soil whose existence is unknown to anyone today State Treasury property? Here, we need only remind ourselves that in the UNESCO-UNIDROIT Model Provisions on State Ownership of Undiscovered Cultural Objects, which was prepared by experts, the element of state property is indicated as being particularly prone to divergent interpretations and raises concerns. In an explanatory report, it was suggested that the text of an act should contain express provisions on undiscovered archaeological property.[147] Based on existing regulations, a model solution determining state ownership was created. Another "sensitive" element is the determination that a thing constitutes ownerless property. For example, the provisions should not apply to a situation where a person buried their own property in order to safeguard it since they were able to deal, in this way, with an archaeological object they owned. The authors of the legal model recommend including appropriate exclusions in domestic regulations that take into account a country's own legal culture and traditions when determining in which situations a thing is not considered abandoned.

Similar doubts may arise when interpreting Article 35 paras. 1 and 2 APGM, which seek to assess the status of undiscovered objects. The wording of these provisions does not permit the view that all archaeological objects located in the ground constitute State Treasury property before they are found or discovered. The adopted solution foresees identification as part of the acquisition of ownership. In a certain sense, the affirmative phrase "constitute property" may suggest that such objects do not "become" property because they are already "owned" by the State Treasury. As to the civil law status of a thing before it is found, Krzysztof Mularski

[147] Expert Committee on State Ownership of Cultural Heritage, Model Provisions on State Ownership of Undiscovered Cultural Objects. Explanatory Report with model provisions and explanatory guidelines, UNESCO, UNIDROIT, 2011, s. 5. https://fr.unesco.org/sites/default/files/unesco-unidroit_model_provisions_en.pdf. Accessed 1 June 2022.

has commented somewhat more broadly and emphatically, arguing against the view,

> certainly rooted in a failure to distinguish between real and nominal definitions, that before a thing is found it is an ownerless thing. It seems that, before being found, a thing is not a 'thing' at all in the meaning given to that term in civil law doctrine; for such an object cannot constitute an object of trade. If this were not the case, rather than creating a structure that raises so many doubts, the legislator would simply have determined that all treasure is simply State Treasury property – not only after the moment it is discovered in certain defined circumstances.[148]

With regard to archaeological property, yet another expression was employed—"constitutes property". It places the emphasis on the moment ownership is acquired in a very different way. In Article 189 CC, archaeological cultural property is described by the phrase "becomes property". With respect to archaeological property, the criterion of exclusion from trade strengthens the value of the property itself as well as the value attributed to it. I believe that archaeological objects are not ownerless things before they are discovered, found or obtained as a result of archaeological research.[149] For objects where it is pointless to search for an owner and that meet the criteria for archaeological property, they remain the "property" of the State Treasury. The finder or discoverer, however, is entitled to receive a reward (Article 34 par. 1 APGM).

Many archaeological objects may never come into human possession, or this may occur only after several centuries—but this does not diminish their importance for civilisation. First, there is no way to separate them from the layers of soil that surround them without carrying out excavation work. Further, it is frequently impossible to determine the moment at which ownership is acquired. Nor can one establish how many such objects there are or the scope of territory in which they are located. It seems doubtful that undiscovered archaeological objects constitute things in the meaning of the Civil Code. While they occupy a specific place in the world, they cannot be directly subject to human control. One can consider, then, three variants. The first is that archaeological objects are things independent of the ground. The second is that they are things and component parts of the ground. The third is that they have no independent existence and constitute material property not constituting things. This last proposal is the closest to a right *in rem* similar to ownership.

According to Edward Muszalski, the object of a right similar to a right *in rem* cannot be "strictly controlled", and those rights "dependent on the joint work of generations of the nation and on the security provided by the state, are subject to much greater limitations for the good of the public".[150] Muszalski refers to public benefit and provides examples of the use of water and fair use in copyright. Such rights are also subject to control and are exercised in cooperation with state

[148]Mularski (2009), p. 648, footnote 41.

[149]Different view: Drela (2006), p. 200. The author believes that undiscovered monuments are res nullius.

[150]Muszalski (1932), pp. 331–332.

authorities. This view is still current, and if we apply it to our considerations, the following findings arise. Archaeological heritage is also protected due to public interest, where the equivalent of common use may be apply to access components thereof in museums. Undoubtedly, there is an additional similarity in such property being subjected to human control. Archaeological objects, however, cannot be expropriated for they belong to the State Treasury. The State Treasury, however, can secure an archaeological object and remove it from a person who acquired it as a result of illegal excavation.

As stated above, archaeological property may be movable or immovable. Among those types that are immovable, some occupy a large surface area and penetrate deep into the ground. In this sense, they are similar to mineral deposits, which may or may not occupy most of the subterranean portion of a piece of land and cause the property to retain no economic significance for its owner. In such a case, the owner's scope of ownership is limited. Moreover, the owner may learn about the existence of an archaeological object at any time and is not able to foresee it.[151] This does not apply to situations where real property is covered by an entry in the register of historical objects. A similar phenomenon in the context of mineral deposits has been described by Roman Mikosz.[152] It should be pointed out that this problem seems to have been noticed in the Decree of 1918 and the Regulation of 1928, although in subsequent legal acts fell silent on the subject of takeovers of real estate.

In the case of immovable archaeological objects set into the ground, their nature and location do not allow them to be moved without detrimental consequences for this would remove them from their original context and cause an irreversible loss of cognitive values for research. The existing area entries on archaeological property impose an obligation on investors to obtain a permit for construction works and provide for archaeological research to be carried out on the property.[153] Where there is no entry of a given area in the register, upon the discovery of objects that may be deemed historical objects, work should be stopped and the competent conservator of historical objects must be notified—or the relevant mayor if this is not possible (Article 32 APGM). It should be added that since archaeological objects constitute State Treasury property, a very interesting situation arises in connection with the costs of maintaining such property. Article 31 par. 1 APGM initially foresaw that the costs of archaeological research should be incurred by the investor. This provision was revoked on the grounds of unconstitutionality,[154] and subsequently a mechanism for co-financing such work was introduced (Article 82a par. 1 APGM). This did not completely relieve investors from having to bear such costs, however.

[151] One can imagine a situation where an archaeologist acquires an estate to conduct research on the property and not disclose this information.

[152] Mikosz (2008), pp. 178 et seq.

[153] In the media, the issue arises particularly in plans to build underground parking lots or conduct archaeological surveys during renovation in the city centres.

[154] Polish Constitutional Tribunal, Judgement of 8 October 2007, K 20/07, OTK-A 2007/9/102, Polish Official Journal (Dz.U.) 2007 No. 192 item 1394; Jagielska-Burduk (2016d), pp. 38–39.

In the case of objects such as vessels, jewellery and money, which can be readily moved, secured and exhibited in a museum, archaeological work leads to their being separated and detached from the ground. Upon consent, they may be put in deposit with a museum or other organisational unit under the procedure of Article 35 paras. 3 and 4 APGM. The current approach towards archaeological property began in relation to water. The example of "ownership" of water was illustrated based on the mineral water production cycle—from deposit to well to factory and, finally, to a bottle standing on a table in a restaurant. The physical properties of liquid and the impossibility of separation it have led to certain formal structures.[155] In relation to archaeological property, it should be emphasised that they may be found in a better or worse state of preservation, depending on their location and the circumstances of their discovery and extraction. What is more, in the case of artefacts such as vessels, these often exist as fragments, and even after joining them together, it is not always possible to restore the original form of an object. Nevertheless, they are always removed from the ground. The conservation work results in independent objects. Here, it is worth citing the postulate of Monika Drela concerning the idea that movable things should be treated as belonging to immovable property. Drela proposes creating a formal connection between certain products of intangible heritage and a given space.[156] This is a very valuable contribution to the discussion on managing world heritage sites, although in my opinion it cannot be used within the scope of the legal regime for managing archaeological property.

This is so because, firstly, archaeological artefacts were often created independently of the other evidence of human existence found in other layers of the ground in the same location. Secondly, with regard to traces of settlements found under the ground, it is usually impossible to excavate them due to the buildings or structures situated above them—including in accordance with the principles of conservation theory. In managing such property, the State Treasury takes measures attributed to an owner of a historical object under Articles 5 and 28 APGM. Given the specific nature of archaeological artefacts and their location in the ground, the type of guardianship exercised over them by the state differs from that applied to a historical building or sculpture. Scientific research and documentation (Article 5 pt. 1 APGM), which entail an obligation to prepare archaeological documentation during construction works and to secure artefacts in the best possible condition (Article 5 pt. 3 APGM)[157] are particularly important in this context. Article 5 is addressed to both owners and possessors. It seems, however, that it is also addressed to the State Treasury as the "owner" of deposits of archaeological property.

The main aim of the provisions contained in Articles 31–35 APGM is to secure archaeological heritage. Protecting archaeological property may be effected by entering immovable property in the register of monuments, the records of a

[155] Agopszowicz (1973), p. 36.

[156] Drela (2017), pp. 41–42.

[157] Drela (2008) shares the view that rescue works can be qualified as care and protection of cultural heritage.

provincial conservator or a municipal spatial development plan. Pursuant to Article 31 par. 1a pt. 2 APGM, apart from works on immovable property, another situation is identified where the nature of current earthworks on a given site may change if archaeological objects are found there and the works could damage or destroy the archaeological property; in such cases, an obligation arises to carry out archaeological research and documentation. Not only must there be a risk of damage or destruction; the research must also be necessary from a heritage protection perspective.[158] Such research is not limited solely to sites where archaeological relics have been identified and granted one of the forms of protection for historical objects. The structure of the provision

> does not therefore limit the obligation to conduct research solely to sites on which archaeological objects are located that are covered by one of the forms of conservation protection; it is necessary to conduct archaeological research also on the grounds of an immovable historical object entered in the register without the requirement that it be an archaeological object. Nevertheless, for the proper application of Article 31 par. 2 [APGM – author], there must exist a conviction as to the possibility of archaeological objects being present on a given site.[159]

It is noteworthy that an investor's documentation drawn up under the procedure of Article 31 APGM is limited in scope. The work conducted and its scope are determined by the provincial conservator of historical objects in accordance with the guidelines contained in Article 31 par. 2. The scope of work may be determined

> solely within the scope in which the construction works or earthworks or a change in the character of existing activities on a site on which archaeological objects are located will destroy or damage them.

The main purpose of the work, then, is to identify and document those objects. One more issue must be mentioned. The Act permits the destruction or consumption of State Treasury archaeological property under the condition that proper documentation is prepared. This situation is similar to that concerning water, which may be used by third parties under the WLA 2017 even though it is the "property" of the State Treasury. Conducting research also requires that a permit be obtained under the APGM. Thus, there is an organised system for protecting archaeological objects, whether their existence has already been ascertained or it is only deemed likely that they are to be found on a given site.

Under the current wording of the Act, I believe it is justifiable to say that undiscovered archaeological property can be treated as material property subject to a right similar to that of ownership. In the future, it would be worth developing a new act of law that would specify and separate the "ownership" of undiscovered archaeological property. The current construction permits archaeological property to be protected in light of the UNIDROIT Convention of 1995. Pursuant to Article 3 pt. 2,

[158] Regional Administrative Court in Wrocław, Judgment of 27 February 2013. II SA/Wr 890/12, LEX no. 1312232.

[159] Regional Administrative Court in Warsaw, Judgment of 29 September 2017. VII SA/Wa 2533/16.

for the purposes of the UNIDROIT Convention, a cultural object that has been unlawfully excavated or retained shall be considered stolen when this is consistent with the law of the state where the excavation took place. In Poland, a plaintiff, meaning the State Treasury, does not need to prove that the object was entered in the national register; it is assumed that it was stolen and constitutes State Treasury property. Unfortunately, the UNIDROIT Convention has not yet been ratified by Poland, though the ratification and accession of states to the UNESCO Convention of 1970 show that this should be seen as a long-term process.

Archaeological property, then, is owned by the State Treasury, which the Act identifies as the sole holder of archaeological objects. Archaeological property constitutes a special category of the components of cultural heritage. It often goes beyond a narrow understanding of national heritage for it can attest to the history of an entire region or of humanity itself. In reference to cases where rights similar to ownership are established over material objects (water, minerals), with regard to archaeological property, sometimes in legal acts the word "ownership" is used improperly. Only when an archaeological object is acquired can one speak of ownership by the State Treasury. The legal existence of an archaeological object after it is discovered, however, permits the belief that a right similar to a right *in rem* continues to exist. Firstly, restrictions appear as to how the object can be disposed of. Ownership may be transferred only on the basis of a decision issued by a provincial conservator of historical objects upon the handover of the object to become the property of the museum in which it has been deposited. This is not the case for a found object, where the handover of ownership takes place by way of an agreement. The way in which this right is managed is similar to the model under which water and minerals are managed, with admission to trade being seriously restricted.

One should also recall the proposals made for amending Article 35 APGM. With the amendment of Article 189 CC in mind, a new wording of Article 35 APGM was proposed, that

> objects that are historical objects, including archaeological objects, accidentally found or obtained as a result of archaeological research, shall become property of the State Treasury.[160]

Certainly, all efforts made to strengthen the system of cultural heritage protection are very important. In this case, though, comparing the legal situation of archaeological objects with that of other artefacts found accidentally or obtained as a result of archaeological research may be, in my opinion, to the detriment of the former. Firstly, in terms of how ownership is acquired, the provision is not formulated identically to the norm provided in the APGM. Broadening the scope of application of this provision is contrary to the existing privileged position of archaeological property. Moreover, determining in an act that the owner of all historical objects found in such a manner is the State Treasury could create a state of uncertainty. At

[160] Trzciński (2016), p. 94.

present, only after establishing that there is no point in looking for the owner of an object does the procedure for the State Treasury to acquire ownership begin, which is not the case with archaeological objects.

In the APGM, immovable archaeological objects are defined as remains of prehistoric and historic settlements, cemeteries, burial mounds and relics of economic, religious and artistic activity. The question arises, then, as to whether archaeological objects constitute a component part of the ground they are located in or property of the State Treasury. Without a doubt, a building that was erected on a site several hundred years ago would comprise a component part of the land in the legal thought behind today's provisions, and the building would constitute part of the landowner's property. As an archaeological object, though, under Article 35 APGM, it constitutes "State Treasury property". There is no reason why it should be treated otherwise. In this way, the traditional civil law solution was rejected in favour of the concept of State Treasury ownership. There is a noticeable similarity to mining ownership encroaching into real estate provisions. The owner of the land is not the owner of the deposits, which, regardless of their location, constitute "mining property". There is no avoiding the fact that it is much more difficult to assess whether we are faced with an archaeological object than it is to determine the location of mineral deposits. Yet it seems that in deciding on such an approach, a legal structure similar to ownership was created, more or less consciously drawing on the structures already existing in the laws on water and mining.

In the literature, the view has been expressed that archaeological objects have the status of *rex extra commercium*, that is, of things excluded from trade.[161] It has therefore been argued that the provisions on the acquisitive prescription of ownership and acquisition in good faith do not apply to them. Monika Drela points out that considering Article 35 par. 6 APGM as a provision of *iuris cogentis* rules out the application of cases of acquisition of ownership other than those foreseen in the procedure included in that provision.[162] In accordance with the provision of Article 35 par. 8 APGM,

> upon an application by a museum director, archaeological objects in deposit at that museum may be transferred as property of that museum on the basis of a decision by the provincial conservator of historical objects.

Maciej Trzciński notes, however, that "the reality seems, however, to confirm that those provisions are not respected".[163] The question arises: are we dealing with a real *res extra commercium* regulation or only with an incomplete form thereof? From the wording of Article 35 APGM, it only follows that after being separated from the ground, an object becomes the property of the State Treasury. This reservation of ownership of archaeological objects for the State Treasury does not automatically make them things excluded from trade. In my opinion, this could only be achieved

[161] Trzciński (2011), p. 205; Drela (2006), pp. 184–189.

[162] Drela (2006), p. 187.

[163] Trzciński (2011), p. 206.

by being explicitly set out in a legal act, as in the case of registered, non-state archival resources.

After being found or discovered, archaeological objects are usually handed over to a museum and, as museum exhibits, are subject to the rules concerning how these can circulate. The very attribution of ownership of archaeological property to the State Treasury does not necessarily mean, in my opinion, that they are excluded from trade but that they are things limited in trade, like museum exhibits.[164] The demand to exclude archaeological objects from trade is fully justified. In the current state of the law, they function as components of public collections. All national cultural property in public collections is covered by a similar regime, though there are large internal differences.

Here, the work on the ratification of the UNESCO Convention on the Protection of Underwater Cultural Heritage, and of the importance of that Convention for protecting archaeological objects, should be mentioned. Due to technological progress, such objects located underwater are becoming increasingly accessible.[165] For years, it has been seen that the ratification of the Convention undoubtedly strengthened the protection of archaeological heritage in this area.[166] Apart from the evident increase in protection at the national level, if underwater archaeological heritage components are obtained illegally, they will be subject to the restitution procedure set out in the UNIDROIT Convention of 1995 (provided it is ratified) if it is not contrary to the law of the country where the excavation took place,[167]

On 24 December 2020, the Act of 27 October 2020 on the Ratification of the Convention on the Protection of Underwater Cultural Heritage, adopted in Paris on 2 November 2001, entered into force.[168] Poland joined 69 other signatories to the Convention. Pursuant to the draft justification of the law,

> (i)n the case of accession to the UNESCO Convention of 2001, it will therefore be necessary to formally and fully introduce the status of *rex extra commercium* for historical objects of the underwater cultural heritage, which will totally exclude them from being sold. This will take place through the inclusion of a relevant provision in the Act on the Protection and Guardianship of Monuments, whose Article 35 par. 1 regulates the already special ownership status of archaeological property. Following up on the provisions of the Convention, the new provision introduced to the act must lead at least to objects classified as underwater cultural heritage being excluded from circulation, sale, purchase or exchange as commercial goods.[169]

[164] Cf. Kowalski (2004), p. 264.

[165] Jakubowski and Trzciński (2019), pp. 151–152.

[166] Zeidler and Trzciński (2009), p. 147.

[167] Cf. Prott (1997), p. 34.

[168] Act of 27 October 2020 on the Ratification of the Convention on the Protection of the Underwater Cultural Heritage, adopted in Paris on 2nd November 2001. Polish Official Journal (Dz. U.) 2020, item 2201.

[169] Draft law on ratification of the UNESCO Convention on the Protection of Underwater Cultural Heritage, drawn up in Paris on 2 November 2001, Print No. 520, 23 July 2020, pp. 6–7.

According to the authors of the justification to the draft, the effect of applying the regime of *res extra commercium* is also reflected in the penalties provided for acts that violate that status. They state in the justification that

> in order to implement the provisions of Article 17 of the UNESCO Convention of 2001, in connection with granting objects of the underwater heritage the status of *res extra commercium*, it will be necessary to introduce penalties for taking possession, circulating or aiding in the disposal or concealment of objects of the underwater heritage. If the introduction of *res extra commercium* status is made through an appropriate supplementation of the provisions of the Act on the Protection and Guardianship of Monuments, the sanction for acts that violate that status should be contained in that act.[170]

Pursuant to Article 2 par. 7 of the Convention, "underwater heritage is not to be commercially exploited". The introduction of a *res extra commercium* status is certainly connected with the views expressed in the literature that

> extracted objects can on no account become objects of commercial trade, nor can they be used for other commercial purposes. That directive is a consequence of the principle adopted in the 2001 convention that the underwater cultural heritage falls within the legal category of *res extra commercium*, that is, it is totally excluded from trade.[171]

This is an important stance with respect to the search for model solutions concerning underwater archaeological heritage in private law. Bartłomiej Gadecki argues that

> the convention does not cover the ownership of the underwater cultural heritage. It excludes the underwater cultural heritage from commercial trade, treating objects as *res extra commercium.*

Similar proposals concerning the state ownership model have been put forward by Patrick O'Keefe.[172] The issue of excluding underwater heritage from trade has also been analysed in the context of the available documents and guidelines on the protection of that heritage and on existing solutions, which do not always include the postulate of exclusion from trade. Patrick O'Keefe provides the example of an auction at Christie's in Amsterdam held in 1986, where porcelain and gold ingots from the wreck of the ship *Geldermalsen* of the Dutch East India Company were sold.[173] In documents concerning soft law, there are provisions that, in a certain way, strengthen the content of the Convention (e.g. in the ICOM Code pertaining to the acquisition of property and in ICOMOS documents).[174] The recommendation most frequently made is undoubtedly state ownership, for the purpose of securing heritage and the global interest in protecting it. In addition, pursuant to Article 3, the Convention does not

---

[170] Draft law on ratification of the UNESCO Convention on the Protection of Underwater Cultural Heritage, drawn up in Paris on 2 November 2001, Print No. 520, 23 July 2020, p. 16.

[171] Kowalski (2014a), p. 337; Kowalski (2014b), pp. 67–68.

[172] Dromgoole (2013), p. 115.

[173] O'Keefe (2013), p. 129.

[174] O'Keefe (2013), p. 140.

"prejudice the rights, jurisdiction and duties of States under international law, including the United Nations Convention on the Law of the Sea".[175]

It should be highlighted that, in the explanation to Article 2 par. 7 of the Convention, reference is made to the duty of states to "prevent intrusive activities directed at underwater cultural heritage aiming at commercial exploitation and avoid commercial exploitation of underwater cultural heritage".[176] The information section of the website of the Convention contains information stating "No regulation of ownership", in accordance with which the Convention does not determine the ownership status of shipwrecks and ownership should be regulated through civil law, other domestic laws or international private law.[177] The document UNESCO-UNIDROIT Model Provisions on State Ownership of Undiscovered Cultural Objects also refers to underwater archaeological heritage. In the explanations to the definition of undiscovered property, it is stated that, in light of the Convention, the ownership of such objects is different from what is proposed in the document and applies to the state signatories to the Convention.[178]

In light of the principles forming an integral part of the body of the Convention, findings on underwater heritage and its commercial exploitation were refined. Pursuant to Rule 2,

> The commercial exploitation of underwater cultural heritage for trade or speculation or its irretrievable dispersal is fundamentally incompatible with the protection and proper management of underwater cultural heritage. Underwater cultural heritage shall not be traded, sold, bought or bartered as commercial goods.[179]

This rule concerns the exclusion of underwater heritage from trade and its loss of the attributes of commercial goods.[180] The rule, however, does not determine ownership. Sarah Dromgoole believes that excluding the issue of ownership from the Convention was a pragmatic move that made it possible for the work on the Convention to progress and for its scope to be extended to include warships.[181] The assumptions of the Convention on protection *in situ* or, in the case of extraction, security, scientific study, maintenance of integrity and public accessibility together

---

[175] Articles 149 and 303.

[176] Operational Guidelines for the Convention on the Protection of the Underwater Cultural Heritage Document CLT/HER/CHP/OG 1 REV, p. 6. https://unesdoc.unesco.org/ark:/48223/pf0000234177. Accessed 1 June 2022.

[177] Principles of the 2001 Convention "No regulation of ownership", https://en.unesco.org/underwater-heritage/2001. Accessed 1 June 2022.

[178] Expert Committee on State Ownership of Cultural Heritage, Model Provisions on State Ownership of Undiscovered Cultural Objects. Explanatory Report with model provisions and explanatory guidelines, UNESCO, UNIDROIT, 2011, p. 5. https://fr.unesco.org/sites/default/files/unesco-unidroit_model_provisions_en.pdf. Accessed 1 June 2022.

[179] Records of the General Conference, 31st session, Paris, 15 October to 3 November 2001, v. 1: Resolutions, Annex Rules concerning activities directed at underwater cultural heritage, 58–61. https://unesdoc.unesco.org/ark:/48223/pf0000124687.page=67. Accessed 1 June 2022.

[180] O'Keefe (2020), p. 315.

[181] Dromgoole (2013), p. 117.

constitute a heavy burden on owners. For this additional reason, although the Convention does not rule out private ownership, in terms of the exercise of ownership rights, state ownership is advisable. Since the Convention covers property that has been under the water for at least 100 years, it is possible for a private entity to come forward as an owner. Sarah Droomgole argues that the ratification of the Convention affects the legal situation of non-state entities that could claim underwater heritage components and points to the article connected with the obligation of states to cooperate in protecting objects found in the sea that are of an archaeological or historical nature (Article 303 par. 1 Convention).[182]

In practice, there is a problem over how the Polish law will make use of the Convention's principle on the exclusion of property from commercial activity. Property taken from the sea that constitutes underwater cultural heritage will be subject to a separate procedure aimed at securing the property and excluding it from commercial use or admission to trade. This does not mean, however, that objects deemed *res extra commercium* (if extracted) constitute State Treasury property. It seems that, if the management of such resources is modelled after the regulations covering archaeological property, museums will be able to acquire ownership. Similarly, it will be possible for one museum to transfer ownership to another museum.

5.6 Ownership of Cultural Objects Entered in the National Register of Lost Cultural Property

The need for changes in civil law in relation to the acquisition of cultural property from an unauthorised person has been discussed in the literature for years.[183] With the amendment of the APGM and the establishment of the National Register of Lost Cultural Property (NRLCP), a new regulation related to cultural heritage appeared in the Civil Code. The changes were formally introduced by the AFP. The explanatory material for the draft indicates that

> proponents, assuming that the existing legal order insofar as it relates to the protection of the cultural property owners' interests is not fully satisfactory, propose the creation of the National Register of Lost Cultural Property and the exclusion of the objects disclosed therein from the operation of the provisions on the acquisitive prescription (Article 174 of the Civil Code) or acquisition from an unauthorised party (Article 169 § 1 and 2 of the Civil Code).[184]

The creation of a new register for cultural objects and their trade can be considered a breakthrough. Certainly, the reason this regulation is considered a

[182] Dromgoole (2013), p. 119.

[183] Kowalski (2004), pp. 257–273; Kowalski (2006), p. 5.

[184] Government Draft on Found Property and Amendments to Certain Other Acts, Explanatory Report, Print No. 2064, p. 2. http://www.sejm.gov.pl/Sejm7.nsf/druk.xsp?nr=2064. Accessed 1 June 2022.

breakthrough is not due to its effectiveness or the design of its legal provisions. It is, however, a long-awaited legal initiative that addresses the issue of trade in cultural property and combats illegal transactions. It can be also considered a first step aimed at positioning cultural objects among other tangible assets on the market. The purpose of cultural heritage protection regulations is to preserve cultural heritage as a resource and ensure that cultural objects do not leave the possession of their owners against their will.

It is important to note the content of the explanation to the draft as it expresses an important and interesting view concerning the significance of private law and its role in the protection of cultural heritage. It states that while the protection of historic monuments falls under the domain of public law, private law nevertheless influences this field

> through some of its institutions, to some extent it influences the functioning of the cultural heritage protection system. The reason for this is the fact that within the meaning of the Civil Code, cultural objects are things, objects of specific rights and carriers of property values. Their non-economic values (aesthetics, memorable value) are meaningless unless they have an impact on price. Civil law exposes only the commercial status of monuments and works of art, although their actual role goes beyond economic significance.[185]

The legal institutions that the authors of the explanation surely had in mind were those specialising on the specific ways of acquiring property, including finding a thing and finding a treasure. Civil law does not deal with the protection of cultural heritage, or at least it did not do so previously. The amendment to the Civil Code, combined with the introduction of the Act on Found Property and the amendments to the APGM, is an important legislative event in this area and somewhat interrupts this state of affairs. The cautious declaration quoted above concerning the relationship between civil law and the cultural heritage protection system is particularly noteworthy. I believe that, in this case, we may speak not only about the influence of civil law but also about the fact that civil law is an integral part of this system. This scope should be expanded by creating new legal constructs and conducting civil law analyses through the prism of cultural property (a component of cultural heritage) rather than from the perspective of entities as parties to contractual or property rights relationships. Only in this way will it be possible to build a national model for cultural heritage protection, drawing on the experience of the Polish legal system and also international law and solutions used in other countries.

The amendment is described in the explanation to the draft as the implementation of international obligations under the 1970 UNESCO Convention on the Means of Prohibiting and Preventing the Illicit Import, Export and Transfer of Ownership of Cultural Property.[186] It is true that the new institution (NRLCP) can be considered further in this context, as any action in this case falls within the framework of the said

---

[185] Government Draft on Found Property and Amendments to Certain Other Acts, Explanatory Report, Print No. 2064, p. 3. http://www.sejm.gov.pl/Sejm7.nsf/druk.xsp?nr=2064. Accessed 1 June 2022.

[186] Lizak (2017), p. 117.

Convention. The amendment was also noted in the report submitted by the state to UNESCO pursuant to its obligation under Article 16 of the Convention in the section concerning new elements related to trade in cultural goods.[187] The construction of the register makes the Polish law look for its own way of creating a legal framework for the protection of cultural heritage. It correspondingly appears that this search is less related to the illegal traffic and looting of cultural heritage items in Syria or Iraq but rather serves as a constant search for ways to strengthen the existing Polish regulation.

At this point, it is necessary to refer to the legislative work carried out on the Act. During one of the relevant legislative sessions, a legislator (participating in the commission's works) presented a proposal to move the proposed regulations to the Civil Code, referring to the principles of legislative technique. Originally, the amendment concerning the exclusion of the application of certain provisions was to be introduced directly into the APMG. In accordance with the wording of the proposed Article 24e in section 1 of the Act, the provisions of Articles 169–170 and 174 of the Civil Code[188] were not to be applied to an object entered in the NRLCP. Paragraph 2 stipulated that an owner's claim under Article 222 para. 1 of the Civil Code[189] (possessory claim) shall not be time-barred if it concerns an object entered in the NRLCP.[190] Despite the fact that the amendment was of a technical and legislative nature, it is my belief that, beyond the issue of legislative technique, it is of a far greater significance.

[187] National Report on the Implementation of the 1970 Convention on the Means of Prohibiting And Preventing the Illicit Import, Export and Transfer of Ownership Of Cultural Property 2011–2015, Poland Report 2015, p. 15. https://en.unesco.org/sites/default/files/poland_2011-15natrep_1970_en.pdf. Accessed 1 June 2022.

[188] Article 174. 1 CC The possessor of a movable who is not the movable owner acquires ownership if he possesses the movable uninterruptedly for 3 years as an owner-like possessor unless he possesses it in bad faith.

[189] Article 174. 1 CC The possessor of a movable who is not the movable owner acquires ownership if he possesses the movable uninterruptedly for 3 years as an owner-like possessor unless he possesses it in bad faith 222 par. 1 CC An owner may demands of any person who has actual control of his thing that the thing handed over to him unless that person has a right to actually control the thing effective against the owner.

Art. 24e. APMG. "1. Provisions of Articles 169-170 and 174 of the Civil Code shall not apply to the thing entered in the National Register of Lost Cultural Property. 2. The claim of the owner provided for in Article 222 paragraph 1 of the Civil Code shall not be subject to time limitations if it concerns cultural object entered in the National Register of Lost Cultural Property."

[190] Legislator Magdalena Klorek pointed out that "it is contrary to art. 2 of the principles of legislative technique, which requires comprehensive regulation of given matters in one act. In our opinion, the exceptions, which are formulated in art. 24e of the amended APMG, constitute exceptions from the rule concerning the acquisition of movable property from an unauthorized party (art. 169 of the Civil Code), from the expiration of encumbrances referred to in art. 170 of the Civil Code, from the rule concerning the acquisitive prescription of movable property (art. 174) and from the rule concerning the prescription of vindication claim referred to in art. 222".

Bulletin No. 3989/VII, Committee on Local Government and Regional Policy (no. 310), Committee on Culture and the Media (no. 162), 27-11-2014, http://orka.sejm.gov.pl/Zapisy7.nsf/wgskrnr/KSP-162. Accessed 1 June 2022.

Firstly, similar changes will need to be made to the Civil Code when regulating the standard of due diligence for acquiring objects on the art market. Secondly, the introduction of the amendment to the Civil Code made these provisions a more visible exception to the rule. Thirdly, these are the first amendments to the Civil Code as far as the safety of trade is concerned, and they represent an important moment in building the future of Polish regulation in the field of cultural heritage protection law.

The NRLCP is maintained by the competent minister for culture and national heritage protection. The NLRCP is referred to in the literature as a meta-register[191] as it covers objects listed in other types of registers. The following movables are subject to entry in the register: monuments entered in the register, monuments entered on the List of Heritage Treasures, museum collections (museums exhibits), library materials and archival materials. The legislator returns to the term cultural property used in the previous APCP.[192] The scope of the definition refers directly to the article defining a monument in the APCP.[193] Within the meaning of the APCP, all objects listed in the register of historic monuments and the inventory of museum collections and those included in libraries, with the exception of materials included in the national archival collection, were considered historic monuments. Archival materials remained outside the scope of the APCP's 1962 definition due to their separate protection, which was provided for in the Act of 29 March 1951 on State Archives.

Goods that can be included in the NLRCP are not excluded from circulation. The circulation of certain goods (museum exhibits) can be linked to the obligation to launch a specific procedure (e.g. sale of museum exhibits) and control it in a certain way. The NLRCP also covers archival materials referred to in Article 1 ANARA. In my opinion, in the case of a loss of an object from the registered, non-state archival record, there is no need to make an entry in the NLRCP because the object is excluded from circulation pursuant to ANARA. As the NLRCP register, is thought to be open and public, it should be verified by potential buyers and market players. This would enable the buyer to check the objects track record and will certainly aid due diligence measures.

Another important issue worth mentioning is the fact that the register covers privately owned cultural heritage items entered in the register of monuments or included in the inventory of museum collections. This is a solution that broadens the scope of application of *res extra commercium*, where the objects covered by this

191 Gredka and Gwoździewicz-Matan (2016), p. 113.

192 Gredka and Gwoździewicz-Matan (2016), p. 100.

193 Article 4 The following cultural property, referred to in the Act as "monuments", are subject to legal protection as provided by the provisions of the Act: "1) entered in the register of monuments, 2) entered in museums to the inventory and included in the libraries, with the exception of materials forming part of the national archival resource, the protection of which is governed by separate provisions, 3) other, if their historic character is obvious, unless they are protected under separate provisions."

regime are state property.[194] Objects listed in the inventory of a museum whose organiser is neither a local government unit nor a state administration body can also be entered in the NLRCP.[195] It is worth mentioning that the unclear relationship between the register and the museum's inventory should be clarified in the nearest future.[196] It is possible to imagine a situation where an object was not entered in the register of historic monuments and was stolen from private property. If the museum was run by the owner, a natural person, the object's presence in the museum's inventory could benefit from such protection. Only cultural objects listed in the inventory are subject to registration.[197] Moreover, the entry of a movable monument in the register of historic monuments can be made *ex officio* only in certain circumstances of threat to the object.[198]

The issue of protection of contemporary works of art remains a problem. Due to the legal definition of monuments, contemporary works are not treated as monuments and therefore are not entered into the NLRCP. There is a tendency to include more and more new objects, both movable and immovable, in the register of monuments. However, a special procedure concerning the protection of the integrity of collections should apply to public and private collections. In the case of museums with contemporary art objects, if these objects listed in the inventory of museum collections are stolen, they will also be able to benefit from the exemptions assigned to the listing in the NLRCP.

From the perspective of the register's functionality, data concerning the objects are crucial. As provided in Article 24b par. 2 APMG, data enabling the identification of a lost item are entered in the register. Only the disclosure of data (information) will allow its verification by the entity that will perform the transaction and exercise due diligence by verifying the register. If due diligence is not exercised, it will be of no significance to the rightful owner as one cannot identify the object. The application for entry should be accompanied by a photograph of the lost property; if it is a

[194] Szafrański (2016), p. 158.

[195] Golat (2008), pp. 11–15.

[196] Jagielska-Burduk (2016e).

[197] Government Draft on Found Property and Amendments to Certain Other Acts, Explanatory Report, Print No. 2064, p. 14. http://www.sejm.gov.pl/Sejm7.nsf/druk.xsp?nr=2064. Accessed 1 June 2022.

[198] Article 10 "1. A movable monument is entered in the register on the basis of a decision issued by the provincial monument conservator at the request of the owner of a monument. 2. The provincial monument conservator may ex officio issue a decision on the entry of a movable monument to the register in case of justified concern of destruction, damage or illegal removal of the monument or removal abroad of the monument of exceptional historical, artistic or scientific value. 3. A movable monument constituting a cultural object referred to in Article 12 par. 1 item 1 of the Act of 25 May 2017 on the Restitution of National Treasures (Polish Official Journal [Dz. U.] 2019, item 1591) shall be registered ex officio. The minister competent for the matters of culture and protection of national heritage shall inform the relevant provincial monument conservator on the existence of grounds for the entry of the monument to the register, providing the data of the monument and the documents necessary for the entry."

monument or mausoleum referred to in paragraph 2 points 1 and 2, it should be in the form of a digital file.

Interestingly, the application for entry does not need to include a photograph of a monument included in the List of Heritage Treasures. Presumably, this issue was overlooked by the legislator during the introduction of the List of Heritage Treasures, or alternatively, due to the planned unique character of the List of Heritage Treasures, the images of these objects will be widely available on the Internet. It does not change the fact that photographs of objects should also be included in the description of the work in the NLRCP. It is also not necessary to present a photo of library materials and archival materials. If there is no requirement for a photograph of library and archival materials, it cannot be assumed that such materials will be included. Given that part of the collection has been digitised, it is possible that additional information (scans) allowing for their identification will be available online and should then also be included in the register.

The entry in the register is primarily based on the owner's loss as a result of criminal activity. According to the APGM, the loss must be due to one of the following crimes: theft, burglary, robbery, aggravated robbery, extortion or misappropriation.[199] However, the catalogue of offences was considered incomplete as it did not include, for example, the offence of fraud, where the previous owner exchanged a cultural object for a non-original one, thus diminishing the object's worth and causing the owner a loss. Moreover, the listed prohibited acts do not cover the offence of theft and appropriation under Article 119 of the Petty Offence Code. The issue of the value of a cultural object will therefore be important in terms of applying for an entry.[200] A correction or amendment of the Act seems necessary in this respect.

The document confirming the acceptance of the notification will contain a description of the object, including its estimated value. However, it may happen that there is a discrepancy between the value of the object accepted by the declarant and the declarant's estimation, in particular when the report is made by a private person. The application may be submitted by the police, public prosecutor, voivodeship conservator of monuments, chief director of the State Archives, owner of the object or person in charge of the organisational unit in whose collection or resources the object has been located (for instance, the director of a museum).

The procedure for the application of an entry is foreseen in tangible (i.e. paper) form. The entry is made on the basis of an administrative decision by the minister, which is immediately enforceable. Criminal proceedings related to the object could be pending (recently launched); only information that notification of an offence has been made is required. Within the meaning of administrative procedure, a party is the owner of an object or an organisational unit in whose collection the object originated. It was rightly resolved that not every organisational unit (museum) will be the

[199] Acts specified in Art. 278 § 1 and 3, Art. 279 § 1, Art. 280–283 or Art. 284 § 1–3 of the Act of 6 June 1997—Criminal Code.

[200] Gadecki (2016), pp. 191–192.

owner of an object (private museums or museums without legal personality, such as some university museums). A party may also be the museum from which an object was stolen and where it was located under an agreement concluded with the actual owner.

The register is kept in a teleinformatic system, and everyone can access it as the register is open to the public. Each time an entry is made, data enabling the identification of the lost item are entered in the register. The date of entry shall be the date on which data included in the decision on entry are entered in the register. In accordance with the provision of Article 24 APMG, "from the date of entry in the NLRCP, no one may plead ignorance of the data revealed in this register". The entry results in a temporary exclusion from trade. It is then impossible to acquire the object in good faith or to acquire it by acquisitive prescription. The protection of certainty of trade and security of transactions is relinquished in favour of the protection of the object. This is a temporary solution, assuming that the object will eventually be found and it will be possible to remove it from the register.

The register is maintained in Polish. In the literature, there is information about a proposal presented at the stage of the legislative process that the register should also be maintained in English.[201] Interestingly, the authors of the proposal were not representatives of the art market, entities cooperating with the market or monument conservation authorities but representatives of the National Library. The remark was very pertinent and, to a large extent, took into account the risks that may arise in the future when establishing the legal status of an object entered in the NLRCP but located abroad. Unfortunately, the suggestion was not met with a proper response. The following example shows that the suggestion deserved to be taken into consideration, even with the awareness of increased costs associated with the creation of an English version of the database. In a case decided by a German court following a claim under the 1970 UNESCO Convention, the issue of the language of the register and its accessibility was raised. It was pointed out that the register of cultural property in Mexico is only available in Spanish and was not available online. This barrier affected the level of due diligence that the court assumed should have been performed. The finding that the registry was not in English or French and was not available online contributed to the court's dismissal of the case.[202]

Although the proceedings before the German court concerned the maintenance of a register of historical monuments, this does not mean that it is not relevant to the functioning of the NLRCP. Without delving into the details of the case, which involve complex facts, including illegally acquired archaeological artefacts and subsequent court proceedings as a result of which two objects were returned to Mexico, it should be noted that the issue regarding the register, its accessibility and

[201] Lizak (2017), p. 127.

[202] Bayerischer Verwaltungsgerichtshof, Beschluss vom 16.07.2010—7 CE 10.109, https://openjur.de/u/625069.html. Accessed 1 June 2022; Kugler (2011), pp. 16–17; The El-Manati-Case: Restituting Mexican Archaeological Artefacts. A precedent in Germany. 6th Session of the Subsidiary Committee of the Meeting of States Parties to the 1970 Convention. UNESCO Headquarters, Paris, 29 May 2018.

its language is very important because this is how its accessibility is assessed. This issue leads to a negative evaluation of the decision of the Polish legislator not to consider an English language register. If the NLRCP is to serve owners in the future and enable proceedings involving the participation of a foreign entity in the proceedings or the illegal export of an object abroad, regulations should be drafted taking these elements and the ongoing internationalisation of trade into account. Although the register has not yet been launched, it is worth considering whether it should be delegated as a task to be carried out by cultural institutions or kept within the framework of ministry departments. One argument in favour of placing the task within the organisational structure of the ministry is the administrative and legal element connected to the issuing of the entry decision by the minister.

Following an entry in the register, a cultural object is not subject to the provisions on the acquisition of ownership from an unauthorised party, nor does a third party's right expire if the object is encumbered with such a right. Moreover, an item entered in the register cannot be acquired by way of acquisitive prescription in good faith. This undoubtedly strengthens the protection of the owner. Assuming that the amendment adopted in 2015 came into force on 21 June 2015 and the regulation to the NLRCP was issued on 19 August 2015, it can be predicted that from the end of 2015, the register should have been operational. Thus, for at least 6 years, owners of cultural property cannot exercise the right of property protection granted to them. The loss connected with the inability to temporarily exclude a stolen object from circulation should be considered somewhat more broadly, beyond the subject of the owner. Is it possible to determine the potential number of objects that, as they are not listed in the register, will be subject to acquisition in good faith or acquisitive prescription? For the years 2016, 2017 and 2019,[203] it is worth referring to the report by Olgierd Jakubowski entitled "Criminal Threats to the National Heritage – An Analysis of the Events of 2019", published in the Santander Art and Culture Law Review journal. The study shows that in 2016, a total of 92 objects were reported stolen and burglarised or lost;[204] in 2017, only five objects were reported subject to theft and burglary;[205] and in 2019, it was 41 cases.[206]

The explanation to the draft refers to the date of the Act's entry into force, stating that the 3-month deadline is related to, among other things, "the need to establish a national register of lost cultural property".[207] To this end, the assessment of the regulation describes the costs that will need to be covered for the new register (NCLPR); in the first year of the Act's effective date, the costs would amount to

---

[203] Unfortunately, it will not be possible to provide information for 2018, in that year the National List of Monuments Stolen or Illegally Exported Abroad was not verifiable.

[204] Jakubowski (2017), pp. 253–254.

[205] Jakubowski (2018), p. 221.

[206] Jakubowski (2021), pp. 221–232.

[207] Government Draft on Found Property and Amendments to Certain Other Acts, Explanatory Report, Print no. 2064, p. 21. http://www.sejm.gov.pl/Sejm7.nsf/druk.xsp?nr=2064. Accessed 1 June 2022.

PLN 100,000–400,000, which is mainly related to the costs of designing and developing an information technology (IT) system. The maintenance of the NLRCP was considered by the ministry as part of an outsourced process. Outsourcing the management of this register to an external entity is interesting, in that the ministry is close to extending this task and entrusting a private entity with the task of monitoring the art market, diagnosing good practices and then disseminating them.

The real effectiveness of the NLRCP in returning an object to its owner depends on the development of good practices in the art market and the impact of initiatives aimed at raising awareness. One can pose the question of to what extent there is awareness of the described NLRCP institution in Poland. I have the impression that the level of this awareness is low, if not marginal. Firstly, the register does not function in practice, as noted by the authors of the commentary on the Civil Code.[208] Secondly, there are no social campaigns that would strengthen the community of market participants. These campaigns are already carried out with UNIDROIT, the World Customs Organization (WCO), ICOM, UNESCO and the European Union in the case of other cultural heritage and art market matters. At the national level, cultural policy actors are also encouraged to conduct dissemination projects. The objectives set for the NLRCP and other institutions related to heritage security will not be achieved without being accepted by the public and made part of wider circulation.

As such, it would be misleading to consider the register as a good tool to reduce market problems. It is also difficult to assess its practical effectiveness since the register has not been set up. However, it is possible to make an assessment of the owners' losses. Hence, there were proposals to delete the new provisions and create a solution directly related to objects in the registers. Attempts to discuss the amendment and analyse various options for applying the provisions often end with proposals to change and simplify the operation of the register and point out defects in the new regulation.[209]

An assessment of the NLRCP as a new register against the background of other existing registers amounts to a finding of artificial multiplication of institutions.[210] I partially agree with this view, but I cannot imagine combining the register with the already existing National List of Monuments Stolen or Illegally Exported Abroad without profound changes. An entry in the NRLCP is followed by specific consequences in terms of the legal status of an object. An entry to the National List of Monuments Stolen or Illegally Exported Abroad is informative, and the entities concerned are administrative bodies, conservation services and law enforcement agencies. Placing together objects from the list of stolen monuments and lost cultural property (that is, merging them) could cause confusion in the use and verification of

[208] Kępiński and Kępiński (2021), pp. 1294–1309.

[209] Gredka and Gwoździewicz-Matan (2016), pp. 112–113; Górniak (2018), pp. 39–40.

[210] Zeidler (2015), p. 170.

the register. The effect of an entry could be "diluted" by the multiplicity of entries from previous years.

The amendment to the Civil Code introduced the register but did not refer to transactions and due diligence in the art and cultural goods market. At this point, it should be added that it seems natural and reasonable that, already at the stage of establishing the register, it would have been worthwhile to combine the debates on the NLRCP and the model of proceeding in the art market with particular consideration of the tools for verifying the status of objects at the national (NLRCP) and international levels. Then further actions could include cultural objects and the transfer of objects between owners with emphasis on the role of future generations in these regulations. The first steps may concern the NLRCP and shaping models of safe transactions on the art market.

The protection afforded to the private owner of a collection is still weaker than that provided to collections owned by state or local government museums. The inclusion of non-public items in the NLRCP and the rejection of the ownership criterion demonstrate the institution's progressiveness. In certain situations, privately owned collections were, after the enactment of the AFP, covered by the strengthened legal regime provided by the ARNCP. However, this depends, among other things, on the owner obtaining a subsidy from public funds. It seems that since the appearance of the NLRCP, it has been possible to set a time limit based on which the Polish law, when creating protection regimes, takes private collections into account. In this respect, it is an innovative solution when compared to other countries. The creation of the institution of the NLRCP was meant to be a response to the search for protection against acquisition in the case of theft. The scope of the NLRCP includes public and private property, making its application wider. This amendment was an attempt to search for our own concept of protecting selected goods on the market, independent of protection models that are binding in other national systems.

5.7 Legal Status of Found Movable Monuments or Archival Materials

The Civil Code provides special regulations on the acquisition of ownership of cultural heritage components through concealment, acquisitive prescription or acquisition from an unauthorised party. Certainly, cultural heritage components are exceptional objects, which is why there are special solutions provided for them. One of these is how found property is treated in the Polish legal system regarding cultural property and the preservation of cultural heritage. The AFP introduced changes in how things that are found may be dealt with. Invoking a ruling by the

Constitutional Tribunal,[211] which found Article 6 of the Decree of 18 September 1954 on the liquidation of unclaimed deposits and unclaimed property unconstitutional,[212] as well as with the adoption of the new Act of 18 October 2006 on the Liquidation of Unclaimed Deposits,[213] in 2014, a legislative activity pertaining to found property, including cultural heritage components, was initiated.[214] The need to set the issue of found property in order became connected with the separation of cultural heritage components as special property against the background of the Civil Code.

Historical objects and archival materials are defined in Article 187 CC as atypical objects requiring separate treatment as well as the participation of external entities due to the need for their protection. How their ownership can be acquired, and by whom, is defined in a different manner than for ordinary property. Pursuant to Article 187 CC, after the lapse of a certain period of time for collection, a found object becomes the property of the person who found it, whereas a found object constituting a historical object or archival material does not share the same fate. After the lapse of the collection period, the thing becomes property of the State Treasury. In other cases, it may become the property of a county. The acquisition of things by concealment, regulated in the chapter "Other Cases of Acquisition of Ownership", currently refers solely to historical objects (monuments) and archival materials. In seeking to establish the attributes of concepts, we must in each case turn to the acts of law: the APGM and the ANARA.

Since the Civil Code entered into force, there has been no amendment to this provision. The original wording of Article 187 CC states that

> (m)oney, securities, valuables and things of scientific or artistic value which are not collected within one year of being called on to do so by a competent authority, and if he cannot be called on, within two years of the day they are found, become State Treasury property.

---

[211] Polish Constitutional Tribunal, Judgement of 16 March 2004 K 22/03, the judgment declared unconstitutional the provisions concerning the liquidation of unclaimed deposits, set forth in Art. 6 of the Decree of 18 September 1954 on Liquidation of Unclaimed Deposits and Unclaimed Property (Dz. U. No. 41, item 184 and of 1964, No. 16, item 94) and the Regulation of the Council of Ministers of 16 March 1971 on decisions on taking over deposits to the State ownership (Dz. U. No. 7, item 78 and of 1984, No. 14, item 61). The judgment points out the lack of a precise identification of the entity competent to issue a decision on the transfer of property ownership to the State Treasury and the procedure therefor.

[212] Decree of 18 September 1954 on the liquidation of unclaimed deposits and unclaimed property unconstitutional. Polish Official Journal (Dz. U.) No 41, item 184 as amended.

[213] Act of 18 October 2006 on the liquidation of unclaimed deposits, Polish Official Journal (Dz. U.) No. 208, item 1537.

[214] Government Draft on Found Property and Amendments to Certain Other Acts, Explanatory Report, Print No. 2064, p. 1. http://www.sejm.gov.pl/Sejm7.nsf/druk.xsp?nr=2064. Accessed 1 June 2022.

In 1996, only one passage was amended, whereby state ownership was changed to State Treasury ownership.[215] How found property can be dealt with was further specified in the Regulation of the Council of Ministers of 14 June 1966 on Found Property.[216]

In the institution of the acquisition of ownership of found property, emphasis has decidedly shifted to objects that have cultural value. Now, only historical objects and archival materials become State Treasury property. In Chapter 4 of AFP, special rules of conduct are provided with regard to things of historical, scientific or artistic value. If a person who finds a thing of historical, scientific or artistic value has no knowledge of the identity of who is entitled to recover it or does not know where that person is, they should promptly hand the thing over to their county administrator (starosta). The obligation to hand things over does not arise with other property; in such cases, the finder need only notify the country administrator of the find. Only then does the county administrator decide whether the finder should hand the object over. Compared with other found property, a distinction has certainly been made for items that have a significant value for the public interest. It should be added that this solution is similar to that applied when dealing with military equipment or documents, which also stand apart from ordinary property.

In an opinion on the draft AFP, a suggestion was made that some of the things mentioned in Article 6 par. 3,[217] such as maps and certain military items, are not significant enough to warrant special conduct by those who find them. Ultimately, Article 5 par. 4[218] made no mention of maps. It is worth noting that the sample types of property enumerated in that provision do not preclude its application to maps as military documents. No similar remarks were made in reference to objects having historical, scientific or artistic value. The value threshold contained in the draft Act, whereby a person who finds an object having a historical, scientific or artistic value of less than 50 zlotys need not hand it over to the relevant county administrator, was also commented upon. That very apt remark was taken into account, and no threshold appears in the version adopted. It is difficult to estimate whether the value of a thing is above or below a certain threshold.[219] Certainly, though, one

[215] Act of 23 August 1996 amending the Act—Civil Code. Polish Official Journal (Dz. U.) 1996, No. 114, item 542.

[216] Regulation of the Council of Ministers of 14 June 1966 on Lost Property. Polish Official Journal (Dz. U.) 1966, No. 22, item 141.

[217] Art. 6 par. 3 If an item is found whose external features or special signs on it indicate that it is military equipment or uniformed equipment or other uniformed services, and if a military or other uniformed services document is found, and in particular a military ID card, a booklet or a military certificate, an appointment card or a military map, the finder shall immediately return the found item to the competent district starosta.

[218] Art. 5, par. 4. Whoever finds an item whose external features or special marks on it indicate that it is military equipment or gear, and in the event of finding a military document, and in particular a military ID card, booklet or certificate or an appointment card, shall surrender the item or document without delay to the competent district starosta.

[219] Warciński (2014a), p. 7; Warciński (2014b), pp. 316–318.

can assume that the average participant in trade will be able to perceive certain things about an object that make it unique; presumably, the Polish legislator had this in mind.

Pursuant to Article 22 of the AFP, if a county administrator suspects that an object has historical, scientific or artistic value, they must notify the territorially competent provincial conservator about the find within 7 days. The conservator of historical objects then has the key role in determining what happens next; within 7 days of being notified, they should inspect the object. The conservator decides whether the object should be classified as a historical object or archival material and whether it should be handed over to a specialised institution for storage. In order to make sure that an object is a historical object or archival material, the provincial conservator may seek the opinion of an expert, a museum competent for the particular type of thing found or a library (for a thing other than archival materials). However, pursuant to Article 23 par. 2 AFP, the provincial conservator of historical objects should seek the opinion of the director of the relevant state archive if it shows from the inspection that the object may be archival material.[220] Whether a thing constitutes a historical object or archival material should be ascertained within 3 days following the receipt of an opinion.

In order to safeguard an object by means of an administrative decision, the conservator may transfer it "for proper storage due to the type of property found to a state or local government museum or library organised by the minister, the head of a central office or local government unit, or a state archive". In this way, the duty to care for the object is entrusted to a specialised institution. If the owner does not claim the object within the statutory time period, it becomes the property of the State Treasury.

Entities that have been entrusted with storage may apply for a transfer of ownership by way of an agreement (Article 25 par. 1 AFP). The structure of Article 25 par. 2 of the AFP, which discusses the fate of archival materials, is noteworthy. If no owner is found, the property is incorporated into the archival resources of the state archive where the provincial conservator of historical objects sent it for storage. Again, particular categories of cultural heritage were distinguished with regard to the procedures for their handling and ownership status. Meanwhile, in the case of museums and libraries, if a thing has become State Treasury property, those institutions may apply for ownership, which is to be transferred to them by way of an agreement.

It seems that the adoption of these two solutions may justify the special status of archival materials and the provision that state archival materials cannot be sold provided in Article 7 ANARA. The procedure for transferring ownership by way of an agreement cannot concern archaeological property discovered in the territory of the country, as discussed further on. It is worth noting the viewpoint of Artur Niewęgłowski regarding the effects of the above provision on non-state and state archival resources. Niewęgłowski shows that in a situation where

[220] The author point to the obligation to consult the expert Niewęgłowski (2015), p. 28.

archival material belonging to the State Treasury is lost, the subjective structure of ownership does not change, even after the lapse of the time period for claiming found property

and

. . .the State Treasury remains their owner without interruption, and neither the finder nor other entities may acquire ownership of them on the basis of the provisions on found property or other civil law regulations.[221]

Yet in another study, the same author admits that, here, we are dealing with things limited in trade, not excluded from trade.[222]

This observation, however, needs to be corrected somewhat. The binding provisions on national cultural property belonging to public collections exclude the application of the provisions on acquisition from an unauthorised party and acquisitive prescription (Article 46 ARNCP), as discussed above in relation to such property. Therefore, the relationship between Article 187 CC and Article 46 ARNCP must be determined. The scopes of application of these provisions are not identical but certainly overlap because some national cultural property falls within the category of historical objects or archival materials. The exclusion contained in the ARNCP will have no effect on acquisitions by the State Treasury. Those provisions protect public collections, which cannot be acquired if they are illegally admitted to trade. The provisions do not coincide with each other, and in the case where a historical object or archival material is found, after the lapse of the time period for collection, ownership is acquired by the State Treasury.

The new wording of Article 187 CC was meant to establish order, specifically by separating property that constitutes archival materials or historical objects from other property that can be acquired by the finder.[223] Museum exhibits are not mentioned in the act, nor are elements of national library resources. This is justified by the relationship between those concepts, best illustrated by Article 11 APGM, pursuant to which no entry in the register of historical objects is made for a historical object entered on the List of Heritage Treasures or museum inventory or that forms part of the national library resources. Thus, the scope of application of the provision (187 CC) also extends to valuable library collections from private collections or libraries that are not included in the national library resources but are protected as historical objects (Article 3 pt. 1 APGM).

Unfortunately, property that cannot be deemed to constitute a historical object now falls beyond the scope of the provision, though it was covered under the previous version. The use of concepts from acts of law on the protection of historical objects and national archival resources is a manifestation of the publicisation of private law. The chosen procedure, however, entails a certain risk for the future. If the conceptual apparatus of any of those acts changes, it will be necessary to make an interpretation that draws on legal acts that are no longer binding.

[221] Niewęgłowski (2015), p. 30.

[222] Niewęgłowski (2016), Art. 7 [Commentary].

[223] Cf. Jagielska-Burduk (2016b), p. 174.

5.8 The Legal Status of the Treasure Trove

A separate model is provided for acquiring ownership of treasure. That institution was not preserved in its original form in the Civil Code. In its current wording, the relevant provision was introduced in the above-cited AFP. Pursuant to Article 189 CC, if property is found under circumstances indicating that it is indeed pointless to look for the owner, it then becomes subject to joint ownership. The finder and the owner of the real estate where the thing was found become co-owners in fractional parts. An exception to this is when the thing constitutes a historical object or archival material, in which case it becomes State Treasury property. This provision refers solely to movable things found on real estate[224] since these may be concealed.[225] As in other cases of things having historical attributes, the finder should promptly hand their find over to the relevant county administrator. Some commentators accept that the provision also covers, apart from things that are hidden and impossible to perceive, "situations where another type of thing was found, but not necessarily hidden (e.g. things cast up by sea waves)".[226]

In the original wording of Article 189 CC, found property and the criteria for distinguishing it were presented in a different way. Treasure was defined as a thing having "considerable material, scientific or artistic value found in such circumstances that a search for its owner would clearly be futile". There was no direct reference to the terminology adopted in acts on the protection of cultural heritage, which allowed the provision to be effectively applied under the regimes of APCP 1962 and APGM 2003. The APCP in force at the time the Civil Code was adopted introduced the basic concept of cultural property, meaning that the legislator more or less consciously did not refer to that terminology. The only change made was to replace state ownership with State Treasury ownership, as in the case of found property.[227]

The attempts made in the literature to interpret this provision led to several postulates *de lege ferenda*. It is worth citing them here in the context of the current regulations.[228] Firstly, it was proposed to amend the provision by introducing a solution on whose basis the ownership of treasure would be acquired "in equal parts by the finder and the owner".[229] With regard to found property having cultural value, two options were suggested. The first involved adding a provision to the Civil Code that would allow things of exceptional historical or scientific value to be acquired by the State Treasury, although the author rightly noted that this could create or maintain a state of interpretive uncertainty and eventually lead to disputes. The

[224] Szydło (2017), p. 386.

[225] Fras and Habdas (2018).

[226] Gudowski (2016).

[227] The Act of 23 August 1996 amending the Act—Civil Code. Polish Official Journal (Dz. U.) 1966, No. 22, item 141.

[228] Mularski (2009), pp. 643–654.

[229] Mularski (2009), p. 652.

adoption of the idea of exceptional historical or artistic value could lead to interpretive problems similar to those created by the already defunct Article 4 APCP, pursuant to which legal protection is granted to cultural property defined as a historical object "if their historical character is obvious" (Article 4 pt. 3 APCP).[230] The second option involved adding to Article 50 APGM "the expropriation of real estate of exceptional value in exchange for compensation equal to its market value".[231]

I will not go into a detailed analysis at this time but will only indicate that the proposed solution for extending the institution of expropriation in the APGM could fail a constitutional test. Caution in approving this proposal is also confirmed by a careful reading of rulings by the Polish Constitutional Tribunal in APGM cases, particularly those concerning the List of Heritage Treasures.[232] The possibility of expropriation currently provided by Article 50 APGM concerns situations where a historical object is under threat and a decision to secure it is not sufficient to guarantee its protection. When one of the risks set forth in the Act—namely destruction, damage, theft, loss or illegal removal from the country—cannot be removed, the conservation protection authority resorts to the institution of expropriation. Only in the case of objects entered on the List of Heritage Treasures does the legislator use the phrase "is taken over", whereas in relation to other movable historical objects, the phrase "may be taken over" is used. This categorical obligation to issue a decision only concerns objects entered on the List of Heritage Treasures, that is, exceptional objects defined in the Act as having special value for cultural heritage. In this light, the proposal for expropriating exceptionally valuable movables seems to violate the right to the protection of property (once lawfully acquired by the finder).

Nevertheless, that proposal was partly taken into account with regard to the joint acquisition of treasure not constituting cultural heritage and is expressed in the current wording of Article 189 par. 1 CC. Yet the direction of the provisions on things having scientific or artistic value was completely changed. Two new concepts were introduced to the Civil Code—historical objects and archival materials—which are of key importance and define the subject of protection in acts of administrative law. In this way, elements concerning cultural heritage protection were put into the Civil Code without being indicated through evaluative criteria. Evaluative criteria did not disappear, though, as the legal definitions of historical objects (Article 3 pt 2 APGM) and archival materials (Article 1 ANARA) refer to them. Without a doubt, however, the scope of application of the provision changed as not everything having material, scientific or artistic value is a historical object or archival material. It is specified what things are to become property of the State Treasury. Exclusively, these are things that have significant value for future generations as material heritage, including those in the form of documentation.

---

[230] Jagielska-Burduk (2011), pp. 57–61.

[231] Mularski (2009), p. 652.

[232] Polish Constitutional Court, Judgement of 25 May 2016, Kp 2/15, OTK-A/2016, item 23.

The very broad scope of treasure that may be appropriated by the State Treasury may raise some doubts. As indicated above, only some historical objects or archival materials have considerable value, whether economic or "historical". From the perspective of the State Treasury and to preserve certain types of property for future generations, it is not necessary to acquire all historical objects or archival materials. As we know, the system of heritage protection is based on a selection of objects to be preserved due to their inherent value, although the burden of protection is distributed between each owner and the state. On the other hand, a solution allowing for no exceptions was adopted for archaeological property. When the provision was formulated, the problem lurking in the background, which was how to finance the care provided to objects, was unnoticed. Perhaps the solution of acquisition by the State Treasury should contain an additional stage in which a decision is issued by cultural heritage protection authorities (i.e. the regional monuments conservator). Such a decision would state whether a given object is to become State Treasury property or whether it should be subject to general rules. In this way, up to the moment a decision is issued, the ownership status of the object would be "suspended". This procedure would require the need to create a rapid communication network between museums interested in the treasure and the relevant provincial conservator of historical objects or even a system similar to the ARCHEO platform of the World Customs Organization.[233] Such a platform could also be used in other areas of cooperation both nationally and regionally. Unfortunately, though, I have the impression that the current law, while simple to apply, will not stand the test of time. It is a pity that the problem of the ownership of historical objects has returned to the discussion on the problem of a lack of storage space or the disproportion between the costs of preserving objects and their value.

It is also worth examining what constitutes treasure and sets of things. The previous wording of the provision was analysed in terms of whether treasure can also be a "set of things" or refers to each thing separately.[234] As described in Chap. 2, how a set of things is dealt with in trade or inheritance can be of vital importance. In terms of the purpose to be achieved by the institution of treasure and what it leads to—namely, the acquisition of ownership by the State Treasury so that a thing can be handed down to future generations—the scope of the ownership acquired (covering one thing or a set of things) is of secondary importance. Yet it is worth checking whether, at present, the law permits the possibility of acquiring several things together, in view of the wording of Article 189 CC, which discusses historical objects and archival materials.

In practice, a find of treasure is not usually one thing but consists of at least several things (parts of jewellery, a collection of coins, a set of ornaments).

[233] ARCHEO, Connect to preserv. http://www.wcoomd.org/-/media/wco/public/global/pdf/topics/enforcement-and-compliance/activities-and-programmes/cultural-heritage/archeo_brochure_en.pdf. Accessed 1 June 2022.

[234] Mularski (2009), p. 644.

Nonetheless, there is no uniform view on treating treasure as a set of things.[235] Pursuant to Article 3 pt. 3 APGM, a movable historical object is a movable thing, a part thereof or a set of movable things. Assuming that the legislator acted rationally in applying the fundamental civil law concept of a thing to historical objects, one cannot infer that ownership of a whole set of movable things can also be acquired. The provision refers to a thing that is a historical object, and it does so with all the consequences entailed. One can imagine a situation where a single item does not qualify as a historical object, but a set of such objects as a whole (e.g. pendants representative of a given period, which makes it possible to determine the state of development of a workshop) deserves to be preserved for future generations. Each separate non-historical object would then become the property of the person who found it and the owner of the real estate on which it was found. In the interest of the public, however, should those objects not become State Treasury property? I believe that the values behind protecting cultural heritage and the purpose of such protection do not justify dispensing with the result of a literal interpretation of the law, especially since voivodeship conservators will have the right to enter a set of things in the register of historical objects *ex officio* where there is a danger of an attempt to export them illegally. In this situation, it would be necessary to amend the provision such that the reference in Article 189 CC to "things" in the plural form would take on the wording "if that thing or things constitute a historical object".

It also seems that one cannot consider treasure as a collection within the meaning of the APGM. Pursuant to Article 6 par. 1 pt. 2 letter b APGM, movable historical objects are collections constituting "sets of objects collected and arranged in accordance with the concept of the persons who established these collections". In administrative court rulings on collections, emphasis has been placed on the element of the concept or idea in accordance with which items were selected, as opposed to a random set of things.[236] Applying this to treasure, one can consider whether, in every situation where it would be futile to search for an owner, one cannot determine whether the items found were gathered together based on the idea of the person who collected them. Since a search for the owner is pointless, it is very likely that it will be difficult to establish the concept behind the collection. The same can be said of archival materials (such as maps and documents hidden underground) since in Article 189 CC, the concept "archival material" is again used in the singular. It seems that, in both cases, the manner in which ownership is acquired did not change in relation to the acquisition of things having scientific or artistic value.

Participants in trade are faced with the difficult task of distinguishing historical objects and, from among these, archaeological objects. One can find an "ordinary" movable historical object, archival material or an archaeological object. The classification of things as archaeological objects is a thorny problem that has serious implications for how legal provisions operate in practice. The legal status of archaeological objects directly affects the manner of dealing with discoveries and

[235] Szydło (2017), p. 386; Fras and Habdas (2018). Different view Mularski (2009), p. 644.

[236] Supreme Administrative Court. Judgement of 13 November 2008, I OSK 1438/07.

excavations or objects brought to the surface of the ground by natural forces or animals (such as the interesting example of historical objects being dug up by moles in the Białowieża Forest[237]). Moreover, the aim of the provisions on the potential ownership of lost property unclaimed by its owner and of archaeological property by the State Treasury is to secure cultural heritage, albeit with the difference that the regulations on archaeological property also protect undiscovered and unidentified objects that may be illegally extracted, exported and admitted to trade on the art market.

The APGM separately regulates finds made during construction and those discovered accidentally. The discovery of an object that may constitute a historical object triggers an obligation to halt construction, secure the object and its location and promptly notify the relevant conservator of historical objects (Article 32 par. 1 APGM). When this is not possible, the authority to which notification should be sent is the relevant local mayor. If archaeological excavations lead to the discovery of a historical object of exceptional value, the provincial conservator may issue a decision to extend the halt in construction, and those in charge of the work will have to put up with this (Article 32 par. 7). In a further article, the obligations of a person who finds an object that may qualify as archaeological property are set. The finder should secure and mark the location of the find and discharge the same notification duty as that provided for a discoverer.

Both a finder and a discoverer are entitled to a reward if they behave in accordance with the directives contained in Articles 32 or 33 APGM. This element of a reward was introduced to encourage entities to notify the relevant authorities about found property. Practice shows, however, that the procedure for handing out rewards is not always conducted properly, and if such cases become widely known, this may effectively discourage people from complying with the duty to notify.[238] The fact that notifications of discoveries and finds are made in the public interest and flexibility is proposed regarding "strictness in maintaining the criteria" was already pointed out by the APCP.[239] But this must not lead to a situation where the finder of a historical object who reports the find after the time period set forth in the Act finds themselves faced with criminal proceedings.[240]

---

[237] https://www.tvn24.pl/wiadomosci-z-kraju,3/puszcza-bialowieska-krety-wyrzucily-na-powierzchnie-slady-osadnictwa,963460.html. Accessed 1 June 2022.

[238] Provincial Administrative Court in Warsaw, Judgment of 14 June 2017, VIII SAB/Wa 38/17, Provincial Administrative Court in Warsaw, Judgment of 5 January 2017, VIII SA/Wa 446/16.

[239] Sieroszewski (1971), p. 67.

[240] Trzciński (2011), p. 209.

5.9 Conclusions

Components of cultural heritage play an important role in satisfying human needs and in developing societies and economies. Those components became recognised in the civil law system only after many, many years. Perhaps that is why various authors discussed this issue even under the previous political system, where state ownership was key in relation to such property. Further changes in the legal regulations in this area were certainly caused by developments in legal thought and case law.

Regulating rights to material property in the form of water or mineral deposits not only meets societal needs but is also important economically. While this has been the case for some time with respect to cultural heritage, it is only relatively recently that a broad view of cultural heritage and the creative industries has been taken. Apart from the history of the art market, here, I have in mind the creation of new jobs in the creative sector or the activities taken at the European Union level concerning the reuse of public sector information, including the use of museum exhibits' images.

Going further, the more attention we pay to the potential of cultural heritage components, the more profound the changes in how they are legally regulated will be. The inclusion of new institutions for the legal protection of cultural heritage in private law and the changes taking place in existing institutions confirm that there has been a kind of breakthrough where elements of cultural heritage will be an area of future legislative activity. One can already detect a certain pattern of development in this area. Some of the changes taking place result from analyses of the system by experts in the country. Without a doubt, certain legislative activities are the result of analyses of the effectiveness of internal law (the institution of treasure, found property), foreign experience and the obligation to implement EU law (national cultural treasure and public collections). It is also noticeable that some solutions are to be withdrawn (e.g. NRLCP), as they are not applied, for example by not creating certain registers; this is also part of building a new legal strategy for heritage protection.

This chapter discussed various ways of acquiring the ownership of cultural heritage components. Regarding the institution of treasure, as well as found historical objects, archival materials and archaeological property, a particular role is played by the State Treasury. The State Treasury acquires ownership over these categories, but it is not possible to estimate what the cost of that solution is. In providing for State Treasury ownership, it is automatically agreed that the state shall incur the costs for managing and protecting such goods. And at the same time, a serious problem arises as to the manner of securing archaeological heritage. Additionally, it has been shown that in domestic law, there is a strengthened regime for property constituting the property of the State Treasury or public institutions. The criterion of national property arises in relation to museum objects, while the term "national cultural property" and the institution of public collections demonstrate that there is a continuity and reinforcement of existing regimes (museum exhibits), as well as the creation of new ones that also encompass property owned by private entities, provided that certain requirements are met.

It has also been pointed out that, up to now, the issues of water and mineral deposits have each been dealt with in a single act of law. This is also the case with now binding laws, including the Water Law and the Geological and Mining Law. Even assuming that the structure of property is internally non-uniform (water, mines, animals), from the beginning, the core of the regulation has been one act governing such atypical kinds of property, while the purpose of the other regulations is to supplement that fundamental act. Those regulations, however, are not devoid of detailed solutions for example, the special legal status of thermal waters being subject to mining ownership. The growing interest in cultural heritage allows one to suppose that there is a good chance of similar developments in the regulations in this area.

The large number of legal constructions regarding cultural heritage results from the variety of its components. Heritage cannot be considered through the prism of civil law issues without reference to those various forms. Hence, the character of a given heritage component determines the civil law regime to which it is subject. Furthermore, technological progress has only increased that heritage by enriching it with new forms. In the future, something that constitutes work but exists solely in the intangible dimension should be afforded legal protection, at least to some extent. The basis of protection, then, will include not merely the expression of the artist's intellectual work but also an object that is deserving of protection due to its value to future generations.

The rights to cultural heritage are not uniform. In the case of heritage constituting material property, there is an internal stratification of rights *in rem* and rights similar to ownership with regard to the components thereof. An example of such a difference is the formulation "ownership of archaeological property", whose form, in relation to undiscovered archaeological property (objects for which there is no way to establish their owner), is more reminiscent of an absolute right similar to that of ownership. In relation to movable historical objects, there are no uniform solutions. And other solutions are adopted for museum objects, archival materials and "ordinary" movable historical and archaeological objects. With regard to archival materials, two categories based on the criterion of the provenance of archival materials are identified. When creating the provisions on inalienability, the legislator imprecisely created two regimes within the system for the protection of national archival resources, and unfortunately, this was not followed by any deeper reflection on the significance of those provisions for other cultural property.

Dealing with cultural heritage in a single act of law may be a remedy for the fragmentation that exists in the current regulations governing cultural heritage, as broadly understood, and in the current structure of rights to cultural heritage. One act, under the working title Cultural Heritage Protection Act or Cultural Property Protection Law, would make it possible for this complex problem to become more accessible to those entities that apply the law. This presents a big challenge, however, since account must be taken of the specific nature of the different types of property (e.g. archival materials, museum objects), and relevant stakeholders must be consulted. Another goal that should be set for is regulatory transparency. An advantageous legislative move would be to locate all the provisions on the ownership of cultural heritage in a separate part of the act, where they would be combined with the provisions on trading in cultural heritage components. The same section should also contain an inalienability clause or the status of *rex extra commercium*. It might also be worth starting from initial assumptions, but ones that cover the whole of the regulations in a comprehensive manner and can act in a certain sense as a roadmap for planning work on individual parts of the legislation.

In the Polish legal system, the potential of the *res extra commercium* regime has not been fully exploited with respect to museums and other collections. Apart from the narrow set of non-state registered state archival resources, the exclusion from trade is not literally expressed in any act of law. The view that some historical objects, and archaeological objects in particular, remain excluded from trade in Polish law is not shared by everyone. It could be effectively questioned if a foreign court wanted to apply a provision of foreign (i.e. Polish) law. Here, in order to remove any doubts, objects should be granted an unequivocal status.

In defining each category of property (museum objects, archival materials, national library resources) and specifying their function, values and interests are invoked that prevail over individual interests. There is a clear line between different institutions, set by the criterion of the organising entity (cultural institutions or other institutions conducting cultural activity). One cannot help but notice that some of the differences in the regulations seem to be completely accidental.[241] The most recent research shows that the dividing line based on the organising entity will not be of key importance in the long run. It may be worth considering to include the construction of *rex extra commercium* in the system for protecting private collections and to create an application procedure;[242] this seems to already have been confirmed by the introduction of the new institution of public collections.

It is also worth arguing in favour of the advantages of a systemic, lasting solution over fragmentary solutions as regards the time period of protection afforded by the NRLCP. Clearly, the *res extra commercium* model is not applied to private collections, and so within this scope, the Polish NRLCP solution goes somewhat farther, though it is limited to historical objects entered in the register. Similarly, the regulation concerning national cultural property found in public collections also takes into account objects constituting private property, while their "public" character derives from receiving funding from public sources.

It seems that only a consolidation of the concept of *res extra commercium* with regard to all or, as discussed above, some state collections will allow that institution to be applied with a further reach. The NRLCP without set and operational register and an unclear regulation on public collections cannot be considered as long-term solutions. Additionally, the functionality of the NRLCP and the registration procedure envisaged are not in line with the latest trends at the international level and do not fit in with activities for combating illegal trade in cultural property in a broader

[241] For instance, the legal status of archive materials in the Polish legal system.
[242] Szafrański (2016), pp. 160–163.

sense. Strengthening the protection granted to owners deprived of their property by adopting trade restrictions serves the public interest in relation to handing such objects down to future generations.

The creation of the protection of national cultural property belonging to public collections and the proposed exclusion of the application of the provisions on acquisitive prescription and acquisition in good faith are very promising solutions. Unfortunately, as things stand today, the difficulty in defining what a public collection is causes legal uncertainty. What is more, no record system for public collections has been implemented (apart from those located in museums), which means that a potential acquirer is not always able to verify the provenance of an object and its potential affiliation with a public collection even when exercising due diligence.

The regime of *res extra commercium* should be unambiguously formulated for cultural heritage components. Given the consequences of being covered by that regime at both the national and international levels, the construction cannot raise any doubts. It is in the best interests of cultural heritage components, specifically that of preserving the integrity of collections and pursuing the release of objects. The introduction of the NRLCP, the implementation of Directive 2014/60 and the protection of national cultural property belonging to public collections constitute important stages in building future law. The NRLCP meets only some of the postulates put forward by Wojciech Kowalski concerning how the law should deal with the trade in cultural heritage components at the domestic level and the creation of different levels of protection based on the criterion of ownership.[243] It is not a fundamental solution that grants an object permanent legal status but only a temporary solution. Moreover, in practice, the register does not work, for objects are not being reported for entry. The concept of public collections, while of a lasting nature, entails the problem of how its components are to be established. Nevertheless, in the future, the protection of other heritage components will inevitably be strengthened by the introduction of provisions on due diligence when acquiring cultural property, which force participants to act in certain ways before concluding a transaction.

With regard to the subjects of civil law relationships, there is a number of ways available to achieve its goal. These emerge from experiences gained from foreign legal systems and from the discussion on the search for a new image of cultural heritage.[244] The experience in the Polish legal system of excluding heritage components from trade is very modest compared with that in other countries. The regulation of trading in national cultural property belonging to public collections goes beyond the previous understanding of public collections. It seems that, as practical problems rise, it will be necessary to return to the definition of public collections and modify it, at least regarding the assessment criterion of the "public character" of a collection, and how the moment a collection gains such status is determined.

The first solution related to the exclusion of a particular property from civil law transactions for public interest but maintaining it in the category of things. This

[243] Kowalski (2004), pp. 257–273.

[244] Jagielska-Burduk (2016c), pp. 44 et seq.

solution may be implemented at several levels and should also consider valuable private objects that are not subsidised through public funds and whose owners submit a relevant application and agree to the consequences of managing inalienable objects. The second solution is to deem cultural property as a separate category of property. This is supported by the specific nature of cultural heritage components. The findings on this potential separation of legal categories are presented in Sect. 6.3. Here, I will only point out that the first (weaker) solution does not rule out the second. One can also make changes "in instalments" and take advantage of stronger solutions only at a later stage of the legal system's transformation. Further, it may be that the first solution connected with the introduction of a *res extra commercium* regime and an analysis of how it functions will constitute a first, preparatory stage leading to a proposal for a new legal category.

The debate over the exclusion of cultural property from the category of things cannot, in my opinion, justify a refusal to hand property over and legitimise "cultural wrongs". The search for new legal solutions concerning rights to movable cultural heritage should consider joint responsibility for property and should go beyond the traditional framework of ownership rights. In particular, it may lead to a continuation of research and a search for an intangible, supranational element in cultural property.[245] This argumentation appeared in discussion on the report *The Restitution of African Heritage. Toward a New Relational Ethics*.[246] The issue of objects taken to French museums during the colonial period and their potential return to their country of origin again brought on a discussion around the legal status of objects in a national museum, which are inalienable in accordance with French law. It is enough to recall that, to date, objects have been removed from French inventories on two occasions, but these instances concerned human remains.[247] Using a similar model for other types of cultural property could mark a breakthrough in the French system as it has been functioning for years and has been described as a model or target system for other countries.

Frederice Sarr and Benedicte Savoy (the authors of the report) examined the status of objects of African origin in French public collections held in museums and prepared model proceedings for how to deal with their return to their countries of origin. The report concerned objects taken to France without the consent of those countries during the colonial period. In their conclusions, the authors proposed a procedure for returning property, divided into three stages: the first, planned for November 2018–2019, was to involve the restitution of objects.[248] They referred to the French regulation on exclusion from trade, which they argued solely concerns

[245] Garnier (2019), pp. 51 et seq.

[246] Sarr and Savoy (2018).

[247] Acts regarding the real status of Maori heads (France, Law No. 2010-501 of 18 May 2010 to authorize the return of *Maori* heads to *New Zealand*) and Venus Hottentot (France, Law No. 2002-323 of 6 March 2002, on the restitution of the remains of Saartje Baartman to South Africa by France, Official Journal of 7 March 2002).

[248] Sarr and Savoy (2018), pp. 63–64.

national property. They also reminded the public about the case of the Maori heads.[249] Because of the unequivocal recommendations it contained on the return of objects, the report was not met with the approval of European states. The range of objects indicated by the authors as subject to return went back to the period before 1970 and involved the introduction of a targeted procedure for the return of objects from the colonial period. The adoption of the proposed model by other countries would require verification and would certainly lead to a reduction in museum inventories. Up to March 2019, none of the objects singled out in the report had yet been returned,[250] including 26 objects (sculptures and thrones) from Benin, whose return had been announced by Emmanuel Macron at a conference on 23 November 2018.[251] In November 2021, 26 objects were finally returned to the Abomey palace in Benin.[252] While the report did not initially lead to proceedings being initiated and the pace is slower than what was declared, this return was nonetheless important in prompting a discussion on objects of rights *in rem* and similar rights and what parties are entitled to cultural property.

A third solution involves the continuation of the existing incidental, fragmentary legislative activity, without a systematic approach. This may seem effective in the short term and may demonstrate dynamic legislative work, but upon analysis, it is not beneficial for future generations. In Poland, there is a proliferation of cultural heritage registers, as well as new forms of protection for historical objects, such as the List of Heritage Treasures. The fact that neither of these institutions functions effectively should send a loud signal to entities involved in the cultural sector, which signal will be read by lawyers in the next century. It also reinforces the conviction that not only society but also political decision-makers themselves do not consider the legal regulation of cultural heritage a priority. It seems, then, that those entities responsible for the form of law on the protection of cultural heritage do not pay sufficient attention to the proposals that have been made in the literature for years, which are supported by research. One cannot fail to notice that this is not the area of legislative initiatives. While in principle the law protects what it considers to be fundamental values, one of which is cultural heritage, this does not adequately translate into the applicable law as it is currently written.

The measures taken to date reveal that there is no systematic approach to the legal protection of cultural heritage. It seems that the experiences of recent years, or more precisely the frequency with which laws are amended, constitute a "heavy baggage". Those experiences could be used to draw conclusions for the future, create a new act of law and strengthen the role of private law in protecting cultural heritage. The progress being made in research on cultural heritage and the fact that reports that

[249] Sarr and Savoy (2018), pp. 73 and 82.

[250] Herman (2019).

[251] Nayeri (2018); Benin artworks: France to return thrones and statues, 2018, 23 Nov BBC. https://www.bbc.com/news/world-46324174. Accessed 1 June 2022.

[252] France returns 26 looted artifacts and artworks to Benin—CNN Style, 2018, 12 Nov. https://edition.cnn.com/style/article/benin-art-returned-scli-intl/index.html. Accessed 1 June 2022.

analyse the binding provisions of law are being prepared confirm that there is an ongoing intensification of activities in the sphere of cultural heritage legislation. Undoubtedly, these studies and analyses are being conducted in parallel with developments in criminal law, administrative law, tax law and international law. The creation of a working group on a new act by the Cultural Heritage Protection Department in the Ministry of Culture and National Heritage and the inclusion of experts from all over Poland in the discussion mark a clear shift in the model used for developing the protection of cultural heritage.

When writing on the new Civil Code, Andrzej Stelmachowski emphasised the reaction of lawyers to the adoption of this legal act. He wrote that

> in legal circles – especially at universities – the entry into force of the Civil Code brought a wave of hope. You have to understand the emotions of the older generation of lawyers, who grew up under a kind of myth. That myth was the desire to create one's own, Polish civil law, which would guarantee stability in relations, and which at the same time would be modern, and represent a high level of legislative technique.[253]

How can this relate to the contemporary challenges in protecting cultural heritage? A heritage code would be the fifth act of law addressing this problem since 1918, anchored in many years of legal thought in the field of administrative law. This very noticeable change concerns the issue of private law, the status of cultural heritage components, new private law institutions and EU Directive 2014/60, which also refers to the ownership of property subject to return. While the goal of both the post-war decree on rights *in rem* and the code of obligations was to unify the law, in the case of the code, the fundamental purpose should be to integrate all of the detailed legal acts. The current system, wherein laws on particular types of property are scattered, should be replaced with a single, central act of law. Then there would be no need to determine the mutual relations among laws or interpret referring provisions, and any future amendments would be made within a single act of law.

References

Agopszowicz A (1973) Własność wód (jej istota i charakter prawny). Zeszyty Naukowe Uniwersytetu Jagiellońskiego. Prace z Wynalazczości i Ochrony Własności Intelektualnej 1: 25–40

Antoniak P (2012) Ustawa o muzeach. Komentarz. LEX, Warszawa

Bednarek M (1997) Mienie. Komentarz do art. 44–55 Kodeksu cywilnego. Zakamycze, Kraków

Chechi A, Contel R, Renold M-A (2011, Oct) Case Jiroft Collection – Iran v. The Barakat Galleries Ltd. Platform ArThemis. Art-Law Centre, University of Geneva. https://plone.unige.ch/art-adr/cases-affaires/jiroft-collection-2013-iran-v-barakat-galleries/case-note-2013-jiroft-collection-2013-iran-v-barakat-galleries. Accessed 1 June 2022

Dobosz P (1997) Administracyjnoprawne instrumenty kształtowania ochrony zabytków. Dajwór, Kraków

Drela M (2006) Własność zabytków. C.H. Beck, Warszawa

[253] Stelmachowski (1980), p. 37.

Drela M (2008) Obowiązek finansowania prac archeologicznych przez inwestora. Glosa do wyroku TK z dnia 8 października 2007 r., K 20/07. PiP 11:138–142

Drela M (2014) Ustalanie prawa własności muzealiów w zasobach publicznych oraz o stosowaniu regulacji prawnych dotyczących likwidacji niepodjętych depozytów przez muzea. In: Jagielska-Burduk A, Szafrański W (eds) Kultura w praktyce. Zagadnienia prawne, vol 3: Muzea a rynek sztuki. Aspekty prawne. Wydawnictwo Poznańskiego Towarzystwa Przyjaciół Nauk, Poznań

Drela M (2017) Zabytkowe części składowe i przynależności a przedmiot wpisu do rejestru zabytków: uwagi de lege lata i de lege ferenda. Roczniki Nauk Prawnych 27(3):27–46

Dromgoole S (2013) Underwater cultural heritage and international law. Cambridge University Press, Cambridge. https://doi.org/10.1017/CBO9781139020503

Francioni F (2017) Cultural property in international law. In: Graziadei M, Smith L (eds) Comparative property law. Global perspectives. Edward Elgar, Cheltenham, pp 374–392

Frankiewicz-Bodynek A (2019) Konstytucyjna regulacja dziedzictwa narodowego oraz dóbr kultury. Wydawnictwo Adam Marszałek, Toruń

Fras M, Habdas M (eds) (2018) Kodeks cywilny. Komentarz, vol 2: Własność i inne prawa rzeczowe. Wolters Kluwer Polska, Warszawa, Lex

Frigo M (2016) The implementation of Directive 2014/60/EU and the problems of the compliance of Italian Legislation. SAACLR 2(2):71–84. https://doi.org/10.4467/2450050XSR.16.019.6127

Fuchs B (2013) Przepisy wymuszające swoje zastosowanie w nowej ustawie – Prawo prywatne międzynarodowe. In: Poczobut J (ed) Współczesne wyzwania prawa prywatnego międzynarodowego. Wolters Kluwer Polska, Warszawa, pp 69–81

Gadecki B (2016) Nowe regulacje dotyczące problematyki zabytków w związku z wejściem w życie ustawy o rzeczach znalezionych. Ius Novum 10(4):186–195

Garnier F (2019) La restitution de biens culturels déplacés: une question patrimoniale non résolue, une solution juridique à trouver. In: Laws and policies for the return of cultural property taken during the colonial control or foreign invasion (19th – mid 20th Century), Disquisition Collection of International Symposium on Frontier Issues of Cultural Heritage Law, 24 October, Pekin

Goettel M (2019) Cywilnoprawne skutki znalezienia dobra kultury, Meandry ochrony dziedzictwa kultury. Aspekty prawnokarne i kryminalistyczne, red. M. Sabaciński, M. Trzciński. Narodowy Instytut Dziedzictwa, Warszawa, pp 19–29

Golat R (2004) Ustawa o ochronie zabytków i opiece nad zabytkami. Komentarz. Zakamycze, Kraków

Golat R (2008) Jak założyć prywatne muzeum. Muzealnictwo 49:11–15

Górecki J (2009) Prawa rzeczowe i posiadanie w projekcie ustawy o prawie prywatnym międzynarodowym. Problemy Współczesnego Prawa Międzynarodowego, Europejskiego i Porównawczego 7:7–21

Górecki J (2015) Ochrona dóbr kultury. In: Pazdan M (ed) Prawo prywatne międzynarodowe. System Prawa Prywatnego, vol 20b. C.H. Beck, Warszawa, pp 999–1001

Górka M (2016) Directive 2014/60/EU: a new legal framework for ensuring the return of cultural objects within the European Union, pp. 29–31. SAACLR 2(2):27–34. https://doi.org/10.4467/2450050XSR.16.016.6124

Górniak K (2018) Szczególna ochrona własności w ramach krajowego rejestru utraconych dóbr kultury. Transformacje Prawa Prywatnego 2:5–44

Gredka I, Gwoździewicz-Matan P (2016) Cywilnoprawne skutki wpisu rzeczy do krajowego rejestru utraconych dóbr kultury. PiP 10:100–113

Gredka-Ligarska I (2019) Uregulowanie własności narodowego dobra kultury, zwróconego na terytorium RP w ustawie o restytucji narodowych dóbr kultury. PiP 8:103–121

Grzybowski S (ed) (1985) System prawa cywilnego, vol 1: Część ogólna. Zakład Narodowy im. Ossolińskich, Wydawnictwo Polskiej Akademii Nauk, Wrocław–Warszawa

Gudowski J (ed) (2016) Kodeks cywilny. Komentarz, vol 2: Własność i inne prawa rzeczowe, 2nd edn. Wolters Kluwer Polska, Warszawa, Lex

Haberko J, Uhrynowska-Tyszkiewicz I (2014) Ustawa o pobieraniu, przechowywaniu i przeszczepianiu komórek, tkanek i narządów. Komentarz. LEX

Herman A (2019, 12 Nov) One year after the Sarr-Savoy report, France has lost its momentum in the restitution debate. The Art Newspaper. Accessed 1 June 2022. https://stage.theartnewspaper.com/2019/11/12/one-year-after-the-sarr-savoy-report-france-has-lost-its-momentum-in-the-restitution-debate

Jagielska-Burduk A (2011) Zabytek ruchomy. Wolters Kluwer Polska, Warszawa

Jagielska-Burduk A (2014) Koncepcja świadomego dysponenta zabytków w polskim prawie ochrony zabytków. In: Zeidler K (ed) Prawo ochrony zabytków. Wolters Kluwer, Wydawnictwo Uniwersytetu Gdańskiego, Warszawa–Gdańsk, pp 311–318

Jagielska-Burduk A (2016a) Fideikomis. In: Jagielska-Burduk A (ed) Mechanizmy prawne zarządzania dziedzictwem kultury. Wolters Kluwer Polska, Wydawnictwo Uniwersytetu Gdańskiego, Gdańsk–Warszawa, pp 238–253

Jagielska-Burduk A (2016b) Formy ochrony zabytków jako mechanizm zarządzania dziedzictwem kultury. In: Jagielska-Burduk A (ed) Mechanizmy prawne zarządzania dziedzictwem kultury. Wolters Kluwer Polska, Wydawnictwo Uniwersytetu Gdańskiego, Gdańsk–Warszawa, pp 171–212

Jagielska-Burduk A (2016c) Nowy wizerunek dziedzictwa – między ochroną a zarządzaniem. In: Jagielska-Burduk A (ed) Mechanizmy prawne zarządzania dziedzictwem kultury. Wolters Kluwer Polska, Wydawnictwo Uniwersytetu Gdańskiego, Gdańsk–Warszawa, pp 44–65

Jagielska-Burduk A (2016d) Ownership of cultural heritage. In: Jagielska-Burduk A, Szafrański W (eds) Legal issues in cultural heritage management. A Polish perspective. Peter Lang, Berlin, pp 29–52

Jagielska-Burduk A (2016e) Problematyka muzealiów – ochrona zabytków w muzeach i kolekcjach prywatnych, raport dla NIMOZ 2016. Gdańsk, pp 107–146

Jagielska-Burduk A, Mularski K (2015) Problematyka reprywatyzacji zabytków ruchomych. Uwagi na marginesie wyroku Sądu Najwyższego z 12 lutego 2012 r. (III CSK 208/11). In: Stec P, Maniurka P (eds) Kolekcje i zbiory muzealne. Problematyka prawna. Redakcja Wydawnictw Wydziału Teologicznego Uniwersytetu Opolskiego, Opole, pp 201–216

Jagielska-Burduk A, Szafrański W (2016) Trust. In: Jagielska-Burduk A (ed) Mechanizmy prawne zarządzania dziedzictwem kultury. Wolters Kluwer Polska, Wydawnictwo Uniwersytetu Gdańskiego, Gdańsk–Warszawa, pp 254–284

Jagielska-Burduk A, Zajęcki M (2013) Przesłanki likwidacji instytucji kultury w nowym ustawowym modelu organizowania działalności kulturalnej. In: Jagielska-Burduk A, Szafrański W (eds) Kultura w praktyce. Zagadnienia prawne, vol 2: Wokół problematyki prawnej zabytków i rynku sztuki. Wydawnictwo Poznańskiego Towarzystwa Przyjaciół Nauk, Poznań, pp 153–165

Jakubowski A (2006) Własność zabytków i dzieł sztuki w prawie prywatnych międzynarodowym. Zagadnienia węzłowe. KPP 2:401–422

Jakubowski O (2010) Kryteria wieku i wartości jako nowy mechanizm określania czy dobro kultury wymaga pozwolenia na wywóz zabytku za granicę. MPCiP 8:288–291

Jakubowski A (ed) (2016) Cultural rights as collective rights: an international law perspective. Brill, Leiden

Jakubowski O (2017) Zagrożenie dziedzictwa kulturowego przestępczością – analiza wydarzeń z 2016 roku. SAACLR 1(3):249–274. https://doi.org/10.4467/2450050XSNR.17.016.7388

Jakubowski O (2018) Zagrożenie dziedzictwa kulturowego przestępczością – analiza wydarzeń z 2017 roku. SAACLR 1(4):215–236. https://doi.org/10.4467/2450050XSNR.18.013.9774

Jakubowski O (2021) Zagrożenie dziedzictwa kulturowego przestępczością – analiza wydarzeń w 2019 roku. SAACLR 1(7):221–232. https://doi.org/10.4467/2450050XSNR.21.001.14590

Jakubowski A, Jakubowski O (2014) Pierwokup przy wywozie dóbr kultury za granicę – analiza kierunkowych zmian w prawie polskim. In: Jagielska-Burduk A, Szafrański W (eds) Kultura w praktyce. Zagadnienia prawne, vol 3: Muzea a rynek sztuki. Aspekty prawne. Wydawnictwo Poznańskiego Towarzystwa Przyjaciół Nauk, Poznań, pp 205–234

Jakubowski O, Trzciński M (2019) Przestępczość przeciwko dziedzictwu kulturowemu – charakterystyka zjawiska. In: Trzciński M (ed) Praktyczne aspekty zwalczania przestępczości

przeciwko dziedzictwu kulturowemu. Wydawnictwo Uniwersytetu Gdańskiego, Gdańsk, pp 85–157
Kaczan D (2016) Cywilnoprawna sytuacja znalazcy oraz przechowującego. Studia Iuridica Toruniensia 18:77–94. https://doi.org/10.12775/SIT.2016.004
Kępiński M, Kępiński K (2021) Art. 169 [Commentary]. In: Gutowski M (ed) Kodeks cywilny. vol 1: Komentarz do art. 1–352, 3rd edn. C.H. Beck, Warszawa, pp 1294–1309
Kono T (2019) Recovery and reconstruction of cultural heritage – the ICOMOS Matrix for case studies. In: Marcinkowska M, Zalasińska K (eds) The challenges of world heritage recovery. Narodowy Instytut Dziedzictwa, Warsaw, pp 37–45
Konstankiewicz M (2015) Zmiany w ustawie z 1983 r. o narodowym zasobie archiwalnym i archiwach wchodzące w życie od 1 listopada 2015 r. Archiwista Polski 3:7–22
Konstankiewicz M (2016) Art. 43 [Commentary]. In: Konstankiewicz M, Niewęgłowski A (eds) Narodowy zasób archiwalny i archiwa. Komentarz. LEX
Kowalczyk BJ (2017) Art 27. In: Zeidler K, Marcinkowska M (eds) Dekret Rady Regencyjnej z 1918 r. o opiece nad zabytkami sztuki i kultury z komentarzem czyli eseje o prawie ochrony dziedzictwa kultury. Wydawnictwo Uniwersytetu Gdańskiego, Gdańsk, pp 208–216
Kowalski W (2004) Nabycie własności dzieła sztuki od nieuprawnionego. Zakamycze, Kraków
Kowalski W (2005) Kolizyjnoprawne problemy restytucji dóbr kultury. In: Ogiegło L, Popiołek W, Szpunar M (eds) Rozprawy prawnicze. Księga pamiątkowa profesora Maksymiliana Pazdana. Zakamycze, Kraków, pp 123–149
Kowalski W (2006) Nabycie dzieła sztuki od osoby nieuprawnionej. PiP 7:5–21
Kowalski W (2010) Trust and res extra commercium. In search of legal instruments to strengthen protection of cultural heritage. In: Habdas M, Wudarski A (eds) Ius est ars boni et aequi: festschrift fur Stanisława Kalus. Peter Lang, Frankfurt am Main, pp 227–242
Kowalski W (2014a) Konwencja UNESCO o ochronie podwodnego dziedzictwa kulturowego przyjęta dnia 2 listopada 2001 r. na 31 Konferencji Generalnej UNESCO. In: Zalasińska K (ed) Konwencje UNESCO w dziedzinie kultury. Komentarz. Wolters Kluwer Polska, Warszawa, pp 312–391
Kowalski W (2014b) Konwencja UNESCO o ochronie podwodnego dziedzictwa kulturowego z 2001 roku. CBU 3–4:66–68
Kowalski W, Zalasińska K (2013) Prawo do wyglądu muzealiów i ich fotografowania. PiP 2:75–86
Kugler R (2011) Die Praxis des Kulturgüterrückgabegesetzes. Vortrag zum Jahreskongress der Deutsch-Mexikanischen Juristenvereinigung e.V. am 14. September 2010 in Berlin. In: Prinz von Sachsen Gessaphe KA (ed) Kulturgüterschutz und politische Entwicklung in Mexiko im Jubiläumsjahr 2010. Jahreskongress 2010 der Deutsch-Mexikanischen Juristenvereinigung e.V. in Zusammenarbeit mit dem Ibero-Amerikanischen Institut Preußischer Kulturbesitz. Ibero-Online.de, Heft 1, Berlin, pp 14–21, https://www.iai.spk-berlin.de/fileadmin/dokumentenbibliothek/Ibero-Online/Ibero_Online_11.pdf. Accessed 1 June 2022
Lizak A (2017) Prawne aspekty utworzenia krajowego rejestru utraconych dóbr kultury. Przegląd Prawniczy Uniwersytetu Warszawskiego 1:115–135. https://doi.org/10.26330/ppuw.2017.01.12
Mikosz R (2008) Uprawnienia górnicze *de lege ferenda* (uwagi na tle projektu nowego prawa geologicznego i górniczego). In: Lisicka H (ed) Prawo ochrony środowiska i prawo karne. Książka jubileuszowa z okazji 40-lecia pracy naukowej Profesora Wojciecha Radeckiego. Wydawnictwo Prawa Ochrony Środowiska, Wrocław, pp 173–194
Mularski K (2009) O skarbach de lege lata i de lege ferenda. Monitor Prawniczy 12:643–654
Muszalski E (1932) Prawo cywilne obowiązujące w b. Królestwie Kongresowem. Księgarnia F. Hoesicka, Warszawa
Nafziger JAR (2016) Trading and returning cultural objects under international law. SAACLR 2(2): 179–194. https://doi.org/10.4467/2450050XSR.16.026.6134
Nayeri F (2018, 27 Nov) Return of African Artifacts sets a tricky precedent for Europe's museums. The New York Times, https://www.nytimes.com/2018/11/27/arts/design/macron-report-restitution-precedent.html. Accessed 1 June 2022

Niewęgłowski A (2014) Obrót materiałami archiwalnymi – zagadnienia wybrane. Archeion 115: 45–72

Niewęgłowski A (2015) Nowa ustawa o rzeczach znalezionych i jej znaczenie dla prawa archiwalnego. Archiwista Polski 3:23–37

Niewęgłowski A (2016) Art. 7 [Commentary]. In: Konstankiewicz M, Niewęgłowski A (eds) Narodowy zasób archiwalny i archiwa. Komentarz. LEX

Nowicka A (2005) Kolizyjnoprawne i jurysdykcyjne zagadnienia naruszeń praw własności intelektualnej. In: Ogiegło L, Popiołek W, Szpunar M (eds) Rozprawy prawnicze. Księga pamiątkowa profesora Maksymiliana Pazdana. Zakamycze, Kraków, pp 225–237

O'Keefe PJ (2013) Commercial exploitation. Its prohibition int the UNESCO Convention on protection of the underwater cultural heritage 2001 and other instruments. Art Antiq Law 18(2):129–148

O'Keefe PJ (2017) Protecting cultural objects: before and after 1970. Institute of Art & Law, Builth Wells

O'Keefe PJ (2020) Underwater cultural heritage. In: Vrdoljak AF, Francioni F (eds) The Oxford handbook of international cultural heritage law. Oxford University Press, Oxford, pp 295–317. https://doi.org/10.1093/law/9780198859871.003.0013

O'Keefe PJ (2007) Commentary on the 1970 UNESCO Convention on the means of prohibiting and preventing the illicit import, export and transfer of ownership of cultural property, 2nd edn. Institute of Art and Law, Leicester

Piątkowski JS (1977) Commentary. In: Ignatowicz J (ed) System prawa cywilnego, Prawo własności i inne prawa rzeczowe, vol 2. Zakład Narodowy im. Ossolińskich, Warszawa

Prott LV (1997) Commentary on the UNIDROIT Convention on stolen and illegally exported cultural objects 1995. Institute of Art and Law, Leicester

Prott LV (2021) Commentary on the 1995 UNIDROIT Convention, 2nd edn. Institute of Art and Law

Purchla J (2010) W stronę systemu ochrony dziedzictwa kulturowego w Polsce. Zarządzanie Publiczne 2(12):69–82

Purchla J (2012) Naród – Dziedzictwo – Pamięć. Zagadnienia Sądownictwa Konstytucyjnego 2(4): 59–68

Rychter AR (2019) Ustawa o drogach publicznych, Lex

Sarr F, Savoy B (2018, Nov) The Restitution of African Cultural Heritage. Toward a new relational ethics. http://restitutionreport2018.com/sarr_savoy_en.pdf. Accessed 1 June 2022

Sax JL (2007) Legal concepts of cultural heritage property. J Rare Books Manuscripts Cult Herit 8(1):67–74. https://doi.org/10.5860/rbm.8.1.279

Sieroszewski W (1960) Zbiór przepisów dotyczących ochrony i konserwacji zabytków. Ministerstwo Kultury i Sztuki, Zarząd Muzeów i Ochrony Zabytków, Warszawa

Sieroszewski W (1971) Ochrona prawna dóbr kultury w Polsce. Ministerstwo Kultury i Sztuki, Zarząd Muzeów i Ochrony Zabytków, Warszawa

Small Z (2020, 6 Oct) T. Rex Skeleton Brings $31.8 Million at Christie's Auction. NY Times. https://www.nytimes.com/2020/10/06/arts/design/t-rex-skeleton-brings-31-8-million-at-christies-auction.html. Accessed 1 June 2022

Stec P (2015) Dyrektywa 93/7/EWG z perspektywy dwóch dekad funkcjonowania. SAACLR 1(1): 103–118. https://doi.org/10.4467/2450050XSR.15.003.3771

Stelmachowski A (1980) Zasada jedności prawa cywilnego (Teoria i praktyka). Przegląd Ustawodawstwa Gospodarczego 2:37–43

Stelmachowski A (2003) Współczesna stratyfikacja własności, muszę do jakiejś biblioteki zadzwonić i zapytać o strony tego rozdziału, bo mam tylko ksero o dziedzictwie. In: Dybowski T (ed) Prawo rzeczowe, System Prawa Prywatnego, vol 3. C.H. Beck, Warszawa, pp 149–202

Stelmachowski A, Zaradkiewicz K (2013) Współczesna stratyfikacja własności. In: Gniewek E (ed) Prawo rzeczowe, System Prawa Prywatnego, vol 3. C.H. Beck, Warszawa, pp 294–336

Szafrański W (2016) Res extra commercium. In: Jagielska-Burduk A (ed) Mechanizmy prawne zarządzania dziedzictwem kultury. Wolters Kluwer Polska, Wydawnictwo Uniwersytetu Gdańskiego, Gdańsk–Warszawa, pp 127–171

Szpunar A (1999) Nabycie własności ruchomości od nieuprawnionego. Zakamycze, Kraków

Szydło W (2017) Art. 189 [Commentary]. In: Gniewek E, Machnikowski P (eds) Kodeks cywilny. Komentarz. C.H. Beck, Warszawa, pp 386–388

Trzciński M (2011) Nielegalny obrót zabytkami archeologicznymi. In: Kowalski W, Zalasińska K (eds) Rynek sztuki. Aspekty prawne. Wolters Kluwer Polska, Warszawa, pp 201–213

Trzciński M (2013) O potrzebach zmian systemu ochrony dziedzictwa archeologicznego. In: Jagielska-Burduk A, Szafrański W (eds) Kultura w praktyce. Zagadnienia prawne, vol 2: Wokół problematyki prawnej zabytków i rynku sztuki. Wydawnictwo Poznańskiego Towarzystwa Przyjaciół Nauk, Poznań, pp 225–243

Trzciński M (2014) Definicja zabytku archeologicznego – problemy i kontrowersje wokół stosowania prawa. In: Zeidler K (ed) Prawo ochrony zabytków. Wolters Kluwer, Wydawnictwo Uniwersytetu Gdańskiego, Warszawa–Gdańsk, pp 115–122

Trzciński M (2016) Ochrona ruchomych zabytków archeologicznych. In: Zeidler K (ed) Raport dotyczący stanu ochrony prawnej oraz kierunków zmian w zakresie prawnej ochrony zabytków ruchomych w Polsce przygotowany w ramach realizacji Krajowego Programu Ochrony Zabytków i Opieki nad Zabytkami na lata 2014–2017 dla Narodowego Instytutu Muzealnictwa i Ochrony Zbiorów. Gdańsk, pp 83–106

Warciński M (2014a, 5 March) Opinia prawna na temat projektu ustawy o rzeczach znalezionych oraz zmianie niektórych innych ustaw, druk nr 2064. Opinia sporządzona dla Biura Analiz Sejmowych. Warszawa, p 7. https://www.sejm.gov.pl/Sejm7.nsf/opinieBAS.xsp?nr=2064. Accessed 1 June 2022

Warciński M (2014b) Opinia prawna na temat projektu ustawy o rzeczach znalezionych oraz zmianie niektórych innych ustaw. Zeszyty Prawnicze 1(41):313–323

Zachariasiewicz MA (2010) O potrzebie wskazania w nowej ustawie o prawie prywatnym międzynarodowym podstawy stosowania przepisów wymuszających swoje zastosowanie. Problemy Prawa Prywatnego Międzynarodowego 7:9–43

Zachariasiewicz MA (2018) Art. 10 [Commentary]. In: Pazdan M (ed) Prawo prywatne międzynarodowe. Komentarz. C.H. Beck, Warszawa. accessed in Legalis

Zalasińska K (2010) Prawna ochrona zabytków nieruchomych w Polsce. Wolters Kluwer Polska, Warszawa

Zalasińska K (2013) Muzea publiczne. Studium administracyjnoprawne. LexisNexis Polska, Warszawa

Zeidler K (2007) Prawo ochrony dziedzictwa kultury. Wolters Kluwer Polska, Warszawa

Zeidler K (2011) Restytucja dóbr kultury ze stanowiska filozofii prawa. O trudnych przypadkach na granicy kultury i prawa. Wolters Kluwer Polska, Warszawa

Zeidler K (ed) (2014) Prawo ochrony zabytków. Wolters Kluwer, Wydawnictwo Uniwersytetu Gdańskiego, Warszawa–Gdańsk

Zeidler K (2015) Krajowy wykaz zabytków skradzionych lub wywiezionych za granicę niezgodnie z prawem oraz Krajowy rejestr utraconych dóbr kultury. In: Zalasińska K, Zeidler K (eds) Wykład prawa ochrony zabytków. Wolters Kluwer Polska, Wydawnictwo Uniwersytetu Gdańskiego, Gdańsk–Warszawa, pp 170–172

Zeidler K, Trzciński M (2009) Wykład prawa dla archeologów. Wolters Kluwer Polska, Warszawa

Zieliński JM (2019) Art. 423 [Commentary]. In: Izdebski H, Zieliński JM (eds) Prawo o szkolnictwie wyższym i nauce. Komentarz. Lex, Warszawa

Chapter 6
Cultural Heritage Protection in Private Law: In Search of New Solutions

6.1 Shared Responsibility for Cultural Heritage

Shared responsibility for cultural heritage is a response to the inability to place the right to property at the heart of the right to cultural heritage. The aim is to present how this notion is recognized in the chosen international acts as a derivative of common heritage notion. It is probable that shared responsibility and its potential could enrich the ongoing debate on cultural heritage. The link with cultural heritage is not always based on property rights and the bond to heritage at large is more spiritual than derived from the legal title.[1] Moreover, in the case of indigenous peoples, we may discuss the notion of collective ownership, which is not only anchored in the right of ownership, but also in the in right to manage goods, and is an integral part of the right to self-determination. Indigenous peoples' claims related to property and land are fundamental, and their fulfilment is meant to enable the physical, cultural, and spiritual survival of these peoples.[2] The holistic nature of indigenous peoples' culture[3] includes tangible cultural heritage, intangible cultural heritage, intellectual property, and land alongside its natural resources. All these components constitute an ecosystem that allows for the functioning and development of indigenous peoples' culture. The holistic approach to indigenous peoples' rights encompassing self-determination, land rights[4] and culture[5] makes it difficult to fit the relationship with cultural heritage solely into the framework of property rights.

In addition, some cultural heritage components as presented in Chap. 3 (space heritage, human remains) cannot be the subject of property rights. This does not

[1] Hodder (2010), p. 870.

[2] Wiessner (2014), p. 177.

[3] Vrdoljak (2014), p. 158.

[4] For instance native title in the Native Title Act 1993. Title was recognized in the case Mabo and others v Queensland (Mabo and others v Queensland (No 2) (1992)).

[5] Wiessner (2010), p. 288 "living within one's roots."

A. Jagielska-Burduk, *Cultural Heritage as a Legal Hybrid*,
https://doi.org/10.1007/978-3-031-04946-0_6

diminish their importance or justify a lack of protection. The contribution of intellectual property rights to the protection of cultural heritage can be considered in yet another way. In cases where the right to heritage is weak, does not exist or is difficult to enforce, intellectual property can serve as a tool to help communities, including indigenous peoples.[6] On the other hand, there are goods that do not fall under ownership, but still are or should be protected. Fiona Macmillan discusses the privatization of rights to heritage, including traditional heritage belonging to communities, and posits whether such a direction is in fact beneficial for heritage conservation in general. Moreover, the relationship between heritage commons and typical property rights is difficult to disentangle[7] and to this extent, the experiences of indigenous peoples showing a successful balance between individual and community rights may be helpful.[8]

It is easier to justify the protection of a given property by referring to a shared responsibility rather than the common heritage or shared ownership argument. Undoubtedly, the common heritage concept, followed by the development of new international legal instruments imposing obligations for States Parties to the cultural conventions to create protection mechanisms, have led to the emergence of shared responsibility as an effective approach. The growth of international law, at least within the law of the sea and the right to common spaces, has been stimulated by the human rights approach and contributed to the evolution of common heritage.[9] In the case of the law of the sea, however, it was easier to create a mechanism for interaction because of the type of resource where the shared responsibility could be implemented. However, within this resource a distinction is made between territorial seas depending on the relationship and proximity of the national territory, to some extent similar to the case with cultural heritage and existing stratification into national, European, world, etc. levels.

---

[6] Macmillan (2020), p. 49.

[7] Macmillan (2020), pp. 53–54.

[8] It seems that the discussion around indigenous peoples can also feed into, or support, the discussion of cultural heritage claimants from a global and national perspective. Prof. Mark McMillan at the "UTS Big Thinking Forum. Competing Sovereignties" used a very vivid example showing the relationship between Aboriginal communities and Australians. He compared 70,000 years of existence of Aboriginal tribes to 7 m, and 350 years since the settlement of the continent by the first arrivals from Europe to 3.5 cm. In this way he demonstrated the strength of the culture and organization of Aboriginal communities and the short-lived nature of the new inhabitants. Speaking of a shared, or rather a shared future, he emphasized that Aboriginal communities can answer many questions, share their knowledge, experience, and support the development of non-Aboriginal communities. The relatively short history of the movement for the protection of the rights of Aboriginal communities, as well as other groups of indigenous peoples, and the difficult process of rebuilding cultural identity mean that in the scale of world heritage, the culture of indigenous and native peoples can be a map for researchers of cultural heritage with marked fragments that should be avoided, and to which special attention should be paid. A statement by Professor Mark MacMillan at the UTS Big Thinking Forum. Competing Sovereignties on 17 January 2018, as part of the Sydney Festival 6–28 January 2018.

[9] Mazzeschi (2014), p. 100.

As provided in Article 136 of the United Nations Convention on the Law of the Sea, "the Area and its resources are the common heritage of mankind."[10] Article 137 of the Convention, which defines the status of the Area and its resources, indicates that "*(a)ll rights in the resources of the Area vest in mankind as a whole.*" The Authority acts on their behalf. These resources are defined as inalienable, although minerals, which may be disposed under certain conditions and in accordance with the rules set out by the Authority, have a different status. This is found in Article 140 of the Convention, which refers to the use and activities in the Area being "*carried out for the benefit of mankind as a whole.*" As provided in Article 149 of the Convention,

> (a)ll objects of an archaeological and historical nature found in the Area shall be preserved or disposed of for the benefit of mankind as a whole, particular regard being paid to the preferential rights of the State or country of origin, or the State of cultural origin, or the State of historical and archaeological origin.[11]

This regulation was analyzed during works on the UNESCO Underwater Heritage Convention and was considered incomplete with regard to its scope, resulting only in a regulation covering the Area and the contiguous zone within the very scope of the subject of protection.[12] Therefore, the objective of the UNESCO Convention was to create protection mechanisms for underwater cultural heritage, thus supplementing the existing regulation.

However, a certain similarity can be found in the relationship between resources and the states where they are located. While the coastal zone or internal seas are under the partial or total influence of states, respectively, the rest constitute waters beyond the jurisdiction of states. Examining cultural heritage from this angle, one can see a similarity in links existing between cultural heritage associated with a state and those that are not a part of the Area. Regarding the management of UNESCO World Heritage sites, one may notice some similarity to the management of the Area, with the difference that, in the case of cultural heritage, this is performed by various entities related to the state where a given place inscribed on the UNESCO World Heritage List is located.[13] Concerning historical and archaeological heritage located in the territory of the Area, they are also intended to serve humankind, although the Convention stresses the preferential rights of the state or country of their origin.

From the outset, archaeologists have viewed archaeological cultural heritage as a common good belonging to all mankind. The concept of common heritage has been analyzed in the literature in terms of the expressions used in international law conventions and documents issued by international organizations. In particular, the

---

[10] United Nations Convention on the Law of the Sea Montego Bay, 10 December 1982, 1833 U.N.T.S. 397.

[11] See about the directive incorporated in Kowalski (2014), p. 315.

[12] Convention on the Protection of the Underwater Cultural Heritage 2001. In: O'Keefe and Prott (2011), p. 131.

[13] Although there are no uniform mechanisms, there are good practices regarding site's management.

feature of commonality has been considered, if it concerns communities or individual entities. Another question refers to the value and diversity of resources; whether only globally exceptional objects should be considered as heritage or whether another definition could be applied. An emphasis on the link between cultural heritage and humanity appears in most cultural conventions. The perspective of humankind heritage is present in both preambles and conventions' texts. However, it does not create a separate legal construction, but a certain confirmation of the resource's global importance. In fact, it can be considered that the humankind dimension of heritage is a permanent part of the global discourse on cultural heritage's future and protection. Due to its great rhetorical significance, it appears in speeches, acts issued by the European Union or international organizations[14] or documents related to the international community's response to threats affecting cultural heritage.

In the preamble to the Hague Convention for the Protection of Cultural Property in the Event of Armed Conflict,[15] reference is made to the cultural heritage of all mankind and it is stated that "*damage to the cultural heritage of all mankind, since each people makes its contribution to the culture of the world.*" Although the phrase "cultural heritage of mankind" does not appear in the rest of the Convention, this concept is key to the interpretation of the convention's provisions.[16] Cultural property objects demonstrating value described as having "*great importance to the cultural heritage of every people*" are protected under the Convention. Article 4 sets out the scope of obligations to respect cultural property located within the territory of the state or within the territory of the other contracting party by

> refraining from using such property and its immediate surroundings and the means designed to protect it for purposes which might expose it to destruction or damage in the event of armed conflict, and by refraining from all hostile acts against it.

On the other hand, the Convention provides the possibility of conferring special protection on cultural property (Article 8). However, granting special protection does not exclude the possibility that certain objects, either because of their location or their use, might not be covered by it.

In the UNESCO conventions, references to common heritage appear quite often. Nonetheless, this does not mean that the same perspective of common cultural heritage is identical each time. The phrases used in the recommendations and declarations differ. Roger O'Keefe draws attention to the existing inconsistency in the relevant terminology.[17] The concept of world heritage in the UNESCO World

---

[14] References to common resources and common good in the Communication from the Commission to the European Parliament, the Council, the European Economic and Social Committee and the Committee of the Regions Towards an integrated approach to cultural heritage for Europe. Brussels 22.7.2014. COM/2014/0477 final.

[15] Convention for the Protection of Cultural Property in the Event of Armed Conflict. The Hague, 14 May 1954.

[16] O'Keefe (1999), pp. 37–40.

[17] O'Keefe (1999), p. 39.

Heritage Convention on the Protection of the World Cultural and Natural Heritage is anchored in its value for all humankind. In the preamble, reference is made to the unprecedented global significance of certain assets by indicating that

> the cultural or natural heritage are of outstanding interest and therefore need to be preserved as part of the world heritage of mankind as a whole.[18]

The international protection regime outlined in the Convention mentions sites of outstanding universal value—i.e., sites selected under the procedure set out in the Convention—however, it does not mean that property that has not been inscribed cannot demonstrate outstanding universal value (Article 12).

The Convention on the Protection of the Underwater Archaeological Heritage, in my opinion, comes closest to the common cultural heritage in a dimension similar to that of the Area. The preamble of the Convention clearly situates underwater heritage as an element and integral part of the cultural heritage of humanity. Furthermore, underwater heritage, seen as "*constituting traces of human existence of a cultural, historical or archaeological nature*" (Article 1) rises to become "*a particularly important element in the history of peoples, nations, and their relations with each other concerning their common heritage.*"[19] The history of cooperation between states, trade or conflict have an undeniable influence on the development of a protection model. The debates on treasure hunting and the "hunt" for underwater riches triggered the need to regulate those issues at the international level. In consequence, a platform for cooperation has been created, enabling cooperation between states as jointly responsible for this unique part of heritage. The Convention refers to models of protection provided by states separately or together and creates a unique regime for archaeological heritage in this Area. For instance, under Article 2 (7) of the Convention, underwater cultural heritage shall not be commercially exploited.

At the EU level, an explicit reference to common cultural heritage is found in Article 167(1) TFEU on cooperation between Member States in the field of culture. The concept of common heritage appears alongside respect for cultural diversity in regional and national dimensions. Consequently, cultures are meant to flourish through mutual understanding and respect for diversity and the richness of the Member States' cultural mosaic. In these activities, the EU undertakes to emphasize the importance of "common cultural heritage." However, among the activities of the Member States that are to be supported and supplemented by the EU, the conservation and safeguarding of cultural heritage of European significance is mentioned in Article 167(2) TFEU. This focus on EU heritage is also reflected in the regulations on the export and import of cultural goods outside the EU. Article 36 TFEU departs from the concept of common cultural heritage. Yet, it can perhaps be perceived as an element allowing for the reinforcement of cultural identity and connection of a

---

[18] Preamble to the Convention Concerning the Protection of the World Cultural and Natural Heritage.

[19] Preamble to the Convention on the Protection of the Underwater Cultural Heritage.

regional or national community with a given good. Restrictions on imports and exports confirm an awareness of the phrase "cultures" used in Article 167 (1) TFEU to emphasize their multiplicity. The reference to national treasures possessing artistic, historical, or archaeological value and their protection justifies prohibitions or restrictions on imports and exports of goods and proves their unique value because of their exceptional link with the Member State concerned.

Sometimes the destruction of an important component of cultural heritage can trigger international action. As far as the integrity of the relevant heritage and its security is concerned, these actions result in building a sense of common responsibility for heritage and raising awareness. The proceedings are also aimed at deterring potential perpetrators of similar destructive acts in the future. Threats to heritage on a global scale due to acts of intentional destruction of historic sites are changing the common cultural heritage approach. The range of war crime proceedings held by the International Criminal Court since 2014 has expanded to include cases of deliberate destruction of cultural heritage. The milestone case concerned Ahmad Al Faqi Al Mahdi,[20] where the perpetrator was accused of destroying nine mausoleums and a historic mosque in Timbuktu.[21] The destruction concerned specific religious sites whose outstanding universal value was confirmed through their inscription on the UNESCO World Heritage List.[22] Under Article 8(2) (b) of the Rome Statute of the International Criminal Court,[23] among the activities considered war crimes under para. (ix), the following are included:

> intentionally directing attacks against buildings dedicated to religion, education, art, science or charitable purposes, historic monuments, hospitals and places where the sick and wounded are collected, provided they are not military objectives.

In *The Prosecutor v. Ahmad Al Faqi Al Mahdi,*[24] a symbolic compensation of 1 Euro was awarded to UNESCO and Mali. It was seen as extremely important from the perspective of heritage holders.[25] This was intended to identify UNESCO as an entity representing the interests of the international community entitled to cultural heritage and benefiting from its protection.[26] It was highlighted that the way in which this symbolic compensation was handed over, apart from acknowledging the losses and suffering of the community, was conceived as a ceremony of forgiveness and remembrance. In this context, a certain idea of common heritage appears, but

[20] The Prosecutor v. Ahmad Al Faqi Al Mahdi, ICC-01/12-01/15.

[21] Wierczyńska and Jakubowski (2017), pp. 695–721.

[22] 12COM XIVA—Inscription: Timbuktu (Mali).

[23] Rome Statute of the International Criminal Court done in Rome on 17 July 1998, United Nations, Treaty Series, vol. 2187, no. 38544.

[24] The Prosecutor v. Al Hassan Ag Abdoul Aziz Ag Mohamed Ah Mahmoud, ICC-01/12-01/18-35-Red2-tENG.

[25] Cf. Meskell (2018), pp. 212–213.

[26] Situation in the Republic of Mali in the Case of the Prosecutor v. Ahmad al Faqi al Mahdi, Public Reparations Order, 17 Aug 2017, par. 90. https://www.icc-cpi.int/CourtRecords/CR2017_05117.PDF. Accessed 1 June 2022.

seen from the side of the international community. In addition, it cannot be overlooked that at the time of the judgment, the structures destroyed in Timbuktu had been rebuilt, at a cost of €2.7 million from funds provided by UNESCO and other entities. Although the jurisdiction of the International Criminal Court is limited, the case has been widely noted, as it represents a new shift in the debate on shared responsibility for cultural heritage and actions taken at the international level. This case also demonstrates a focus on the community and the values attributed to heritage sites, as pointed out by Lucas Lixinski.[27]

An important novelty at the level of proceedings before the International Criminal Court is the inclusion of elements relating to movable cultural heritage in the arrest warrant in the *The Prosecutor v. Al Hassan Ag Abdoul Aziz Ag Mohamed Ag Mahmoud.*[28] The act lists the destruction of valuable manuscripts and sculptures, issues that go beyond those mentioned in Article 8(2) of the Statute. Although it is clear that the proceedings and subsequent verdict will not address this part of the accused's crimes, the fact that this loss and destruction relating to movable cultural heritage is included can be seen as a sign of change, or even a broadening of the perception of war crimes by highlighting the destruction of movable cultural property.

An important manifestation of shared responsibility is the idea of safe havens[29] and the protection of the cultural heritage of refugees. ICOM's *International Observatory on Illicit Traffic in Cultural Goods*[30] platform and the EU CULTNET[31] cooperation can be posited as examples of the international community's cooperation in the fight against the illicit traffic of cultural goods. In this case, the notion of shared responsibility for cultural heritage is visible as well. This approach makes it possible to recreate a shared responsibility and, consequently, jointly cover costs and implement preventive and rescue measures.

The ALIPH Foundation[32] based in Geneva is a good example of cooperation between states, experts, and private entities. The foundation was established in 2017 and operates under Swiss law. Its mission is to financially and substantively support projects related to heritage preservation. The first project in which the foundation was involved concerned its support for the Mosul Museum in Iraq. The foundation's mission statement is "*to keep heritage sites around the world safe in conflict or post conflict regions.*" Through a wide range of activities, including the implementation of preventive, emergency and post-conflict projects, the foundation is another

[27] Lixinski (2019a), pp. 593–594.

[28] *The Prosecutor v. Al Hassan Ag Abdoul Aziz Ag Mohamed Ag Mahmoud.* ICC-01/12-01/18.

[29] Lasik (2018).

[30] https://www.obs-traffic.museum/. Accessed 1 June 2022.

[31] Draft Council Resolution on the creation of an informal network of law enforcement authorities and expertise competent in the field of cultural goods (EU CULTNET). Brussels, 4 October 2012. http://register.consilium.europa.eu/doc/srv?l=EN&f=ST%2014232%202012%20INIT. Accessed 1 June 2022.

[32] https://www.aliph-foundation.org/en. Accessed 1 June 2022.

example of a shared responsibility formula with a strong contribution by private actors.

It is much more difficult to embrace the common ownership of cities or cultural heritage sites. It is even more complicated to determine the rules to exercise this property right. An acceptable solution intended only for individual assets[33] is more likely than implementation of a broad common cultural heritage concept. It is perhaps safe to say that the idea of common heritage is an inseparable part of the common/shared responsibility for this heritage. The Communication from the Commission to the European Parliament, the Council, the European Economic and Social Committee and the Committee of the Regions Towards an integrated approach to cultural heritage for Europe[34] touches directly upon this type of shared responsibility. It indicates that "*(c)ultural heritage is a shared resource, and a common good*" and thus "*(l)ooking after our heritage is, therefore, our common responsibility.*"[35] This obligation, which stems from a responsibility for both geographically close and distant cultural heritage components, cannot be fulfilled without targeted educational campaigns and reinforcement of international cooperation. Building awareness finally leads to the acceptance of the common interest in cultural heritage preservation, and stimulates future effective actions.

The very concept of shared responsibility is burdened with several risks. First, it derives from issues connected with establishing the scope of responsibilities. Going further, the amount of funds that should be allocated for works on threatened or destroyed cultural heritage depends on scope, and further influences implementation. A similar problem arises from fund allocation when the good is not threatened, but still requires some measures to be taken. Another risk concerns problems that come from the management and use of certain heritage components. This is most noticeable in conservation and reconstruction, which as a complex process includes both the tangible and intangible dimensions, together with ongoing processes in the community.[36] The World Heritage List shows this twofold situation as well. It foresees the inclusion in the international protection regime together with the prestige. On the other hand, it may put a target on this heritage. Moreover, the focus on heritage protection in certain regions is seen as disproportionate with regard to the assistance provided to the population.[37]

In *Playing darts with a Rembrandt*, J. L. Sax introduced the idea of a game causing damage where the target is a valuable painting, thus challenging the property

---

[33] See *Spitzenobjekte* Jagielska-Burduk (2011), p. 300.

[34] Communication from the Commission to the European Parliament, the Council, the European Economic and Social Committee and the Committee of the Regions Towards an integrated approach to cultural heritage for Europe. Brussels 22.7.2014. COM/2014/0477 final.

[35] Communication from the Commission to the European Parliament, the Council, the European Economic and Social Committee and the Committee of the Regions Towards an integrated approach to cultural heritage for Europe. Brussels 22.7.2014. COM/2014/0477 final, par. 1.1, p. 2.

[36] Meskell (2018), pp. 191–192.

[37] Meskell (2018), p. 192.

rights to cultural property.[38] In *A Future in Ruins. UNESCO, World Heritage, and the Dream of Peace,* Lynn Meskell attempts to show that World Heritage Sites are similar targets. A similar phenomenon can be seen in relation to movable cultural components. In international discussions concerning whether to return an object located in a museum as a result of colonization, this particular argument is often raised. It is based on the fact that the country from which the object was taken will not guarantee proper protection and conservation. In this way, the movable cultural object is seen as "better" and "held in custody." Therefore, it is presented as not fitting into its original whereabouts and requiring security that cannot be provided in its place of origin. The natural question comes up—Whose responsibility and how should it be shared? This supplements the famous question *Whose heritage*? and keeps the debate open.

The core of shared responsibility resembles stewardship.[39] The trust doctrine was invoked many times in terms of cultural heritage management. Fiduciary assets could be combined with shared responsibility when it comes to the management of cultural resources. It would bypass the problem connected with the transition of property rights. It is, however, impossible to separate cultural heritage from elements of identity, nation, and community. All this influences the recognition of common heritage. In the case of common heritage and the subject of rights, it is impossible to accept a claim based solely on property rights.[40] The process of searching for a new right to heritage is a complex one. For instance, a World Heritage Site is both a part of global heritage and constitutes an essential element of a certain local community. It seems necessary to refer to the divided ownership to apply existing legal institutions from property law. For example, the owner and the superficiary have rights to the same property. The owner (*dominium directum*) can be treated as society at large. This enables one to think of heritage as a national good, or humankind's, if we treat it in terms of the good of all humanity. The utilitarian owner (*dominium utile*), on the other hand, will remain the disposer of the good at all times. To some extent, this relationship reflects the current arrangement and treatment of cultural heritage as a national good and the cultural heritage component's holder.

The concept of shared responsibility for cultural heritage should be implemented by considering the heritage surrounding and the community closest to it and, in the case of claims for movable objects, taking into account its origin. Heritage management mechanisms in national and international law should be used for this purpose. Preservation actions should take place parallel to contribution to other goals set out in the 2030 Agenda for Sustainable Development. There, a balance and care for values should be intact. At the same time, private law support should consist of defining the status of assets in the legal system and strengthening the argument for the importance of these assets. Since cultural heritage is subject to protection regardless of property rights, and is considered as part of world or national heritage,

[38] Sax (1999).

[39] Carpenter et al. (2009), pp. 1022, 1048, 1028–1029.

[40] Macmillan (2013), pp. 363–364.

perhaps leaving heritage outside the category of things is a natural consequence of strengthening the regime of its protection at the national and international levels.

6.2 Private Property in Cultural Heritage Protection

The importance of private law in cultural heritage protection mechanisms and the private sector's participation and its initiatives are important parts of the debate on the future of cultural heritage. This section aims to show the place of the private sector and, in particular, private ownership in the protection of cultural heritage. Over the years, the participation of private actors in the preservation of cultural heritage has evolved. It demonstrates responsibility towards future generations and confirms a new obligation arising from the principle of shared responsibility for cultural heritage.

By creating an organizational and legal framework for organizing cultural protection, financially supporting cultural heritage conservation, and preparing inventories, states fulfil two important obligations. On the one hand, it allows states to participate in the protection of their heritage legacy and, on the other hand, it enables them to access heritage for individuals and communities. In many national legal regulations, private holders must allow access to cultural heritage, as it is one of the conditions for receiving financial support for conservations works.

The involvement of private property and private owners are integral parts of the history of cultural heritage protection. The principle of *noblesse oblige*[41] was followed by the founders of the first Polish museum, Świątynia Sybilli [Sybilla Temple] in Puławy,[42] as indicated in documents regarding fideicomisum, e.g., the Gołuchów entail[43] or the Sieniawa entail. The latter included the most famous Polish painting available to public in Cracow, Dama z gronostajem [Lady with an Ermine], and the most valuable Polish war loss, Młodzieniec Rafaela [Raphael's Young Man]. Using the foreign example of Stonehenge, the most distinctive cultural heritage site in Great Britain, it must be stated that until 1918 it was still the property of a private individual. The problem of securing and enclosing the site due to the threat of destruction was debated in terms of access to the site.[44] Eventually the site was transferred to the state with several conditions, including that the site be open to the public. The last private owner, Cecil Chubb, repeatedly stressed the importance of free access for local residents to the site.[45]

---

[41] Sax (2005), p. 1130.

[42] Zalasińska (2013), p. 24.

[43] Projekt Ordynacji Gołuchowskiej, Proponowany dokument erekcyjny, manuscript 845, 18–36, Polish Library in Paris. See more Jagielska-Burduk (2016b), pp. 238–253.

[44] English (2002), p. 6.

[45] Chippindale (2012), p. 176.

Access to cultural heritage is implemented through various instruments. There are many mechanisms, including those based on cooperation between private and public entities, which can improve cooperation. The model of cooperation between collectors and museums or respect for the will of private donors have been discussed very often.[46] The history of collecting points to many negative examples.[47] The access to cultural heritage in its tangible and intangible dimensions, or to cultural heritage subject to public or private ownership, plays a significant role in the search for a new status for cultural heritage.

Nowadays, to enable access to cultural heritage in the United States, exhibitions are organized during the summer months, during which objects from private collections are displayed.[48] On the other hand, private palaces in Rome are opened to a wider audience as part of their cooperation with *Turismo Culturale Italiano* and the *Palazzi di Roma a Porte Aperte* project, with its first edition taking place in 2012.[49] This is favored by the Italian law for the protection of historical monuments, more specifically by Article 38 of the Code of Cultural Monuments and Landscapes of the Italian Republic (Codice dei beni culturali e del paesaggio).[50] Under the Article cited, full or partial participation of the state in the costs of conservation or restoration is connected with ensuring public access to cultural assets. The arrangements shall be inserted in contracts or agreements between the Ministry and the owners.[51] This obligation of enabling access has a temporary nature and depends on the type of work carried out, together with the artistic and historical value of the property and existing goods. The fact that contracts and agreements are delegated to the municipality and the metropolitan city on whose territory the properties are located makes it possible to implement "Open Gateway to Heritage" programs similar to *Palazzi di Roma a Porte Aperte.*

In the post-COVID-19 era, it seems that while maintaining the sanitary regime and restrictions related to the access to certain places or objects, a new proposal may be addressed to private owners. Perhaps one should consider providing online walks, tours, short lectures, and posting digitized works on the Internet by the owners if supported by the state. So far, the activities undertaken by museums and other institutions engaged in cultural activities could serve as a model. We can imagine a situation in which the owner of a private monument accepts a grant and one of its

[46] History of Feliks Mangha Jasieński collection in: Sztuka jest ryzykiem dla inwestora i dla artysty, Z profesorem Krzysztofem Pomianem rozmawia Janusz Miliszkiewicz, *SAACLR* (2015) 1(1), p. 44.

[47] Cf. Jagielska-Burduk and Markowski (2011) and examples: Charitable Fund of Sir Denis Mahon, collection of Helga and Walter Lauff given in the document UNIDROIT, item No. 13 on the agenda: Draft Triennial Work Programme 2017–2019. Comments and suggestions received by the Secretariat, p. 5.

[48] Szafrański (2012).

[49] http://www.turismoculturale.org/. Accessed 1 June 2022.

[50] Kodeks dóbr kultury i krajobrazu Republiki Włoskiej. Introduction and translation A. Moś. Wydawnictwo Uniwersytetu Gdańskiego, Gdańsk–Sopot 2017.

[51] A similar model is used in Poland when it comes to the support from local government and from the ministry.

conditions is to prepare educational or awareness-building materials available online. It will certainly involve additional costs and the need to cooperate with experts, but undoubtedly, it may also help in gathering information about the works carried out and co-financed with public funds. It seems that it would be a good idea to create an online platform coordinated by one of the national cultural institutions—in Poland I would suggest the National Heritage Institute. All the materials would be published on the platform, which would make it much easier for the public to browse content.

Regarding ownership, it should be emphasized that private property is subject to special protection, and in the case of cultural heritage is further subjected to a unique test, the outcome of which is pivotal for future generations. Determining the costs covered by the owner and the acceptance of those costs, ultimately balancing between public interest and private interests, are particularly visible in exercising ownership rights to monuments/cultural heritage. The treatment of private entities as custodians of heritage, and at the same time the lack of elements balancing the additional burden of costs, makes it legitimate to assume that the components of cultural heritage, due to its incorporated values, are not typical examples of things within the meaning of Civil Code.

So far, the Polish Constitutional Court[52] and European Court of Human Rights have dealt with issues related to cultural heritage ownership, and more specifically the protection of private property owners.[53] As presented before only in one examined case, the Constitutional Tribunal has found an infringement of constitutional norms regarding the lack of co-financing mechanism. The judgment of the ECHR in *Potomski and Potomski v. Poland* draws attention to the need to provide protective mechanisms not only for cultural heritage, but also for private actors that decide to withdraw from monument management and ownership. If an individual is entitled to access cultural heritage, and become its holder, they should also have the right to reject this right. It is important, especially if exercising property rights, given the limitations connected with cultural heritage protection, as it results in financial and organizational burdens that cannot be removed.

Bearing in mind the different pace of national laws, their evolution, and ongoing changes, it is possible to determine what stage of legal development we are currently at. The question of whether cultural heritage ownership withstands the pressures of time and decision-makers and whether the scope of obligations imposed on the private owner arises in this context. It will not be referred to as a "*disgrace* of constitutional guarantees" but will remain as a form of provocation (*Una discgrazia*

[52] Polish Constitutional Tribunal, Judgement of 8 October 2007 (ref. no. K 20/07, OTK-A 2007/9/102); *Judgment of the Constitutional Tribunal* of 25 May 2016 (ref. no. Kp 2/15, OTK ZU no. A/2016, item 23).

[53] European Court of Human Rights, Judgment of 29 March 2011 in Potomska and Potomski v. Poland 33949/05, LEX No. 784737; European Court of Human Rights, Judgment of 4 November 2014 in Potomska and Potomski v. Poland, 33949/05.

costituzionalmente garantita).[54] There, policy makers are reluctant to introduce changes that may result in overburdening the owner. Additionally, in the search for new solutions, we can move within constitutionally possible mechanisms. However, a proposal for a new legal instrument or a standard-setting instrument can offer a new approach and ultimately spur changes in national legislations.

In the face of threats to cultural heritage, the role and involvement of private actors increases. A good example of this contribution is private collections that formed a core of the existing public collections.[55] There is no doubt that, in the long term, private collections become public. This public feature is not only connected with exhibitions, but also in terms of their ownership status through donations or wills.[56] I wish to point out that this is a gradual shift of cultural heritage resources to public resources.[57] In part, this ensures a greater guarantee of their preservation, but it should not be a temptation for policymakers to take steps to accelerate this long-term process.[58] An acceptable reason might be that the collection is endangered. Each time, however, the issue should be considered on a case-by-case basis, especially since the clear shift towards the inclusion of private actors is highly likely to continue in the future.

Private owners make numerous attempts to protect their collections or individual objects. An owner may not only ensure security through actual actions, i.e., through conservation work, making inventories, and commissioning scientific work, but also through an appropriate choice of legal institutions "in which to dress his collection." It is not a secret that the most prominent collectors analyze the management models of their collections for tax, inheritance, and market purposes. Similarly, but to a lesser extent, owners of historic properties, especially those used commercially for tourism, make similar decisions. Although these solutions result from the adopted resource management model, they can be considered private law forms of protection used on the owner's initiative. These forms of management do not only implement protection. Among the available mechanisms, one can distinguish legal institutions whose role in managing cultural heritage has been significant for years. For instance, within the scope of possibilities allowed by law, the owner may establish a foundation, an association, a museum, or a commercial company.

One can analyze cultural heritage as related to safeguarding assets and planning and resource management. This approach leads to cultural heritage commodification and treating it as an investment asset whose integrity, provenance, or legality (collections) is an essential element of the owner's plans and strategies. On the other hand, regardless of motives, the search for favorable regulations fulfilling the

[54] The expression used in the title of the article by Pontiroli (2014), p. 97 and borrowed from a formulation by Merusi (1975), p. 434.

[55] Jagielska and Szafrański (2008).

[56] Cf. on inheritance of collections: Dembska (2007).

[57] Jagielska-Burduk (2016e), pp. 94–96.

[58] For example, the institution state's pre-emptive right in case of permanent export of an object abroad and the existence of a special fund to manage the funds allocated for this purpose.

owner's intention is standard in the case of other goods. However, we should not overlook that in the case of cultural property, the interest in securing the objects by the owner, in using this asset for individual purposes, will not always be in line with the interest in its protection and passing it on to future generations. Similarly, intangible heritage and its popularization is often linked to a commercial goal, with problems arising as to who should benefit from commercial activities. The Guidelines to the Intangible Cultural Heritage Convention[59] point to the commercial activities associated with this heritage. It is considered in terms of the individual development and strengthening of regional markets.[60] In addition, the importance of this activity for raising awareness of this heritage is emphasized and attention is drawn to the risk of abuse and to ensure that commercial exploitation does not interfere with the meaning and purpose of intangible cultural heritage for the community. Responsible cultural heritage commoditization can constitute an element of social and economic development strategies, and the cultural heritage itself is seen as a catalyst for development.

Public-private cooperation was the subject of the recommendation of the Parliamentary Assembly of the Council of Europe on the private management of cultural heritage.[61] In the recommendation, the state's role is to safeguard cultural heritage. However, the state is also expected to act as an initiator and the driving force for new models for cultural heritage development with the private actors' participation. The report on the recommendation sets out the private actors: private individuals, trusts, associations, foundations, churches, NGOs and companies.[62] In each country, there are specific rules related to how such entities function, but it is important to note their institutional diversity and their relationship with the state, which may be determined by specific regulations (e.g., the relationship between the state and the church, issues of financing religious heritage).

At the heart of the recommendation is the desire to define responsibility for cultural heritage with a clear reference to a "notion of common responsibility whether of Europe or of mankind, as well as the responsibility of the state."[63] The report indicates that young democracies from Central and Eastern Europe, for which public-private partnerships are a new phenomenon, will be particularly interested in

---

[59] Operational Directives for the implementation of the Convention for the Safeguarding of the Intangible Heritage, 8.GA (2020).

[60] Operational Directives for the implementation of the Convention for the Safeguarding of the Intangible Heritage, 8.GA (2020) Para 107 (l, m), Para 116.

[61] Recommendation Council of Europe Parliamentary Assembly 1730 (2005) The private management of cultural property adopted by the Parliamentary Assembly on 25 November 2005.

[62] Council of Europe Parliamentary Assembly, For debate in the Standing Committee, Doc. 10731, 24 October 2005, The private management of cultural property, Report Committee on Culture, Science and Education Rapporteur: Baroness Hooper, United Kingdom, European Democrat Group. http://assembly.coe.int/nw/xml/XRef/X2H-Xref-ViewHTML.asp?FileID=11062&lang=EN. Accessed 1 June 2022.

[63] Recommendation Council of Europe Parliamentary Assembly 1730 (2005) The private management of cultural property adopted by the Parliamentary Assembly on 25 November 2005, Par. 1.

this issue.[64] The main goal of the recommendation is to encourage states to involve private entities in managing cultural heritage and to move away from public party-dominated cultural policy. The text further deals with management, including the need to draw up guidelines on best practice for public-private partnerships and conduct an analysis of regulations.[65]

It should be noted that at the international level, trusts, waqf and foundations are being considered in the context of cultural property.[66] The importance of cultural heritage management remaining in private hands and the problems with collections' legal regulation become noticeable at the international level. In the Recommendation for the Protection of Movable Cultural Property of 1978, the protection of movable cultural property belonging to private entities or individuals is as important as those belonging to the state and "all this property constitutes an important element of the cultural heritage of the nations concerned."[67] A separate paragraph of the Recommendation is devoted to private collections (Para 14). According to the Recommendation, states should ensure the protection of private collections by taking measures in line with their respective national laws and constitutional systems. Among the mechanisms to be considered are inventories of collections, granting access for curators and technicians to advise owners and study collections and setting up an institution advising on security measures and other services.[68] The Recommendation mentions the incentives for the objects' conservation or fiscal benefits for those planning a bequeathment or donation to museums and similar institutions. The latter is still underdeveloped in many countries, although it is clear that many countries use this property to stimulate and wisely manage the changes in the cultural sector. Unfortunately, Poland is only at the beginning of this road when it comes to targeted tax and fiscal incentives. The practice of creating a foundation that is in close cooperation with a museum and merges private and public collections in joint

[64] Council of Europe Parliamentary Assembly, For debate in the Standing Committee, Doc. 10731, 24 October 2005, The private management of cultural property, Report Committee on Culture, Science and Education Rapporteur: Baroness Hooper, United Kingdom, European Democrat Group. http://assembly.coe.int/nw/xml/XRef/X2H-Xref-ViewHTML.asp?FileID=11062&lang=EN. Accessed 1 June 2022.

[65] In Poland, a handbook for owners and users of historic monuments prepared by the National Heritage Institute may serve as an example of this task.

[66] "Private Collections: Historical and Legal Perspectives" in collaboration with the International Society for Research and Cultural Heritage (ISCHAL), Institut des sciences sociales du politique (ISP), BonelliErede law firm, Institut – Droit Ethique – Patrimoine (IDEP), Institut d'études de droit public (IEDP), Università degli Studi di Milano and Université des Etudes de Genève. 16–17 March 2017. Panel: table on institutional instruments (foundation, trust, waqf) Chaired by Véronique MAGNIER, professor at the Université Paris Saclay, director of the IDEP, Giovanna FORLANELLI ROVATI, vice-president of the Fondazione Luigi Rovati, Monza Jean-Claude GANDUR, president of the Fondation Gandur pour l'Art, Geneva. https://www.unidroit.org/english/news/2017/170316-private-collections/programme-e.pdf. Accessed 1 June 2022.

[67] UNESCO Recommendation for the Protection of Movable Cultural Property adopted on 28 November 1978 by the General Conference of UNESCO (para. 3).

[68] In Poland, this role is fulfilled by the National Institute of Museology and Collections Protection.

projects such as exhibitions, organizing donations and promotion projects is not yet popular.

The Recommendation on the Protection and Promotion of Museums and Collections, their Diversity and Role in Society adopted on 17 November 2015 by the General Conference of UNESCO, prepared in collaboration with ICOM, is another important document in recognizing the role of private collections.[69] Although it is mostly devoted to museums, it also refers to non-museum collections. Para. 5 of the Recommendation defines a collection as a set of natural and cultural, tangible and intangible, ancient and contemporary objects. It is added that each Member State should define for itself how it understands a collection within its own national regulation for the purposes of the Recommendation. The role of collections not held in museums is directly addressed in paragraph 32. They should be protected and promoted with a view to preserving their integrity to better represent the cultural diversity of the countries' heritage. To this end, states may cooperate in their conservation, research and promotion activities and providing access to these collections.[70] At the national regulatory level, states should consider appropriate legal, technical, and financial measures to prepare strategies and policies to implement the recommendations.

Another important moment for private art collections was UNIDROIT's tasks for 2017–2019 (continued 2020–2022), among which are studies on private collections, the issue of national regulation and the relationship between collectors and the state. The proposal was made in 2016 by the representative of Mexico.[71] There is no doubt that this initiative is in a sense naturally assigned to UNIDROIT, as in contrast to the UNESCO 1970 Convention, the UNIDROIT Convention confers on private entities the right to claim restitution. In this way the emphasis is shifted to the owner, including private ones. This indirectly confirms the exhaustion of the formula of the state as the exclusive guardian of cultural heritage and confirms a shift at the international level. At the same time, undertaking research in this area by UNIDROIT is a signal for national legislators that the problem of private collections goes beyond the level of national regulations and national cultural policy.

Although the private collections task was given a low priority,[72] its assignment to UNIDROIT allows us to assume that we may be dealing with the beginning of new work that will help develop a model for the functioning of private collections, one

[69] UNESCO Recommendation on the protection and promotion of museums and collections, their diversity and their role in society adopted on 17 November 2015 by the General Conference of UNESCO 2015.

[70] Original text: The collections defined in paragraph 5, when held in institutions that are not museums, should be protected and promoted to preserve the coherence and better represent the cultural diversity of those countries' heritage. Member States are invited to cooperate in the protection, research, and promotion of those collections, as well as in promoting access to them.

[71] Report of the UNIDROIT Governing Board meeting, 2016 95th session C.D. (95) 15, Rome, 18–20 May 2016, pp. 42–43.

[72] Report of the UNIDROIT Governing Board meeting, 2016 95th session C.D. (95) 15, Rome, 18–20 May 2016, p. 48.

that will cover not only the status of the collection, but also the implementation of its public functions. The so-called difficult cases reviewed previously have proven that the problem of private collections should not be ignored, and the participation of private collectors in the global art market makes private entities the guardians of cultural heritage of global significance. The need to offer activities aimed at raising "international collectors' awareness," particularly in countries where large collections of cultural goods are located, was mentioned earlier in 2010 during the 40th anniversary of the UNESCO 1970 Convention.[73]

The activity of private actors has also been raised in terms of threats to cultural heritage, and more precisely, illegal trading. Para. 23 and 24 of UN Security Council Resolution 2253 (2015) refer to cooperation with private sector actors in the field of verification of cultural property and checking databases in efforts to combat the financing of terrorism.[74] The involvement of private actors in activities related to cultural property is necessary, since funds from the illegal sale of cultural goods are believed to be the second largest source of funding for ISIL (Daesh).[75] Private participation is therefore not only present in peacetime, but when heritage is threatened and used for terrorist activities. Taking steps at the international level to include private actors, analyzing national solutions, and trying to develop model public-private relations are important elements in the development of cultural heritage protection law.

Attention should be paid to the participation of actors in the protection of cultural heritage considered at the level of international governance of cultural heritage and the inclusion of groups and individuals in this process.[76] However, this process is not exclusively beneficial. It may be burdened with risks; for instance, NGOs that are supposed to represent communities including indigenous peoples could abuse their position.[77] The presence of public and private actors in the field of tangible heritage preservation is necessary. In the case of intangible heritage, private entities play an additional role, acting as the depositaries of heritage. In the latter case, it is not possible to preserve and document this heritage without cooperation.

The involvement of private actors in the protection of heritage is independent of the property right. There are different stakeholders and interested parties that are not bound with heritage through property rights. However, the owner or holder of cultural property has many more obligations imposed by public and private law in comparison to property rights for regular goods. Cultural heritage law mirrors the current social situation and development of societies. Considering the role of private property shows the trend of sharing the costs of protection between the private and public sectors. The presence of private actors in the protection of heritage is not

---

[73] Prott (2011), p. 439.

[74] Security Council resolution 2253 (2015) of 17 December 2015.

[75] Statement by Omar Malhas, Jordan's Minister of Finance at the UN Security Council on 17 December 2015, https://www.un.org/press/en/2015/sc12168.doc.htm. Accessed 1 June 2022.

[76] This problem was presented in the monograph Lixinski (2019b).

[77] ILA Report.

equal globally, and in some countries, partnerships are still not sufficiently used in the field of culture.[78] Private ownership is an important element in the future of cultural heritage law. Ignoring private sector regulations can only harm cultural heritage in the long term. The existing tensions regarding additional obligations, reporting or permit obligations, which impose new limitations on the art market, will be present for years. Hence, new concepts should consider the valuable elements of cultural heritage, regardless of the owner's profile, and even assume that in this narrow scope the "knot" (link) based on property law and private actors' participation can form the strongest foundation for new legal constructions.

6.3 No "Res"? Dereification of Cultural Heritage: Future or Myth

The process of legal emancipation for cultural property is in progress, and is characterized by a new perception of certain goods. At the same time, new regimes and instruments of protection have appeared, which may be viewed as derivatives of that process or its supplements. Transposing the above onto cultural heritage, we can see that, it is not a typical good to which legal relationships apply in terms of regulation. In view of its characteristics, it forces parties in a legal relationship to behave in a certain way, which manifests in specific conduct regarding the acquisition of the object in question, the way permitted acts are typified in legislation, or even additional provisions for contracts. Furthermore, the welfare of cultural heritage, and in particular situations where it is in jeopardy, may increase the obligations of administrative authorities to take certain actions. It is this location of cultural heritage components outside the typical arrangement of civil law actors which, in view of the autonomy of contractual parties, may freely shape the contents of a legal relationship and illustrates this good's special nature. Similarly, to an object of a property law relationship, a cultural heritage component also stands out against the background of other goods. As a result, a good determines the entity-related right of the owner and not the other way around, and the desire to have a good at one's disposal without any restrictions or preserving its integrity may lead to incurring criminal liability.

The Polish legislature is undoubtedly still searching for ideas on how to shape a new cultural heritage regime, and to this end it has introduced changes to private law and initiated discussions regarding subsequent amendments. Introducing elements related to cultural objects and attempts aimed at strengthening the cultural heritage

[78] Council of Europe Parliamentary Assembly, For debate in the Standing Committee, Doc. 10731, 24 October 2005, The private management of cultural property, Report Committee on Culture, Science and Education Rapporteur: Baroness Hooper, United Kingdom, European Democrat Group. http://assembly.coe.int/nw/xml/XRef/X2H-Xref-ViewHTML.asp?FileID=11062&lang=EN. Accessed 1 June 2022.

protection regime in private law constitute an important stage in the search for the status of cultural goods in private law. Publicization of civil law or, as some researchers indicate, hybridization of the law, is conducive to a debate on cultural heritage. Likewise, a debate on the future of cultural heritage is also enhanced by the phenomenon of civil law fragmentation. Both these phenomena, in conjunction with the proven disintegration of the law of cultural heritage protection, allow one to conclude that a significant part of the discussion revolving around cultural heritage has been transposed onto the significance of civil law in its protection. This is an excellent opportunity to think about the essence of cultural heritage and to point out at least a few dispersed (and not always discerned) indications provided by the Polish legislature treating cultural heritage as a separate legal category.

Considering the introduction of dereification, the first thing that becomes apparent is the issue of the purpose that it is supposed to serve. A question that also arises is whether the new construct is actually needed and whether the assumed goal could not be achieved by means of other traditional methods. Each new, unique solution may face the allegation that the change is superficial and does not contribute much to legal practice in reality. On the other hand, dereification of cultural heritage may be treated as the manifestation of a legal revision of the systemization of tangible goods that has been used to date. In the case of cultural heritage protectors, it would be difficult to expect their spectacular participation in protests for heritage, as is the case with protests attended by animal rights activists. Similarly, however, disputes my arise between civilians and the rest of the world favoring the protection of the status quo.[79] Many things indicate that the ground for change has been systematically prepared, and the final decision will rest with the legislature and will depend on the success of the legislative process that has already been initiated. Within the scope presented in previous chapters, certain heritage components do not constitute objects under property law, so no interference on the part of the legislature is needed. What is needed in that respect is to organize the method of record-keeping for certain goods and mechanisms subjecting them to protection, since certain heritage components, including tangible ones, no longer fall within the category of objects. Moreover, archaeological artifacts in APGM require special attention and protection before their excavation, although they are not covered by the doctrine of possession and distinguished legally as yet. Dereification of cultural heritage may be considered similar to the case of animal rights solely with regard to a certain portion of cultural heritage collections. The development of the theory of law in respect of a legal entity's status, as well as related challenges, appear in the case of the debate on animals,[80] and they will certainly be also present in deliberations on cultural heritage. However, it is not determined whether this will be limited solely to movables or immovables. Experiences from abroad related to the special regulation of

[79] About animals in the Polish legal system Łętowska (1997), pp. 72–73.
[80] Pietrzykowski (2017), p. 4.

waters or forests,[81] although they are still treated as something unique, are very important supplements in the perception of new dimensions in cultural heritage.

In the case of cultural heritage, it is of vital importance to place emphasis on a good and its interests. As part of this altered perspective, which is undoubtedly visible in public law and provisions concerning cultural heritage protection, the search for a new perspective on cultural heritage in private law is supplementary. By this, I refer to the private law response to the anthropocentric definition of cultural heritage in the Faro convention,[82] which is said to be a manifestation of the new philosophy of protection.[83] In said convention, in Article 4(b) there is a reference to the obligation of individuals and society to protect heritage and responsibility for that heritage, which is in line with the framework of thinking about shared responsibility for heritage. Under Article 2 of the Convention, cultural heritage is a group of resources inherited from the past which people identify, independently of ownership, as a reflection and expression of their constantly evolving values, beliefs, knowledge, and traditions. It includes all aspects of the environment resulting from the interaction between people and places through time. Resources given to current generations are deemed to constitute heritage important for communities,[84] irrespective of their ownership or title. Seeing a human being at the center of the definition[85] of cultural heritage certainly satisfied the expectations of lawyers dealing with international law. Civil lawyers have once more been "removed"; in other words, the attempts to make property law arrangements have been neutralized, as they do not impact heritage and the right to it as such.

In the light of private law, this is needed to balance the needs of heritage as a legal good subject to protection and, on the other hand, a good which, apart from its significance for humanity and future generations, may also be important and play a significant role for each person who may dispose of it. A question should be posed as to why cultural heritage could not be treated as an object, and a distinction should be drawn between three separate areas in which this can be considered. Namely, the areas concerning the following: the right of ownership and its exhaustion, the perception of cultural heritage from a social perspective, and characteristics of cultural heritage. One may refer to the constitutional values and obligations of each person having cultural heritage as at his or her disposal at a given time, as well as the questions that arise about the compliance of such restrictions with a given constitution. At the same time, one should refer to the ownership right as a right in rem concerning cultural goods and the discussion revolving around the exhaustion of that right. The Polish experience indicates that each restriction of an ownership or investment process should be considered from the perspective of the co-responsibility of the state for monuments and the protection of cultural heritage.

[81] Legal regulations in India, Australia, New Zealand, see Sect. 4.2.2.

[82] Jagielska-Burduk (2016a).

[83] Zalasińska (2015), p. 73.

[84] Therond (2012), p. 165.

[85] Jagielska-Burduk (2016a).

Changes will be a natural consequence of an individual accepting responsibility over cultural heritage at their disposal and their obligation towards future generations, as well as transposing what has already been discerned in that dimension onto the level of a new legal construct. Shared responsibility, or elements of a temporary nature, are referred to in Polish court rulings and justifications of legal acts. Therefore, it may be concluded that the Polish legislature has prepared a quite solid ground as a starting point for subsequent legislative actions. The origin of the changes can be found in cultural heritage itself, and more precisely in its characteristics, which make a given component worth preserving. All of the above results in the legislature starting to treat a given good differently in view of its characteristics, creating a division in various legal regimes concerning a part of the resource, and the state or another entity designated as responsible for managing that resource or its most important part.

Searching for a new right to monuments or cultural heritage has been broadly analyzed in the literature of the subject. The first question about the fourth estate was posed by Richard Crewdson.[86] Usually, while looking for solutions, the status of a good as such has not been changed, but the type of right has been adjusted. The legal concept is adjusted to the needs of heritage (trust, *fidei commissum*, disposition) indicating the exhaustion of the ownership right. In research concerning legal mechanisms of cultural heritage management, there have been deliberations on a universal knot which combines the present and the past in managing cultural heritage and attempts made to liberate heritage from the ownership knot.[87] In the research presented in this publication, concentrating on the characteristics of a good and the method of the state's dealing with similar goods having a special value and considered to be a common good, I have noticed that the category of cultural heritage in certain areas is similar to resources considered to be a national good, including waters and minerals. Furthermore, similarly to the case of legal regulations concerning tangible goods not considered as objects, cultural heritage is characterized by a significant variety of components. Consequently, it will require "tailor-made" solutions for individual components of heritage. Dereification is one of them.

A good subjected to dereification should be a one that stands out among others. Undoubtedly, that condition has been satisfied. The intangible value of cultural heritage is the extra-economic value of the good. It is beyond any doubt that the economic value of a good is frequently related to its intangible value, justifying its enhanced protection. In that context, one should refer to the constitutionalization of heritage and cultural goods, making them legally protected goods at the constitu-

[86] Crewdson (1984), p. 126; Williams (1978); Weidner (2001). In the Polish legal scholarship: Kowalski (2005), pp. 125–127; the concept of protecting the interests of successors in: Jagielska-Burduk (2011), pp. 281–286; the notion Ethernal Rombus and future generations: Szafrański (2015), pp. 161–168; Jagielska-Burduk (2016d), pp. 77–79.

[87] Jagielska-Burduk (2016c), pp. 178–184.

tional level.[88] This is a starting point for adducing the perception of cultural heritage as a common good as an argument for dereification. In Poland, the broadest deliberations concerning the common good are conducted from the perspective of constitutional law and the place of cultural heritage among the values protected in the Constitution. Literature has noted that rulings of the Polish Constitutional Tribunal referring to the common good with regard to heritage mention elements of cultural heritage or activities undertaken with a view to protection of heritage as the common good.[89] Unquestionably, cultural heritage is a good which, as something subject to protection, is indicated by the constitution and is examined as the common good. This has also been recognized by the legislature while justifying new mechanisms protecting certain heritage components

> (c)ultural goods, although they are owned by individual private and public entities, constitute common goods in the social sense. That is because they participate in shaping the historical and cultural awareness of the national community.[90]

The legislature permits interference with the ownership right with a view to the protection of a constitutional value, but the scope of such restrictions should always be evaluated from the perspective of the proportionality principle in each case. Restrictions as to the right of ownership, private ownership included, are therefore justifiable by the need to protect the common good and to protect the freedom and rights of another entity, and "(i)n order for such freedom to be attained, actions of public authorities aimed at protection of monuments are indispensable."[91] This is also visible in rulings of administrative courts, which frequently quote the reasons for the judgment of the Regional Administrative Court in Warsaw of 23 April 2009 as strengthening the actions of conservation services and the obligations of owners of monuments

> thus a monument ceases to be just and only a private good of its owner, whose interests are for that reason significantly restricted, and the substance of the statutory restriction is signalled by the provision of Article 140 of the Civil Code.[92]

In turn, one should recognize a reference to the European Union regulations in rulings of the Constitutional Tribunal. The Constitutional Tribunal, in its judgment

[88] On the definition of cultural heritage and "flexibility in the process of applying law": Zeidler (2004), p. 353; about cultural heritage being a part of national heritage and separate category of protected goods: Florczak-Wątor (2016), pp. 288–289 and on the constitutional legal framework: Frankiewicz-Bodynek (2019), pp. 112–154.

[89] Cf. Frankiewicz-Bodynek (2019), pp. 259–260.

[90] Governmental draft of the act on the found objects and amending other legal acts. Justification, Print no. 2064, p. 3. http://www.sejm.gov.pl/Sejm7.nsf/druk.xsp?nr=2064. Accessed 1 June 2022.

[91] Polish Constitutional Court Judgement of 8th October 2001, OTK-A 2007/9/102, http://isap.sejm.gov.pl/isap.nsf/DocDetails.xsp?id=WDU20071921394. Accessed 1 June 2022.

[92] The Polish voivodship administrative court in Warsaw of the 23rd of April 2009, I SA/Wa 48/09, LEX no. 550267.

of 25 May 2016,[93] referred to European Union law and Article 36 of the Treaty of the functioning of the European Union[94] while mentioning export restrictions.

Focusing on the object meets the assumptions of both concepts proposed by John H. Merryman: the national concept and international concept concerning the justifiability of the freedom of the flow of goods and their transfer outside the borders of countries, boiling down these concepts to a common denominator. The international theory revolves around the object as a good that may change owners, be transferred outside borders, and should be made available to the public and should be subject to conservation and protection. That position is defined as object-centered, as opposed to the national concept, referred to as nation-centered.[95] Elements related to the access to a good, taking care of it, and ensuring its safety are similar to those that were used for justifying the dereification of animals. In turn, the assumptions underlying the concept concerning the special connection between a given good and the nation (i.e., the territory of a given country), result in the need to maintain it within geographical borders and constitute a carve-out from the principle of the free movement of goods. In that respect, if a given good is viewed as having a special value, therefore, it should not leave the borders of the country permanently. One can derive important arguments in favor of the dereification of cultural heritage and its suggested scope from both these concepts. First, it is important to organize the protection of a given good in such a way that it is not damaged and remains available for society. Second, if we are to treat a given cultural object as a treasure for all nations, one should concentrate on the elements whose connection with the country is undeniable and measurable. At present, such an indication among cultural property may include, for example, a prohibition on permanent export. It should be mentioned that such prohibition covers both state-owned and private-owned objects. One cannot skip the reference to a certain supplement of the construct proposed by John H. Merryman and created by Lucas Lixinski. The latter author performed some research on cultural heritage and legal regulations in the context of including society in its management. Apart from the dichotomy and focus on the object or the nation, he proposes going beyond and accepting, apart from the state, other stakeholders for heritage. He suggests a participation model at the level of management of cultural

---

[93] Polish Constitutional Court Judgement of 25th May 2016, Kp 2/15, OTK-A 2016/23. http://isap.sejm.gov.pl/isap.nsf/download.xsp/WMP20160000792/T/M20160792TK.pdf. Accessed 1 June 2022.

[94] "[. . .] the use of restrictions on the rights of owners of movable monuments, and in particular restrictions on the right to dispose of a thing, is recognised by the primary law of the European Union. The protection of national treasures of artistic, historical or archaeological value constitutes a premise justifying derogation from prohibitions or restrictions on imports, exports or transit, provided that it does not take the form of arbitrary discrimination or a disguised restriction on trade between Member States (Article 36 of the Treaty on the Functioning of the European Union, OJ C 326 of 26.10.2012, p. 47; hereinafter: TFEU). Undoubtedly, therefore, the objective of the challenged provision can be regarded as systemically legitimate."

[95] Merryman (1994), pp. 64–65.

heritage in international law and concentrates on the construct of society.[96] In addition to that element of connection with cultural heritage, one may infer a conclusion about the necessity to treat it as a good which goes beyond the ordinary scheme and method of realizing cultural rights.[97]

Treating cultural goods as special goods is reflected in international law instruments as well as EU law. To prove the atypical character of regulations, one should indicate a claim for return that can be made. In the UNESCO 1970 Convention, a claim for return is made by a state party to that convention by diplomatic means. The state making the request covers all the costs related to the return of the requested cultural goods. Nevertheless, the scope of cultural property subject to return is limited to property originating from public institutions and satisfying the criteria indicated in Articles 1 and 4 of the convention. Another model was implemented in the 1995 UNIDROIT convention, where in the case of illegal export, the claim for return is made by the state (Article 5 of the Convention) and in the case of theft by the state or the owner.[98] In the explanatory report to the Convention, it was emphasized that it adopted a new solution (departing from the construct of good faith for the benefit of due diligence) in view of the special nature of cultural goods.[99] In turn, EU Directive 2014/60 assumes that a request may be made by a Member State before the competent court in the Member State in which a given good is located (Article 6). These instruments pay attention to the applied constructs concerning the entity making the request and granting the right to claim the return to states.

It further demonstrates an interest of the state and, moreover, a public interest in retrieving such objects. In the case of the UNESCO 1970 Convention, these are goods belonging to public collections, but in the remaining cases, the claim may concern the return of a privately-owned good. This stresses the extra-ownership nature of cultural property and its belonging to the national heritage of a given state. These concepts of claims show two layers of heritage—one at the global level, and another consequently duplicating the existence of a claim of a state at the level of the European Union. So, do such regulations allow us to deem that, apart from ownership, we also have another right that the state is entitled to? Going even further, if this is the case, how should we treat the right of the state to request returns granted by international conventions, which do not apply retroactively, as compared to the rights of states and their demands made with regard to cultural objects which are not covered by these instruments?

In the case of disputes concerning cultural heritage, a special role in the parties' attempt to reach an agreement is played by alternative dispute resolution methods. They allow for the removal of legal obstacles concerning issues such as limitation

---

[96] Lixinski (2019a), pp. 577–580.

[97] Jakubowski and Jagielska-Burduk (2021).

[98] Schneider (2016), pp. 154–157.

[99] UNIDROIT Convention on Stolen or Illegally Exported Cultural Objects: Explanatory Report prepared by the UNIDROIT Secretariat, Uniform Law Review, 2001, no. 1, p. 502.

periods, evidentiary difficulties, differences between legal systems, and omit the issue of the non-retroactive application of international conventions. Furthermore, they allow parties to resolve a dispute in a way that considers the interests and positions of both parties and dedicating adequate attention to the very good they concern.[100] In respect of cultural goods, apart from the path provided by the UNESCO 1970 Convention, the states may use alternative dispute resolution methods. There is the Intergovernmental Committee for Promoting the Return of Cultural Property to its Countries of Origin or its Restitution in Case of Illicit Appropriation operating at UNESCO, and the Rules of Procedure for Mediation and Conciliation were adopted in 2010.[101] What should also be noted is the activity of WIPO, including the rules for mediation prepared in cooperation with the International Council of Museums (2012)[102] and as part of the initiative "WIPO ADR Services for Specific Sectors."[103] Moreover, the first Court of Arbitration for Art (CAfA) has been operating since 2018, which is supposed to be a permanent forum for conducting arbitration and mediation proceedings with respect to cultural property. The creation of separate mechanisms for the resolution of disputes dealing solely with such issues points to the need to draw experts from the specific area of law to these institutions, as well as in assessing provenance and the evaluation of works, resulting in that a separate system for dispute resolution around cultural goods. What is more, the use of alternative dispute resolution methods allows for the adoption of solutions that would not be possible to achieve in court proceedings, and which constitute solutions considered as morally justifiable. The history of cultural heritage, which is part of the history of humankind, makes it inevitable for various interests to arise, which must be reconciled. Such interests must consider the interest of the good and its safety. Common management of the good at the center of a potential dispute[104] allows for the separation of ownership rights from other valid titles. In that respect, a separate system for dispute resolution enhances the possibility to implement a shared responsibility for cultural heritage and justifies its special status.

It is beyond any doubt that enormous resources of cultural heritage constitute an object of state ownership. In the case of Poland, the relevant body is the State Treasury or units of territorial local government. The state ownership model is introduced here with regard to archaeological artifacts. A question that arises is whether a distinction between public domain goods and private domain goods can be

---

[100] Chechi (2020), p. 719. See also Cornu and Renold (2010), pp. 1–31.

[101] Intergovernmental Committee for Promoting the Return of Cultural Property to its Countries of Origin or its Restitution in Case of Illicit Appropriation, CLT-2010/CONF.203/COM.16/7, https://unesdoc.unesco.org/ark:/48223/pf0000192534_eng. Accessed 1 June 2022. Cf. Urbinati (2014).

[102] ICOM-WIPO Art and Cultural Heritage Mediation. https://www.wipo.int/amc/en/center/specific-sectors/art/icom/rules/. Accessed 1 June 2022.

[103] WIPO Alternative Dispute Resolution (ADR) for Art and Cultural Heritage, https://www.wipo.int/amc/en/center/specific-sectors/art/. Accessed 1 June 2022.

[104] The object legal status remains the same and it is in the perpetual deposit in the museum located in the country of its origin.

maintained if one wants to justify dereification or, in the case of defining public collections, whether inclusion of private goods should be considered. Although co-responsibility and protection of cultural heritage by the state and members of society at large are assumed, it is easier to imagine a change in that resource. On the other hand, strengthened protection regimes are currently being prepared as regimes incorporating the protection of goods originating from private actors. This happens because the value of such goods is considered separately from the ownership right—at the social level, as a good whose fate is important not only for the owner but also for society when viewed from the national or international perspective. Answering this question, one should concentrate on the object of regulation and not on the entity being regulated. *Ipso facto,* common ground should be indicated for private goods and public goods (public goods include those that do not constitute an object and may not be the subject matter of ownership rights such as waters and minerals). At the same time, similarly to other tangible goods that are not objects, it is possible to formulate higher requirements with regard to goods being public property.

Dereification of some immovable monuments and considering certain complex multi-component goods as live and dynamic organisms could strengthen the process of retrieving goods from their inventory. In that case, even the valid acquisition of an ownership right to a chandelier, tiled stove, glass case, or stained glass originating from a manor would have to be confronted with the right of the manor represented by attorneys-in-fact to preserve the latter's integrity and undeniable historical connection. Attention should also be paid to the fact that an element related to the acquisition of an ownership right can always be rebutted and depends on a court's findings for a particular case. The creation of certain formal fictions would allow a quick process for the return of goods. In a certain sense, such a connection between an establishment and its inventory has an intangible dimension, and in that respect, it is similar to the native title, which is not always tantamount to the ownership status. Of course, avoiding or, in certain situations, looking for solutions that bypass deliberations on the ownership right may sometimes result in avoidance of liability. On the other hand, if these are solutions that are proven in the practical dimension, they should also be considered as falling within the scope of solutions that should appear alongside and in support of alternative dispute resolution methods.

Finally, one cannot avoid referring to the concept of personification of certain components of cultural heritage. A debate as to the personification of animals and artificial intelligence occurs while conducting debates of a philosophical nature, but also, for example, in the area of the analysis of copyrights and the status of a creator—in both these cases, there has been a search for new solutions. It is true that in the case of artificial intelligence, people are still considering its use for the public good, although the use of artificial intelligence in creative work and the creation of works sold at auctions of works of art undoubtedly constitutes an element of artistic activity. It is different in the case of animals, as the essence of legislative changes is the willingness to safeguard animals and their rights. The idea of personification may find an additional justification in religious beliefs, similarly to considering a river as a person or an ancestor. In practice, such a formal construct of a fictitious natural person will need to be combined with an appropriate system of representation. An excellent example in the area of cultural heritage is treating a stolen statuette as a person.

In the case Pramatha Nath Mullick v. Pradyumma Kumar Mullick (1925), the Privy Council (acting as a judicial body hearing appeals from the High Court in Calcutta) dealt with the transfer of a statuette of an idol. Taking care of the idol was a task that had been passed from generation to generation within the family of the founder who endowed the idol. What is important for the protection of cultural heritage is that the rights and interests of the idol were protected by its representative, a guardian of the prayer house. His decision to move the idol caused a reaction from female worshippers who believed that their cultural rights would be infringed by the transfer of the idol.[105] The Council found that the idol was not a movable object and not subject to private ownership.[106] In that case, two elements appeared: the first was related to the confirmation of the idol's status as an entity of the law under Hindu law and customs, and the second was related to the juxtaposition of the interests of the idol and its worshippers, who did not want to allow the change of location to proceed. Ana Vrdoljak describes the case to illustrate the right to appear before courts and tribunals to protect cultural rights in the individual and collective aspects, as well as the interest of entities in managing idols as an element of cultural heritage.[107] Against the background of this case, one may wonder whether each transfer of an idol would infringe the rights of the worshippers or whether a transfer for safekeeping would be permitted. This is best illustrated by the situation of goods which are placed in museums and originally obtained in periods of colonization, and claims made, for example, by African countries for the return of such goods. A frequently mentioned argument is the issue of the security of the objects and making them available to the public.

The legal personality of idols is accepted in certain jurisdictions, while a similar status concerning animals or artificial intelligence has not been accepted yet.[108] A discussion about granting animals or artificial intelligence the status of legal entities has a considerably broader global dimension. One cannot omit, however, the fact that even as regards the dereification of animals, the legislation of states does not occur at the same time. Thus, this cannot be an argument in favor of withholding the search for new legal concepts. The creation of an arrangement in which a tangible good is at the center and is represented by a human being has additionally heated the discussion. Even considering the specificity of legal systems, one can discern the common value of a solution concerning the religious and cultural sphere or incorporating this into the tangible object of values (endowing), which makes it a special good. The analysis of the idol's status and legal persons in both cases seems fictional, but in the former case we deal above all with a religious justification, in reference to tradition and customs, and in the latter case we have the legal construct of legal

[105] Vrdoljak (2016), p. 285.

[106] Solaiman (2017), pp. 167–168.

[107] Vrdoljak (2016), p. 285.

[108] Solaiman (2017), p. 157.

entities.[109] Just like legal persons operate through their bodies, the idol operates through each of its guardians. A visible religious and cultural dimension is of vital importance in this case. Granting a legal personality to a river and treating it as a natural person, or in other cases as a legal person, allows one to act in the interests of these goods through attorneys-in-fact or guardians.

Although the personification of cultural heritage at the legal level seems remote, educational programs on cultural heritage frequently use such a rhetorical figure while describing certain goods by referring to their durability and the fact that they are witnesses of history. Although their relevance or function changes over the years, they are still observers of human history and last alongside subsequent generations.

References

Carpenter KA, Katyal SK, Riley A (2009) In defense of property. Yale Law J 118(6):1022–1125

Chechi A (2020) Alternative dispute settlement mechanisms. In: Vrdoljak AF, Francioni F (eds) The Oxford handbook of international cultural heritage law. Oxford University Press, Oxford, pp 718–736. https://doi.org/10.1093/law/9780198859871.003.0030

Chippindale C (2012) Stonehenge complete. Thames & Hudson, London

Cornu M, Renold M-A (2010) New developments in the restitution of cultural property: alternative means of dispute resolution. IJCP 17(1):1–31. https://doi.org/10.1017/S0940739110000044

Crewdson R (1984) Cultural property – a fourth estate? Law Soc Gazette 18:126

Dembska R (2007) Problemy dziedziczenia kolekcji w świetle polskiego prawa spadkowego. In: Szafrański W (ed) Wokół problematyki prawnej zabytków i dzieł sztuki, vol 1. Wydawnictwo Poznańskie, Poznań, pp 125–129

English P (2002) Disputing stonehenge: law and access to a national symbol. Entertain Law 1(2): 1–22. https://doi.org/10.1080/14730980210001730401

Florczak-Wątor M (2016) Art. 5 [Commentary]. In: Safjan M, Bosek L (eds) Konstytucja RP, vol 1: Komentarz do art. 1–86. C.H. Beck, Warszawa, pp 278–290

Frankiewicz-Bodynek A (2019) Konstytucyjna regulacja dziedzictwa narodowego oraz dóbr kultury. Wydawnictwo Adam Marszałek, Toruń

Hodder I (2010) Cultural heritage rights from ownership and descent to justice and well-being. Anthropol Q 83(4):861–882

Jagielska A, Szafrański W (2008) Darowizny na rzecz muzeów. In: Szafrański W (ed) Wokół problematyki prawnej zabytków i dzieł sztuki, vol 2. Wydawnictwo Poznańskie, Poznań, pp 69–80

Jagielska-Burduk A (2011) Zabytek ruchomy. Wolters Kluwer Polska, Warszawa

Jagielska-Burduk A (2016a) A new image of heritage protection or management. In: Jagielska-Burduk A, Szafrański W (eds) Legal issues in cultural heritage management. A Polish perspective. Peter Lang, Berlin, pp 165–178

Jagielska-Burduk A (2016b) Fideikomis. In: Jagielska-Burduk A (ed) Mechanizmy prawne zarządzania dziedzictwem kultury. Wolters Kluwer Polska, Wydawnictwo Uniwersytetu Gdańskiego, Gdańsk–Warszawa, pp 238–253

Jagielska-Burduk A (2016c) Formy ochrony zabytków jako mechanizm zarządzania dziedzictwem kultury. In: Jagielska-Burduk A (ed) Mechanizmy prawne zarządzania dziedzictwem kultury. Wolters Kluwer Polska, Wydawnictwo Uniwersytetu Gdańskiego, Gdańsk–Warszawa, pp 171–212

[109] Solaiman (2017), pp. 176–177.

Jagielska-Burduk A (2016d) Prawo własności dziedzictwa kultury. In: Jagielska-Burduk A (ed) Mechanizmy prawne zarządzania dziedzictwem kultury. Wolters Kluwer Polska, Wydawnictwo Uniwersytetu Gdańskiego, Gdańsk–Warszawa, pp 69–96

Jagielska-Burduk A (2016e) Umowy darowizny, użyczenia i depozytu. In: Jagielska-Burduk A (ed) Mechanizmy prawne zarządzania dziedzictwem kultury. Wolters Kluwer Polska, Wydawnictwo Uniwersytetu Gdańskiego, Gdańsk, pp 97–126

Jagielska-Burduk A, Markowski D (2011) O lwowskich zbiorach Bolesława Orzechowicza. Acta Universitatis Nicolai Copernici Zabytkoznawstwo i Konserwatorstwo 42:25–38. https://doi.org/10.12775/AUNC_ZiK.2011.012

Jakubowski A, Jagielska-Burduk A (2021) Cultural rights. In: Sellers M, Kirste S (eds) Encyclopedia of the philosophy of law and social philosophy. Springer, Dordrecht. https://doi.org/10.1007/978-94-007-6730-0_826-1

Kowalski W (2005) Kolizyjnoprawne problemy restytucji dóbr kultury. In: Ogiegło L, Popiołek W, Szpunar M (eds) Rozprawy prawnicze. Księga pamiątkowa profesora Maksymiliana Pazdana. Zakamycze, Kraków, pp 123–149

Kowalski W (2014) Konwencja UNESCO o ochronie podwodnego dziedzictwa kulturowego przyjęta dnia 2 listopada 2001 r. na 31 Konferencji Generalnej UNESCO. In: Zalasińska K (ed) Konwencje UNESCO w dziedzinie kultury. Komentarz. Wolters Kluwer Polska, Warszawa, pp 312–391

Lasik P (2018) Zabytki na uchodźstwie – safe haven jako narzędzie wielopoziomowej współpracy międzynarodowej na rzecz ochrony dóbr kultury. SAACLR 1(4):189–214. https://doi.org/10.4467/2450050XSNR.18.012.9773

Łętowska E (1997) Dwa cywilnoprawne aspekty praw zwierząt: derefikacja i personifikacja. In: Szpunar A (ed) Studia z prawa prywatnego. Księga pamiątkowa ku czci Profesor Biruty Lewaszkiewicz-Petrykowskiej. Wydawnictwo Uniwersytetu Łódzkiego, Łódź, pp 71–92

Lixinski L (2019a) A third way of thinking about cultural property. Brook J Int Law 44:563–612

Lixinski L (2019b) International heritage law for communities exclusion and re-imagination. Oxford University Press, Oxford. https://doi.org/10.1093/oso/9780198843306.001.0001

Macmillan F (2013) The protection of cultural heritage: common heritage of humankind, national cultural 'Patrimony' or private property? NILQ 3(64):351–364. https://doi.org/10.53386/nilq.v64i3.355

Macmillan F (2020) Intellectual and cultural property: between market and community. Routledge, London

Mazzeschi P (2014) Human rights and the modernization of international law. In: Lenzerini F, Vrdoljak AF (eds) International law for common goods. Normative perspectives on human rights, culture and nature. Hart, Oxford, pp 89–101

Merryman JH (1994) Nation and the object. IJCP 3(1):61–76

Merusi F (1975) Art. 9 [Commentary]. In: Zanichelli N (ed) Commentario della Costituzione. Roma Società Editrice del Foro Italiano, Bologna

Meskell L (2018) A future in ruins. UNESCO, world heritage, and the dream of peace. Oxford University Press, Oxford

O'Keefe PJ, Prott LV (eds) (2011) Cultural heritage conventions and other instruments. A compendium with commentaries. Institute of Art and Law, Builth Wells

O'Keefe R (1999) The meaning of 'Cultural Property' under the 1954 Hague Convention. Netherlands Int Law Rev 46(1):26–56. https://doi.org/10.1017/S0165070X00002084

Pietrzykowski T (2017) Introduction. In: Kurki VAJ, Pietrzykowski T (eds) Legal personhood: animals, artificial intelligence and the unborn, Law and philosophy library, vol 119. Springer, Cham, pp 1–5

Pontiroli L (2014) Una disgrazia costituzionalmente garantita: note critiche sullo status iuridico dei bieni culturali private. In: Negri-Clementi G, Stabile S (eds) Il diritto dell'arte, vol 3: La protezione del patrimonio artistico. Skira, Milan

Prott LV (2011) The fight against the illicit traffic of cultural property: the 1970 Convention: past and future, 15–16 March 2011. IJCP 18(4):437–442. https://doi.org/10.1017/S094073911100035X

Sax JL (2005) Imaginatively public: the English experience of art as heritage property. Vanderbilt J Transnatl Law 38(4):1097–1140

Sax JL (1999) Playing Darts with a Rembrandt: public and private rights in cultural treasures. University of Michigan Press, Ann Arbor. https://doi.org/10.3998/mpub.16038

Schneider M (2016) The 1995 UNIDROIT Convention: an indispendable complement to the 1970 UNESCO Convention and an inspiration for the 2014/60/EU Directive. SAACLR 2(2): 149–164. https://doi.org/10.4467/2450050XSR.16.024.6132

Solaiman SM (2017) Legal personality of robots, corporations, idols and chimpanzees: a quest for legitimacy. Artif Intell Law 25(2):155–179. https://doi.org/10.1007/s10506-016-9192-3

Szafrański W (2012) Publiczne aspekty kolekcji prywatnych. In: Jagielska-Burduk A, Szafrański W (eds) Kultura w praktyce. Zagadnienia prawne, vol 1. Wydawnictwo Poznańskiego Towarzystwa Przyjaciół Nauk, Poznań, pp 43–58

Szafrański W (2015) Mity i patologie obrotu dziełami sztuki. SAACLR 1(1):135–172. https://doi.org/10.4467/2450050XSR.15.005.3773

(2015) Sztuka jest ryzykiem dla inwestora i dla artysty. Z profesorem Krzysztofem Pomianem rozmawia Janusz Miliszkiewicz. SAACLR 1(1):41–48

Therond D (2012) 4. Europejskie Forum Dziedzictwa, Wrocław, 10–12 października 2011 rok. Ochrona Zabytków 3–4:165–167

Urbinati S (2014) Alternative dispute resolution mechanisms in cultural property related disputes: UNESCO mediation and conciliation procedures. In: Vadim V, Schneider H (eds) Art, cultural heritage and the market. Ethical and legal issues. Springer, Heidelberg, pp 93–116

Vrdoljak A (2016) Standing and collective cultural rights. In: Jakubowski A (ed) Cultural rights as collective rights: an international law perspective. Brill, Leiden, pp 272–287

Vrdoljak AF (2014) Human rights and cultural heritage in international law. In: Lenzerini F, Vrdoljak AF (eds) International law for common goods. Normative perspectives on human rights, culture and nature. Hart, Oxford, pp 139–175

Weidner A (2001) Kulturgüter als res extra commercium im internationalen Sachenrecht. De Gruyter, Berlin

Wierczyńska K, Jakubowski A (2017) Individual responsibility for deliberate destruction of cultural heritage: contextualizing the ICC judgment in the Al-Mahdi case. Chin J Int Law 16(4):695–721

Wiessner S (2010) Re-enchanting the world: indigenous peoples' rights as essential parts of a holistic human rights regime. UCLA J Int Law Foreign Aff 15(239):239–288

Wiessner S (2014) The cultural dimension of indigenous rights. In: Lenzerini F, Vrdoljak AF (eds) International law for common goods. Normative perspectives on human rights, culture and nature. Hart, Oxford, pp 175–192

Williams S (1978) The international and national protection of movable cultural property. A comparative study. Oceana Publications, Inc., Dobbs Ferry

Zalasińska K (2013) Muzea publiczne. Studium administracyjnoprawne. LexisNexis Polska, Warszawa

Zalasińska K (2015) Nowa filozofia ochrony dziedzictwa w Konwencji ramowej Rady Europy w sprawie wartości dziedzictwa kulturowego. In: Pływaczewski W, Gadecki B (eds) Ochrona dziedzictwa kulturalnego i naturalnego. Perspektywa prawna i kryminologiczna. C.H. Beck, Warszawa, pp 63–73

Zeidler K (2004) Pojęcie "dziedzictwa narodowego" w Konstytucji RP i jego ochrona prawna. Gdańskie Studia Prawnicze 12:343–353

Chapter 7
Conclusions and Projections

The issues presented in the publication against the background of international and EU laws show current challenges and pitfalls in searching for national legal models. The reference to the rights of tangible goods not considered objects, together with the holistic perception of cultural heritage, confirms that legal regulations have a long history created in stages. Challenges to cultural heritage are challenges not only for international law lawyers but also for national lawyers and policymakers. The role of the latter is of key relevance during the ratification and implementation of international conventions or the transposition of EU law. Exploring potential areas for development and searching for innovative solutions could be successful avenues for lawyers dealing with cultural heritage in their respective countries.

The area of cultural heritage in civil law covers only a part of the deliberations on the law of cultural heritage protection. Nevertheless, this is very important, and what depends during deliberations is frequently the determination of the entity that has the good at its disposal and the possible methods of protection. Even in view of varied or undetermined ownership status, it is necessary to secure at least a part of heritage for future generations. The status of a good is treated slightly differently in international conventions, which are more concerned with the obligations of states parties and international cooperation. For instance, in the prepared model documents, it is left at the legislature's discretion how to construct the state ownership of archaeological artefacts and potentially include human remains within the scope of that legal regulation.[1] The latitude of the national legislature as to arrangements concerning the status of a cultural good and rights in rem to natural and cultural heritage somehow forces one to think about the legal status of heritage components in civil law and, subsequently, the right to it. Going beyond typical deliberations on cultural heritage at the private law level was necessary in the case of goods that undoubtedly

[1] Model Provisions on State Ownership of Undiscovered Cultural Objects. Explanatory Report with model provisions and explanatory guidelines, UNESCO-UNIDROIT, 2011. http://www.unesco.org/new/en/culture/themes/restitution-of-cultural-property/standards-for-ownership/. Accessed 1 June 2022.

A. Jagielska-Burduk, *Cultural Heritage as a Legal Hybrid*,
https://doi.org/10.1007/978-3-031-04946-0_7

constitute a component of cultural heritage and that are not objects within the meaning of civil law.

The deliberations presented in the publication indicate that cultural heritage is a diverse resource requiring attention on the part of the legislature and forcing one to look at the world from a bird's-eye-view perspective. In terms of the status in civil law, one can differentiate between tangible and intangible goods which belong to the resource of cultural heritage. That division shows that the intangible nature of cultural heritage will force a different perception of that heritage in private law. We can, nevertheless, separate certain elements that will occur in most cases: holistic approach to cultural heritage, an ownership right or another absolute right to a given good sometimes similar to the management of a common thing, the possibility of copyright protection of certain goods, as well as the necessity to determine contemporary entities qualifying as beneficiaries so that they can have access to heritage and the possibility of its continuation. The work presents challenges for heritage related to the appearance of new creations of cultural goods as a result of technological progress or changes in the perception of given goods or incorporating new spheres into the heritage of humanity. In that respect, civil law is not always able to provide a clear answer as to the status of a given good. Some issues (e.g. participation of artificial intelligence (AI) in the creation of cultural property) are currently subject to debate on the basis of national law, but there are also areas (e.g. space heritage) where the management and identification of such heritage should be initiated at the international level.

The situation of heritage components in civil law is affected by a holistic approach to cultural heritage and a clearly indicated natural component. The natural component of cultural heritage shows that as regards its protection, it is necessary to refer to the protection of the environment and its relevance in the life of human beings. The similarity between branches of cultural heritage law and environmental law[2] and the path of its development, which is somehow common but occurs within a certain time span, shows that cultural heritage cannot be considered without a reference to environmental law.[3] At the level of international law, one can recognise the view that heritage protection law constitutes a part of a bigger whole, namely international environmental law.[4] It seems that in the national dimension, this area has not been sufficiently researched, and deeper research in that respect would constitute an excellent foundation for new legal acts. Eventually, this could lead to an enhanced synergy between the activities of ministries through the creation of independent teams and at the level of territorial local government units; departments essentially combine these two areas in practice.

However, research concerning cultural heritage in civil law does not illustrate the challenges that come into being without a reference to copyright law, public law, EU law and international law. Constant tensions around the substance of cultural

[2]Zeidler (2014), p. 29.

[3]Ciechanowicz-Mclean (2014).

[4]Blake (2015), p. 117.

heritage as a subject matter of law are generated by the overlapping of legal regimes, the interdependence of protection for future generations and the protection of intangible heritage, as well as the rights of an individual or the community under existing legal mechanisms. Even the example of intangible heritage confirms that with its differentiation, one may deliberate on protection at the level of copyright and intellectual property, rights of an individual and the community, and adopted national solutions, which are not uniform. In addition, the need to refer to environmental protection shows that without adopting a broader perspective, we cannot deliberate on the future of cultural heritage.[5]

In civil law, it is possible to discern opportunities to strengthen the protection of certain goods, which will be related to the acquisition of cultural goods and their trade. An example of the manifestation of the above concerns new Polish legal provisions on the impossibility of acquisitive prescription of an ownership right or the acquisition of ownership from somebody who does not have a title in respect of national cultural goods belonging to public collections. Another turning point in legislative activities will undoubtedly be the introduction of the duty to exercise due diligence when trading in cultural goods on the art market. That model of conduct, consisting in proving due diligence while acquiring a good and which allows the award of damages, was included in the act governing the restitution of national cultural property. The next step should be its incorporation into the civil code. It is even more desirable as that change will constitute the implementation of accepted and recommended standards in the art market at the international level.

It is not possible to conclude that cultural heritage has not changed over time and that the only changes occurring in the resource are related to our new perception of reality. On the one hand, it seems that what we consider to be heritage has always existed and surrounded us. It was only with the development of science concerning heritage that humanity learned how to separate its new manifestations, going from concentrating solely on tangible creations to separating manifestations of intangible heritage and its subsequent identification, documentation and promotion. Elements of that heritage have been present for a long time, but it was not until initiatives arose at the international level that the introduction of protective regulations at the national level was to a certain extent initiated. Furthermore, that process depends on the specificity and history of a given country, including the issue of the protection of indigenous people's culture. On the other hand, circumstances like technological progress, works of art in the digital sphere, AI in the creative process, trading in non-fungible tokens (NFTs) and rising apparent speculations in that segment of the market confirm that changes in art—the typical resource of cultural heritage—are somehow a reflection of the technological progress of humanity and its development. Cultural heritage has constantly been assuming new forms and is constantly changing. Nevertheless, new forms of cultural heritage have occurred and have contributed to this resource, while new manifestations pose a challenge to existing law, which in its existing form may be used to protect heritage or be adequately adapted.

[5] Fromageau (2020).

A question that arises each time is how to define heritage and who it belongs to. Can we, while creating a map of beneficiaries, reconcile various interests, and which interests should be given priority? The state is unable to protect the entirety of heritage, either as part of its own actions or in cooperation with private actors. Intuitively, one should support a solution based on the protection of the most important part of cultural heritage resources. As a result of the adoption of such a model, some valuing criteria occur, such as the element of evaluation of the authority applying the law while imposing restrictions on the owner related to the extension of a building or the denial of a permit to export a cultural object permanently. Apart from the selection of the most valuable goods, what is perceivable is the creation of legal frameworks for the protection of selected goods, somehow "tailor-made" and adjusted to their status (for example, the protection regime for public collections in the form of *res extra commercium* in France) and, moreover, the fragmentation of cultural heritage protection. An interesting example is the Polish Act on the Frederic Chopin Heritage, where the protection of tangible and intangible cultural heritage related to the composer was integrated. Another factor affecting the strengthening of protection is the application of selective solutions with regard to goods that are particularly susceptible to damage, for example archaeological artefacts.

What has recently drawn the interest of the media and shocked art critics has been a group's provocative act consisting in setting a Banksy artwork on fire and subsequently uploading a video documenting that event on YouTube.[6] The work was later sold as an NFT for a price nearly four times higher than the purchase price of the original in its tangible form. The intent of the group was to show the detachment of art from the material world. A masked man set the object on fire using a lighter and subsequently calmly observed the process of the object's transformation into ashes. What is more, the very fact of creating an NTF of the work has no connection to the artist's economic copyrights. Perhaps the use of the work as an NFT is to show the multi-dimensional nature of art and the limitations of copyright in accessing and using it. One of the hardest questions that must be answered by decision-makers is the question of ensuring the stability of heritage. In an advertisement for the work titled "The Life", Marina Abramović says:

> I believe that art of the future is art without objects (tangible objects – note by the author), this is just pure transmission of energy between the viewer and artist.[7]

She indicates that the future of performance is virtual reality (VR) and digital space. NFT art also exists solely without objects, which is not a problem for its acquirers and which does not discourage people from investing in it. Both tangible and intangible creations may be perceived as non-durable, so a question arises about their durability and the carrier used. The lack of a material substrate may lead to the

---

[6] Film Authentic Banksy Art Burning Ceremony (NFT), https://youtu.be/C4wm-p_VFh0. Accessed 1 June 2022.

[7] "I believe that art of the future is art without objects. this is just pure transmission of energy between the viewer and artist". https://www.christies.com/features/Marina-Abramovic-The-Life-10193-3.aspx. Accessed 1 June 2022 (film, 0:0–0:13).

trap that there is nothing to protect, while it is the intangible good that is subject to protection.

Is this really the approach that will be applied in the future with regard to heritage? In that respect, a new type of uncertainty concerning durability will arise. How can we ensure the "long life" of a good in the digital space? Will the entity with the good at its disposal and the guardian of that good construct security precautions of the network where the good is placed, or will it be possible to make a copy of the file even without the author's consent? Will we be able to enclose a certain non-live part of heritage in a memorial "snowglobe"? Are we close to converting the familiar snowglobes sold as memorabilia with a plastic Wawel castle in Cracow into an intelligent ball that can connect to the castle at any time via VR glasses? How fast will we move from art without objects to accessing heritage in a digital and intelligent dimension? Will we replace access to heritage in the tangible dimension with online access? The risk I see is related to the commercialisation of heritage. However, access to heritage at the level of intangible values has been inevitably transferred to the Internet or applications, which is why we should also look for heritage management models by means of such tools.

An internal evaluation conducted by the decision-makers of the Act on the Protection and Guardianship of Monuments (APGM) and the entire Polish cultural heritage law resulted in discarding some solutions as unnecessary or even defective. As a result, drafts for legislative amendments are being prepared. For example, the liquidation of the List of Heritage Treasures is being planned,[8] which is meant to be a collection of the most valuable Polish movable cultural objects.[9] As a form of monument protection providing restrictions on owners, it was assessed in terms of compliance with the constitution,[10] and the new provisions were not deemed non-compliant. The legislature decided to eliminate what has not proven to be effective in recent years or what has never been applied in practice. It is difficult to reconstruct, however, whether financial issues constitute an important part of the decisions made. The legislature resigns from certain legal concepts for several reasons: first, it may be because it has the burden of the former regime on it, and second, it is more and more visible that there has been an attempt to search for a new path for the cultural heritage protection law. Third, new challenges have constantly arisen in the area of international law as new standards have been implemented and declarations have been made regarding the ratification of international conventions. Poland has actively participated in the debate concerning cultural heritage in the international forum, at the institutional and academic levels, which is why we can

[8]Govermental draft law on amending Act on the Protection and Guardianship of Monuments Act and Certain Other Acts, UD247, Justification to the draft, p. 1 https://legislacja.gov.pl/projekt/12356151. Accessed 1 June 2022.

[9]Jagielska-Burduk (2016).

[10]Polish Constitutional Court Judgement of 25th May 2016, Kp 2/15, OTK-A 2016/23. http://isap.sejm.gov.pl/isap.nsf/download.xsp/WMP20160000792/T/M20160792TK.pdf. Accessed 1 June 2022.

talk about a high level of advancement in works creating the foundations for the construction of the Polish concept of cultural heritage protection.

One may have the impression that apart from the conversations behind the scenes, a hidden criticism of certain statutes, including the Act of 25 May 2017 on the Restitution of National Cultural Property (ARNCP), the issues connected with cultural heritage have not been exhausted and recently have not been visible enough in public debate. This is somehow justified by the current situation, where society has been occupied with the issue of COVID-19 and its consequences in the social and economic aspects. A social dimension also covers culture, which, although it was only available online for some time, is of vital importance in the area of tourism and economic development. Polish cultural institutions have faced difficult choices these days as the annual budget did not provide for a near-total lack of revenue from sales of tickets. On the other hand, one can observe the attitudes of citizens, who wish to exercise their right to enjoy cultural goods, as was proven by the long lines to visit museums after they were opened in February 2021 and then closed again for a few months. Culture and heritage also form an important resource in the process of dealing with new challenges, which have been extended for an indefinite time with COVID-19.

It is worth quoting Audreu Azoulay, who stated, referring to the pandemic: "Let us reaffirm the primacy of education, science, culture and knowledge to help us surmount crisis."[11] It is beyond any doubt that culture can help us overcome the crisis, although indirectly. It then becomes a tool that is an important good in itself. A similar approach may be noticed in amendments to the document

> Council Conclusions on the Work Plan for Culture 2019–2022[12] concerning strengthening the role of culture in the attainment of the goals of the Sustainable Development Agenda and the use of the full potential of culture in development.[13]

In a certain sense, one can conclude that heritage protection is a noble act, but needs that are related to safety and health take precedence. It is true that culture is of vital importance when overcoming difficulties, but the fundamental goal will be the survival of humanity. Therefore, it is important to continue research and protect cultural heritage taking holistic approach. The current phenomenon of incorporating natural components into the protection of cultural heritage has begun to accelerate that process.

---

[11] "Let us reaffirm the primacy of education, science, culture and knowledge to help us surmount crisis" UNESCO Snapshots, 2020. https://unesdoc.unesco.org/ark:/48223/pf0000375163. Accessed 1 June 2022.

[12] Council conclusions amending the Work Plan for Culture (2019–2022), ST/14984/2018/INIT, OJ C 460, 21.12.2018, pp. 12–25. https://eur-lex.europa.eu/legal-content/GA/TXT/?uri=CELEX:52020XG0609(03). Accessed 1 June 2022.

[13] Council conclusions amending the Work Plan for Culture (2019–2022), ST/14984/2018/INIT, OJ C 460, 21.12.2018, pp. 12–25. https://eur-lex.europa.eu/legal-content/GA/TXT/?uri=CELEX:52020XG0609(03). Accessed 1 June 2022; Holtorf (2020), p. 22.

The burden currently placed on the legislature is related to both the past and the future, i.e. to what extent state budgets and international budgets will be able to take into account the costs of maintenance for heritage already held as a public resource and its new components. Additionally, to what extent will it be possible, relying on these budgets, to create financing mechanisms for actions concerning cultural heritage undertaken by private actors? It is hard to expect from subsequent decision-makers that there will be an open declaration in that respect. Looking into the future of cultural heritage, it should be discerned that the axis of the discussion will be formulated around the safety of societies and health. Cultural heritage will therefore play an important function, allowing governments to handle these difficulties. On the other hand, cultural heritage is also defeated by COVID-19 as APGM does not apply to

> designing, construction, reconstruction, renovation, maintenance, and demolition of building structures, including a change in the method of use in connection with COVID-19 prevention measures.[14]

Attention should be paid to the fact that even though this special legal regulation has been noted, it has not given rise to increased discussion.[15]

The extension of public cultural heritage resources is at present an inevitable process. It is also certainly an important element of the debate about the future of museum keeping and, more specifically, the management of such resources. On the other hand, digital heritage is gaining prominence, which also constitutes a challenge for protection and inventories. Simultaneously conducted activities in the area of digitalisation of tangible heritage serve purposes other than record keeping and documenting. What is separated is the intangible value of the heritage, together with what can be transferred into the virtual space. At the same time, the presence of tangible cultural heritage on the Internet allowed access to culture during the COVID-19 lockdown period. Reports concerning museums during this time show that these institutions, despite organisational and financial problems, undertook many activities online, as presented in the United Nations Educational, Scientific and Cultural Organization (UNESCO)[16] and International Council of Museums

[14] Act of 2 March 2020 on special solutions related to the prevention, counteraction and eradication of COVID-19, other infectious diseases and emergencies caused by them. Polish Official Journal (Dz. U.) 2020, item 374. The provision was expanded by the Act of 31 March 2020 on amending the Act on special solutions related to preventing, counteracting and combating COVID-19, other infectious diseases and crisis situations caused by them and some other acts. Polish Official Journal (Dz. U.) 2020, item 568.

[15] Wybranowski (2020).

[16] World Museums Report 2021: UNESCO report: Museums around the World in the face of COVID-19 – UNESCO Digital Library, UNESCO, Paris 2021, https://unesdoc.unesco.org/ark:/48223/pf0000376729_eng. Accessed 1 June 2022.

(ICOM)[17] reports, and the future will show to what extent these activities will remain a part of the permanent offer of such museums.

What is inevitably coming is the moment when one will not be able to consider the inclusion of cultural heritage components in state resources as a rescue for cultural heritage. In view of potential financial problems, it is hard to conclude that public ownership is always the best solution. At present, not all immovable monuments owned by the state treasury or territorial local government units are in good condition. Projects financed with EU funds covering revitalisation constitute only a partial solution. The increasing costs related to the maintenance of the ever-growing cultural heritage resource will be taken over by subsequent decision-makers. Considering the above, it is hard to determine at what point the funds for heritage protection will prove insufficient.

What may happen is therefore a reversal of the situation and a slow return to the overwhelming participation of private actors in cultural heritage protection. Undoubtedly, the participation of private actors in shaping the beginnings of organised cultural heritage protection is undeniable. Currently, pursuant to Article 5 of the Constitution of the Republic of Poland, such activities are co-performed by the state. *Ipso facto*, a return to the total transfer of responsibility for cultural heritage to private actors is not possible under the currently applicable law. It will, however, proceed in a discreet way by introducing new forms of protection and valuation of cultural heritage components. Cultural heritage may be compared to a house inherited from one's ancestors, whose layout, location and interior were not subject to our consideration. The state required to protect cultural heritage will not have the possibility to reject that heritage. It may only construct new forms of protection. The state may alternatively implement new policies concerning changes to heritage and the adaptation of immovable cultural heritage to new needs and functions, as well as creating a classification of its most valuable components. It will not be allowed, however, to remove heritage entirely, which is in line with the judgement of the European Court of Human Rights in the case *Potomski Potomska v. Poland*[18] and should be implemented in the case of private actors.

In that case, considering a selected portion of cultural heritage components as a separate legal category (the fourth estate) may be an important argument for the changes in the system of cultural heritage protection law in Poland. A reconstruction of arguments in favour of the new approach to certain cultural goods and carving out a new legal category allows further practical research in that respect. Theoretical deliberations, placing them in the discourse concerning movable and immovable goods, including the issue of special regulations of "living rivers", and showing these solutions in the context of foreign experiences allow us to wonder to what extent such instruments are compliant with the national concept of cultural heritage

[17] Museums, museum professionals and COVID-19: follow-up survey. REPORT Museums, museum professionals and COVID-19: follow-up survey, ICOM 2020, https://icom.museum/wp-content/uploads/2020/11/FINAL-EN_Follow-up-survey.pdf. Accessed 1 June 2022.

[18] *Potomska* and *Potomski* v. Poland, 33949/05, ECHR judgement 4 November 2014.

protection. Current legal circumstances allow me to conclude that the application of that legislative solution, if any, may apply solely to a narrow portion of goods, and the construct of shared responsibility and dereification as an idea highlighting the intangible value of cultural goods will determine the direction of legislative measures. One cannot also rule out the possibility that such a legislative solution may be introduced at the international level if we consider a selection of the most valuable cultural objects or continue research concerning space heritage and the separation of the most important part of that resource. Although the suggestions of covering selected goods with a special regime under an international agreement have been made for quite a while, there has been no international legislative initiative in that respect. Each time, a problem with the right to a given component of cultural heritage will arise, together with the obvious context of national rights *in rem* applicable in the given country where the good is located.

In principle, what would be closest to the solution being analysed is the Polish case, where the List of Heritage Treasures as a form of protection is applied regardless of the owner (public/private) but solely in view of the special value of national cultural heritage. It seems that the new classification of objects of civil law relationships and that method of searching for solutions should be initiated in national law; therefore, a starting point could be the experiences related to the introduction of the List of Heritage Treasures and axiological assumptions underlying the work on that unused form of monument protection.

Last but not least, a question that may be posed is whether world-renowned masterpieces will be replaced by digital files in the future. It is certainly hard to imagine that this could happen in the foreseeable future. But it may be a good idea to use objects known to society and create an application for the youngest members who could take care of and protect a masterpiece. I am of the opinion that this, alongside board games, cards and workshops, would be an important tool for raising awareness of the importance of cultural heritage.[19] That is because only building a true connection with cultural heritage by means of available tools may lead to the next generation not rejecting the heritage of the past.

References

Blake J (2015) International cultural heritage law. Oxford Scholarship, Oxford. https://doi.org/10.1093/acprof:oso/9780198723516.001.0001

Ciechanowicz-Mclean J (2014), Kształtowanie się gałęzi prawo ochrony środowiska jako wzór dla prawa ochrony dziedzictwa kultury. In: Zeidler K (ed) Prawo ochrony zabytków. Wolters Kluwer, Wydawnictwo Uniwersytetu Gdańskiego, Warszawa–Gdańsk, pp 34–41

Fromageau J (2020) The interactions between intangible cultural heritage and environmental law. In: Cornu M, Vaivade A, Martinet L, Hance C (eds) Intangible cultural heritage under national and international law. Going Beyond the 2003 UNESCO Convention. Edward Elgar

[19] Jagielska-Burduk et al. (2021).

Publishing, Cheltenham–Northampton, pp 1–11, pp 69–80. https://doi.org/10.4337/9781839100031.00014
Holtorf C (2020) Post-corona archaeology: creating a new normal? Eur Archaeol 66:18–23
Jagielska-Burduk A (2016) List of national treasures. In: Jagielska-Burduk A, Szafrański W (eds) Legal Issues in Cultural Heritage Management. A Polish Perspective. Peter Lang, Berlin, pp 68–73
Jagielska-Burduk A, Pszczyński M, Stec P (2021) Cultural heritage education in UNESCO cultural conventions. Sustainability 13(6):3548. https://doi.org/10.3390/su13063548
Wybranowski M (2020, 13 July) Zabytki bez ochrony. Winna specustawa covidowa. Gazeta Prawna. https://prawo.gazetaprawna.pl/artykuly/1485953,tarcza-antykryzysowa-zabytki-prawo-budowlane.html. Accessed 1 June 2022
Zeidler K (2014) Prawo ochrony dziedzictwa kultury jako nowa gałąź prawa. In: Zeidler K (ed) Prawo ochrony zabytków. Wolters Kluwer, Wydawnictwo Uniwersytetu Gdańskiego, Warszawa–Gdańsk, pp 23–33

The manufacturer's authorised representative in the EU is Springer Nature Customer Service Centre GmbH, Europaplatz 3, 69115 Heidelberg, Germany. If you have any concerns regarding our products, please contact ProductSafety@springernature.com

Printed and bound by CPI Group (UK) Ltd, Croydon, CR0 4YY
28/09/2026
02224088-0017